Between the end of the Middle Ages and the Industrial Revolution, the long-established structures and practices of European agriculture and industry were slowly, disparately, but profoundly transformed. *Transitions to capitalism in early modern Europe* narrates and analyzes the diverse patterns of economic change that permanently modified rural and urban production, altered Europe's economic geographies, and gave birth to new social classes. Broad in chronological and geographical scope and explicitly comparative, the book introduces readers to a wealth of information drawn from throughout Mediterranean, east-central and western Europe, as well as to the classic interpretations and current debates and revisions. The study incorporates recent scholarship on world economy, proto-industry, women's work, and consumption, and it discusses at length the impact of the emergent capitalist order on Europe's working people. Also included are lists of suggested readings which direct students to the latest research on a wide variety of subjects.

NEW APPROACHES TO EUROPEAN HISTORY

Transitions to Capitalism
in Early Modern Europe

NEW APPROACHES TO EUROPEAN HISTORY

Series editors
WILLIAM BEIK *Emory University*
T. C. W. BLANNING *Sidney Sussex College, Cambridge*
R. W. SCRIBNER *Harvard University*

New Approaches to European History is an important new textbook initiative, intended to provide concise but authoritative surveys of major themes and problems in European history since the Renaissance. Written at a level and length accessible to advanced school students and undergraduates, each book in the series will address topics or themes that students of European history encounter daily: the series will embrace both some of the more "traditional" subjects of study, and those cultural and social issues to which increasing numbers of school and college courses are devoted. A particular effort will be made to consider the wider international implications of the subject under scrutiny.

To aid the student reader scholarly apparatus and annotation will be light, but each work will have full supplementary bibliographies and notes for further reading: where appropriate chronologies, maps, diagrams and other illustrative material will also be provided.

The first titles in the series are

1 MERRY E. WIESNER *Women and Gender in Early Modern Europe*

2 JONATHAN SPERBER *The European Revolutions, 1848–1851*

3 CHARLES INGRAO *The Habsburg Monarchy 1618–1815*

4 ROBERT JÜTTE *Poverty and Deviance in Early Modern Europe*

5 JAMES B. COLLINS *The State in Early Modern France*

6 CHARLES G. NAUERT, JR *Humanism and the Culture of Renaissance Europe*

7 DORINDA OUTRAM *The Enlightenment*

8 MACK P. HOLT *The French Wars of Religion, 1562–1629*

9 JONATHAN DEWALD *The European Nobility, 1400–1800*

10 ROBERT S. DUPLESSIS *Transitions to Capitalism in Early Modern Europe*

Transitions to Capitalism in Early Modern Europe

ROBERT S. DUPLESSIS

Swarthmore College

CAMBRIDGE
UNIVERSITY PRESS

Published by the Press Syndicate of the University of Cambridge
The Pitt Building, Trumpington Street, Cambridge CB2 1RP, United Kingdom

Cambridge University Press
The Edinburgh Building, Cambridge CB2 2RU, United Kingdom
40 West 20th Street, New York, NY 10011-4211, USA
10 Stamford Road, Oakleigh, Melbourne 3166, Australia

First published 1997

Printed in the United Kingdom at the University Press, Cambridge

Typeset in 10/12pt Plantin

A catalogue record for this book is available from the British Library

Library of Congress cataloguing in publication data

DuPlessis, Robert S.
  Transitions to capitalism in early modern Europe / Robert S. DuPlessis.
    p.   cm. – (New approaches to European history; 10)
  ISBN 0 521 39465 1 (hb). – ISBN 0 521 39773 1 (pb)
  1. Industries – Europe – History.   2. Industrialization – Europe – History.
3. Agriculture – Economic aspects – Europe – History.
4. Capitalism – Europe – History.   I. Title.   II. Series.
HC240.D82   1997
338.094 – dc21   96–50037
                                                                      CIP

ISBN 0 521 39465 1 hardback
ISBN 0 521 39773 1 paperback

VN

Contents

Illustrations

Maps

Preface

The subject of this book is the economic history of Europe during three and a half tumultuous centuries, focusing on agriculture and industry. It is organized so as to offer the reader a narrative of developments in the major states and geographical areas over time on the one hand, and an analysis of general trends and structural changes that affected Europe as a whole on the other. On each of the multitude of subjects upon which it touches, a vast amount of scholarship exists. To assist students who wish to pursue themes further, suggested readings have been provided at the end of each chapter.

Economic history can be a difficult, even a frustrating, field to study. It is characterized less by dramatic events and famous individuals than by processes that take place over extended periods of time, begin and end at dates that are almost impossible to pinpoint, and involve the efforts of people who mostly remain anonymous. Yet economic history can also be exciting, for it reveals the manifold ways that human beings have acted within the constraints and opportunities offered them by geography, resource endowment, demography, institutions, values, and beliefs in order to produce the goods and services that they need and want. Like every significant discipline, moreover, economic history is replete with controversies generated by scholars seeking both to extend their empirical knowledge and to refine their theoretical understandings. Many of these debates are discussed in this book. Attending to them indicates the state of current research and conceptualization.

This book presumes no prior knowledge of economics, but it may be helpful to define here the most frequently used terms (others are defined when they appear in the text). To begin with, growth and development need to be distinguished analytically, even if the distinction is not always clearcut in practice. *Growth* pertains to an increase in output, to quantitative change. Because such expansion may be accompanied by an increase in population, scholars differentiate between aggregate growth (expansion of the total output of a society), which may or may not result in improvement for individuals, and per capita growth, achieved when aggregate expansion of output exceeds population increase. Unfortunately, in the early modern period the shakiness of our demographic information usually makes it difficult to determine whether the latter has occurred, even when the evidence points to the former. *Development* refers to qualitative change or, as it is frequently termed, structural change.

Both growth and development involved alterations in the ways in which the *factors of production*, the inputs into the production process, were employed. Three factors are usually distinguished: land, labor, and capital. Land refers, of course, to property used for cultivation, pasturage, woodland, and so forth, but it can also mean other natural resources, such as ores. Labor is physical or mental work directed towards production. Capital, too, is a broad term, encompassing not simply the funds employed in production but also tools, equipment, and other property used to create more wealth. Care needs to be taken not to confuse *production* (total output of goods and services of an enterprise, farm, or entire society, often used synonymously with output) with *productivity*, which is output per unit of time (hour, day, etc.). In turn, productivity can be further subdivided. Productivity of labor signifies the output of products divided by the number of workers; of land or agriculture, the output of farm products divided by the amount of land in use. Growth involves increasing the amount of production but does not necessarily entail rising productivity.

Industry is often thought to signify mechanized production; in this book, however, it refers to all processing of raw materials to make non-agricultural goods and services for sale in the market. Therefore, in the pages that follow, industry is at times used synonymously with *craft* and *trade*, particularly when manual labor is involved. Both *workers* and *artisans* perform manual labor, though in this book the former term is generally reserved for those with little skill who are employed for wages, and for all those working in mechanized factories, whereas the latter connotes skilled workers laboring at home or in smaller shops, whether or not they were self-employed and belonged to guilds. *Peasants* and *farmers* may also be used interchangeably, signifying those who work the land. At times, the terms suggest different social relations, a peasant being someone who has to pay the landlord a form of tribute (whether in cash, kind, or services) in order to remain on the land, whereas a farmer is an owner or a tenant owing only land rent. Peasant often carries overtones of subsistence agriculture, but here it includes those who produce for the market.

Finally, the terminological conventions used below need to be pointed out. The first time that foreign terms are employed, they are italicized, but thereafter they are printed in Roman type. Names of provinces, cities, towns, villages, and geographical features such as rivers are given in the form currently common in the English-speaking world; but for states I have used the name(s) current in the early modern period. Thus what has been known as Belgium since 1830 is referred to below as the southern Netherlands or (depending on the specific era) the Spanish or Austrian Netherlands. The northern Netherlands becomes the Dutch Republic or the United Provinces from the later sixteenth century. Before the mid-nineteenth century, Germany and Italy were geographical expressions, although enjoying a good deal of linguistic and cultural unity; in this book, the many states that comprised them are grouped together (as Italy and western and eastern Germany) for some purposes, although for others regions are distinguished. The various kingdoms of Spain were dynastically united, but economically diverse; Castile, the largest, and Catalonia, the most dynamic, are treated separately here.

All scholarship is to some extent a collective endeavor, but a synthesis like this one is unusually dependent on the contributions of many others. Many of the works that I have found especially useful are cited in the suggested reading at the end of each chapter. But I have not listed there the numerous books and articles in languages other than English upon which I have repeatedly drawn. Such works are essential reading for anyone wishing to explore in greater depth many of the topics discussed in this book, for which the English-language literature is unsatisfactory or nonexistent.

A number of scholars both European and North American have supplied readings, given parts of my manuscript helpful and critical readings, or otherwise provided aid. For such assistance, I would particularly like to thank James Amelang, Pierre Boulle, Francis Concato, Daryl Hafter, Martha Howell, Catharina Lis, Guido Marnef, Joyce Mastboom, John Munro, Hugo Soly, and Herman Van der Wee. I have benefited greatly from comments by the editors of the series "New Approaches to European History" – most of all from a detailed and unsparing critique by Bill Beik – and from suggestions made by an anonymous reader. Richard Fisher at Cambridge University Press has been unfailingly supportive and patient and Vicky Cuthill has helped smooth the production process. All of them share the credit for whatever virtue this book has; I alone am responsible for its shortcomings. I would also like to thank the students in the various incarnations of my course History 24 who over the years have helped to sharpen my ideas and pointed out new ways of thinking about the rise of capitalism. I hope that this book will be useful to their successors. My deepest gratitude goes to the two people to whom the book is dedicated: my wife Rachel, for being patient, and our daughter Koré, for not.

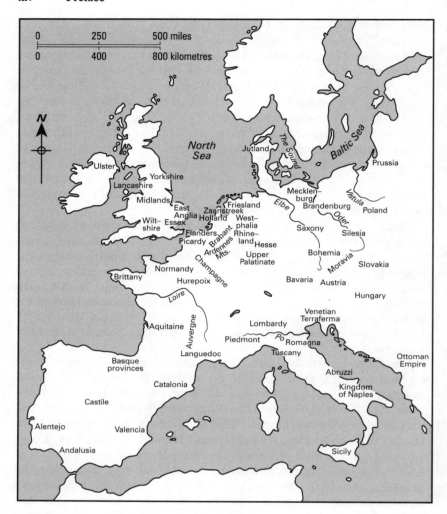

1 Regions mentioned in the text

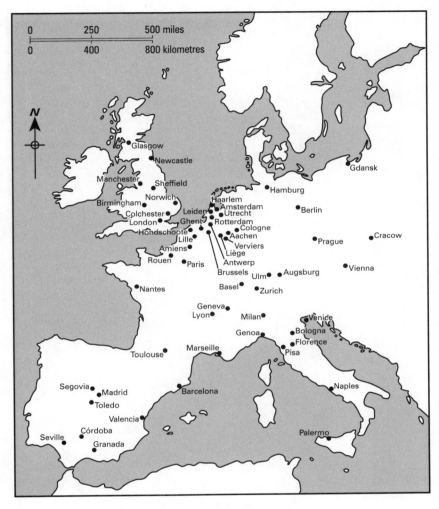

2 Towns and cities mentioned in the text

Part I

1   Themes and theories

In 1800, nine out of ten Europeans lived in small towns and villages, where most engaged, as their ancestors had since Neolithic times, in farming. The landed aristocracy remained the dominant social and political class, rarely involved directly in production yet nevertheless receiving much of the economic surplus. Artisans who worked in their homes or small shops using hand-powered tools made most manufactured goods. Modest levels of productivity, along with poorly developed commercial institutions, communications, and transport, hobbled the operation of markets and kept living standards low for the majority of the populace. These circumstances have prompted many historians to label the economy of Europe in the several centuries preceding the Industrial Revolution "traditional" or "pre-industrial," thereby emphasizing both its continuities with the medieval past and the profound rupture represented by subsequent factory-based mechanization.

Significant changes also marked the European economy between the mid-fifteenth and late eighteenth centuries, however. Innovative crops and practices boosted agricultural output, while many farmers held land by novel forms of tenure. Industry spread into new areas, particularly in the countryside, where countless villagers spun thread, wove cloth, or drew nails in addition to raising crops and tending animals. Many of these rural producers, as well as numerous urban artisans, were dependent wage-earners, their goods sold in distant markets by entrepreneurs who adopted new techniques for doing business more efficiently and profitably. By the end of the period, mechanized factories were springing up, most thickly in England, but also in many areas of the Continent. City folk had adopted novel consumption goods and patterns, and their country cousins were following suit. The number of Europeans had at least doubled from 60 to 120 million; in Britain and Scandinavia, population increased more than three times. Urbanization – measured as the proportion of population living in towns of more than 10,000 residents – followed a similar course. It rose from just over 5 percent around 1500 to 10 percent in 1800, and even more in northwestern Europe: from 3 percent to 20 percent in England and Wales, from 15 percent to nearly 30 percent in the Netherlands. Historians pointing to these developments often define the economy as "early industrial" or "proto-industrial," playing down the novelty and abruptness of mechanization by linking it to a long period of cumulative, slow change.

Each of these characterizations, as we shall see, identifies important attributes of the economies of the time: continuities as well as disjunctions must figure prominently in any economic history of Europe's "early modern" period (roughly 1450–1800). Particularly in comparison with succeeding decades, the economic life of the era was not marked by rapid change. Numerous long-established structures and practices visibly persisted. Behind, beside, and even within them, however, Europe experienced both growth and development as a series of far-reaching changes permanently modified its economies. Agricultural and industrial output increased and became more varied, so Europeans could buy not only new foodstuffs and manufactures but also a greater quantity of goods to which they had long been accustomed. Peasant agriculture still predominated, yet commercial farming was altering the face of the countryside. Despite the endurance of regulated artisan handicrafts, the roots of industrialization were sinking deep, and throughout Europe there emerged full-fledged industrial regions boasting large enterprises that employed hundreds if not thousands of workers, most of them rural folk, among whom women and children bulked large. The pace of demographic advance and urbanization was slow and erratic by later standards, but a new network of cities that could promote economic growth was being constructed. As merchants created a polycentric commercial system and new ships and techniques significantly reduced costs, international trade routes both spread broadly across the globe and bound the regions of Europe more closely together. Europe's economic center of gravity, since antiquity located in the Mediterranean, shifted to the North Atlantic. Most of all, European agriculture and manufacturing underwent an epochal transformation, as capitalism reorganized production in country and town alike.

Definitions of capitalism are legion, contentious, and give rise to disparate and often incompatible explanations of economic history. Some scholars take an expansive view, beginning their story in classical antiquity and encompassing all manifestations of profit-seeking trade, investment, and production. Others focus much more narrowly, whether by equating capitalism with a single quality – such as competition, markets, the predominance of money in exchange – or by identifying this form of economic structure with modern factory industrialization as originally exemplified by England during the Industrial Revolution.

The definition used in this book regards capitalism as a specific way of organizing the production of material wealth. In a capitalist economy, individuals and groups who possess capital assets – in the form of money, credit, land, productive equipment, and stocks of raw materials – use these resources to hire laborers for wages and set them to work turning out agricultural and industrial goods (commodities) for sale in the market, where profits are realized. Competition among capitalists induces and rewards innovation to cut costs and raise productivity. Commodity, financial, land, and labor markets, long-distance trade, and rational profit-seeking assume increasing importance in a capitalist economy. But what sets it apart from other economic systems are the relations obtaining between entrepreneurs – who may come from any class and occupation – and workers, who may till the land, tend vines or trees, or herd animals, as well as toil in a factory, in a garret, or on a construction site. These relations of production are manifested in the arrangements by which craft, industrial, and agricultural workers are employed and paid, as well as in those by which tenants hold farms.

Historically, the rise of this new economic system was a complex and pervasive process, eventually involving nearly every facet of economic life throughout Europe. It was also protracted, stretching across the entire early modern period. In fact, although this era saw capitalism achieve dominance in Europe, the transformation had begun in the Middle Ages, and it continued well after 1800. The development of capitalism entailed a revolution in economic relations, institutions, and attitudes; on occasion involved violence on the part of proponents and opponents alike; and gave birth to new social classes. None of this occurred quickly or abruptly, however. The novel form of production grew up within the old, gradually supplanting rather than suddenly and dramatically overthrowing it. Hence its date of birth and critical moments of maturation are, as we shall see, difficult to specify, though its attainment of mastery cannot be gainsaid.

Nor, finally, was the advance of capitalism steady or uniform. On the contrary, it was a decidedly uneven procedure. Taking place in an environment marked by fluctuating economic trends, it suffered disruptions, crises, even reversals, and was continuously challenged by established forms of economic organization. Not surprisingly, then, the process unfolded in disparate fashion across nations, regions, and sectors of the economy; even within the same industry or farming district capitalist and non-capitalist methods might be found cheek by jowl. Hence in exploring the emergence and eventual hegemony of capitalism, it is necessary to trace a variety of transitions across time and space.

These properties of the transitions to capitalism and the contexts in which they occurred have suggested the scope, subject matter, and shape of this book. It begins (Part I) by depicting agriculture and craft production in the mid-fifteenth century. Besides providing a benchmark against which subsequent change can be measured, the anatomy of the European economy at the close of the Middle Ages reveals both pronounced common features and striking diversity. A snapshot taken in about 1450 also identifies constraints and opportunities that powerfully molded developments during the following three centuries of fluctuating growth and transformation.

That process unfolded across the two periods examined in Parts II and III. The first, which scholars often label "the long sixteenth century" (1450/70–1620/50), was a time of mainly quantitative growth, although structural reorganization began in a few parts of Europe. These changes accelerated during the second period (1620/50–1780/1800), a time of initial crisis and subsequent growth. Capitalist relations penetrated deeply but unevenly into both agricultural and industrial production, thereby setting the stage for factory industrialization while consolidating regional economic disparities. The effects of these transformations on Europe's working people are explored in Part IV, which concludes with a brief look back at the era of transitions and ahead to the gradually emerging factory order.

In order to reveal both general patterns of economic restructuring and the manifold shapes and tempos that they took in specific settings, this book is geographically, organizationally, and socially broad as well as chronologically expansive. It ranges from the feudal estates of Poland to the teeming cloth districts of England, from Mediterranean latifundia to minuscule market gardens in Flanders, from Dutch industrial zones to New World slave plantations. Capitalism first prevailed in lands around the North Sea, but it had repercussions across the Continent – and indeed beyond. In addition to the common features among these disparate places and institutions, we will also explore the manifold different ways in which crops were cultivated, animals bred, and goods manufactured. Some of these arrangements proved transitional to capitalism; others impeded its appearance. Each implied a characteristic set of social relations, so we shall encounter not only wage-earners and entrepreneurs but journeymen and masters, serfs and lords, day-laborers and tenant farmers. All were engaged at once in weaving cloth, printing books, growing grain, or herding sheep, and – though rarely by design – in promoting, modifying, or obstructing fresh ways of organizing production.

Explanations of the rise of the new economic system date back to the eighteenth century, when its outlines were starting to become clear. Two of the original interpretations deserve attention by virtue of their considerable influence on later scholarship. In his epochal *Inquiry into the Nature and Causes of the Wealth of Nations*, published in 1776, Adam Smith (1723–90) emphasized the interdependent processes of market expansion and widening divisions of labor. Because, Smith held, humans have an innate "propensity to truck, barter, and exchange" in order to obtain most of the goods and services they require,[1] they engage in exchange, and in order to trade most advantageously they specialize in tasks in which they excel. When generalized throughout society, the resulting divisions of labor enhance skills, stimulate innovation, and raise productivity, unleashing continuous growth and development. In Smith's reading of history, such economic dynamism had sprung from unimpeded exchange among individuals, groups, and eventually nations. He knew, of course, that public authorities and private bodies had repeatedly attempted to shape the economy through regulations, monopolies, tariffs, and the like, but the inevitable consequence, in his eyes, had been to divert land, labor, and capital from their most productive uses, thereby frustrating improvement. Thus to promote the true wealth of nations – the full development of agriculture, industry, and commerce – individual initiative, competition, and free trade had to be allowed to flourish: this was both the achievement and the substance of the new order.

Smith and his fellow "political economists" traced the advance of capitalism to the onset of conditions that liberated purportedly inherent human qualities and to the beneficent operation, in market transactions, of an "invisible hand" that brought the common good out of the conflicting self-interest or "self-love" of all individuals.[2] To Karl Marx (1818–83), capitalism was powerful and dynamic, a superior form of production that promoted economic growth far above anything possible in the agrarian feudalism that had preceded it. However, he attributed its appearance not to the release of natural, unchanging human predispositions but to specific economic, political, and legal measures that by creating new relations among those involved in production reconfigured their attitudes and behavior. To Marx, capitalism is not a system of free exchange among equal participants all of whom realize equivalent benefits once emancipated from artificially imposed fetters. On the contrary, it is an order of structured inequality between wage-earners ("proletarians") who lack productive property and capitalists who control such resources. In order to earn subsistence, workers do not specialize and enter a market based on the division of labor. Instead, they sell their only property, their labor – or, more precisely, the productive power embodied in it – to

---

[1] Adam Smith, *Inquiry into the Nature and Causes of the Wealth of Nations* (Modern Library edn., New York, 1937), p. 13.   [2] Smith, *Wealth of Nations*, pp. 423, 14.

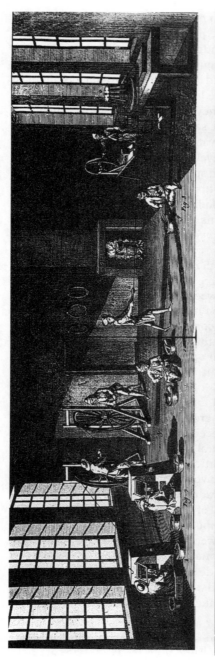

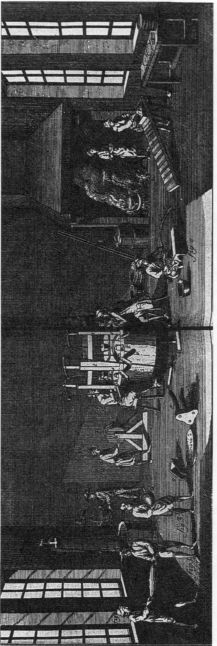

1 As an example of the division of labor, Adam Smith cited the eighteen operations involved in pinmaking. He was probably thinking explicitly of the description in Denis Diderot's *Encyclopedia*, in which these plates originally appeared.

entrepreneurs. It is these capitalists who organize production and exchange the resulting goods in the market, earning a profit by extracting
greater value (in Marxist terminology, "surplus value") from the labor
they buy than they pay out in wages. New and more productive divisions
of labor and specializations were an outcome rather than a cause of the
emergent system.

The genesis of capitalism lay in the process that Marx called "original"
or "primitive accumulation." At once destructive and creative, original
accumulation was an economic, social, political, and cultural phenomenon that involved both town and country, industry and agriculture,
expropriation and concentration. For capitalism to arise, Marx argued,
capital – both in the form of assets like land and equipment, and in the
form of specie and credit – had to be amassed by individuals who invested
it productively rather than consuming it. This step was carried out by
landlords and big tenant farmers who dispossessed impoverished aristocrats and peasants of their holdings, by merchants who crushed artisanal
guilds, and by merchants and adventurers who operated the lucrative
slave trade, exploited or outright looted colonies, and practiced usury.
They were assisted by government laws, monopolies, taxes, and debt; far
from the state being a brake on or enemy of capitalism, Marx held, it was
one of its principal progenitors and servants. The efforts of these diverse
groups often resulted in intermediate forms of production such as
industry based in rural households and large, unmechanized but increasingly capital-intensive workshops; they also took a long time to come to
fruition. Still, by the later eighteenth century original accumulation had
given birth to the capitalist mode of production.

To help interpret the rich and varied information that scholars have
assembled about the early modern economy, the chapters that follow will
draw repeatedly though critically upon Smith and Marx and upon the
debates that they have provoked. We shall also make use of several other
perspectives that are currently shaping historians' understanding of
European economic history in the centuries before mechanized factories:
those focused on the world-system, on class structure, on proto-industry,
on consumption, on women's work, and on work experience. All borrow
from – and contribute to – disciplines beyond economic history, including
developmental economics, cultural anthropology, and feminist theory.
And while each is incomplete, taken together they both cast new light on
neglected aspects of the early modern economy and encourage reconsid-
eration of subjects long in the foreground.

The "world-system" approach is represented most prominently by the
work of Immanuel Wallerstein. This interpretation springs in part from
Marx's postulate that capital derived from commercial exploitation of

colonial possessions was both the prime solvent of Europe's feudal order and a source of its capitalist successor. It also amplifies Smith's argument that the growth of trade furthers the division of labor, combining this with recent theories that capitalist economic development in favored areas necessarily bred underdevelopment elsewhere. According to Wallerstein, the rise of capitalism in western Europe (the "core" of a new world economy) was achieved by the exploitation of other regions, notably eastern Europe and the colonized New World (the "periphery"). Together with an intermediate "semi-periphery," these regions constituted a global division of labor characterized by a unified market but sharply differentiated forms of labor: free in the core, coerced in the periphery. In this asymmetrical economic system, inherently unequal trade, backed up by similarly unbalanced power relations, transferred the surplus generated in the periphery to the core where it built sustained capitalist development.

Drawing on Marx's insistence on the importance of peasant dispossession, the work of Robert Brenner locates the principal dynamic for early modern economic change in class structure (and attendant class struggle) in the countryside. Brenner focuses on social relations among nobles and peasants that were founded on unequal property ownership and expressed in peaceful and violent interactions mediated, in a variety of fashions, by state institutions and policies. The different outcomes of this interplay, he maintains, accounted on the one hand for divergent patterns and levels of growth both within the western European core and between western and eastern Europe, and on the other for the eventual advent (or frustration) of capitalism. In contrast to world-system theory, which considers capitalism global in origin as well as in consequences, Brenner's analysis situates its mainsprings within Europe.

Scholarship on proto-industrialization, which has both Smithian and Marxist roots, emphasizes interconnections among widening markets, rural populations seeking wage-earning employment, and entrepreneurs' search for cheap labor. Highlighting rural, household, and regional changes, studies of what one team of historians has dubbed "industrialization before industrialization" argue that Europe's capitalist development sank deep roots in the countryside, involved all members of peasant families in production of marketed goods, and both relied upon and enhanced interrelated regional economies with distinctive specializations. By insisting that organizational restructuring had to precede technological innovation on a broad scale, such explanations also underline that the rise of capitalism must be understood as a process rather than an event.

Inquiries into consumption reintroduce a surprisingly disregarded aspect of economic activity. According to these accounts, capitalist transformation proceeded not simply (and in some versions not mainly) from enhanced supply – notably increased amounts of labor and capital that resulted in more and cheaper goods – but also from new patterns and levels of demand. This scholarship thus understands the expansion of consumer markets across the early modern period less as the consequence of rising output than as a (even the) leading cause of that growth.

Research on women's work, a central component of the burgeoning literature on gender relations, has explored links between families' economic behavior and novel modes of organizing production. Feminist scholars have likewise investigated the ideological, institutional, and material forces that governed the types of labor assigned to women, the pay they received, and the status they derived from it. These historians bring out the often paradoxical effects of capitalist development on women in the peasantry and artisanate, as well as in the nascent working class.

The study of work experience and of the vaguer if more inclusive topic of "work culture" also forms part of broader historiographical trends, in this case what has frequently been called "history from below" and the closely allied subject of popular culture. Analyses inspired by these schools of thought have sought to recover the outlooks, expectations, and actions of pre-industrial working people in their own terms. In so doing, these historians have revealed an array of institutions, practices, and beliefs – many of which now strike us as bizarre or even repellent – that encouraged or hampered economic transformation.

To examine the rise of capitalism is to investigate the origins of the economic order that continues to dominate Europe and increasingly the world. But it is also to court epistemological danger. Knowing how the story has "come out" in the present can all too easily lead into a teleological and deterministic account of the origins of that result. This is not an easy problem to avoid in early modern economic history, because the very terms of discussion tend to imply movement towards the present, as the phrase "early modern" indicates. Similarly, "pre-industrial" and "proto-industrial" acquire their logic retrospectively, from the vantage point of industrialization.

This book does not entirely avoid the trap of teleology. It does, however, seek to demonstrate that the ascendancy of capitalism was by no means ineluctable, and that no single path of development constituted a model against which others are to be measured. By attending to a broad range of regions, structures, sectors, and patterns of economic change between about 1450 and about 1800, it attempts to recapture the diversity and contingency of economic development during those centuries. From this standpoint, capitalist industrialization was part of, if eventually dominant over, a spectrum of possibilities.

SUGGESTED READING

Of the political economists, the great founding text, Adam Smith, *An Inquiry into the Nature and Causes of the Wealth of Nations* (many modern editions), is most relevant for the concerns of this volume. Book III is the most explicitly historical; chs. I–III of Book I discuss the division of labor in a context of expanding markets. An important critique of the views of the political economists, together with an alternate explanation of the rise of market society, is Karl Polanyi, *The Great Transformation* (New York, 1944). In their bulk, the three volumes of Karl Marx, *Capital, A Critique of Political Economy* (orig. publ. 1867–94; many English translations and editions) can be intimidating. For historical materials, see especially vol. I, chs. 14, 26–32, and Vol. III, ch. 20. A fine selection from the difficult *Grundrisse* [*Foundations of the Critique of Political Economy*] (1857–58), complete with a superb introduction, is in Karl Marx, *Pre-Capitalist Economic Formations*, ed. E. J. Hobsbawm (New York, 1965). For Immanuel Wallerstein's work, see his *The Modern World-System*, 3 vols. to date (New York, 1974–89); Robert DuPlessis, "The Partial Transition to World-Systems Analysis in Early Modern European History," *Radical History Review*, no. 39 (1987), presents an evaluation. *The Brenner Debate: Agrarian Class Structure and Economic Development in Pre-Industrial Europe*, ed. T. H. Aston and C. H. E. Philpin (Cambridge, 1985), includes both Brenner's work and commentaries by other scholars. R. J. Holton, *The Transition from Feudalism to Capitalism* (London, 1985), provides a good review of many of the preceding interpretations. Works on proto-industry, consumption, women's work, and work experience are listed at the end of later chapters.

Some of the broader works of scholarship that have informed both this chapter and the entire book, and which amply repay further study, include Fernand Braudel, *Civilization and Capitalism, 15th–18th Centuries*, 3 vols. (1979; Engl. trans. New York, 1981–84); *The Cambridge Economic History of Europe*, vols. IV–V (Cambridge, 1967–77); Ralph Davis, *The Rise of the Atlantic Economies* (Ithaca, NY, 1973); Jan de Vries, *The Economies of Europe in an Age of Crisis* (Cambridge, 1976); de Vries, *European Urbanization, 1500–1800* (Cambridge, Mass., 1984); Peter Kriedte, *Peasants, Landlords and Merchant Capitalists. Europe and the World Economy, 1500–1800* (1980; Engl. trans. Leamington Spa, 1983). In economic history as in economics in general, much of the path-breaking scholarship appears in journals. Some, like *Economic History Review*, *Explorations in Economic History*, *Journal of Economic History*, and *Journal of European Economic History*, include a broad range of topics and periods; others, like *Textile History* and *Agricultural History Review*, specialize in particular sectors. More general scholarly journals such as *Past and Present* and *Social History* also regularly publish important articles on early modern European economic history.

2 Medieval legacies

The middle of the fifteenth century provides a good vantage point from which to locate the salient characteristics of Europe's economies at the dawn of a new era. For the previous century and a half, Europe had suffered through the protracted "late medieval crisis": repeated famines and epidemics (including, in 1347–50, the notorious Black Death) that killed between a third and a half of its people; abandoned fields and deserted villages; diminished manufacturing and mining output; disrupted trade; destructive wars and rebellions. But now the dark clouds were lifting. Hunger and plague had abated, if not vanished, so population had stabilized; in some places, births had begun to outnumber deaths. Plows bit deep into long-neglected fields, and as axe-blows resounded and windmills groaned, forests were cleared and marshes were drained for cultivation. From dawn to dusk looms hummed in urban workshops, while peasant wives and daughters set hands and feet to spinning wheels, and mining families labored to open fresh seams. Their security once again better assured, merchants hastened by ship and pack train to the farthest reaches of Europe and on into neighboring Africa and Asia. Few years were free from the clash of arms. But the most baleful conflict, the interminable Hundred Years' War between England and France, mercifully wound up.

Against this backdrop of incipient but fragile recovery, this chapter outlines the economies of Europe. Looking successively at agriculture and industry, it describes the ways in which production was organized on farm and in workshop; the relations obtaining between peasants and artisans on the one hand and landlords and masters on the other; and the conditions that defined and differentiated groups of producers, as well as the ties that bound them. We shall see that vigorous initiatives promoted change in countryside and town, but we shall also observe that many forces – often more powerful – helped perpetuate existing structures and practices.

14

Peasants and lords

As befitted an area that had seen countless migrations, invasions, and changes of regime and legal codes, and which encompassed a bewildering variety of topographies, climatic conditions, and soil qualities, the agrarian practices and structures that had evolved in Europe across the Middle Ages were extremely complex. Broad patterns in the ways that land was owned, occupied, and worked can nevertheless be discerned. Some property was "allodial," freely owned by those who inhabited and farmed it and, at least in principle, subject to neither monetary nor other charges to any superior. The greatest proportion of land belonged, however, to landlords who did not themselves cultivate it but derived their income from the peasants who did. All lordly estates yielded their owners rents. But most had feudal (seigniorial) rights attached as well. Enshrined in law and custom, these rights were upheld in the seigniors' own courts or, if necessary, by the threat or use of force. Although serfdom had disappeared from most of Europe, feudal rights survived. They permitted lords to levy dues on the produce of the land, to demand payments when peasants sold, exchanged, or bequeathed holdings, to collect fees for the peasants' mandatory use of seigniorial monopolies such as ovens, wine-presses, and mills, to demand market fees and bridge tolls, and to charge for the civil and criminal justice administered in their courts.

Land was held by peasant families in individual "tenements," tenures or holdings subject to specific conditions although usually exploited in accordance with collective regulations enforced by communal institutions. Effective possession of most land resided, then, in the hands of the peasantry, which enjoyed hereditary usufruct so long as it fulfilled the obligations imposed by lords. The confusion of ownership and occupancy, not to mention disagreements over the nature and level of appropriate lordly charges, ensured continuous conflict over the division of the surplus generated by the peasantry. At the same time, extensive customary and written rights and organized village communities, together with control of the land and agricultural production, not only allowed peasants a good deal of autonomy in their daily lives but gave them powerful weapons for negotiating with or even defying seigniorial demands.

The manorial system

Lords' land was organized into manors (seigniories). The proprietors might be individuals or collectivities, and, although mainly lay nobles and princes, also comprised ecclesiastical institutions, clergy, and, increasingly, bourgeois such as merchants, financiers, lawyers, and notaries. A manor generally belonged to a sole lord (who could own more than one of them), but sometimes a single manor was subject to several lords. The boundaries of a manor ordinarily coincided with those of a village, yet some manors included more than one settlement, whereas others contained just a portion of a single village, so in size they ranged from a few to thousands of acres.

Manorial territory was typically split into two parts of unequal size: the lord's "demesne" and the peasants' holdings, which in the aggregate were much larger. Neither farming practices nor technology distinguished them, however: similar crops were planted, livestock raised, rotations followed, and implements used on both parts. In the earlier Middle Ages, demesnes employing slaves, serfs owing labor services (*corvées*), and paid workers had produced large amounts of foodstuffs. But from the twelfth century onwards, lords had faced stiffening peasant resistance to corvées, rising wages, and difficulties in obtaining slaves; concurrently, population growth resulted in greater demand for land, pushing up rents. In the circumstances, many lords had granted or sold freedom to slaves and serfs, exchanged ("commuted") labor services for payments in cash or kind, and leased their demesnes to cultivators.

Well before the end of the Middle Ages, therefore, the peasant tenement had become the basic unit of agricultural production on the demesne as well as on the rest of the manor. A holding was usually occupied by one household consisting of a nuclear family, augmented as need be by a spouse's aged parent, by live-in servants, or by local or migrant farmworkers. In mountainous areas, several related nuclear families might reside together in a house and work a single holding in the arrangement that historians often refer to by its French name, *frérèche*.

Each holding contained a dwelling with attendant yard and outbuildings, along with its own fruit and vegetable garden, in which also might be cultivated industrial crops like madder and flax, or new ones such as turnips and clover. In addition, a tenement included arable (cropland) and access to the other resources of the manor: pasture, meadow, waste, forest, and waterways. These were not found equally across Europe, however, giving rise to disparate agrarian structures. Primarily pastoral regions, where most of the land was devoted to grazing, covered much of Scandinavia and the Celtic-speaking areas (notably Scotland, Ireland, Wales, Brittany) and were also found throughout upland Europe. More often, arable predominated. Some arable districts specialized in tree and vine crops, horticulture, or industrial crops; in fact, the most recent research suggests that a greater degree of agricultural specialization prevailed throughout medieval Europe than had previously been suspected. Cropland was principally employed, however, for growing the cereals (mainly wheat and rye, though also barley and oats, which could grow on the poorest land) used in the bread, gruel, and ale that were the staples of the popular diet. These grain fields were usually farmed on a triennial or "three-course" rotation of winter crops, summer crops, and fallow; on light, thin soils, however, two-course rotations were preferred, with fallow every second year.

As a rule, cereal regions lacked sufficient pasturage to support large numbers of livestock. Supplies of manure, far and away the leading fertilizer, were therefore limited, helping to keep arable productivity low. On average, the "yield ratio" (the amount of grain harvested compared to the amount sown) was just 4 or 5: 1, a tenth of today's figure. After setting aside seed for the next year's planting, a typical holding could feed only one or two people besides the five-person household that worked it. Low arable productivity thus required most Europeans to work the land. Other food sources did exist, however, even in essentially monocultural districts. Besides their gardens, peasants often cultivated peas, beans, and other legumes in corners of their larger fields or on land left fallow; olive groves flourished throughout the Mediterranean basin; and virtually every country boasted vineyards. Foodstuffs were also bought with income from the sale of specialized crops, including those that most peasants planted on spare bits of land.

Holdings in some grain areas had little but cropland. But they were the exception. In most regions, possession of a tenement conferred rights to common pastures and wastes – those, that is, accessible to all tenants of the manor. On them grazed horses, oxen, cows, and sheep that supplied whatever dairy products, wool and hides, hauling power, and manure to which most peasants had access. Tenants likewise had claims to a share of hay from common meadows, took building materials, fuel, nuts, and game from woodlands – where their pigs, the most common source of meat, also foraged – and fished in the manor's waterways. Lords typically claimed ownership of forests, fishponds, and streams and demanded recompense for their use, but peasants evaded payment whenever possible. So from the lords' perspective poaching was pervasive, although the peasants viewed it differently.

Peasants in mainly cropland districts usually lived in nucleated villages or hamlets surrounded by large open arable fields divided into numerous plots; an individual holding routinely included plots scattered among several fields. Over time, rules had developed to regulate plowing, sowing, harvesting, and grazing on fallow in the open fields, as well as the use of common resources. In pastoral areas, too, and in regions where individual cropland was separated by fences, hedges, or other enclosures, access to

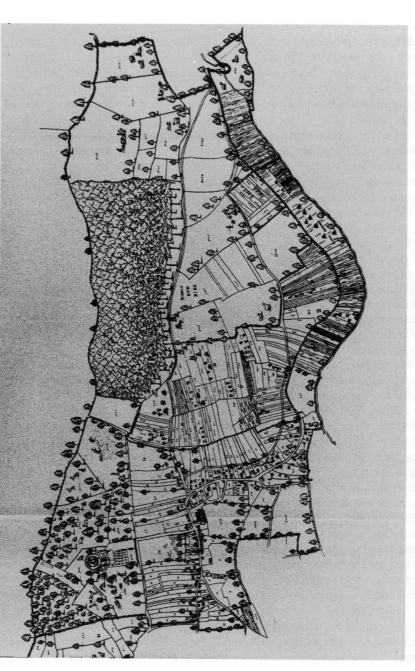

2 This map of the English manor of Laxton (Nottinghamshire) depicts the several components that composed it. They include the lord's house in the upper left; the village dwellings and gardens along the roads in the center left; the arable fields, mainly divided and cultivated in strips; the numerous meadows and pastures; the woods for timber, for hunting game, and for grazing. Although difficult to discern, both women and men are having just to the left of the manor house.

common lands was controlled by limits or "stints" placed on the number of stock that each household could graze.

Initially, perhaps, landlords had enforced the regulations that mandated the sharing of common resources. But by the later Middle Ages, if not earlier, village communities, embodied in periodic assemblies of heads of households, discharged this and other important administrative duties such as levying taxes, managing the parish church's land, and, in frontier and other thinly populated areas, dividing and leasing vacant land to settlers. These functions conferred a good deal of power on village communities, enabling them to play a vital role in the defense of peasant interests against landlords, tax collectors, and other officials. The performance of these tasks also promoted communal solidarity, as did practices like trading labor among households or teaming up individual families' draft animals to pull village-owned plows. Villages, which usually coincided with parishes, also celebrated carnival, processions, and similar collective rituals and festivities.

Villages were not, however, egalitarian, nor was the peasantry homogeneous. To begin with, gender disparities were deeply rooted. Of course, the bulk of peasant holdings required the labor of all household members save the underage or infirm, and female earnings were especially vital to the survival of smallholders and the landless. For these reasons, many scholars have considered the Middle Ages a golden era for peasant women, a time when they achieved equality by virtue of making essential contributions to family subsistence. Recent studies generally reject this view, however, arguing that despite the significance of their economic role, medieval rural women occupied a subordinate position grounded in work patterns, property relations, the patriarchal household, and widely prevalent beliefs.

No inflexible, prescribed gender-based division of labor obtained in the countryside, and family crises, exceptionally heavy seasonal demands, or labor shortages (as in the years following epidemics) could temporarily override habitual patterns. Among the poor and on farms raising the greatest variety of crops, jobs tended to be less segregated by sex. Yet conventional if informal norms associated specific tasks with one sex or the other; women's work was complementary to rather than interchangeable with men's. Whereas men plowed and herded, women gardened, cared for animals, and performed domestic chores.

Women also enjoyed fewer opportunities for wage labor than men, and found it difficult to establish a secure and recognized position in the labor market: employers preferred to hire men and took on women only when male labor was unavailable. When employed, moreover, women normally held the less skilled, unspecialized jobs that paid low wages and were frequently part-time and seasonal; women also typically worked close to home, whereas male laborers could move farther afield. And even when women held the same jobs as men they could count on earning less. The experience of female grape pickers in Languedoc (France) shows the effects of several of these factors. In 1349–50, immediately after the Black Death, they earned 80–90 percent of their male colleagues' wage; by the later fourteenth century, after the labor shortage had ended, their pay dropped to half of men's (save at harvest, when it rose to 60 percent), where it remained for centuries.

Women's access to and control over land was likewise restricted. Most inheritance customs favored males, although in some places a woman might receive up to one-third of her father's holding. A married woman was usually cotenant of the family holding, but she was the junior partner, for her husband administered the property in his capacity as head of the household. Unmarried women and widows could hold land in their own right in a few regions. In most cases, however, they were unable to transfer land freely, lest it leave the patrilineal family, and they faced pressure to marry, remarry, or turn the holding over to an adult son. Such demands seem to have become acute in the century after the Black Death. On the English manor of Havering (Essex), for instance, women formed 7.5 percent of all tenants holding in their own right in 1352–53; a century later, that group included no women at all. Unless they were widows and heads of households, moreover, women were excluded from the village communities that made important decisions about many aspects of peasant life. Whatever a woman's authority within her family, or her indispensability to the operation of the holding, it was rarely translated into sanctioned power in the public arena.

Village social distinctions also arose from tenurial arrangements that could differ substantially among the peasants of the same settlement or even among the several pieces of property that a single household held. Variations in such matters as the length of leases, the terms under which they could be renewed or bequeathed, the level of rent and dues, and the rights of landlords to levy arbitrary fees or "entry fines" when heirs took up a holding resulted in dissimilar degrees of peasant security and prosperity. Disparities in the size and quality of holdings, inheritance of land and capital, skill and other personal characteristics, and just plain luck likewise helped to create stratified farming populations. Three broad groups can be distinguished: a minority of well-to-do farmers; a throng of small to middling peasants; and a sizable body of landpoor and landless.

At the top stood the small group often designated by the English term "yeomen," who with the assistance of paid laborers produced for the market as well as for their families' subsistence. Their origins can be traced far back into the Middle Ages, but they came into their own in the wake of the epidemics, wars, and other calamities that afflicted Europe in the fourteenth and early fifteenth centuries. Adding to properties they owned outright, yeoman families leased abandoned tenements or took on demesnes that were rented out intact, enabling them to assemble large holdings – 100 acres or more of arable in grain-growing areas, even bigger farms in pastoral districts. Favorable court decisions that confirmed their property rights helped to solidify their position.

In the mid-fifteenth century, yeomen confronted an unenviable conjunction of low grain prices and high wages for farm workers. Yet yeomen proved adept at adjusting to the new conditions. Where possible, they cut labor costs by converting arable to pastoral. On their remaining cropland, they emphasized industrial crops, such as flax, hemp, dyestuffs, and oleaginous seeds, not to mention fruits, vegetables, and other specialty foodstuffs, for which demand remained buoyant. Yeomen throve most of all in the vicinity of sizable urban centers and among stock breeders. They constituted, for example, one-fourth of the tenants on Havering manor, supplying cattle, sheep, and wood to nearby London.

The same conditions that challenged yeomen helped those at the bottom of the rural hierarchy, that quarter or even third of villagers that contemporaries deemed poor: the landless, the "cottars" or cottagers who lived in dwellings with only gardens attached, and the occupants of puny tenements. Reliant on paid employment to make ends meet, they benefited from higher wages and depressed grain prices. Although scarcely affluent, in the 1450s many enjoyed a higher standard of living than their predecessors had for many decades. A male English agricultural laborer, for instance, had to work only eleven hours to earn a market basket of food that had demanded thirty-two hours of toil in 1310–20, and a similar tripling of real wages has been noted in regions across Europe. In many rural areas, too, industrial by-employments yielded additional income. Because of gender divisions of labor and wage inequities, however, poor peasant women – many of them widows – gained less; although their real wages rose, they remained below men's.

Conditions in mid-fifteenth-century rural Europe also smiled on the majority of peasant families, those cultivating small to medium-sized farms of 10–30 acres. Requiring minimal use of expensive hired labor, these farms were productive enough not only to assure their households' subsistence but frequently to send a surplus to market; like their yeomen neighbors, those with access to urban consumers might diversify out of grain into more specialized and lucrative crops. Generally depressed rents also contributed to their good fortune. Even those with quite small family farms could more than get by, thanks to the healthy wages they received for the agricultural and craft work that they often took on.

Overall, then, European peasants were prospering on the eve of the long sixteenth century. Many of their landlords, in contrast, faced gloomier prospects. Prior to the fourteenth century, rising demand, prices, and population had encouraged lords to expand their manors onto previously uncultivated land and to raise rents and dues on existing holdings. Subsequent market contraction, price decline, monetary instability, and demographic collapse foreclosed these possibilities. Leases in kind lost value as prices fell, while currency devaluations lessened the worth of cash rents. To repopulate deserted holdings, or to keep tenants from absconding, lords had to cut rents or grant long leases – for two or three lives, or even in perpetuity – at rates set with an eye on contemporary deflationary trends; they also reduced feudal dues. Rents in mid-fifteenth-century England and central Italy, for instance, were commonly just 60 percent of their level a hundred years earlier and were even more depressed in northern Germany. Across the same period, the so-called *champart* levy decreased from one-sixth to one-twelfth of the grain crop around Paris and disappeared entirely in the Lyon region. High wages and low prices likewise made demesne grain cultivation unprofitable.

Some lords counted on military adventure to recoup their losses and thus were eager recruits for the many wars that disturbed Europe in the century after the Black Death. Others became notorious highway robbers. But many accepted assistance from sovereigns who garnered political support by alienating royal lands, revenues, and offices to nobles and granting them pensions and tax exemptions. Crown beneficence became, in fact, essential for some nobles' survival. With princes' backing, too, lords used the substantial political and juridical authority that they retained to continue collecting an array of feudal levies, including "socage" or "tallage" taxes owed by all non-noble tenants; transfer and inheritance fees; market, bridge, and other tolls; fees from lordly monopolies; and judicial fines from seigniorial courts. Some lords, however, showed more imagination in the face of economic difficulties. In England, for example, landowners added vacant holdings to their demesnes – not, for the most part, to hazard direct cultivation, but to attract tenants by offering large holdings with adjustable rents and fees in place of tenures with fixed rights, obligations, and payments. Seigniors in central Italy and southern France (and to a lesser extent elsewhere) favored sharecropping (*mezzadria* or *métayage*), whereby they furnished land, buildings, tools, livestock, seed, capital, and, if necessary, food in return for half their tenants' produce. Although the farms specialized in labor-intensive arboreal and arable crops like mulberries, fruit, and grapes, these yielded higher profits than grain, and sharecropping landlords avoided paying high wages or having to collect rents at depressed levels.

At the end of the Middle Ages, peasants thus owed lords a complex of cash and in-kind ground rents, along with, in most cases, feudal charges and fees. They also paid ecclesiastical tithes (in principle, one-tenth of field crops; in reality, the proportion and the items taxed varied considerably) and central state taxes. Scholars estimate that in the late Middle Ages the majority of peasants handed over a quarter to a third of their gross yield to landlord, priest, and prince; the bulk of what remained was required for the family's consumption and the following year's planting or breeding. Still, a growing amount entered the market.

With the income thereby obtained, a number of peasants were able to undertake agricultural improvements such as better seed or breeding stock, drainage systems, or more effective plows, and they found tenurial arrangements flexible enough to accommodate their new ways. Nevertheless, in many places strong obstacles to innovation persisted. Seeking to assure that the majority of tenants would continue to enjoy access to the range of collective resources required for subsistence, villages often bitterly opposed landlord and yeoman attempts to enclose land, amalgamate strips, convert arable to pasture, drain marshes, clear wastes and forests. In addition, many peasants clung to time-tested practices, whether because the tried and true was most profitable or, as many scholars have held, because villagers valued a customary standard of living more than risking change in return for the promise of increased income or consumption. Landlords also seem rarely to have encouraged innovation. Although some fostered new economic activities, most devoted their efforts to defending or extending their traditional rights and revenues. Placing prestige and power above profit, moreover, they tended to engage in conspicuous consumption that would enhance their social and political standing rather than investing in their properties. Over most of Europe, then, the interplay of peasant production and substantial landlord surplus appropriation, and of village organization and seigniorial authority, underlay the continued vitality of traditional agrarian structures and routines.

Lords, peasants, and cash crops

Late medieval European agriculture was not entirely closed or immobile, however. Nearly all peasants had to buy some goods in the market. This was particularly true in specialized pastoral, wine, and horticultural areas. But even those peasants who raised and processed most of their own food, made their clothing, repaired farm buildings and equipment, and gathered the fuel they burned could only obtain necessities such as salt or iron from beyond their holdings. Cash levies imposed by lord, church, and state also forced peasants to generate marketable surpluses or find supplementary wage work. Demographic recovery and higher real wages, which translated into rising demand for foodstuffs and raw materials, had the same effects. A proliferation of market towns and villages – around 1450, Germany had some 4,000 – allowed these influences to permeate deep into the countryside.

Yet while market forces were widely felt, only in a few distinctive regions had commercial farming become dominant by the mid-fifteenth century. Each was densely populated and heavily urbanized relative to Europe as a whole, creating concentrated demand for the produce of the land as well as a ready supply of labor. In each, too, the village community had traditionally been weak, which eased the introduction of new practices. Several variants of market-oriented agriculture can be distinguished, according to size of productive units, conditions of tenure, crop specialization, and the roles of peasants and lords in promoting commercialization. Although involving but a limited amount of Europe's land, and employing only a small proportion of its peasantry, they do indicate the possibilities for development present within agriculture as the Middle Ages drew to a close.

Commercial agriculture based on large farms and strong landlord leadership had developed in several parts of the Mediterranean basin. On the riverine plains of northern Italy, where urban political and economic dominion over the surrounding countryside (*contado*) facilitated the rise of sizable regional markets, noble, ecclesiastical, and bourgeois investors assembled units of up to 250 acres. These were operated by tenant households assisted by numerous farm workers, many of them seasonal migrants from towns or mountainous regions. To extend their political power while strengthening the economic foundations of their states, rulers like the Visconti and Sforza dukes of Milan assisted landlord-sponsored agrarian change. They promoted major canal and irrigation projects, as well as the introduction of new crops, at the expense of open fields, common pasture rights, small peasants, and more traditionally minded seigniors.

Some of these large properties went in for conventional grain-based farming, others for cattlebreeding. But many, with an eye to urban demand, turned to large-scale dairying and lucrative food and industrial crops such as rice, grapes, olives, fruit, vegetables, hemp, mulberries, and dyestuffs. All invested capital in seed, stock, and buildings and systematically used advanced if labor-intensive methods. These included "interculture," whereby vines and mulberry trees – the cultivation of which required relentless hoeing, plowing, and tending – were planted in grain fields; "water meadows" that, by dint of repeated flooding and mowing, produced several harvests of hay a year; and the cultivation of rice in specially constructed fields that demanded continuous maintenance. Despite the high cost of labor and capital investment, these farms achieved impressive levels of productivity – on intensively cultivated irrigated fields, for example, four or five woad crops could be harvested each year – and yielded handsome profits.

Substantial farms also characterized the commercial agriculture found in southern Italy (Sicily and the mainland Kingdom of Naples) and Andalusia in southern Spain, where huge estates or *latifundia* had arisen in the aftermath of military conquest and civil disorder between the twelfth and fourteenth centuries. Some latifundia were operated as single units employing day laborers. Others were divided into farms of 125–250 acres that were leased for short terms, often on sharecropping tenures. Both tenants and laborers lived in populous villages into which the rural population had been regrouped to facilitate lords' control.

Although olive groves, sugar cane plantations, mulberry trees, saffron fields, and vineyards were to be found in latifundia areas, most of the land was devoted to cereals, cattle, and sheep. Traditional crops did not, however, imply backward agriculture. Sicilian grain yield ratios were as high as 10:1, and latifundia owners regularly deployed large amounts of capital and credit in production, as well as employing free and mobile wage labor. Individual landlords were attentive to estate organization and the sale of agricultural commodities on urban and export markets, and the landlord class, which easily bought and sold fiefs and divided its patrimony among heirs, welcomed wealthy merchants and urban patricians into its ranks. Governments played a particularly noteworthy role in the commercial agriculture of these regions. Not only did they organize and regulate grain marketing, but they provided the necessary legal and institutional setting for the transhumant sheepgrazing practiced in these hot, dry climates. In Spain, the *Mesta* or herders' association had been set up in the thirteenth century to adjudicate between herders and sedentary populations, establish migration routes between summer pastures in northern Castile and Léon and winter grasslands in Andalusia and Estremadura some 450 miles to the south, and collect tolls for the Crown and fees for the military orders that owned the main southern grazing lands. The Kingdom of Naples founded a similar body termed the *Dogana* in 1447, centered on the royal customs house at Foggia, in Apulia.

In the regions along the North Sea known as the Low Countries or Netherlands, it was the peasantry that initiated and directed commercial farming. Small-scale intensive agriculture relying upon household labor was practiced throughout the provinces of east Flanders and Brabant in what is today Belgium and northern France. In this area of partible inheritance and historically dense populations, half the farms were just 5–8 acres in size by the mid-fifteenth century. Yet these small holdings proved viable in this highly urbanized and commercialized region. The third of the total population that lived in towns furnished concentrated demand in accessible markets, as well as night soil for fertilizer. Trade along road, canal, and river brought a growing stream of grain from nearby west Flanders, Hainaut, and Cambrésis, allowing east Flemish and Brabantine farmers to diversify into other crops and livestock.

Although subject to moderately strong lordship, peasants in this area enjoyed both long leases and weak collective regulations that left nearly complete control over agriculture in their hands. In this context, they had slowly and steadily introduced the innovations that exemplified what became known as "Flemish farming" or *petite culture*. Abandoning fallow or reducing it to as seldom as once in every seven or eight years, they planted fodder crops like turnips, buckwheat, vetch, and spurry on the formerly idle land; the requisite hoeings also served to clean the soil. In addition, they alternated cereals and legumes (peas and beans); created temporary meadows for livestock by putting arable under grass for three to six years and then returned the well-fertilized land to crops; farmed waste and other marginal plots for brief periods followed by long rests; and quickly planted and harvested turnips between fall reaping and spring sowing. Flemish farmers also took up new tools: harrows to break up clods and uproot weeds, plows adapted to local soils, the scythe that harvested faster than the sickle it replaced.

As a result of generations of experimentation, these smallholders had become both highly productive grain growers and suppliers of increasing quantities of meat and dairy products for human consumption, along with wool, leather, flax, hemp, dyestuffs, and hops for urban industry. Already around 1300, lands near Lille yielded up to two and a half bushels of wheat an acre, as compared with the European norm of less than a bushel; and though this achievement may have been exceptional, yields of 1.6–1.9 bushels per acre were noted in neighboring districts of Flanders and Brabant during the late fourteenth and fifteenth centuries. So productive was the intensively worked, abundantly fertilized land that it could sustain the cultivation of flax, notorious for rapidly depleting the soil. Indeed, a flax-growing family that engaged in some handicrafts on the side – as many did – could survive on a holding as small as a single acre.

A nearly independent peasantry and weak lordship shaped the commercial agriculture that was beginning to emerge in the northern Netherlands provinces of Holland, Utrecht, and Friesland. In order to attract colonists

to this swampy frontier wilderness, eleventh- and twelfth-century seigniors had been forced to offer personal freedom as well as low, fixed cash
rents and dues. From the beginning, therefore, peasants enjoyed nearly
complete ownership of their holdings, which they freely bought, sold,
leased, and mortgaged. By the late fifteenth century, they owned as much
as 50 percent of Holland's land, more than any other social group; the
nobility had no more than a tenth. Because, moreover, nearly all noble
holdings were widely scattered and did not include strategic land such as
commons and forests, lords lacked an adequate material basis for
dominating the peasantry. Towns controlled the provincial representative
assemblies or "estates" and juridical feudalism was weak, so northern
Netherlands lords were also unable to acquire extra-economic means of
gaining income.

Anemic lordship did not entail strong village communities, however; if
anything, the very absence of conflictual relationships between seigniors
and tenants inhibited the development of collective institutions that might
have helped form common interests and practices. What is more, the land
was settled, "impoldered" (drained and turned into viable fields and
pastures), and worked in individual canal-enclosed family farms without
common arable fields to regulate cooperatively. The most important
collective organizations were the drainage boards or *waterschappen* that
undertook the never-ending tasks of maintaining windmills, pumps,
canals, and related facilities. Yet while legally autonomous and elected
and managed by the peasants, and thus wholly independent of lordship,
the waterschappen had nothing to do with the kinds of agricultural
regulation that structured communal institutions and solidarities elsewhere in rural Europe.

In the mid-fifteenth century, most Dutch farms remained too poorly
drained and frequently flooded to support a family or fully utilize its labor,
thereby foreclosing both self-sufficiency and specialization. Instead,
peasant households in the northern Netherlands engaged in a variety of
pursuits – grain growing, dairying, market gardening, fishing, peat
digging, transport – and thus were considerably less efficient or productive
than the farmers of northern Italy or nearby Flanders and Brabant. But
dairying and livestock herding, already leading agricultural activities,
promoted a monetized and market-oriented rural economy, since so
many foodstuffs and other items had to be bought. Forms of intensive
cultivation were beginning to appear, and so were the trading and
transport facilities needed to bring in grain and carry out bulky agricultural commodities.

These regions of commercial agriculture presented a variety of options
for change that were to be more widely adopted – albeit usually in

modified form – in subsequent centuries. But it is important not to overestimate either their extent in or their impact on late medieval Europe. At best a tenth of the peasantry produced primarily for the market, and only a tiny minority of landlords promoted commercial farming with capital, novel crops, new forms of estate organization, or revised tenancies. Agrarian innovation was mainly restricted to Europe's peripheries, whereas in the core long-established structures and practices remained robust. Property relations, judicial authority, and political power enabled the great majority of landlords to continue to collect incomes without directly involving themselves in agricultural production. Village organizations enforced norms and regulations that fostered communal solidarity and stability. Admittedly, they might also impede the introduction of new ways of exploiting communal resources. Yet the possibilities for growth within traditional agriculture were far from exhausted. In fact, the availability of land and work in a context of moderate rents and prices made the end of the Middle Ages a time of broad peasant prosperity, curtailing the constituency for structural change across most of rural Europe.

Masters and workers

In the late Middle Ages, European industries had a number of distinctive attributes, many of which persisted into the early modern period. Overall, as well as in most specific locations, the making of textiles was the largest single industry; the apparel, leather, food processing (especially grain milling and beer brewing), and construction trades also provided significant employment. Most production was carried on in small dispersed artisan shops, in which working capital in the form of raw materials and wages far exceeded the fixed capital embodied in plant and equipment. Because technological change was halting, pressure on wages was the preferred means of cutting production costs, although attempts were made to obtain cheaper raw materials, usually by switching the area from which they were bought. At the same time, labor markets and mobility – particularly in urban areas – were constrained by corporate and other rules. In mining, metallurgy, and milling, proximity to supplies of raw materials or sources of inanimate energy usually determined industrial location. In contrast, the many crafts whose raw materials could be readily transported, and whose motive power was provided by humans and animals, were much more widely dispersed. Their siting owed more to the availability of labor (whether skilled or cheap), satisfactory commercial and transport facilities, sufficient food supplies, and the weight of government or corporate regulations, laws, and privileges.

Virtually every industry was strongly affected by the rhythms of agriculture. Demand for manufactures rose when abundant harvests lowered food prices; conversely, in a subsistence crisis industrial jobless-ness spread as consumers were forced to devote more of their income to foodstuffs. What is more, the peasant majority supplied much of what it consumed, limiting demand for industrial goods. For all that, manufac-turing for sale took place in town and country across medieval Europe. Much output consisted of lower quality goods for local or regional customers, but there was also a considerable international trade in European products. Some were expensive luxuries, like Flemish scarlets, fine Cordovan leather from southern Spain, Milanese armaments, or Venetian glass, destined for a restricted, widely dispersed clientele. Yet large quantities of goods for middling- or even lower-income consumers also travelled long distances: to take just one example, cheap woollen "says" from the Low Countries were available from the Baltic to the Mediterranean.

Mobility and innovation

The industrial geography of medieval Europe was fluid. In the early Middle Ages, most manufacturing was rural and employed farm families as well as specialized artisans. Young peasant women, for example, often fulfilled labor services to their lords by making cloth in workshops or *gynaecea* built for that purpose. After about 1000, however, much industry shifted to towns to tap more abundant and skilled labor, larger amounts of capital, concentrated demand, better transport, and more efficient com-mercial facilities. Nevertheless, some manufacturing always remained in the countryside, for certain areas were blessed by plentiful raw materials, cheap energy sources such as water and wind, or abundant labor. As the Middle Ages drew to a close, in fact, rural production was flourishing once again.

Some of the growth in rural manufactures came at the expense of towns. In England, once-proud textile cities such as Winchester, Lincoln, and Stamford lost out to villages in East Anglia, the West Riding of Yorkshire, the Cotswolds, and other districts. Yet rural industrial growth did not necessarily cause urban decline; city and countryside often prospered together. The woollens of Exeter and Norwich, for instance, coexisted with intense cloth manufacturing in surrounding villages. Sometimes both town and country made the same kinds of goods, usually of middling or lesser quality: in south Germany, innumerable villages wove flax and cotton "barchents" (fustians) alongside Ulm and Augsburg. More often, some form of regional division of labor developed. Towns usually specialized in goods involving costly equipment or raw materials, high skill levels, elaborate finishing, or close supervision, while villages focused on simpler items made of cheaper materials. These might be versions of urban products, but they might be quite distinct, especially where cities had secured local monopolies for their own goods. Thus Florence, Venice, and Milan took up fine drapery, silks, and other rich fabrics, leaving inexpensive woollens to weavers in the contado. Rural and urban artisans might also perform different stages in the production of the same goods; frequently city merchants or artisans organized village manufacture. Thread was washed, spun, combed, and bleached in the countryside; cloth was woven, dyed, and sheared in town. Similarly, rural folk smelted and refined metals but urban workers made most weapons, tools, hardware, and jewelry. In short, industry in town and country was as likely to be interrelated as antagonistic.

Reflecting the mobility of capital in search of greater profit, the effects of competition, and the results of social conflict and political upheaval, manufacturing also shifted within and between regions. In the Low Countries, for example, the towns and villages of Artois pioneered the making of standardized woollen cloth for export during the twelfth century, but in the decades around 1200 much of the industry migrated to Hainaut and Flanders. By about 1300, it had moved again, this time to large cities in Brabant; in the following decades it relocated to smaller cities in that province and Flanders; and by the fourteenth century it had expanded into the province of Holland.

Why specific locations blossomed and then declined is not entirely clear. Some areas apparently began to make cloth simply to garner a share of the high profits that early centers were earning; some of these imitators succeeded, while others failed. Other places, however, seem to have taken up textiles because they enjoyed what economists call "comparative advantage," wherein the abundance of one or more factor of production promotes manufacture of goods that intensively use that plentiful factor. Over time, nevertheless, the initial advantage – skilled or cheap labor; capital in the form of ready credit or excellent marketing facilities; fine wool or another raw material – diminished as industrial growth drove up its cost or reduced its availability, so a new location became more attractive and the migration resumed. Such a pattern was not unique to the Low Countries: already by the fourteenth century their primacy in the international fine-woollens trade had been successfully challenged by manufactures from northern and central Italy, which in the next century ceded it to England.

Medieval artisans had few links to scientific learning, yet they made a number of technological advances that promised productivity gains. As

3 This depiction of glass manufacture in Bohemia about 1420 shows its
location in the countryside near local supplies of glass sand and wood,
the peasants who transported the raw materials, and the small group of
artisans who exploited the works collectively and performed the several
stages involved in production.

compared to boats with overlapping or "clinker" planking, ships of the new "carvel" (caravel) type, in which boards were fitted side by side over beams and then caulked, saved on construction outlays by using less wood. Lighter and larger than clinker-planked ships, carvels sailed faster and carried larger cargoes per crew member, so they reduced unit transport costs. Iron-making furnaces using water-driven bellows reached higher temperatures than traditional bloomeries, enabling molten metal to absorb carbon. The resulting pig iron, which could be cast into molds or further refined, was both harder and much less expensive to produce than bloomery iron. Innovations in clothmaking were particularly significant. The horizontal loom turned out three to five times as much cloth as the vertical; and the spinning wheel, with a fixed and thus faster moving spindle, doubled or tripled output as compared with the distaff and spindle.

New technologies generally spread slowly, however. Sometimes this was because innovations threatened jobs: fullers, who beat cloth with their feet, bitterly opposed the introduction of mills with hammers driven by water power. Quality concerns also delayed the adoption of new machines. The spinning wheel was often rejected because it gave flimsy, irregular thread unsuitable for the warp in expensive cloth. Technological change could also impose unwanted patterns of work and sociability: whereas a spindle could be carried around and operated during other activities, the wheel confined the spinner to the home, so even artisans not producing warp thread objected to it.

A more common and acceptable form of innovation involved the use of existing technology to make new products. Typically these were variants of established goods that employed novel, cheaper, or fewer raw materials and smaller amounts of skilled labor. The development of new types of woollen fabrics is a case in point. Expensive woollen broadcloth or "old drapery" was woven on two-person looms from the finest English wool, fulled for up to five days, carefully napped (teaselled) and trimmed smooth by highly skilled shearers wielding great scissors, then dyed for up to a week using costly ingredients (dyestuffs and wool together accounted for three-quarters or more of total production costs). In contrast, most "new drapery" could be sold for just half the price of the best broadcloth (which it carefully and closely imitated) because it used less and cheaper wool and simplified finishing techniques. "Light drapery," a bewildering variety of fabrics often generically known as "say," utilized the lowest grades of wool and often mixed in linen, hemp, cotton, goat hair, and other cheap yarns. Woven on one-person looms, given little or no fulling, and left unteaselled and unsheared, light drapery sold for between 5 and 35 percent of the price of the best woollens, 20–60 percent of that of the inexpensive varieties of new drapery. So despite impediments to the diffusion of technological change, geographical mobility and new product development enabled medieval manufacturers to reduce costs and thereby appeal to a broader clientèle.

Work sites and structures

Medieval Europe was dotted with mines, forges, kilns, papermills, shipyards, and other specifically industrial locations. A few were large – Sicilian sugar refineries employed forty to fifty people – but most enterprises were much smaller. The rich Central European silver mines, for instance, were worked by four or five men who banded together to exploit a seam. Even the greatest manufacturing site of the age, the Venetian Arsenal where the communal galleys were built, was not a single, unified enterprise. Instead, scores of independent skilled masters each employed a few assistants to fabricate the many distinct components required for a ship. A central managerial staff existed only to monitor quality and organize final assembly.

Most goods, in any event, were produced in dwellings or in shops attached to them. The typical shop was small, operated by a trained artisan assisted by family members young and old, an apprentice, and a handful of wage laborers or even household servants. This reliance on cheap labor facilitated the dominance of dispersed petty production. So did the low levels of capital investment required. Most crafts used simple, inexpensive, and manually powered machinery. Supplies could be purchased through "trade credit" (by which payment was deferred until finished products had been sold), intrafamily loans were common, and dowries often brought artisans cash and equipment. Guild and municipal regulations also favored small shops run by individual masters. The most common measures limited output per shop, restricted the number of apprentices or workers a master could employ, and forbade anyone who was not a master to operate a workshop.

Most urban artisans practiced one often highly specialized trade. A dozen or more separate crafts were involved in making a broadcloth; woodworkers were subdivided into carpenters, wheelwrights, cabinetmakers, turners, wet coopers, dry coopers, and still others. Yet within shops the division of labor was usually flexible, and each person performed a variety of manufacturing and marketing tasks. Household members were not, moreover, necessarily engaged in just one craft, although the one for which the head of the family had acquired specific skills and equipment typically predominated. Women in particular frequently practiced several trades – often in areas, like food preparation and the making of cloth and clothing, that were related to domestic tasks – depending on their domestic imperatives, and the resources they had available. Ale, for example, could be brewed using common kitchen implements; spinning could be interrupted for child care. But some women – wives as well as the widowed and the never-married – worked outside their households at everything from bleaching to tailoring.

Full-time artisans could be found in the countryside; in addition, many peasants who raised crops with markedly seasonal demands for labor worked in crafts during slack agricultural periods. Conversely, peasant laborers often had to leave off manufacturing during sowing and reaping. Much rural industry also operated irregularly for other reasons. Water-driven mills, for example, stopped when streams ran low in late summer. But since this was the period when grain, grapes, and other crops had to be brought in, industrial and agricultural work could dovetail nicely. Women were especially likely to be involved in rural manufacturing, often part-time and on a piece-work basis, due to the enormous amount of labor needed in the preparatory stages of textile production. Each say loom, for example, required the output of four spinning wheels, and up to ten spinners were needed for each linen weaver. Indeed, linenmaking provided many jobs for women in the countryside, for they were often responsible for every step in the production process, from raising the flax through bleaching the woven cloth.

Statutory workdays typically stretched from sunrise to sunset, although specified breaks for meals and rest reduced the actual time worked. Winter days were considerably shorter than summer, because working by candlelight was usually forbidden to reduce the danger of fire. Wages in winter were also up to 30 percent below summer levels, indicating that pay was based on hours worked, even though it was formally calculated by the day and paid weekly. The workweek was conventionally set at six days. Fifty or so religious holidays interrupted the year, however, so a fully employed artisan could work 250–70 days a year, or about five days a week. But because of interruptions due to weather – particularly in the many crafts carried on outdoors or dependent on water power – injury, illness, or trade cycles, most workers put in fewer days' work.

By the fifteenth century, most urban trades were organized into guilds or "corporations" recruited along occupational lines; rural crafts usually were not. Some guilds had roots in voluntary associations ranging from lay religious societies to criminal syndicates; others were established by municipal or princely governments. Many, however, sprang up as spontaneous, autonomous unions of masters attempting to enhance their personal liberties, regulate competition among themselves, and mediate differences with other social groups; only later were their rules and privileges ratified by public authorities. Irrespective of their specific origins, guilds were juridically defined, semi-public bodies endowed with diverse social, cultural, and political attributes. Religious, charitable, and festive activities, conducted by brotherhoods or "confraternities," were always central to their identity. To advance their members' collective interests, guilds regularly engaged in politics, whether as well-organized (and, because they staffed the urban militias, customarily well-armed) pressure groups or as constituent elements of the urban polity. In Flanders, northern Italy, and Germany, some large and rich guilds had won representation in municipal governments; in many towns, a citizen wishing to participate in politics had first to enroll in a guild.

Despite these functions, guilds were primarily hierarchic economic institutions that regulated producers and production for the benefit of the crafts and, more specifically, the masters who dominated them. Only those men and (in a few trades) women who had successfully completed apprenticeship in the manner prescribed by guild rules and had amassed sufficient capital to buy the requisite tools, open a shop, and purchase admission to the guild were permitted to make and sell the goods reserved to that corporation. Guilds also helped masters recruit and discipline their labor force. They reserved the training of apprentices to guild masters, prescribed the content and length of the education that apprentices were to receive, and examined candidates at the end of their term of apprenticeship, usually by requiring the satisfactory fabrication of a more or less elaborate "masterpiece." Journeymen and other wage-earning employees, both male and female, likewise fell under the jurisdiction of guilds, which set up hiring procedures, fixed wage rates, regulated laborers' mobility, and whenever possible crushed autonomous worker organizations.

To protect masters against competitors inside as well as outside their crafts, guilds deployed a variety of strategies, including local or regional monopolies, output quotas, restrictions on workshop size, and limits on entrepreneurs' investment in manufacturing. They also mandated quality standards to assure trades a good reputation that would attract customers. At times, corporations sought masters' security by resisting any change in products or procedures. But new methods that cut costs, or innovations that enhanced a craft's competitive position by expanding the variety of goods offered or improving their quality, were welcomed when regulations could be devised to give all masters a share in the benefits.

Guilds were fundamental to the medieval industrial economy, but the sheer bulk of their surviving records and their multifaceted role in public life can create an exaggerated sense of their strength, solidarity, and inclusiveness. For one thing, it often proved impossible for corporations to implement monopolies and other privileges, even within a city's walls. There were always guild masters who flouted production limits, cheated on standards, allied with merchants or other entrepreneurs, or made goods that rightfully belonged to other trades. In addition, numerous artisans remained outside the corporate structure. Some were in so-called "free" trades; others lived in seigniorial enclaves or suburbs beyond the reach of municipal law. Many more lived in villages, and indeed the absence of guilds is often thought to have been a powerful inducement for industry to grow up in or relocate to rural locations. But the point ought not to be overstated. Village crafts producing for export were also regulated in order to assure merchants and consumers that quality standards would be maintained, and urban restrictions were often no more extensive or rigid than those in the countryside.

Women, whether rural or urban, constituted the largest group discriminated against by guilds, kept out as much by custom as by written rules. To be sure, many medieval women were employed in manufacturing, even though their participation was frequently hidden by conventions that only specified husbands' or fathers' occupations. Women wove silk in numerous cities: in 1455, "the silk women and throwsters" (those who twisted silk fibers into thread) of London boasted that they were "more than a thousand," including "many gentlewomen," who "lived full honorably and . . . [kept] many households" on the income they earned in their crafts.[1] Nor were they alone. Women practiced every specialty from combing to dyeing in the Spanish cloth industry, spun gold thread in Cologne, fabricated fine ironwork in England, made tapestries in Paris. Moreover, women had helped found some guilds, and women artisans aided by apprentices and wage laborers had long operated their own shops. Labor shortages that had emerged in the aftermath of the Black Death and later fourteenth-century epidemics had proven especially favorable for women: many had been taken on as apprentices and thereafter attained mastership. But by the mid-fifteenth century it had become very difficult for a woman to work as an independent guild mistress.

Admittedly, in a handful of French and German cities a few guilds in trades producing luxury textiles like cloth-of-gold and silk were primarily or even exclusively female. Nearly all, however, were administered by men, who also took charge of all political matters relating to the crafts. In addition, husbands or other male relatives usually marketed the goods made by guildswomen. Elsewhere, women were rarely corporate mem-

[1] *Rotuli Parliamentorum*, V: 325, quoted in *Not in God's Image*, ed. Julia O'Faolain and Lauro Martines (New York, 1973), p. 159.

bers on their own, since guilds were organized around units of production led by men. A widow who was a head of household might be permitted to join a guild and carry on her late husband's trade. But frequently she could only participate for a limited time and then had to remarry a master or journeyman from the same craft or lose her right to practice it; furthermore, some crafts explicitly barred widows. Little wonder that widows comprised just 2–5 percent of guild masters or that the majority of women were relegated to serving as the vast, cheap, flexible work force required in such labor-intensive tasks as washing, combing, carding, and spinning. Most picked up their training informally, and the women who did enter apprenticeship rarely attained journeyman status.

It seems, too, that women were increasingly forbidden access to the few guilds formerly open to them, though why this happened is controversial and the reasons may have differed from town to town. In some places, women lacked sufficient funds to pay entry fees that became steeper as corporations became oligarchic. Other women apparently found the increasingly formal work rules imposed in numerous trades incompatible with family responsibilities. Women were also likely to be pushed out of guilds that got involved in formal political institutions, which had never welcomed a female presence. Of course, many women continued to find employment. But more and more had to work illegally – and thus with fewer protections and at lower wages – for masters or merchants who chafed at corporate restrictions on the expansion of their businesses.

Beyond these geographical and gender exclusions, at the end of the Middle Ages corporations were marked by a widening gap between ethos and actuality. Many guilds fell under the control of wealthy hereditary elites closely allied to, if not identical with, the merchant and patrician oligarchies that ruled cities; as a result, they served more to levy taxes, shoulder charitable services, and police the laboring population than to defend the interests of the majority of masters. In the fifteenth century, in fact, it seems that many new guilds were formed by civic and royal authorities mainly to help administer urban society and economy. For their part, apprentices were liable to be treated not as masters in training but, because they received little or no pay beyond room and board during their terms, as very cheap laborers at a time when a tight labor supply was helping wage workers raise their rates. Thus apprenticeship was prolonged years beyond the time needed to impart the appropriate skills. Masters' children, in contrast, were favored by exemptions from both formal apprenticeship and the often substantial mastership fees.

Journeymen experienced most sharply the dichotomy between ideal and reality. Having successfully completed their training, journeymen could and routinely did perform exactly the same work as the masters who hired them. Yet many found upward mobility into the ranks of masters blocked because they lacked sufficient capital to pay guild fees, buy tools and raw materials, and rent a shop. Formal and informal exclusionary practices ranging from rules favoring masters' sons to agreements among employers also helped to keep mastership in the hands of a relatively small group. In fact if not in name, journeymen were being turned into permanent wage earners.

Within a single town or village – even within the same trade – relations of production might vary considerably. On the basis of degree of autonomy, three broad categories of workers can be distinguished: independent artisans, artisans employed in "putting-out," and dependent wage-earners. The boundaries between groups were fluid, however, and an individual might move among them over the course of a career or even participate in two at the same time. At one extreme stood those artisans – many of them guild masters – who had charge of the production process from the purchase of raw materials to sale of the commodity, whether to another artisan for further manufacture, to a merchant, or to the final consumer. These independent artisans customarily owned their shops and tools, although equipment that demanded large capital outlays, like kilns, forges, and mills, was often leased. Autonomous artisans most often worked in crafts producing for the local market. But they were also found in export-oriented trades organized into the system known as "small commodity production" or the *Kaufsystem*. In this arrangement, textile weavers, for instance, bought thread in the market, wove it in their households, and then sold the unfinished cloth to merchants for further processing. To protect artisans' autonomy, the urban Kaufsystem relied on corporate and municipal rules that gave them privileged access to raw materials supplies, limited shop size, and forbade merchants and others from outside the guilds to invest in production. An analogous although less regulated system existed in the countryside. Village weavers could raise raw materials on their own holdings or on commons, or purchase them directly from neighbors, and they sold the woven textiles to itinerant merchants or in nearby town markets.

Many artisans, among whom were also to be found numerous corporate masters, enjoyed semi-independence at best, for they were employed in putting-out arrangements (also commonly referred to as "outwork" or "domestic" systems, or called by their German name, the *Verlagssystem*). In putting-out, artisans contracted to manufacture a commodity or perform a stage in production (e.g., weave, full, or dye a piece of cloth) using equipment they owned or rented, aided if necessary by workers they hired; materials were supplied by the entrepreneur or *Verleger*, who typically paid piece-rates.

In principle, virtually any craft could be organized on a putting-out basis, but it was most likely to be found in situations where entrepreneurs – usually merchants – could monopolize access to imported raw materials and non-local consumers and thereby force producers to work for them. Domestic systems were also common in trades where working capital and credit requirements exceeded artisan resources, whether because of the substantial sums needed to purchase expensive materials like raw silk, or because a process such as the soaking of hides for leather immobilized funds for so long, or, as in many export industries, because of the considerable interlude between the completion of manufacture and receipt of payment.

Over time, the credit and advance payment characteristic of outwork could turn an artisan into a virtual wage laborer dependent upon a single employer. Yet such a situation was neither general nor necessarily permanent. Many artisans worked for more than one Verleger and, depending on the state of the business cycle and their judgment about opportunities for profit, switched between outwork and production of commodities that they personally sold in the market. Some carried on both at the same time. Other artisans simultaneously worked on contract and subcontracted to others, or combined contract work with trading, and this sometimes became the avenue by which they themselves became entrepreneurs or merchants.

The Florentine woollens industry indicates the complexities possible in a Verlagssystem. Merchants specializing in – and earning most of their profits from – trading wool, dyestuffs, and finished cloth furnished the necessary capital but were not involved in production. Rather, they supplied raw materials and working capital on credit to master artisans (dyers, shearers, or – most commonly – weavers) known as *lanaiuoli* (in English, "clothiers"), the entrepreneurs who coordinated the actual making of the cloth. Lanaiuoli operated central shops, yet these were small, with on average only seven workers in addition to family members. Several of these employees – usually women – were paid day or piece rates to weigh, pick, beat, comb, and card the raw wool, although these tasks might also be performed by workers employed directly by the guild (the *Arte della Lana*) that incorporated all woollens-related crafts. Most central shop employees, however, were engaged in accounting and administration. They bought and distributed raw materials, made sure that work was carried out in a timely manner and at acceptable levels of quality, and handled sales of finished cloth.

After combing or carding, the wool was sent to specialized artisans. In the preparatory stages of washing and spinning, these were mainly peasant women under the purview of two types of yarn dealers. *Stamaioli* put out combed wool to be spun by spindle and distaff for use in the warp: a say needed 40 pounds of warp thread, the output of forty women working eight days each. *Lanini* took care of carded wool for the woof; it could be spun more rapidly on the wheel, so the 70 pounds needed for a say could be completed by eight women each spinning for seven days. The thread then passed to a weaving shop, more likely in the fifteenth century than in the past to be in the countryside, though many remained in the city. Once warpers and weft-winders had mounted the thread on the loom, a weaver and his or her assistant took six weeks to make a say, just half that time for a cheaper "perpignan" cloth (a silkweaver, in contrast, needed five or six months to turn out a fancy brocade). Finishing tasks, like fulling, shearing, and dyeing, were done in the shops of urban masters who boasted their own capital, equipment, and employees and worked for many entrepreneurs. Finally, the cloth was inspected and sealed by Lana officials, then dispatched to market.

The least autonomous workers of all were those employed by a master or merchant entrepreneur for a wage: whereas putting-out producers sold the products of their labor, dependent workers sold only their labor. Comprising not only semi-skilled and unskilled workers, but also most women (no matter what their proficiency), along with some apprentices, journeymen, and even ruined masters, this was a heterogeneous group laboring under disparate conditions. On rare occasions, medieval entrepreneurs sought to establish large shops in which wage-earning employees using tools and equipment supplied by the owner carried on many or all stages of production. But most towns and guilds discouraged these attempts, instead favoring small shops and separate trades. As a rule, moreover, entrepreneurs themselves looked askance at big units. Aware that labor and raw materials accounted for most production costs and that, as a result, few if any gains could be realized from controlling production processes, they avoided tying up much capital in fixed investments like manufacturing equipment or buildings. The bulk of entrepreneurial capital remained in circulating or working form – in raw materials, advances for wages, and goods in shipment – and profits came overwhelmingly from commercial and credit transactions. Thus most wage-earners, like most putting-out workers or independent artisans, labored in small shops.

Such workers might have long-term contracts or get hired by the week or day; they might use their own tools or their employers'; they worked at a variety of industrial sites. Paid according to piece rates or by time, their wages could vary by gender, by the inclusion of meals or residence in the employer's house, or by advances that bound them almost as servants. Over time, specific places and times had emerged as informal "hiring halls" or had been explicitly established for that purpose, and competition for work existed, magnified by the presence of migrants, pauperized masters, and failed journeymen. But free labor markets, closely attuned to changes in supply and demand, were slow to appear. Their emergence was hampered by guild and municipal regulations, by the continuing importance of personal relations for obtaining jobs, and by widely prevalent notions that there existed correct wage levels fixed by custom. Thus wages tended to be "sticky," remaining unchanged for years or even decades, whereas prices were more volatile.

For all that, the supply of labor did affect wages, and this fact generally favored workers in industry at the end of the Middle Ages (just as it favored their agricultural counterparts). Around 1450, they enjoyed real wages that had at least doubled over the previous century, thanks to low prices for grain, the central determinant of the cost of living, and a tight labor market. The declining cost of cereals also freed a larger proportion of consumer spending for manufactures, which helped maintain industrial wage levels and employment. To be sure, short-term crises combining high prices and joblessness recurred every two or three years, in some industries intensified competition put a damper on wage growth, and even in expanding trades the pace of work may have accelerated, as employers more closely supervised expensive labor. Nevertheless, evidence of more comfortable domestic interiors, as well as more widespread and more regular consumption of white bread, meat, and wine, suggest that on the whole workers' standard of living was rising.

Late medieval European manufacturing encompassed, then, an impressive variety of institutional forms, work relations, and labor conditions. The unskilled wool beater employed for piece-rates by Florence's Lana guild had a work experience unlike that of the independent female ironmonger of the English Midlands; a rich goldsmith in Paris was a producer of a different stripe than a village flax spinner in East Prussia. Guilds provided much of Europe's manufacturing structure, job training, and industrial discipline, not to mention important charitable, religious, and convivial services. By virtue of sex, location, or occupation, however, much of the labor force found itself outside of corporate rules, protections, and controls. Yet whether corporate or free, autonomous or outworking, urban or rural, the small household shop (or, as in mining, shipbuilding, and a few other trades, the small work unit) producing limited amounts of goods in time-honored ways remained dominant. Often it was championed by guild and municipal regulations grounded in widely accepted beliefs about proper economic, social, and moral behavior. According to these presumptions, small units best promoted quality, provided an adequate livelihood for the mass of producers, upheld contemporary ideals of independence, curbed the sin of avarice, and encouraged societal stability. Even when institutionalized support was lacking, moreover, small units found favor among both entrepreneurs unwilling to tie up fixed capital in production and artisans anxious to keep as much control as possible over the production process. During the next three centuries, this resilient structure vitally shaped Europe's capitalist transitions.

Constraints and opportunities

Formidable problems confronted European economies at the close of the Middle Ages. The dominant agrarian structure made it difficult to improve productivity. Custom, law, village communities, and their own values and interests restricted the ability of most landlords and many peasants to experiment with new crops, tools, and practices or to reorganize their properties. Large numbers of tenants with subsistence-level output and inadequate capital resources seldom engaged in market transactions. Uncertain and fluctuating consumer demand discouraged industrial change. So did corporate, government, and popular intervention on moral, social, and political grounds. Apprentices and journeymen faced curtailed possibilities for upward mobility within crafts, while women's labor status deteriorated. Many long-established trades dwindled or were entirely abandoned.

Yet the period also contained opportunities for change and spawned initiatives meant to take advantage of them. Real wages were high, cereal prices low, and much land available on favorable terms. Some areas responded by specializing in pastoralism, as well as in raw materials and foodstuffs more lucrative than grain. Besides increasing the range of agricultural goods available to consumers and industry, these strategies enhanced the commercialization of the countryside and promoted divisions of labor within and between regions. Eastern Sicilian peasants, for example, produced wine, oil, and livestock for sale on the western parts of the island, which sent them grain. New industrial ventures began, too. Some involved luxury goods. Thus Mechelen (Brabant) not only emphasized expensive woollens but developed such crafts as the making of fine leatherware and fur garments, dyeing, carpet weaving, and bell casting. At the same time, the manufacture of cheap linens and woollens penetrated further into villages across Europe, providing employment for poorer peasants, stimulating food production and marketing, and supplying local and regional consumers as well as export markets.

Whether all this added up to anything more than a reshuffling of existing activity is hard to tell in the absence of reliable statistics. Barchent weaving flourished in south Germany and Switzerland, yet fine German linens lost markets in the Low Countries and even at home to aggressive producers in Flanders and Hainaut who had seen their own cheap linen crafts wither. On the eve of the "long sixteenth century," European agriculture and industry embodied both diverse possibilities for change and powerful impulses favoring continuity. Which of them were to come to fruition, and why?

SUGGESTED READING

The best place to get a sense of the vast scholarship in medieval economic history is the three volumes of *The Cambridge Economic History of Europe*. Vol. I, *The Agrarian Life of the Middle Ages* (Cambridge, 1966), and Vol. II, *Trade and Industry in the Middle Ages* (Cambridge, 1987), are now in their second edition; see also Vol. III, *Economic Organization and Policies in the Middle Ages* (Cambridge, 1963). A briefer collective work is the *Fontana Economic History of Europe*, Vol. I. The *Middle Ages*, ed. Carlo Cipolla (London, 1972). Norman J. G. Pounds, *An Economic History of Medieval Europe* (London, 1974), and Georges Duby, *Rural Economy and Country Life in the Medieval West* (Columbia, SC, 1968; orig. French publ., 1962) are useful works of synthesis, although by now inevitably becoming dated. For national overviews, see J. L. Bolton, *The Medieval English Economy, 1150–1500* (London, 1980); Judith Brown, "Prosperity or Hard Times in Renaissance Italy?" *Renaissance Quarterly*, vol. 42 (1989); and Richard Goldthwaite, *Wealth and the Demand for Art in Italy, 1300–1600* (Baltimore, 1993), Part I.

England is particularly well served for agricultural history by *The Agrarian History of England and Wales*. Vol. III. *1348–1500*, ed. Edward Miller (Cambridge, 1991). For more specialized studies see C. J. Dahlman, *The Open Field System and Beyond* (Cambridge, 1980), a new economic history approach; Martin Cosgel, "Risk Sharing in Medieval Agriculture," *Journal of European Economic History*, vol. 21 (1992); and Zvi Razi, "Family, Land and the Village Community in Later Medieval England," *Past and Present*, no. 93 (1981). Regional studies have a long and proud tradition; among the best of those published recently are Christopher Dyer, *Lords and Peasants in a Changing Society* (Cambridge, 1980); Marjorie McIntosh, *Autonomy and Community: The Royal Manor of Havering, 1200–1500* (Cambridge, 1986); Mark Bailey, *A Marginal Economy? East Anglian Breckland in the Later Middle Ages* (Cambridge, 1989); and Larry R. Poos, *A Rural Society after the Black Death: Essex, 1350–1525* (Cambridge, 1991).

Most of the numerous French regional monographs have not been translated, but English-language readers can sample the genre thanks to the translation of Guy Bois' stimulating *The Crisis of Feudalism. Economy and Society in Eastern Normandy c. 1300–1550* (Cambridge and Paris, 1984; orig. publ. 1976). Coverage in English of the rest of Europe is similarly spotty. However, the development of Andalusia can be traced in John Edwards, *Christian Córdoba. The City and its Region in the Late Middle Ages* (Cambridge, 1982); Edwards, "Development and 'Underdevelopment' in the Western Mediterranean: The Case of Córdoba and its Region in the Late Fifteenth and Early Sixteenth Century," *Mediterranean History*

Review, vol. 2 (1989); and E. Cabrera, "The Medieval Origins of the Great Landed Estates of the Guadalquivir Valley," *Economic History Review*, 2nd ser., vol. 42 (1989). Teofilo Ruiz, *Crisis and Continuity: Land and Town in Late Medieval Castile* (Philadelphia, 1994), gives some flavor of the abundant and superb recent studies on the economic history of this kingdom, nearly all of which have yet to be translated. For Italy, see especially Stephan Epstein, *An Island for Itself. Economic Development and Social Change in Late Medieval Sicily* (Cambridge, 1992). Two valuable essays that evaluate sharecropping quite disparately can be found in *Florentine Studies*, ed. Nicolai Rubenstein (London, 1968): David Herlihy, "Santa Maria Impruneta: A Rural Commune in the Late Middle Ages," and Philip Jones, "From Manor to Mezzadria: A Tuscan Case-Study in the Medieval Origins of Modern Agrarian Society." See also Douglas Dowd, "Economic Expansion of Lombardy 1300–1500: A Study in Political Stimuli to Economic Change," *Journal of Economic History*, vol. 21 (1961). For the Dogana, see John Marino, *Pastoral Economics in the Kingdom of Naples* (Baltimore, 1988).

Late medieval urban economies are the subject of R. H. Britnell, *Growth and Decline in Colchester 1300–1525* (Cambridge, 1986); and Charles Phythian-Adams, *Desolation of a City. Coventry and the Urban Crisis of the Late Middle Ages* (Cambridge, 1979). Two excellent recent studies discuss working life: Christopher Dyer, *Standards of Living in the Later Middle Ages: Social Changes in England, c. 1200–1520* (Cambridge, 1989) and Heather Swanson, *Medieval Artisans* (Oxford, 1989). In *The Building of Renaissance Florence* (Baltimore, 1980), Richard Goldthwaite provides an in-depth study of the Florentine construction trades in the later Middle Ages. Material on the emergence of urban wage labor can be found in Steven Epstein, *Wage Labor and Guilds in Medieval Europe* (Chapel Hill, NC, 1991); for wage systems, see essays in *Labour and Leisure in Historical Perspective*, ed. Ian Blanchard (Stuttgart, 1994) and in *Hours of Work and Means of Payment: The Evolution of Conventions in Pre-Industrial Europe*, ed. C. S. Leonard and B. N. Mironov (Milan, 1994). Other influences on late medieval economic life are discussed in R. H. Britnell, *The Commercialisation of English Society, 1000–1500* (Cambridge, 1993).

Of all industries, the textile trades have been most studied. Among the best recent works are Maureen Mazzaoui, *The Italian Cotton Industry in the Late Middle Ages, 1100–1600* (Cambridge, 1981); A. R. Bridbury, *Medieval English Clothmaking* (London, 1982); Herman Van der Wee, "Structural Changes and Specialization in the Industry of the Southern Netherlands, 1100–1600," *Economic History Review*, second ser., vol. 28 (1975); Florence de Roover, "Andrea Banchi, Florentine Silk Manufacturer and Merchant in the 15th Century," *Studies in Medieval and Renaissance History*, vol. 3 (1966); and the collected studies of John Munro, *Textiles, Towns and Trade: Essays in the Economic History of Late-Medieval England and the Low Countries* (Aldershot, 1994). Recent research is superbly surveyed in the *Cambridge History of Western Textiles*, ed. D. T. Jenkins (Cambridge, 1997). For other industries, see Richard Unger, *The Ship in the Medieval Economy 600–1600* (London, 1980); and *English Medieval Industries*, ed. John Blair and Nigel Ramsay (London, 1991), which is wide-ranging, profusely illustrated, and contains excellent bibliographies.

Recent works have begun to explore medieval women's work experiences in depth. Two collections of essays range over rural and urban labor: *Women and Work in Preindustrial Europe*, ed. Barbara Hanawalt (Bloomington, Indiana, 1986); and *Women and Work in Preindustrial England*, ed. Lorna Duffin and Lindsey Charles (London, 1985). For an uneven synthesis, see David Herlihy, *Opera Muliebria. Women and Work in Medieval Europe* (New York, 1990). More successful are focused monographs, such as Martha Howell, *Women, Production, and Patriarchy in Late Medieval Cities* (Chicago, 1986), which examines the Low Countries and Germany; and P. J. P. Goldberg, *Women, Work, and Life Cycle in a Medieval Economy. Women in York and Yorkshire c. 1300–1520* (Oxford, 1992). Margret Wensky, "Women's Guilds in Cologne in the Later Middle Ages," *Journal of European Economic History*, vol. 11 (1982), and Grethe Jacobsen, "Women's Work and Women's Role: Ideology and Reality in Danish Urban Society, 1300–1550," *Scandinavian Economic History Review*, vol. 31 (1983), are valuable brief studies.

For analyses that emphasize the flexibility of urban economic regulations and institutions, see Robert DuPlessis and Martha Howell, "Reconsidering the Early Modern Urban Economy," *Past and Present*, no. 94 (1982); Richard Mackenney, *Tradesmen and Traders. The World of the Guilds in Venice and Europe, c. 1250–c. 1650* (Totowa, NJ, 1987); and Marci Sortor, "Saint-Omer and its Textile Trades in the Late Middle Ages," *American Historical Review*, vol. 98 (1993).

Part II

Introduction: The long sixteenth century

In the history of the European economy, the term "long sixteenth century" denotes an extended cycle with two phases. Originating in 1450/1500 and continuing until 1550/70, almost a century of widespread and imposing growth was marked by rising agricultural and industrial output, trade, rents, and incomes, and was accompanied by sustained demographic expansion and urbanization. As Claude de Seyssel wrote in 1519 (he referred to France, but the terms of his sunny description could be widely duplicated), "many big cities that had been half empty are today so full that it is hardly possible to find space to build houses . . . [M]any places and large regions that were uncultivated and lay fallow or wooded are now entirely cultivated and occupied by villages and houses."[1] This broad expansionary stage was followed by nearly as general a deceleration, until by 1620/50 advance had come to a halt virtually everywhere and most of Europe had entered what is often referred to as "the crisis of the seventeenth century." A century after Seyssel, Sir Edwin Sandys' gloomy words in the English House of Commons accurately reported a state of affairs destined to be repeated for decades throughout Europe: "Looms are laid down . . . The farmer is not able to pay his rent . . . The fairs and markets stand still."[2]

The long sixteenth century was also the age when restless Europeans discovered the New World, circumnavigated the globe, and settled far and wide around the world; fundamentally – and often bloodily – reformed their religious beliefs and ecclesiastical institutions; strengthened monarchic government and rebelled against it; evolved a radically new cosmology and brutally persecuted witches; and widely exploited a host of epochal inventions such as printing and gunpowder. Many scholars have interpreted it as an era of equally sweeping economic change. They have pointed to the so-called "price revolution" – led by grain prices that

---

[1] *La Grande monarchie de France*, quoted in F. Bayard and P. Guignet, *L'Economie française aux XVIe, XVIIe et XVIIIe siècles* (Gap and Paris, 1991), p. 89.
[2] Commons debate, 26 February 1621, printed in *Seventeenth-Century Economic Documents*, ed. J. Thirsk and J. P. Cooper (Oxford, 1972), p. 1.

increased as much as sevenfold in nominal terms – that purportedly caused a profound redistribution of income and property; to an "agricultural revolution" that at least in England renewed structures and techniques, setting off rapid growth in productivity; and to the blossoming forth of a "capitalist world-economy" centered on Europe.

Closer study has modified these claims. The long sixteenth century was indeed a time of dramatic initiatives. But its economic accomplishments were more modest, their impact slower to be felt, and the degree of change less far-reaching, than is often imagined. The price rise helped stimulate economic expansion and redistribute income, but it averaged just a few percent a year, many years saw little or no inflation, and prices of other foodstuffs, industrial raw materials, and manufactures mounted much less than cereals. Most of all, inflation was just one of a multitude of forces affecting development. Recent research has downgraded the depth, breadth, and novelty of the changes that transpired in agriculture, whether in England or on the Continent. And although Europe's trading routes certainly spread, they did not yet constitute an articulated system. So while capitalist relations extended their reach, existing structures and practices channelled, limited, and in many cases thwarted impulses pushing for innovation and transformation. The long sixteenth century comprised an important period in European economic history. Much of its significance lies, however, in the ways in which the established orders shaped new forces. Why and how this process unfolded is the subject of Part II.

3 Agriculture: Growth and the limits of development

As Europeans in the years after 1450 vigorously exploited the possibilities for growth bequeathed by later medieval agriculture, advance proceeded briskly for many decades. By the second half of the sixteenth century, however, it was petering out in all but a few favored areas. Of the many innovations attempted, few took root and fewer still promoted important structural changes. What was the nature and extent of the long wave of growth and decay? How and why were existing practices and forms of organization challenged? Why were they so seldom supplanted by substantially new ones? Who were the proponents of change, and who its opponents? What interests and policies motivated them? And what allowed them to succeed or caused them to fail?

To answer these questions, this chapter examines the contours of the protracted agrarian cycle, the factors that lay behind the admittedly rare instances of development, and the forces that limited and frustrated transformation. It focuses on the landlords and peasants whose resources, initiative, and resistance determined the directions that agriculture would take. Several general trends arose from the common features of Europe's agrarian societies that we have previously identified. At the same time, disparate topographies, tenurial arrangements, inheritance customs, and communal forms, as well as early modern Europe's array of political structures and fiscal pressures, also assured that specific countries, regions, even small districts, would follow distinctive trajectories. It is impossible for this book to explore fully that diversity. But to understand both the broad themes and the significant differences that defined the agrarian long sixteenth century, we need to analyze comparatively the three major European economic zones: the Mediterranean basin, long both the center of gravity of Europe's economy and home to its most advanced agriculture; western Europe, which was starting to assert economic primacy; and the east central lands, which followed a unique path of their own.

Agricultures new and old

The Mediterranean Basin

Spain

Sharing fully in the secular European upswing, an increasingly productive, diversified, and market-oriented agriculture flourished throughout Spain from the later fifteenth century to the 1570s. In Castile, the biggest and most populous kingdom, some cereal farms achieved yield ratios of 8 or 9: 1, among the highest of the age. Grain, olives, and grapes – the staples of Mediterranean husbandry – were grown widely across the peninsula, and most areas had developed profitable specializations as well. Castile was known for wool, Aragon for saffron, the northwestern provinces for cattle, while the kingdoms along the Mediterranean coast produced large amounts of raw silk, fruits, vegetables, rice, and sugarcane. Commercial agriculture had previously been restricted to big estates, but now individual peasants took it up with gusto.

Spanish agriculture benefited from trends in population, industry, commerce, and transport that boosted demand throughout Europe during the growth phase of the long sixteenth century. It also profited from some unique advantages. The number of urban dwellers – about 6 percent of 6.8 million people around 1500, nearly 12 percent of 8.5 million a century later – more than doubled, and many were engaged in vigorous textile industries that used Spanish-raised wool, silk, and other raw materials. Wholly new markets opened up in the overseas colonies conquered and settled in these years. Industrial growth elsewhere in Europe likewise stimulated the Spanish countryside. Fine merino wool from Castile was Spain's leading, and fastest-growing, agricultural export; having surpassed English wool in quality, it was in high demand among both old and new drapery weavers. Bruges, staple city for Spanish wool shipped to the Low Countries, alone took an average of 13,000 sacks (each weighing about 220 lbs) each year in 1510–20; by 1550, the annual figure had climbed to 70,000 sacks.

Despite these achievements, the general agrarian downturn that set in during the later sixteenth century did not spare Spain; rural Castile's depression, in fact, proved as deep and stubborn as any in Europe. The 2.5–2.8 million transhumant sheep that had grazed in Castile before 1550 fell to just 1.6 million in the early 1630s; to judge by wool exports, which in the 1660s stood at less than half their 1570s levels, sedentary flocks must also have contracted from the million or more head estimated for the first half of the sixteenth century. Grain output dropped, too, by 30–50 percent between 1580 and 1640. Neither wool nor grain was to equal its mid-sixteenth-century level until several decades into the eighteenth century. Precise data are not available for other crops, but it is suggestive that many peasants gave up once-thriving specializations.

These agricultural problems have been considered pivotal to the general economic (and later political and military) decline that gripped Spain as the seventeenth century progressed, so their causes have long been vigorously debated. Slumping foreign demand is often cited, and there is some truth in this claim. Because sheepherding depended heavily on sales abroad, it suffered when piracy and blockades during wars with France and the long "Dutch Revolt" or "Eighty Years' War" (1566–1648) disturbed shipments to the Low Countries. To be sure, for several decades rising exports to Italy and France compensated somewhat for the loss of Castilian wool's major market, but by the end of the sixteenth century, textile industries throughout Europe shifted increasingly from fabrics using merino fleeces to those woven from inferior, often local, wools. Colonial markets languished, too, as settlers began to raise more of the food they ate. Domestic conditions, however, were decisive for Spanish agriculture's decay.

Many historians posit a "Malthusian crisis," the outcome of a widening imbalance between population and natural resources. As demand and prices rose during the sixteenth century, most Spanish peasants had responded not by improving their farming practices but by bringing more land under the plow, in particular by converting pasture, waste, and woodland to arable. This process could not, however, be sustained indefinitely. Much newly cultivated land was of marginal fertility and quickly depleted, and even good soil deteriorated from inadequate manuring as the extension of cropland at the expense of grazing compelled herds to shrink. By the later sixteenth century, grain yields began to dwindle, eventually sinking as low as 4:1.

This account is persuasive as far as it goes. But it does not explain why decades of vigorous demand and ascending prices failed to evoke significant investment and innovation. What blocked agricultural improvement? Many early modern Spaniards, followed by numerous later scholars, identified two culprits: the wheat and barley price maximum or *tasa*, and transhumant pastoralism as institutionalized in the Mesta. The tasa, designed to prevent profiteering in time of dearth, was charged with impoverishing the peasantry by making grain production unprofitable. For its part, the broad coalition of monarchy, landowners, merchants, and foreign cloth manufacturers that benefited from sheepherding was accused of destroying cropland and ruthlessly subordinating arable to pastoral interests, thus preventing the development of a balanced and productive agriculture.

In light of recent research, however, both appear much less culpable than previously imagined. The tasa turns out to have been frequently suspended, riddled with exemptions, and widely evaded. Despite some notorious instances when flocks deliberately were permitted to ruin valuable vineyards and olive groves, on the whole sheep did not cause much damage, and many localities actually welcomed them for the manure they left behind. The Mesta's power also should not be overestimated. Admittedly, in 1501 the Crown had ordered that Mesta flocks should henceforth be permitted to graze forever at the original – usually low – rent on any land they had used even once, and in 1633 commanded that all pasture converted to crops since 1590 be put back under grass. Yet these decrees proved ineffectual. Court rulings increasingly sided with arable farmers in disputes with grazers, and ostensibly far-reaching Mesta privileges did little to protect herders from spiralling pasture rents or exclusion from land reserved for sedentary village flocks. Restoration of pasture in the seventeenth century came about not because of government mandates but because farmers relinquished marginal fields (ironically, grazers then also left them empty, because demand for wool was depressed). From all evidence, the arable and pastoral sectors advanced and languished hand in hand across the long sixteenth century.

Price-fixing and pastoralism were not, then, at the root of Spain's agricultural problems. The fundamental causes are rather to be found in the siphoning of resources out of the agrarian sector by a powerful landlord class and a monarchy seeking revenue and political support. These conditions vitally affected patterns of land acquisition, capital accumulation, and seigniorial authority so as to block agrarian improvement.

Until the 1560s, Spanish taxes had declined in real terms; the expansion and defense of the worldwide Habsburg empire were financed by the Crown's share of the gold and silver mined in its American colonies and by massive borrowing. In the following decades, however, this system proved inadequate, so the costs of the drawn-out Dutch Revolt – not to mention maritime campaigns against the Turks and involvement in France's Religious Wars – led to sharp increases. Existing sales taxes (notably the *alcabala*) mounted at least two and a half times between 1561 and 1590, then jumped a similar amount in the next three decades. But even this fell short of filling the gap, so a new tax, the *millones*, was created in 1590; within a decade, its rate had been doubled, and it rose rapidly again during the 1620s and 1630s.

The millones had been conceived of as a levy on wealth, but collection was delegated to local authorities, typically well-to-do individuals who quickly devised expedients to shift the burden off their shoulders. In particular – and most harmful to the majority of peasants – they sold communally administered lands known as *baldíos* or *tierras baldías*, commons where peasants enjoyed the right to pasture sheep and draft animals and to gather manure for their arable fields. Beginning in the 1570s, and continuing into the seventeenth century, about 40 percent of baldíos were auctioned off. Some peasants were able to buy and enclose baldíos by mortgaging their holdings, and others managed to rent some of the now private property. Nevertheless, both groups faced significantly increased costs for fields they had formerly used for free – and just at a time when sales taxes were skyrocketing and demand for agricultural goods was starting to contract. Many baldío purchasers, unable to keep up payments, defaulted and lost all their land, "forcing them," as tenants from the Castilian village of Ceinos de Campos claimed, "to leave the homes and localities where they were born and, with their wives and children, wander through foreign lands."[1] Similarly, the many communities that sought to recover some commons by acquiring baldíos – often from speculators at steep markups – fell massively into debt and usually were forced to resell or lease them to aristocratic and clerical landlords.

Baldío sales thus served both to impoverish peasants and to concentrate land ownership: between them, nobles and ecclesiastical institutions came to control two-thirds or more of the countryside. Other government policies heightened their dominance. To secure political loyalty – and to raise additional funds – the Crown alienated lucrative jurisdictions; public authority was privatized along with public land. Monarchs also turned a blind eye when landowners usurped wastes and forests. In these ways, some great nobles became even greater. The Mendoza dukes of Infantado eventually held sway over nearly 800 towns and villages, while the Duke of Medina Sidonia's estates covered most of the modern province of Huelva and a large part of neighboring Seville province.

Nobles who encountered financial difficulties – whether because of costly service at court or on the battlefield, or simply because of lackadaisical estate management or even wasteful spending – could count, moreover, on being rescued by Crown largesse, including tax exemptions, pensions, debt remission, and, most remunerative of all, participation in royal tax collecting. Although his case was certainly unusual, in 1566 the Count of Benavente derived 74 percent of his income from administering royal imposts, as against 13.5 percent from ground rents and 12.5 percent from seigniorial jurisdictions and fees.

Yet this redistribution of land and capital into the hands of the landed elites failed to induce even the wealthiest and most solvent among them to

---

[1] Quoted in Bartolomé Yun Casalilla, *Sobre la transición al capitalismo en Castilla. Economía y sociedad en Tierra de Campos (1500–1830)* (Salamanca, 1987), p. 285.

invest much in agricultural improvement. Many devoted their resources to "political investment," acquiring municipal offices or court posts that conferred power, status, and considerable opportunity for profit. But even those who put their money in land did not pursue innovative measures for long. To be sure, in the early sixteenth century, some latifundia owners in the Guadalquivir valley of Andalusia planted vineyards and olive groves on demesnes previously devoted to grain and hired full-time wage earners, supplemented by seasonal migrants, to cultivate them. As time went on, however, they did not follow up their initial investments but divided their properties and let them to sharecroppers or tenants; the estate owners themselves became rentiers. In the rest of Spain, where large-scale demesne agriculture had never existed, landlords also focused on maximizing rental income rather than on improvement. In particular, they replaced perpetual leases, which typically had fixed rents, with short-term leases that were repeatedly raised.

The existence of powerful rentier landlords would not necessarily have doomed agricultural development if the peasantry had retained the wherewithal to act on its own. But that was a big if, and it decreasingly held true in Spain. Rents multiplied fivefold between 1500 and 1600, becoming relatively heavier in the later part of the century – just when crop yields fell and formerly free baldío land had to be paid for. By the 1580s, rent commonly took 30 percent of the peasant harvest. When taxes, tithes, and seigniorial dues were added in, peasants owed half or more of their gross output. To meet current expenses, many were obliged to borrow by means of *censos*. These short-term, high-interest loans (often obtained from landlords), secured by mortgages on their holdings, kept peasants in virtual debt peonage.

By that point, most villagers were in serious difficulties. One-fifth or more were landless – a half or even three-quarters in much of Andalusia. They hung on as day laborers whose wages increasingly fell behind the rising cost of living even when jobs were to be found; where demesnes were divided and leased, their employment opportunities became even bleaker. Impoverishment, begging, often vagabondage also faced that half of villagers classified as smallholders. In the best of times, their plots averaging 12 acres or less barely provided subsistence, yet the stratagems they had devised – keeping livestock on the commons, selling produce from their gardens, spinning thread and weaving cloth, working for wages on larger farms – became less viable as baldíos were privatized, urban population shrank after 1600, and the Spanish economy slowed down. Even many of the once well-off peasants, that 20–25 percent (at most) of villagers whose 12–25 acres and team of oxen had allowed them to achieve respectable yields and marketable surpluses, now had to sell crops at a discount before harvest and surrender mortgaged land as they struggled to keep afloat.

Thus as government and landlords' exactions intensified, capital did not flow into agricultural improvement. Instead, it was deployed into financial, seigniorial, fiscal, and especially rent exploitation. Landlords sought not to enlarge the agricultural surplus but – with considerable success – to carve themselves a larger slice of the existing pie. By the late sixteenth century, the combined weight of their levies blocked rural initiative, even on the part of once dynamic middling peasants. Because no significant innovations had been introduced, only extensive growth had been achieved, and once the ecological limits had been reached agriculture slipped quickly into reverse.

The only bright spot in this increasingly grim picture was the market-oriented peasant agriculture found in Catalonia. Although Catalan farmers paid substantial tithes and seigniorial dues, their rents were fixed at low rates and, by virtue of a 1486 royal decree, they enjoyed enviable security of tenure. Equally important, taxes remained stable. With less of their output appropriated by state and landlord than their counterparts elsewhere in Spain, middling Catalan peasants prospered by raising a widening variety of crops for consumers both in nearby towns and abroad. Unfortunately, Catalonia formed the exception. A similarly flourishing peasant-based agriculture in the Kingdom of Valencia was badly disrupted when in 1609 the Crown expelled (largely for religious and political reasons) the christianized Muslims or *moriscos* who had been the most productive farmers. It will come as no surprise to learn that morisco lands were seized and given to their lords, whose debts were also forgiven. As this example indicates, bad as Spain's agricultural decline was to begin with, perhaps even worse was the way in which it entrenched structures and practices that seriously complicated future recovery.

Italy

The robust commercial agriculture that had distinguished medieval Italy continued to flourish across most of the sixteenth century. Lombard pastel was prized in England, Sicilian grain provisioned Iberia. Most Italian agricultural output was, however, consumed within the peninsula itself. The people of the many – and expanding – towns and cities were fed by specialties such as saffron from the Abruzzi, Sicilian sugar, cattle from the Roman Campagna, and rice from the Po Valley, not to mention the wheat, olive oil, and wine produced in nearly every region. Domestically raised wool, silk, flax, and dyestuffs supplied Italy's already formidable textile industries, which experienced a new burst of prosperity. Strikingly, the number of Dogana sheep, and the amount of wool sold, nearly quadrupled between 1550 and 1612.

During this expansive period, many peasants prospered, and some managed to assemble good-sized farms by purchasing holdings from less fortunate villagers or by subletting noble and ecclesiastical properties. But an increasing amount of land was bought by townspeople who held, as Leon Battista Alberti put it, that a "farm is, first of all, profitable and, second, a source of both pleasure and pride."[2] As early as 1498, Florentines held two-thirds of the arable in the Mugello district north of the city (peasant proprietors had barely a ninth), and thereafter the dominion of urban capital steadily extended deeper into the countryside. By 1548, Venetians had purchased one-third of the land around their subject city of Padua; half a century later, Florentines possessed more than 30 percent of the best land in the contado of Pisa (which they ruled), and another fifth belonged to Pisa residents.

As the long sixteenth century drew to a close, however, signs of weakness multiplied throughout rural Italy. In many areas, there emerged throngs of day laborers whose real wages constantly sank, whereas the ranks of well-off peasants shrivelled. Tenants in regions where mezzadria predominated became entangled in webs of debt that few could escape. Because population pressure – 10.5 million Italians in 1500 had become 13.1 million in 1600 – kept land scarce and expensive, few peasants could hope to obtain better terms by changing landlords. At the same time, agricultural output stagnated or even declined. Dogana herds, for instance, contracted sharply after 1612. Productivity deteriorated as well: wheat yields in the Romagna, an admirable 7–8:1 in 1510–19, had fallen to 5:1 by the 1590s. That decade was, in Italy as in most of Europe, especially dismal, but the outlook did not brighten with the dawn of a new century. Already in the 1570s, steep levies and dwindling output made it impossible for many peasants to fulfill their obligations to landlord and state, so rent and tax moratoria had to be granted along the length and breadth of the peninsula. Even so, rural folk went under in record numbers in the years around 1600, and many lost their holdings or survived only by taking on new debt. After 1580 in some areas, after 1610 in nearly all, the vitality went out of Italian agriculture.

Research into Italian agricultural history lags behind that devoted to industry, trade, and finance, so the causes of agrarian distress are not fully understood. But several important factors have been identified, most of which had their roots in the cities that retained their long-established economic and political hegemony over the countryside. To begin with,

[2] Leon Battista Alberti, *The Family in Renaissance Florence, Book Three* (*I Libri Della Famiglia*, c. 1434), trans. Renée Neu Watkins (Prospect Heights, Ill., 1994), p. 62.

from the later sixteenth century many of the leading Italian urban crafts began to founder (as we shall see in chap. 4), while town populations were widely decimated by plague in 1630 and may have been stagnant or dropping even before that time. These trends inevitably had negative repercussions on the agrarian sector, heavily oriented as it was towards city produce and raw materials markets. To a large extent, for instance, the near-collapse of leading Italian urban woollen textile industries helps account for the shrinking of Dogana herds.

Government policies exacerbated the situation. Seeking to assure sufficient cheap raw materials and foodstuffs for city residents and thereby to counteract both the spreading economic slowdown and ongoing inflation, town magistrates commanded farmers in the contado to sell in urban markets at fixed – and low – prices, while simultaneously restricting exports of agricultural commodities. Although of negligible value in overcoming the economic troubles, these steps helped discourage peasant production.

Most harmful were landlords' transfers of resources out of agriculture. Landlord – largely urban – capital remained as crucial to Italian agriculture in the long sixteenth century as it had been in the Middle Ages. Like their medieval predecessors, particularly in the first two-thirds or so of the sixteenth century many owners made substantial and costly improvements that boosted output as well as their income. Around Padua, and elsewhere in the *Terraferma* (the Republic of Venice's mainland territory), urban patricians and the government they controlled built extensive dams, dikes, drainage canals, roads, and bridges to turn formerly pestiferous marshes into lush fields. One hundred thousand holdings had been created by 1575, each said to be worth fifty times as much as before reclamation. Similarly, the group of entrepreneurs who leased land from the Ospedale Maggiore (General Hospital) of Florence constructed an elaborate irrigation system so that the peasants who sublet the holdings could rotate grain and forage crops, the latter destined for carefully selected dairy cows. On a smaller scale, too, individual landowners often combined scattered plots into more efficient consolidated farms, upon which they built new houses and outbuildings for their tenants.

Increasingly, however, Italian landlords found little need to invest in order to profit handsomely, thanks to the brisk demand for both land and agricultural goods. Many landowners converted long fixed leases into short-term adjustable rents, which doubled in real terms in the century before 1580; by requiring that rents be paid in kind, landlords could also gain from sales in urban markets. Landlords raised seigniorial levies considerably, too, and some even succeeded in reintroducing a form of serfdom. Although high and rising ground rents were their main burden, such tenants or *vassi* were subject as well to lordly justice and monopolies, owed labor services, and had to accept restrictions on the sale of their crops, their physical movement, even their marriage partners.

Bullish demand for peasant holdings and the produce of the land also made mezzadria contracts increasingly popular with landlords, for besides selling what they acquired as in-kind rents, they stood to benefit from the high interest rates they charged tenants for advances of seed and cash. As a result, this form of tenancy, long common in a few areas, spread widely. Initially, sharecropping channeled capital into the countryside and might lead landlords to oblige peasants to plant new crops. In some places, it continued to do so across the long sixteenth century: around Florence, sharecropper sericulture provided raw silk for the one industry that long remained healthy. More often, however, mezzadria gradually deprived tenants of both means and incentives to improve.

The rents, dues, loans, and other levies that progressively impoverished the peasantry meant that land remained an attractive outlet for urban capital. Terraferma reclamation projects were launched up until 1610, in the later sixteenth century Lombard land prices rose twice as fast as inflation, and the price of an estate in the Kingdom of Naples went up nearly eightfold between 1553 and 1624. But by the later sixteenth century few citydwellers who owned farms and estates invested much in productivity-enhancing improvements. Some – like the owners of Sicilian sugar plantations who no longer adequately maintained the replanting cycle, irrigation systems, and refineries essential to ongoing operation – actively disinvested. More commonly, however, rural properties were milked for funds that supported lavish expenditure on palaces, churches, art, and other forms of conspicuous consumption.

Commercial agriculture that hinged on landlord capital and initiative brought, then, disappointingly little lasting development to rural Italy. Growth was based largely on expanding the amount of land under cultivation (typically through reclamation) and (by extending mezzadria and emphasizing in-kind rents in other forms of tenancy) on increasing the proportion of produce sent to market. Given continuing strong demand for land and agricultural goods, landlords could resort to traditional peasant-squeezing; at the same time, governments that favored urban consumers, artisans, and taxpayers tightened the screws on rural communities. Landlords and magistrates alike were backed up by courts that strictly enforced contracts and by militias and other policing mechanisms that sternly repressed peasant protests whether individual or collective.

For many years, Italian agriculture was able to support the rising level of exactions, but when the flow of urban capital slowed, the countryside lacked the means to assume the role heretofore undertaken by landlords. As in Spain, the exceptions to the general picture of decay were few and far between. Yet whereas Catalonia was testimony to the potential inherent in peasant production, the most enduringly successful agriculture in Italy, found in the Duchy of Milan and around a few other cities, owed its vigor to continuing infusions of urban capital, bolstered by state aid and leadership. More commonly, however, resources were diverted away from the land, so even extensive growth came to a halt.

Western Europe

France

Following the end of the Hundred Years' War in 1453, French agriculture embarked upon a century of expansion. Deserted holdings were farmed again, forests felled (a third of France was woodland in 1500, a quarter in the mid-seventeenth century), fishponds dug. Cereal production, as measured by tithe payments of grain, perhaps doubled in many areas by the 1540s. Industrial, horticultural, vine, and tree crops, planted in many regions, were sold widely to domestic and foreign consumers. The cultivation of grapes extended throughout the area around Bordeaux, whose port provided ready access to customers in England and the Low Countries, while the expansion of the textile industry at home and abroad stimulated woad growing in the southwestern provinces.

Earlier than in the Mediterranean, however, French agriculture began to show signs of stagnation or even decline. In a few districts, tithe returns languished from the 1540s; in the next few decades, downturn became common. It is a matter of debate how much the Religious Wars (1562–98) aggravated existing problems or originated new ones, but it is clear that the countryside experienced serious and prolonged difficulties during the period of conflict. Besides the destruction suffered by individual farms, rural communities fell deeply into debt both to hire defenders against marauding troops and to repair the damage that despite precautions inevitably occurred. As a result, at the same time that baldíos were being auctioned in Castile, many French villages had to sell off their common lands, a move that had similarly adverse effects on the numerous peasants who had relied on them for vital supplementary arable, pasture, fuel, and fertilizer.

Recovery did ensue with the return of peace in 1598. In the opening decades of the new century, grain output revived smartly and wine production, lackluster at best since the 1550s, rose by at least half. Yet the revival was never robust – not until the late eighteenth century did grain tithe yields around Beaune (Burgundy) return to 1540s levels, for example – and ceased by 1625–30. In the next few decades, harvests repeatedly failed and famine stalked the country. Across the long sixteenth century, in sum, French agriculture described – albeit with a precocious and distinctive curve – the same overall arc of initial and pronounced growth followed by marked decline as the Mediterranean lands.

The reasons for this agrarian pattern were likewise a combination of the unique and the conventional. Middling peasants with single-family farms initially took the lead in promoting growth. Thanks to low, fixed in-kind rents and the availability of unused land in the aftermath of a century of war, they could expand their holdings to 25 acres or more. In addition, village communities, in concert with the emerging monarchic state that sought to counterbalance noble power, succeeded in maintaining customary rights to woodlands, meadows, and the like at nominal rates. And – as in Castile – the tax burden on the agrarian sector actually lightened from the early 1480s to the late 1540s. In consequence, some of these peasants managed (as their name of *laboureurs* or plowmen indicates) to purchase horses or oxen, produce for the market, and accumulate a modest but advancing store of material possessions.

Even during their late fifteenth- and early sixteenth-century heyday, nevertheless, many middling peasants faced pressures that ultimately undermined them. Having failed to enlarge their feudal incomes, and possessing small demesnes – which in lower Normandy, for example, comprised just 5–10 percent of arable – landlords were determined to reverse decades of declining revenues by fattening their rent rolls now that conditions permitted. Many succeeded. After 1511, for instance, ground rent for farms north of Paris, heretofore the equivalent of about one-thirtieth of the gross crop, jumped to an eighth; it was a sixth by the late 1560s. By the early seventeenth century, tenants here, as elsewhere in France, commonly owed up to a third of their gross crop, which came out to a half of the net (after, that is, taxes and tithe had been paid and seed for the next planting set aside). In these years, moreover, a new levy appeared: a cash payment each time the lease was renewed; once instituted, the fee was repeatedly raised.

The Religious Wars delivered a harsh blow to middling peasants. Many lost their holdings entirely, while others had to accept onerous sharecropping contracts. Still, a thin stratum of rich laboureurs not only survived but throve in adversity by assembling large farms employing day laborers. In the grain-growing Hurepoix region south of Paris, to take just one instance, the village elite operated properties composed of a core of 25–50 acres that they owned outright and as many as 250 additional acres that they rented – often after failing plowmen's families were evicted. Farm labor was abundant – the ranks of cottagers and the landless were swelled by downwardly mobile laboureurs – and cheap: in the 1570s, reapers' purchasing power was just a third of its level a century before, and still dropping. Admittedly, farm workers' real wages recovered nearly 50 percent during the early seventeenth century postwar reconstruction, a time when middling tenants also staged a comeback thanks to rent rebates and cheap loans. But for both groups the respite proved cruelly short-lived; after 1625, the tide of peasant dispossession and slumping earnings rolled back in. Around 1550, middling and small plowmen had preponderated in the villages of the Hurepoix, but by 1660, cottagers and wage earners comprised the great majority.

The emergence of the laboureur elite also owed much to a profound shift in patterns of property ownership. Whereas in the later Middle Ages peasants had effectively owned a large proportion of French land, after about 1550 urban lawyers, merchants, and office-holding "robe" nobles, together with some members of the traditional "sword" nobility and high clergy, bought massive amounts of peasant property. The trend towards peasant dispossession had started earlier in the vicinity of big cities, but from the mid-sixteenth century it swept across France, continuing through good years and bad, and encompassing both feudal land and that exempt from seigniorial dues. Thus at Avrainville in the Hurepoix, where in 1546 peasants owned 47 percent of the village's land and Parisians 19 percent, by the 1660s the shares were reversed: city residents now held 57 percent, villagers just 20 percent. As the late sixteenth century Lyon humanist Guillaume Paradin expressed it, "The poor laboureurs, lacking enough to eat, were constrained to put their lands up for sale at rock bottom prices to rich people, who thereby acquired good lands and vineyards for a morsel of bread."[3]

Often the new owners amalgamated formerly separate farms into big consolidated units. But even when they did not, they commonly rented out several holdings to a single peasant. In either event, several families were likely to be displaced while the top laboureurs accumulated tenancies. Evidence from la Neuville-Chant-d'Oisel in Normandy is instructive. Between 1413 and 1635, the top 5 percent of villagers tripled the amount of arable land they held: 17 percent of the total at the first date, it had become nearly 57 percent at the second. From the 1580s to the 1630s, when change was most rapid, this stratum increased its share of tenancies by some 70 percent. In contrast, the middle 50 percent saw its part halved, while the landless and nearly landless class grew to include one-sixth of all residents. The greater availability of pasture and waste combined with less acute population pressure to slow the process of polarization in France's

[3] Quoted in Philip Hoffman, "Taxes and Agrarian Life in Early Modern France: Land Sales, 1550–1730," *Journal of Economic History*, vol. 46 (1986), p. 38.

stock-raising central provinces. In the south, however, peasant differenti-ation followed a trend similar to that observable in Normandy and elsewhere in the north.

Yeoman-style laboureurs had, in short, ready access to the factors of production needed for agricultural development. At a time when more and more peasants were hard pressed to achieve bare subsistence, the richer laboureurs, well supplied with land, capital, and cheap labor, could invest and innovate. Their economic dominance allowed them to take control of village institutions, which they frequently exploited for their own advantage: they juggled assessments to lower their taxes, and in order to produce more goods for the market, they reserved the remaining communal pastures for their livestock and appropriated common arable for their crops. But they also introduced new commercial crops or diffused existing ones more widely: maize and silk in the south and southwest, livestock in Brittany, vineyards throughout Languedoc, Aquitaine, and the western Loire. They, too, were at the forefront of adopting new land-use patterns, more complex rotations, and irrigation.

French agriculture thus appeared headed along a third path, neither the commercialized peasant agriculture of Catalonia nor the capital-intensive farming controlled by urban landlords that was characteristic of Milan and its northern Italian emulators but an agrarian order founded on yeoman initiative. This scenario was, however, destined to come to fruition only in a few areas. Following a script with which we are now well acquainted, escalating state levies, added to the rising rents and other fees demanded by landlords, drained capital from the countryside, discourag-ing peasant innovation while failing to stimulate landlord investment. Heavy charges also – a specifically French twist – led many rich laboureurs to abandon farming for rentiership.

Taxes had begun to go up in the second half of the sixteenth century, but the pace accelerated sharply soon after 1600; the real per capita burden quadrupled between the 1560s and the 1630s. Sales taxes such as the impost on salt shot up after 1607, and direct taxes more than doubled just between 1625 and 1634. In much of the country, land owned by urban bourgeois as well as by nobles was exempt from taxation, and even in provinces with the *taille réelle* (where exemptions belonged to the land, not to its owners) non-peasant propertyholders developed all sorts of stratagems to lower their payments to insignificance. Thus as the nobility's and bourgeoisie's share of land grew (in the Norman village of St-Ouen-de-Breuil, for instance, by the early seventeenth century over three-quarters of the land was in the hands of people who did not pay imposts), and more and more villagers became too poor to pay, the lion's share of the escalating charges fell on plowmen. In addition, landlord sales of produce in urban markets were free of the heavy excise taxes that peasant sellers owed. (Little wonder that wholly in-kind rents became all the rage with seventeenth-century landowners.) Besides taking needed resources from peasant pockets, this grossly unequal distribution of the tax load both induced peasants to sell and made land especially appealing to non-peasant purchasers. Even those farmers who did not sell increasingly shied away from improving their farms, since better stock, drainage systems, or new tools that would have raised productivity also inevitably caught the tax collector's eye.

For reasons that the Spanish and Italian cases have made all too familiar, very little of the surplus extracted from French villagers was productively invested in agriculture. Even infrastructural investment, such as road-building, which might inadvertently have helped the agrarian sector by lowering transportation costs and enhancing the possibilities for commercialization, was minimal. The government squandered most of its abundant revenue on military adventures, notably the Thirty Years' War (1618–48), redistributing much of the remainder to nobles and well-to-do bourgeois in the form of offices, commissions, and outright grants. Landlords devoted their incomes chiefly to conspicuous consumption and the purchase of additional land. Few showed much interest in improving their properties, nor felt much pressure to do so, since they could profit from sales of produce and rents that continued to mount well past 1650.

For their part, more and more wealthy laboureurs saw little point in devoting much energy to agriculture. Instead, they became *marchands-laboureurs* or *fermiers-receveurs*, operating both independently and as intermediaries between landlords and subsistence peasants, cottagers, and day laborers. Their considerable incomes came less from their land than from collecting rents and seigniorial dues, farming taxes and tithes, and extending mortgages and usurious loans to their much more numerous poorer neighbors. Whenever possible, they sent their sons into commerce or the law, or married them into the lower nobility. To be sure, some plowmen found it worth remaining farmers because as tenants of exempt landlords they could also pay much reduced taxes. But if not all laboureur enterprise was thwarted, it was the work of a decreasing minority. So although examples of agricultural development can be discerned in rural France, their impact was muted during the long sixteenth century.

England

Scholars have long contended that English agriculture underwent several fundamental transformations during the long sixteenth century. Together they constituted a veritable agricultural revolution which, it is held, endowed English farming with an advanced structure and practices that made it far more productive than its Continental counterparts. Tenurial and organizational innovations have received much attention, notably although not exclusively from Marxists. In this view, ruthless landlords – mainly from the purportedly rising gentry (lower nobility) – seeking to profit from rising prices engendered by demographic and commercial growth imposed oppressive rents and overrode custom in order to evict peasants from farmstead and village; then they formed substantial holdings rented at market rates to tenants employing wage labor. Although a minority of peasants prospered by taking on the new farms, most were dispossessed of their means of production and turned into proletarian cottagers and day laborers. The prime example of the process of original accumulation, the reorganization of the English countryside created a new class structure, helped concentrate capital in entrepreneurial hands, and powerfully stimulated the development of the domestic market, where labor, means of subsistence, and raw materials were bought and sold. It thus provided the social relations and material conditions necessary for capitalist farming and, eventually, industrialization.

Other historians place more emphasis on technical change. The "floating" of water meadows (in which rerouted streams repeatedly flooded grasslands) tripled hay output by preventing winter freezes and provoking early springtime growth. New crops such as carrots, turnips, cabbage, and potatoes, along with "artificial" (introduced) grasses like clover and sainfoin, provided forage and winter fodder. More selective breeding gave fatter sheep and cattle. Permanent fields, whether arable or grass, were replaced by convertible husbandry (also known as "alternate" or "up-and-down"), in which land rotated every few years between brief interludes of arable cultivation and longer periods as pasture, thereby augmenting output of livestock and industrial crops without diminishing grain supplies. Draining fens and marshes yielded new land, while more frequent manuring improved the old. Taken together, these innovations are said to have at least doubled per-acre yields.

That many of these changes occurred is indisputable. But whether they happened as widely or as quickly as was once thought, and whether they had the impact once claimed for them, is now hotly debated. What was once regarded as a series of breakthroughs leading to continuous agricultural development was in reality, many scholars have recently suggested, a grab bag of more limited and partial advances that had just about ceased by the mid-seventeenth century. Important innovations did appear in many parts of England, but only a few farmers adopted them, so nothing resembling an agricultural revolution took place.

Nowhere is the revision of the scope and consequences of sixteenth-century agrarian change clearer than in the treatment of enclosure, long considered to epitomize and explain English agrarian development. Enclosure was the process of fencing, hedging, ditching, or otherwise cordoning off hitherto open ground, thereby restricting or extinguishing common cultivation or grazing thereupon. It could be followed by conversion of arable to pasture, as happened frequently in the early sixteenth century in response to buoyant wool prices: this was the period when, with some justice, many English people agreed with Thomas More that sheep "devour men" or, as a late sixteenth-century epigram had it, "Sheep have eaten up our meadows and our downs, / Our corn, our wood, whole villages and towns."[4] But enclosure could equally occur so as to facilitate a switch to arable or the introduction of convertible husbandry, as was increasingly true after 1550, when grain prices shot up. No matter what the outcome, however, to be economically viable enclosure generally entailed amalgamating the scattered strips characteristic of medieval peasant farming into a single holding. Enclosure redefined property rights as well, for private owners and their tenants rather than communal regulations determined how the new plots were used.

Often accompanying enclosure – although also taken independently – were several other disruptive innovations. They included "engrossment," the combining of two or more farms into one; "rack-renting," which was, strictly speaking, levying a rent equal to the full annual value of a property, but in common parlance signified imposing an extortionately high rent; boosting entry fines (lump sums owed at the beginning of a lease) tenfold or more overnight; appropriating or encroaching on village wastes and forests. Sometimes enclosure was the work of peasants seeking to try innovative practices or crops barred from collectively regulated land or, more mundanely, carving out additional fields or protecting their holdings from lords' excessive use of the right of foldcourse (temporary pasturage of sheep on peasant land). But most enclosures were carried out by landowners seeking increased profits from big herds of sheep or higher rents from large consolidated farms.

Historians have traditionally accepted that enclosures and related steps were both unsettling and rewarding. Admittedly, freeholds, about one quarter of tenancies across England, had little to fear. Boasting de facto ownership in return for a quitrent set in the Middle Ages and by now nominal, freeholders enjoyed virtually absolute security from eviction and could dispose of their land as they wished. But so-called "unfree" or

---

[4] Thomas More, *Utopia* (orig. publ. 1516; New York, 1975), p. 14; Thomas Bastard, "Chrestoleros" (1598), in *Tudor Economic Documents*, ed. R. Tawney and E. Power (London, 1924), Vol. III, p. 81.

"customary" tenures were more threatened, particularly "copyholds," the largest category. Many were subject to adjustable rents and entry fines and were terminable at the landlord's discretion upon the death of the current tenant. Customary tenants also often lacked written documentation to substantiate their claims. Hence a determined encloser could cause acute tenurial and social upheaval and radically alter relations between lords and peasants. According to a 1549 report, for example, in one village that had undergone enclosure half the former tenants had been obliged to abandon their holdings, while the rest now held on terms that left them wholly at their landlord's mercy.

At the same time, most scholars – even those who, echoing contemporaries, condemn the brutality of the process – have concluded that enclosure enhanced agricultural productivity. Lords and tenants alike are thought to have been more willing to invest in new crops, additional fertilizer, better tools, improved drainage, and superior buildings now that they were no longer forced to share the rewards of innovation. Cultivation could be tailored to the specific characteristics of individual farms. Losses due to the easy spread of animal diseases and inability to breed selectively in intermingled herds, careless farming practices on adjacent plots, and time spent travelling among scattered strips all could be reduced. Larger engrossed farms are also presented as enjoying economies of scale in terms of labor and equipment. The high rents that enclosed plots commanded are taken as proof that enclosure recommended itself to both landlords and tenants.

Recent studies suggest, however, that enclosure's costs and benefits were circumscribed during the long sixteenth century and that the gains that were achieved in that period were not peculiar to the agriculture practiced on enclosed farms. To begin with, enclosure activity was quite localized, with two-thirds occurring in the Midlands. With soil suitable for both grain and livestock, this increasingly crowded region was uniquely vulnerable to ceaselessly rising demand for food and raw materials emanating from nearby London, whose population jumped from 40,000 in 1500 to 200,000 a century later and reached 400,000 by 1650. Yet throughout England as a whole, only about 10 percent of cultivable land was enclosed between 1500 and 1650, most of it in the early seventeenth century. The later Middle Ages had seen considerably greater activity: by 1500, as much as a third of enclosure had already taken place, mainly, and with little controversy, in the largely pastoral and lightly populated northwestern counties. Much more was to occur after 1650. During the sixteenth century, many landlords lacked sufficient funds to undertake enclosure, and before the 1570s or so few peasants had the requisite skills and resources. Then, too, royal courts frequently favored tenants in disputes over manorial custom and curbed entry-fine increases. At the village level, peasants effectively employed rent strikes and various forms of intimidation.

Furthermore, enclosure is no longer viewed as a cataclysm that destroyed an egalitarian, harmonious peasant society but as a process that solidified divisions based on property ownership and wealth already present within medieval villages. Members of the existing yeoman elite – freeholders on lands their ancestors had acquired after the Black Death or tenants with long-term renewable leases at fixed rents – were most often in a position to take on or create enclosed farms. Conversely, the already broad stratum of less prosperous peasants suffered the bulk of enclosure's injuries, for they lost access to common fields and encountered great difficulty finding available land they could afford to rent. Nor did enclosure alone exacerbate social disparities. On the manor of Cheshunt (Hertfordshire), where 20 percent of the tenants already held slightly more than half the land in 1484, but boosted their share to 70 percent in 1562, the trend towards concentration was due essentially to transfers among tenants.

The productivity gains attributable to enclosure have also been reassessed. According to some calculations, yields on enclosed farms rose 10–25 percent for wheat (though more for barley, oats, and sheep), and output per unit of labor increased by an equal proportion. The greater rent rises that some landlords realized were due not only to rising productivity but also to a shift in power that enabled landowners to arrogate a larger share of the expanding surplus. At the same time, scattered-strip, common-field agriculture has come to be regarded more positively. The varieties of drainage conditions, soil quality, and exposure prevailing on dispersed parcels within just a single manor or village provided the only available insurance against storm, disease, or other natural catastrophe that might strike any individual plot. Common-field farming also spread capital costs, allowed all involved to benefit from limited resources such as manure and pasture, and could force the lazy to keep up to communal norms. Most important, much more growth occurred on common-field holdings than has usually been recognized. On their own plots, peasants were free to grow what they wanted, how they wanted, as long as they followed the same plowing, sowing, and harvesting schedule as their neighbors. So changes commonly associated with enclosure – such as careful attention to seed quality, harrowing, fertilizing, and livestock breeding – also transpired in some common fields. Improvements were more likely on enclosed farms, in short, but there was no necessary link between them; nor did common-field agriculture inevitably, or even typically, denote backwardness. Above all, while both enclosure and changes in open-field farming aided whatever agrarian progress came about across the long sixteenth century, neither led to dramatic, irreversible advances.

The contributions of improving landlords were similarly restricted in scope and force. Parallel to the tendency among tenants, so among landowners possession was becoming more concentrated. Thanks in large part to purchases from the Crown of church properties seized during the Reformation, the gentry as a whole probably doubled its share of land between the mid-fifteenth and late seventeenth centuries; at the latter date, gentry owned perhaps half of English cultivated acreage. Yet despite their greatly enhanced resources, only a minority of these – or any other – landlords undertook major capital improvements or even engaged in land reclamation; in general, investment and innovation were left to tenants. Entrenched long leases, paternalistic relationships, and ideals of good lordship may have stayed the hand of some landowners; others found their incomes sufficient or, on the contrary, were so hard-pressed that they sold confirmations of customary rents and fines or conversions of copyhold into freehold. Doubtless, too, many knew that attempts to innovate risked provoking costly lawsuits or violence: in 1607, the hard-pressed Midlands erupted into revolt, and the drainage of the eastern fens so disturbed traditional communities that after decades of recalcitrance they openly rebelled during the Civil War of the 1640s. But like their Continental brethren, most English landlords focused on raising rents. They did not set out to establish agrarian capitalism nor even commercial farming but – with marked success – to enhance their revenues in the way they knew best.

Among the tenants in whose hands lay most of the initiative for innovation were some smallholders who specialized in dairying, market gardening, and (before the government banned it in the 1670s to assist colonial planters) tobacco. Yet most had too precarious a livelihood to hazard experimentation and indeed managed to survive only by maximizing cereal cultivation, usually by reducing their livestock herds, which over time depleted the soil. Much more significant were the accomplishments of yeomen and large tenants who accumulated property thanks to enclosure, inheritance of favorable tenures, and purchases from less fortunate villagers. In some places their share of land increased dramatically: at Chippenham (Cambridgeshire), for instance, the number of farms with 90 or more acres tripled from two to six between 1544 and 1636, whereas smaller holdings dropped from forty-three to eighteen. Over England as a whole, yeomen owned about a fifth of the land in the 1430s, a quarter to a third in 1690.

Yeomen sought to profit from expanding market opportunities and rising prices produced in large part by a growing and urbanizing England, where population more than doubled between 1500 and 1650 (as against an increase of just 17 percent on the Continent), the proportion dwelling in towns with 10,000 or more residents expanding from 3.1 percent to 8.8 percent across the same period (once again a rate of increase far above the European mean). Therefore they pioneered the planting of legumes; greatly expanded the cultivation of specialized foodstuffs and industrial raw materials; built water meadows; reduced fallow. At least in Norfolk, they achieved their greatest successes with much more closely integrated pastoral and arable husbandry in which new fodder crops permitted a doubling of livestock per acre. Besides greatly increasing the output of meat, butter and cheese, and wool – not to mention the supply of vital draft animals – the larger herds allowed intensified manuring that substantially raised grain yields.

For all that, England's agrarian situation was far from rosy. The ranks of the landpoor and landless were swelling explosively: across twenty-eight manors, cottages with gardens accounted for 11 percent of holdings before 1560, 40 percent after 1620. Many became agricultural laborers, whose real wages were cut in half between 1500 and 1650. Even the highest grain yields, achieved about 1630, only equalled medieval peaks, and after that date they began to slip; moreover, the gains had never kept up with the expansion of demand, so inflation in England, as in the rest of Europe, developed apace until population levelled off and then dipped in the second half of the seventeenth century. Not until the late seventeenth and eighteenth centuries did English cereal yields embark on massive and continuous advance that surpassed population increase. Moreover, many innovations in crops and farming methods were very slow to catch on. Although carrots, turnips, and clover initially appeared on a few farms around 1600, they did not enter into widespread cultivation for many decades. Similarly, water meadows remained scarce and inefficient before the 1640s, and yeomen frequently abandoned convertible husbandry after a period of experimentation.

By the end of the long sixteenth century, notable first steps towards tenurial reorganization and technical modernization had been taken in the English countryside. Yet their effects had not bitten deep. England's agriculture was only marginally more productive than France's, and in the former as in the latter growth in output still owed more to extending the area being cropped and grazed than to innovation. As on the Continent, too, customary rights and tenures were under attack but were far from vanquished, and small and middling holdings remained most common. Some of their tenants had become viable commercial producers, but many were marginal, and below them was a burgeoning class of impoverished rural proletarians. The best medieval knowledge and practices were more widely disseminated but not yet surpassed. In contrast to France and the Mediterranean lands, England's government skimmed off less of the agricultural surplus, so yeomen, large tenants, and landlords retained more resources, which they were to deploy with great success in the eighteenth century. But before that, both in structure and in practices English agriculture resembled nothing so much as its western European neighbors, and in efficiency ranked behind the Netherlands.

The Low Countries

The specialized, highly commercialized peasant-led agriculture that had emerged in several provinces during the later Middle Ages took hold throughout the Low Countries in the course of the long sixteenth century. Domestic demographic and industrial growth, together with mushrooming international trade in which Netherlands merchants took an increasingly active role, spawned plentiful market opportunities that farmers turned to their advantage. Thus they expanded grain cultivation as demand waxed in the early sixteenth century: in Flanders, cereals covered 47 percent of arable land in 1507–20, 63 percent in 1541–50. Conversely, when meat and dairy prices surged after the 1550s, peasants shifted from grain to mixed cereals and livestock farming or even converted arable to permanent pasture. Again, in response to the needs of cities and crafts, they cultivated industrial and horticultural crops more widely. A vast expansion in the acreage devoted to oleaginous plants like rape and cole-seed, for instance, fed the explosive growth of oilmills in the Zaanstreek, north of Amsterdam, which increased from two in 1610 to forty-five in 1630 and at least triple that number later in the century.

Tenurial security uncommon for Europe encouraged peasant initiative. Nearly a half of all land (although less of the most fertile) was in peasant hands. But even when they did not own the land they farmed, peasants in the Netherlands enjoyed customary rights assuring that neither an occupant's death nor an owner's sale of a property would end a family's tenancy. Leases were normally renewed for generations, terminating only when no relative could be found to succeed. On these de facto hereditary holdings, more and more farmers not only implemented the intensive cultivation practices developed in medieval Flanders and Brabant (see chap. 2) but also continually experimented to find more productive crops and methods. They perfected a fallowless rotation of flax, turnips, oats, and clover, and also planted nitrogen-rich clover on meadows in place of grasses and legumes. Indefatigable tinkering raised the efficiency of their plows and harrows, while improvements in windmill technology enabled fields to be drained more thoroughly, thereby significantly enhancing both soil quality and output of produce. And, far more than their fellows elsewhere in Europe, Low Countries peasants fertilized their fields with dung, nightsoil, and other waste matter, much of it carefully gathered from towns.

Netherlands farmers benefited, too, from landlord and government levies that were generally more moderate than those prevailing elsewhere in Europe. In the southern provinces (those that remained under Habsburg dominion after the Dutch Revolt and today form Belgium) nobles and ecclesiastical institutions owned much land, as they had in the past. Nevertheless, many lords saw their wealth and power ebb, particularly those with the least land. Already at the outbreak of the Revolt, the precarious situation of this group had earned them the sobriquet of "Beggars" from dismissive Spanish officials, and their condition only worsened thereafter. Many were forced to take out loans and mortgages and sooner or later started selling off land both to peasants and to urban bourgeois. At the same time, the central government steadily chipped away at the seigniorial jurisdictions – and profits – of even the greatest nobles. Most of all, rents lagged behind inflation before and even more during the long decades of unrest; landlords' inability to force them up is perhaps the clearest indication of their slipping power.

The costs of government also did not unduly burden the southern Netherlands countryside. Urban excises, taxes on industrial products, loans, and remittances from the country's Spanish overlords covered many state expenses. Furthermore, the multitude of cities in these provinces lacked the political authority and military capability to exploit the agricultural sector in the ways and at the level of their counterparts in Italy, that other highly urbanized land. Yet urban capital flowed into the land across the period; it was particularly important for financing expensive projects such as the waste clearance and poldering that added 10–20 percent to the cultivated area of the south.

Conditions were even more auspicious for peasant initiative in the northern and eastern provinces that became the independent Dutch Republic and rapidly assumed European economic primacy. With the partial exception of the much less populous, poorer, and less productive east, feudalism had always been exceptionally weak in this region, and nothing in the long sixteenth century strengthened it. Like their southern brethren, the urban merchants who began to put some of their massive wealth into the countryside showed little interest in seigniorial authority and income – nor even in agriculture. Rather, they viewed land purely as a liquid investment, and an excellent one at that. So while they were recurrently willing to fund large-scale reclamation projects – between 1540 and 1664 (apart from the war years 1565–89), an average of 3,625

4 This painting from about 1600 gives a rare contemporary view of the characteristic compact individual Dutch farms with long, narrow impoldered pastures and meadows bordered on each side and bisected by drainage canals that also served for transport and travel. These farms outside the city of Enkhuizen, north of Amsterdam, specialized in dairy products for nearby urban markets.

acres was impoldered annually from the Republic's lakes, marshes, and peat bogs – they often sold the properties to farmers once the work was completed.

The decentralized Dutch state was, moreover, financed mainly by taxes and loans that fell much more heavily on trade and urban consumption than on the countryside. And although cities did not shrink from actions to try to stamp out competing rural industry, they did not hamper agriculture. On the contrary, they promoted increasingly integrated provincial or even wider markets to supply their burgeoning populations. (Dutch towns quadrupled in size between 1500 and 1650; at the former date they held a sixth of the Republic's people, at the latter a third.) Through the cities, too, Dutch farmers were linked to interregional and especially international trade, which had as important repercussions on agriculture as on the rest of the country's economy. Sharply rising imports of grain, which constituted the core of the so-called Baltic "mother trade" of Holland, had the greatest consequences, for they permitted countless peasants to cease cultivating cereals on their own holdings. Numerous

villages that had reported extensive arable devoted to grain in the fifteenth century had none in the seventeenth. Instead, they concentrated on more remunerative industrial crops, hops, horticulture, dairying, and the raising of hogs and cattle that became highly prized throughout the Continent.

Low Countries agriculture was the most productive in Europe during the long sixteenth century. The accounts of the Frisian farmer Rienck Hemmema, for example, reveal grain and milk yields that were double or triple those achieved by his contemporaries outside the Netherlands. The results attained in parts of medieval Flanders and Brabant were not, to be sure, exceeded. But the practices that had previously made high yields possible in a few districts were now widely diffused and passed into general use throughout all but the most backward areas. In England, in contrast, and even more in France and the Mediterranean, stronger landlord structures and weaker connections to long-distance trade restricted the growth of specialization and kept advanced agriculture confined to more limited areas.

In the southern Low Countries, these innovations helped support – albeit at a very modest standard of living – a multitude of tiny farms whose occupants survived by a combination of arable farming, dairying, horticulture, and raising flax that they also spun and wove. By the early 1570s, 50 percent of peasant households in eastern Flanders occupied less than

2.5 acres, and fragmentation had also gone far in Brabant and around Liège. But it was on the medium-sized, compact, enclosed family holdings characteristic of Holland, Zeeland, Friesland, and Utrecht that intensive market-oriented Netherlands farming unleashed its full potential. In these core provinces of the Dutch Republic, peasants were able to relinquish the varied tasks from fishing to carting from which they had pieced together a living in the Middle Ages. Many of these activities – as well as the vital and labor-intensive job of maintaining the Republic's waterworks – were taken up by rural folk who no longer engaged in agriculture; other villagers who lacked land found employment in shipping and fishing. Those who remained farmers devoted their time fully to agricultural pursuits that provided them a standard of living unequalled in rural Europe of the time. Dutch farm families amassed impressive quantities of clothing, curtains, books, mirrors, silver, even paintings. Here it became clear what the peasantry was capable of accomplishing in an environment that did not stifle their initiative nor deprive them of needed capital. It proved, however, much more difficult to export this agrarian model than its produce.

Western Germany

The mosaic of economies, societies, and polities that constituted Germany west of the Elbe ordained that the region's individual agrarian histories would vary appreciably. Nevertheless, similarities in relations of production and surplus appropriation that transcended these boundaries dictated that improvement would be spatially and quantitatively limited. The greatest progress was registered in the urbanized and commercially active zones along the North Sea coast (including those stretching up into Denmark) and in the Rhineland. There, advances that were transforming agriculture in the neighboring Netherlands began to take hold: experimentation with superior tools, more careful selection of seed and breeding animals, prolonging the period between fallows to six or eight years. Immigrants from the Netherlands promoted land reclamation for dairying along with the cultivation of more intensively fertilized industrial and horticultural crops.

Elsewhere, however, innovation was neglected. Admittedly, demand emanating from the many cities that saw their industries blossom, a long-distance trade boom, and populations double or more began to orient even isolated areas toward production for the market. Yet extensive agrarian growth remained the norm, achieved initially by repeopling vacant holdings and later by draining or clearing previously uncultivated tracts. Publicists might urge better manuring, deeper plowing, plant grafting, and the like, but the audience for their writings was narrow – not least because many wrote in Latin.

Rising princely and seigniorial exactions further hampered change. Admittedly, many sovereigns instituted *Bauernschutz* (peasant protection) policies that prohibited excessive rent increases and expulsions from tenancies and ratified or even mandated the practice of impartible inheritance. But if these steps helped to keep peasants on the land, their primary goal was to assure the existence of farms upon which governments could impose higher taxes – as they did. Despite Bauernschutz, moreover, landlords managed to take advantage of mounting land hunger to triple ground rents while also considerably raising entry fines and feudal dues. Before the end of the sixteenth century, German peasants – like their French counterparts – owed state, lord (and often church) at least one-third of their gross yield.

Little of what they paid returned to the land. Often imitating a French or Habsburg monarch, even petty German princes were intent on building up their armies, bureaucracies, and courts. For their part, landlords channeled their incomes into spectacular Renaissance castles that soon dotted the countryside and into other forms of conspicuous consumption. Capital that did come back to the villages usually took the form of loans and charity, which at best enhanced paternalistic domination rather than stimulating agricultural development.

In these circumstances, peasants were unable to raise productivity; yield ratios of 5 : 1 remained typical until the eighteenth century. The great majority sank into poverty. In the southwestern County of Hohenlohe, the bottom 60 percent of villagers controlled one-third of assets in 1528 but just a sixth in 1581. By that point, over half of the County's peasantry was no longer self-sufficient in grain, so the soaring prices they faced in the marketplace could only spell spiraling debt, loss of yet more land, even starvation. In desperation, some cultivated wastes, but the fertility of such land was low and bestowed few if any rights to common pastures and manure, guaranteeing constantly diminishing yields. More and more peasants were unable to obtain any land at all. In Hohenlohe, the proportion of cottars doubled between 1553 and 1581, when they comprised nearly a fifth of villagers. When lucky, they could find a little seasonal work; more often, they had to beg grain from their lords.

Along with, and to a substantial degree profiting from, the immiseration of the peasant masses emerged a rural elite that concentrated land and wealth into its hands, married only within its own circle, and politically dominated the village communities. By 1581, the top tenth of the Hohenlohe peasantry held 43 percent of assets, up from 27 percent in 1528. Many sold foodstuffs in regional and local markets; others had sufficient capital to start growing hops, increasingly in demand as beer gained popularity, or to fatten cattle for sale in German and Netherlands cities. But on the whole their approach to farming remained traditional, and they were attracted more to money-lending and subletting than to investing – in which, of course, they resembled big tenants in France or, for that matter, landlords across Europe. Most of all, like too many peasants of every stratum and location in western Germany, they confronted not only heavier taxes but escalating seigniorial pressure in the form of plowing, hauling, and labor services, death duties, manorial monopolies, and yet other feudal obligations. By 1600, tenants of some Rhineland abbeys owed the services of a wagon, four horses, and two youths for twenty-four days each year, not to mention a variety of payments.

These impositions sharply curtailed the ability and willingness of even the best-off peasants to undertake agricultural improvements. They also suggest the momentous impact of similar yet much greater changes taking place east of the Elbe.

East central Europe

In the mid-fifteenth century, the agriculture of east central Europe (present-day Poland, eastern Germany, the Czech Republic, and western Hungary) strongly resembled that prevailing to the west. Demesne cultivation was waning and the peasant family farm had become the basic unit of production. Even great estates such as those found in Hungary, where sixty magnates held two-fifths of all villages, were conglomerates of small holdings worked by peasants who also enjoyed rights of access to woods, pastures, meadows, wastes, and other common lands. As elsewhere in Europe, too, most peasants lived in nucleated village communities boasting significant administrative autonomy and collective jurisdiction over farming practices, typically exercised through assemblies led by wealthy "headmen" (*schulzen*). Serfdom had all but disappeared by the later thirteenth century, so peasants enjoyed personal freedom, secure tenures with rights of sale and inheritance, and dues and rents often fixed at low traditional rates. Payments in kind and cash constituted the bulk of peasant obligations, and satisfying labor dues required only a few days per year. In Bohemia, where many lords engaged in commercial pisciculture, *robot* (corvées or labor services) might even be fulfilled cleaning ponds or building and stocking new ones.

During the long sixteenth century, however, east central European agriculture – and with it the entire society of the region – diverged radically from that in the west. This striking difference resulted from the reimposition of serfdom, the central feature of a new agrarian structure that became the rule throughout the area east of the Elbe. Lords expropriated

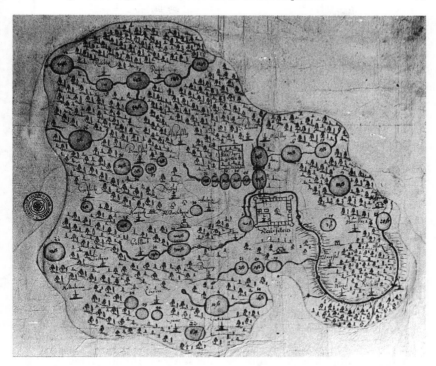

5 The commercial fish ponds on this Bohemian estate were built and maintained by peasants fulfilling their labor services to the lord who dwelt in the castle located in the center right of the map.

peasant holdings to enlarge their demesnes (a process often designated by its German name, *Bauernlegen*), used law and force to tie peasants to the soil, imposed or intensified corvées, and vastly enhanced their seigniorial rights and jurisdictions.

Like its medieval predecessor, the "second serfdom" or "neoserfdom" obliged peasants to perform unpaid corvée labor on their lords' demesnes and subjected them to lordly economic, judicial, and often personal control. Unlike medieval feudalism (or its early modern western survivals, which mainly took the form of seigniorial charges), however, the *Gutsherrschaft* that emerged in east Elbia was heavily commercialized: perhaps three-quarters of all crops were marketed. Reenserfed peasants' corvées were therefore directed mainly towards producing agricultural goods for lords to sell at home and abroad; in addition, serfs had to hand over to their lords a hefty share of the surplus generated on their individual holdings, and this produce likewise went to market. Scholars have long emphasized the importance of foreign demand. Around 1460, 6,000 tons of Polish rye were dispatched to the west each year; a century later, 70,000 tons; by the 1590s – when disastrous shortfalls in Italy brought new customers – as many as 185,000 tons; and in 1618, the peak year, 200,000 tons. Neighboring countries likewise sent thousands of tons, making cheap grain – rye prices in Gdansk (Danzig) averaged about half those in Amsterdam – east central Europe's leading export item. Western purchases of east central livestock, wine, and a few industrial crops also expanded smartly. At least as far as cereals were concerned, however, sales within the region were probably much greater. According to one estimate, demesne farms, which nearly monopolized grain exports, sold four or five times as much on local markets.

The new market-oriented feudal system grew, then, in response to the same increase in demand felt throughout Europe. But its roots lay in the late medieval crisis of the fourteenth and early fifteenth centuries, which had struck east central Europe with unusual force. Dramatic shifts in the balance of economic and political power that emerged in those years – and intensified during the long sixteenth century – gave landlords decisive advantages over peasants. As a result, peasants in east Elbia were largely unable to resist landlord efforts to create a coerced labor force, so agrarian commercialization in that region developed within a structure of neoserfdom, whereas in western and southern Europe it depended on free labor.

To begin with, massive numbers of peasant holdings deserted by virtue of plague or other calamity reverted to landlords, who absorbed them into their demesnes while simultaneously consolidating a broad range of feudal rights and jurisdictions into their hands. In addition, incessant wars and internecine family struggles made sovereigns more dependent on the landowning classes for monetary grants, military assistance, and political backing. Subsequently, the Reformation allowed many aristocrats to expropriate church lands while giving them mastery over parliaments ("Estates"), where churchmen had previously sat alongside them, once ecclesiastical hierarchies and religious institutions had been dissolved. Cities that might have checked an assertive nobility were simultaneously weakening. Symptomatic of waning urban influence (and ebbing princely domination), the Hanse, an association of towns that had long controlled Baltic trade with the west, suffered growing disunity and had to look on impotently as desperate monarchs granted exemptions from taxes, export duties, and longtime city monopolies to noble landowners, permitting them to engage in commerce on their own. Finally, the strength and solidarity of village communities diminished. This occurred in part because of conflicts among peasants of disparate levels of wealth and property, in part because many lords cowed or evicted the schulzen who symbolized and represented village interests. Overt peasant resistance thus became harder to organize and less likely to succeed. Taken together, these changes accorded landowners a disproportionate share of land and of public and private authority as against the peasantry and its allies.

In the long sixteenth century, east Elbian lords used their new property and power to levy labor and crops, which in a period of rapidly growing demand were much more profitable forms of surplus appropriation than rent collecting. The distinctive domestic conditions and market opportunities obtaining within the various east central European lands ensured, however, that each area would introduce the new agrarian order in a somewhat different manner and at an uneven pace. A brief overview of the major states indicates both specific features and general trends.

Developments in Poland and adjacent eastern Germany followed similar paths. As early as the thirteenth century, grain had been shipped west from this area, but it was in the sixteenth century that exports burgeoned from the large expanse of territory where the Elbe, Vistula, and Oder rivers and their tributaries reach far into the interior. Increasingly important to Mediterranean consumers, inexpensive Baltic rye also became integral to Dutch agrarian specialization and commercial expansion: through the port of Gdansk flowed almost 80 percent of Amsterdam's rye imports, and Gdansk also accounted for about half of its Dutch partner's total trade. Yet domestic demand, fueled by internal colonization and (particularly in eastern Germany) urbanization, always surpassed foreign sales.

Cereals were provided in quantities that mounted impressively – more than fiftyfold from the mid-fifteenth to the late sixteenth century – because of the concomitant imposition of serfdom. The bulk of marketed grain always came from peasants' own plots, upon which lords placed progressively higher levies, finally taking up to half of gross output. But more and more rye (along with smaller amounts of hemp, flax, and livestock) were furnished by lordly demesnes worked by corvées. In Poland, demesnes eventually covered a quarter of cultivated land and, as peasants were forced to relinquish wage labor for unpaid services, provided half to two-thirds of landowners' incomes. On estates in the Korczyn district, peasants were paid for 35 percent of the days of work they performed in 1533/38; plowing, hauling, and other draft services accounted for the remainder. But by 1600/16, wage labor amounted to just 15 percent of the days worked, draft services 40 percent, coerced manual labor 45 percent. In the early seventeenth century, middling holdings throughout Poland owed an average of three corvée days per week by two people and a team of oxen; even more during plowing, harvesting, and other busy times. Labor services in eastern Germany increased correspondingly. Mecklenburg peasants owed only a few days of service a year around 1500, but half a century later they were liable for one day a week and by 1600 three days per week. All peasant children not employed on their parents' holdings had to work on their lord's estate for at least several years at minimal pay.

The waning of central state authority facilitated these transformations, for it allowed nobles to become virtually absolute rulers of their estates. As a common saying had it, "the prince's dominion stops at the manor gates." In Prussia, the ruling religious Order of the Teutonic Knights, already enfeebled by the Thirteen Years' War (1453–66), dissolved in 1525, to be replaced by chronically impecunious princes dependent on Estates that fell firmly under the control of estate-owning nobles (*Junkers*). The Jagiellonian monarchy of Poland, increasingly beholden to nobles to fight the Turks, came to an end in 1572, after which the noble-controlled parliament or *Sejm* deliberately elected weak kings. Conversely, in Brandenburg, where the monarchy retained more power, the weight of neoserfdom was considerably lighter.

The Bohemian nobility, which had amassed substantial power in the aftermath of the early fifteenth-century Hussite religious wars, succeeded in legally binding peasants to the land as early as 1487. During much of the sixteenth century, pisciculture, which required little labor, remained the leading demesne activity. Bohemia, lacking easy access to cheap waterborne transport, never became a major grain exporter, sending abroad only about 1,800 tons annually even in the peak years (1597–1621). Most of lords' income came from in-kind rents, so even in the late sixteenth century the maximum corvée was twelve to fifteen days a year and was frequently commuted to a monetary payment. Still, lords were becoming increasingly market-oriented, as demonstrated by the expansion of their demesnes until by 1600 they occupied 20 percent of the land; on them were grown grain, grapes, hops, fruit, flax, and other commercial crops for Prague, Vienna, and nearby towns. And when the Thirty Years' War (1618–48) devastated the countryside, impoverished the peasantry, and undermined village and city authority alike, nobles were able to use the military resources they now commanded to install full-blown neoserfdom.

Hungarian landlords won complete ownership of all holdings in 1514, after suppressing the largest peasant revolt in Hungary's history; the same law directed each farmstead to contribute one day of labor services each week. During the early sixteenth century, demesne-corvée agriculture was little practiced, however, as landlords continued to receive most of their income in the form of in-kind levies on peasant-raised livestock, wine, and grain. Nevertheless, lords augmented the flow of saleable agricultural produce into their hands by raising rents and fees, farming ecclesiastical tithes, and establishing rights of preemption that obliged peasants to sell to them at prices lower than those current in the open market.

By mid-century, growing demand and inflationary pressures were encouraging lords to increase supply and cut costs. They sought to achieve these goals by extending cash-crop feudalism. Labor services were boosted: after 1550, peasants were required to work two days a week during plowing, sowing, haying, and harvest times, and also whenever hauling had to be done; in the late sixteenth century, three days of corvée a week was common and, as in Poland, the use of wage labor dwindled. By the first half of the seventeenth century, corvée-based demesne agriculture had become the dominant farming system, and serfs under seigniorial jurisdiction formed more than 90 percent of the population. In this environment, landlords were able to win a near-monopoly over wine sales and, by securing exemptions from – or simply ignoring – taxes and customs dues, shoulder aside peasant competitors in the livestock trade, which accounted for 50–60 percent of total Hungarian sales abroad. Even though geography discouraged grain exports from Hungary, landlords also expanded demesne cultivation of cereals. The estate of Gyula, for instance, which in 1519 collected 225 florints from selling grain received as rent, in 1557 realized 2,808 florints, mainly from demesne production. Demesne-grown grain was marketed to the landpoor and landless who had previously bought from peasants, to residents of nearby specialized wine and cattle districts, and to the army that expanded ceaselessly during decades of protracted warfare with the Turks.

So although a growing proportion of east central European farm output went to market – some Polish magnates organized their own transport networks and in partnership with urban and foreign merchants shipped and marketed produce of smaller landlords – the region's agriculture became increasingly feudal across the long sixteenth century. Lords' revenues arose from labor services, forced sales, and seigniorial dues, fees, and monopolies that were assured and enhanced through legal and other forms of non-economic coercion. Because of their political and economic hegemony and their control of very cheap labor, east central landlords saw even less reason to invest in agricultural innovation than their western or Mediterranean peers. It made much better sense for them to purchase additional land, villages, and serfs. On their side, few peasants could invest even if they had wanted to. Heightened labor and other services kept them from devoting sufficient time to their own holdings. At the same time, enforced sales and noble monopolies curbed peasant access to competitive markets, further raising their costs while diminishing their incomes. More and more peasants who had once produced marketable surpluses found it hard to achieve subsistence; families came to rely on the vegetables, pigs, poultry, and the like raised by wives and daughters.

Neoserfdom was, however, not merely an exploitative system but an inefficient one. Output gains that were achieved were temporary, the result of bringing abandoned or previously untilled land under the plow. With extensive monoculture the norm, and investment negligible, productivity could not be sustained. Average grain yields, 5:1 at most to begin with, had fallen to 4 or even 3:1 by the early seventeenth century. Livestock were equally mediocre. Whereas pigs in Lombardy averaged 150 lbs, they were lucky to reach 100 lbs east of the Elbe. And although with rare exceptions peasants proved helpless to prevent enserfment, they impeded the smooth operation of the agrarian order by hiding crops, working carelessly, physically attacking overseers and owners, arson, and, when all else failed, flight.

Market-oriented feudalism was not, then, an avenue forward; it did not come close to achieving the results registered in contemporary western Europe and in fact continued practices that had long been forsaken elsewhere. It responded to growing demand, but only by impoverishing the peasantry and the land – and even then the majority of landowners could afford no more than a handful of serfs. As was evident at the time, and became even more obvious later, this distorted and restrained not only immediate material improvement but also long-term economic growth.

Why did development rarely accompany growth?

Beginning in the second half of the fifteenth century and continuing for many decades, farmers from Scotland to Sicily brought more rye, beef, olive oil, wine, apples, peas, carrots, wool, flax, madder, and an abundance of other produce to market in hamlet, village, town, and city. This impressive growth in output was very largely the result of putting more land into cultivation, whether obtained by draining marshes, carving holdings out of virgin forests, restoring farmsteads abandoned in the wake of fourteenth-century epidemics, or converting meadow and waste. Inadequate resources were devoted to intensifying production or even maintaining the soil, especially when inexorably mounting demand for grain to feed the thickening populace – fewer than 61 million Europeans in 1500 but 78 million a century later – cut into pasturage and the crucial fertilizer with which it furnished arable fields. After initial advance, yields stagnated, then in many areas began to slip. So no matter how many additional acres were brought under the plow or grazed by livestock, extensive growth could not keep pace with rising population. The widening disparity was reflected in prices that advanced steadily, with more pronounced increases every few years and, with numbing regularity each decade, sharp spikes that crushed the already wretched poor. Nearly everywhere in Europe, agrarian expansion slowed, then ground to a halt by the end of the long sixteenth century.

Not only did growth stop, but even where it was most pronounced only a modest degree of development occurred. That noticeable changes transpired widely across European agriculture during the long sixteenth century cannot, of course, be denied. Commercialization involved Catalan family farms and east Elbian demesnes, Languedoc vineyards and Northumberland pastures. Changes in tenancy shaped enclosed English farms, Mediterranean sharecropping tenements, and east central demesnes. Landholding became more concentrated, and village communities weakened. Combined with rising prices, these trends benefited not only great latifundium and serf-holding magnates but also the well-off peasant elite that flourished virtually everywhere, including even east central Europe, where despite their unfreedom a handful of serfs accumulated tenancies, livestock, and cash far in excess of their fellows. Concomitantly, the throng of landpoor and landless enlarged, hanging on to cottages with scraps of garden, squatting on waste, or huddling in turf-covered, half-underground hovels.

In scattered instances, these changes promoted development. Enhanced commercialization made possible the specialization characteristic of the most productive agricultures from the North Sea to the Mediterranean. A few wealthy landowners provided capital to help expand the supply of land, and others – a much smaller group – invested to raise productivity. Yeomen frequently took the lead in introducing new crops, tools, and practices. The swelling crowds of marginal peasants were available as constantly cheaper wage labor on big farms: in the early seventeenth century, the purchasing power of male agricultural laborers was just half its level of a century earlier; women, paid as little as a third as much as men even for the same work, fared yet worse.

More commonly, however, the changes had very different results, reinforcing or even creating obstacles to development. A greater orientation to the market, as well as new forms of tenancy, most often facilitated higher lordly levies and, in east central Europe, were accompanied by sweeping economic and social regression. Rich peasants tended to divert resources into usury, tax-farming, and, aping their social superiors, costly styles of life. Increasingly impoverished peasants, whether dependent on wages or owing corvées, curbed the growth of the market for more specialized and more profitable agricultural goods. As inexpensive workers, they weakened any impetus on their employers' part to relinquish existing labor-intensive procedures, no matter how inefficient, and as recipients of various types of credit they absorbed funds that otherwise might have been put to more productive use.

But it was landlord and state policies that bore most responsibility for the generally disappointing level of European agricultural development across the sixteenth century. Most landowners raised rents, granted advances and other forms of credit, and heightened seigniorial levies, all known and secure means of taking advantage of the clamor for holdings and their produce. The minority of landlords that on occasion invested in improvements, moreover, often discontinued them and retreated to traditional forms of enhancing their returns from land. To be sure, landowners often lacked the wherewithal to undertake projects requiring substantial capital; their frantic rent and seigniorial offensives sprang more from a need to replenish incomes that had dwindled during the late medieval peasant Golden Age than from any modernizing impulse. Many also had different priorities. For them, land and its revenues were means to the ends of political power and social prestige, so it was to these goals that they directed their capital. In either case, it made perfect sense to avoid investments like water meadows or convertible husbandry that they poorly understood and that would take a while to bring returns. Better to stick with the well known, the clearly and quickly lucrative – purchasing property and squeezing peasants. Their aversion to risk was damaging to agrarian development but entirely rational from their perspective.

Rentier landlords did not have to impede agricultural development, so long as at least some of those who actually worked the land were in a position to innovate. After all, European peasants of the sixteenth century were for many long years blessed by growing demand, rising prices, stronger transportation and marketing systems, and reasonable knowledge of progressive techniques. Too seldom, unfortunately, did they enjoy access to necessary resources to embark on improvements or to the requisite tenurial conditions to assure them of receiving the rewards of their labor and initiative. For in addition to landowners who were tightening the screws, they faced escalating taxes – much of the revenue from which ended up in lordly pockets – and frequent disruption and destruction due to princely wars. So as vital resources were transferred out of the agrarian sector, paralyzing indebtedness and insecurity rather than fecund and dynamic enterprise became the peasant norm.

In the long sixteenth century, growth, change, and decay predominantly occurred within – indeed, they fortified – existing economic and social structures. Throughout western and southern Europe, singular regions were to be found, of course, where modifications went further and agriculture retained some vigor. Each was marked by tenurial, communal, seigniorial, and political arrangements that were exceptional by European standards. In particular, their structures restrained the appropriation of the peasant surplus, easing the retention or fostering the inflow of capital and providing some assurance that peasants would benefit from their own initiatives. Thus they permitted, at times encouraged, innovation and investment, usually – although as Milan's example shows, not always – under peasant leadership.

On balance, nonetheless, it is the limits of these anomalous areas that prove most striking. Even in the lands around the North Sea, which we know from hindsight were the earliest to break through the constraints on agrarian development, transformation remained more promise than achievement at the end of the long sixteenth century.

SUGGESTED READING

Many of the issues discussed in this chapter are central to the general works listed at the end of chap. 1; more specific studies are given here. For Spain, the most up-to-date accounts are to be found in *The Castilian Crisis of the Seventeenth Century: New Perspectives on the Economic and Social History of Seventeenth-Century Spain*, ed. I. A. A. Thompson and Bartolomé Yun Casalilla (Cambridge, 1994); most essays include material about the long sixteenth century. David Vassberg, *Land and Society in Golden Age Castile* (Cambridge, 1984) covers baldío sales, although its conclusions need some modification in light of work reported in *The Castilian Crisis*. Italian agricultural history can be approached through Maurice Aymard, "From Feudalism to Capitalism in Italy. The Case that Doesn't Fit," *Review*, vol. 6 (1982), and Joanne Ferraro, "Feudal-Patrician Investments in the Bresciano, and the Politics of the Estimo, 1426–1641," *Studi Veneziani*, new ser., vol. 7 (1983).

Translations of some classic regional works provide fine introductions to French agricultural history: Emmanuel Le Roy Ladurie, *The French Peasantry 1450–1660* (Aldershot, 1987); Pierre Goubert, *The French Peasantry of the Seventeenth Century* (Cambridge, 1986); Goubert, "The French Peasantry of the Seventeenth Century. A Regional Example," in *Crisis in Europe 1560–1660*, ed. T. Aston (London, 1965). Among recent reassessments, Hilton Root, *Peasants and King in Burgundy. Agrarian Foundations of French Absolutism* (Berkeley, Ca., 1987); James Collins, *Classes, Estates, and Order in Early Modern Brittany* (Cambridge, 1994), ch. 1; and Philip Hoffman, *Growth in a Traditional Society. The French Countryside, 1450–1815* (Princeton, NJ, 1996), should be consulted.

The Agrarian History of England and Wales. IV. *1500–1640*, ed. Joan Thirsk (Cambridge, 1967), remains the best inclusive account focused on this period; for a longer overview, see Mark Overton, *Agricultural Revolution in England. The Transformation of the Agrarian Economy 1500–1850* (Cambridge, 1996). For the debate over enclosure, consult R. H. Tawney, *The Agrarian Problem in the Sixteenth Century* (London, 1912); Joyce Yelling, *Common Field and Enclosure in England, 1450–1850* (Hamden, Conn., 1977); Stefano Fenoaltea, "Transaction Costs, Whig History, and the Common Fields," *Politics and Society*, vol. 16 (1988); and

Robert Allen, *Enclosure and the Yeoman* (Oxford, 1992). Eric Kerridge, *The Agricultural Revolution* (London, 1967), and Kerridge, *Agrarian Problems in the Sixteenth Century and After* (London, 1969), which contains documents, emphasize technical innovations. The best local study is Margaret Spufford, *Contrasting Communities. English Villagers in the Sixteenth and Seventeenth Centuries* (Cambridge, 1974). See also Paul Glennie, "In Search of Agrarian Capitalism: Manorial Land Markets and the Acquisition of Land in the Lea Valley, 1450–1650," *Continuity and Change*, vol. 3 (1988); and R. W. Hoyle, "Tenure and the Land Market in Early Modern England," *Economic History Review*, 2nd ser., vol. 43 (1990). The papers in *English Rural Society, 1500–1800*, ed. John Chartres and David Hey (London, 1990), cover a number of topics relevant to the long sixteenth century. G. E. Chambers, *The Gentry. The Rise and Fall of a Ruling Class* (London, 1976), focuses on a key group of landowners. Bruce Campbell and Mark Overton, "A New Perspective on Medieval and Early Modern Agriculture: Six Centuries of Norfolk Farming c. 1250–1850," *Past and Present*, no. 141 (1993), emphasize the gradualness of change.

Jan de Vries, *The Dutch Rural Economy in the Golden Age 1500–1700* (New Haven, 1974), and de Vries, "On the Modernity of the Dutch Republic," *Journal of Economic History*, vol. 33 (1973), are superb introductions to agriculture in the Low Countries. Also valuable are B. H. Slicher van Bath, "The Rise of Intensive Husbandry in the Low Countries," in *Britain and the Netherlands*, I, ed. J. S. Bromley and E. H. Kossman (London, 1966); and H. G. Koenigsberger, "Property and Price Revolution (Hainault, 1474–1573)," *Economic History Review*, 2nd ser., vol. 9 (1956–57). Thomas Robisheaux, *Rural Society and the Search for Order in Early Modern Germany* (Cambridge, 1989) is one of the few studies in English that focuses on this period; useful material can also be found in *Germany. A New Social and Economic History. Vol. I. 1450–1630*, ed. R. Scribner (London, 1996).

There is an abundance of fine scholarship available in English on east central European agriculture in this period. Among the most notable recent works are Linda Blodgett, "The 'Second Serfdom' in Bohemia. A Case Study of the Rozmberk Estates in the Sixteenth Century," in *The Peasantry of Eastern Europe*, ed. I. Volgyes (New York, 1979); J. Topolski, "Continuity and Discontinuity in the Development of the Feudal System in Eastern Europe (Tenth to Seventeenth Centuries)," *Journal of European Economic History*, vol. 10 (1981); Topolski, "Sixteenth-Century Poland and the Turning Point in European Economic Development," in *A Republic of Nobles. Studies in Polish History to 1864*, ed. J. K. Fedorowicz et al. (Cambridge, 1982); Heide Wunder, "Serfdom in Later Medieval and Early Modern Germany," in *Social Relations and Ideas. Essays in Honor of R. H. Hilton* (Cambridge, 1983); W. W. Hagen, "How Mighty the Junker? Peasant Rents and Seigneurial Profits in Sixteenth-Century Brandenburg," *Past and Present*, no. 108 (1985); Ian Blanchard, "The Continental European Cattle Trades, 1400–1600," *Economic History Review*, 2nd ser., vol. 39 (1986); Richard Hoffmann, *Land, Liberties, and Lordship in a Late Medieval Countryside. Agrarian Structures and Change in the Duchy of Wroclaw* (Philadelphia, 1989). Still useful are the articles by L. Makkai, B. K. Kiraly, W. E. Wright, and A. Kaminski in *Slavic Review*, vol. 34 (1975). A provocative if difficult Marxist analysis can be found in Witold Kula, *An Economic Theory of the Feudal System. Towards a Model of the Polish Economy, 1500–1800* (London, 1976).

Several excellent documentary collections give access to the words of farmers and landlords (as well as artisans and entrepreneurs) of the time: *Tudor Economic Documents*, ed. R. H. Tawney and E. Power (London, 1924), 3 vols.; *English Economic History. Select Documents*, ed. A. Bland *et al.* (London, 1925); *Seventeenth-Century Economic Documents*, ed. J. Thirsk and J. P. Cooper (Oxford, 1972). The two latter works have modernized the spelling and language of the selections they reprint.

4   Artisans and entrepreneurs

Trends and causes

Industrial output, like agricultural, increased smartly across nearly all of Europe from the second half of the fifteenth century to the third quarter of the sixteenth. No aggregate figures exist to provide a comprehensive overview, but data on textiles, the premier industry across Europe, suggest the extent and breadth of expansion. At Venice, where barely 2,000 woollens had been produced each year before 1520, output rose to nearly 29,000 in 1602. In Castile, Segovia's clothmakers thought themselves fortunate to turn out 3,000 cloths in a good year before 1550, yet by 1580 the yearly norm was almost 13,000. Further north, at Amiens (France), taxes levied on says yielded barely 500 livres per annum in the early 1520s, but more than 1,800 livres in the late 1530s, a level that was maintained or exceeded for the next half century. Annual English exports of shortcloths (a notional category), 30,000–40,000 in the 1450s, were on average more than 120,000 a century later; and although similar figures are lacking for subsequent years, London alone exported more than 100,000 a year until about 1615. Mining and metallurgy also progressed remarkably. Annual coal shipments from Northumberland and Durham counties (England) were about 45,000 tons in 1508–11, in excess of 500,000 in 1655–60. Copper and silver production grew impressively throughout Germany and east central Europe; the Almadén (Spain) mercury mine tripled output during the sixteenth century. Of the 460 ironworks operating in France in 1542, 400 were said to have been established in the previous fifty years. And although quantitatively less well documented, many other industries from beer to paper, glass to soap, flourished as well.

Ebullient demand promoted both rural and urban industries: cheap knives in villages around Sheffield (England), for instance, and better ones in the city. Crafts emerged in heretofore non-industrialized locations. Once a small farming village with a few part-time weavers, Hondschoote counted 10,000 inhabitants by the 1560s and was one of Europe's leading textile centers, with an annual output of nearly 100,000 says. Previously insignificant trades bloomed: Falun (Sweden), of little note before 1570, was by 1650 pre-eminent in European copper mining. Not to be outdone, numerous prospering industrial centers opened wholly new industries. To its renowned silks, high quality woollens, leatherwork, and glassware, Venice added printing and sugar refining.

Much growth entailed the rebirth of industrial centers and regions that had languished during the late medieval crisis. The resurgence of numerous once outstanding but recently lethargic woollens cities in the southern Netherlands thanks to expansion of crafts making less expensive fabrics is exemplified by the experience of Lille in French Flanders. Previously one of the leading old drapery centers of Europe, it had seen its industry slide nearly into oblivion due to competition from nearby villages, towns in the neighboring province of Brabant, and abroad: by 1516 there may have been as few as five active drapery weavers in Lille. But a switch to new drapery revived production, which increased tenfold between the 1530s and 1550 and set a secular record in 1560. At the same time, light drapery (in this city woven by both "sayetteurs" and "bourget-teurs") began a remarkable and longer-lasting ascent. Before 1500, output of fabrics made by sayetteurs yielded less than 500 livres tax a year, but it paid more than 5,000 livres in 1552, nearly 8,000 livres in 1580; in 1608, the number of velveteens, a monopoly of bourgetteurs, was six times greater than in 1541 (when figures were first reported). The most impressive growth of all was registered by luxurious appearing but inexpensive changéants, woven by artisans in both corporations: from about 2,000 cloths a year in the early 1540s, output reached 175,000 in 1619.

Italian cloth production underwent a similar renascence. Annual output of Florentine woollens rose from 10,000–12,000 pieces in the 1430s to 30,000 or more in the 1560s–70s, and its history was far from unique. In fact, northern and central Italy and the southern Low Countries, the traditional industrial heartlands of Europe, reinforced their position during the expansionary years, despite the opening of new maritime routes. The revival of the continental overland routes connect-ing the Mediterranean and the North Sea – the most populous and urbanized parts of Europe – and the rise of great international trade fairs along them, both assisted and symbolized the primacy of the existing industrial cores.

Growth was, however, far from continuous. Whereas Venetian output was about 20,000 woollens a year in 1566–69, it fell to fewer than 13,000 during the next four years. Similarly, the number of changéants made in Lille during the later 1550s was just a fifth of those turned out in the 1540s. In those cities, production soon recovered brilliantly – going on, in fact, to set new records – but many industries never participated in the advance. As woollens output jumped tenfold in rural Yorkshire between the 1460s and 1590s, the city of York's production dwindled. The northern Low Countries' once great old drapery likewise died out. At Leiden, output of broadcloth (*lakens*) shrivelled from 29,000 pieces in 1521 to fewer than 1,100 in 1573. Holland's other significant industry – the brewing of beer – also withered: Gouda's output, for example, fell from 290,000 vats per year in the 1480s to 47,000 in 1571. Still, for nearly a century circumstances like these, though locally or regionally momentous, remained anomalous and circumscribed.

Both demand and supply factors promoted industrial growth. Exploration, conquest, and settlement brought European goods to non-western areas. In the sixteenth century, these new markets most keenly affected industries that supplied Spanish possessions in the New World, for the volume of shipping between Seville (whence all trade with Spanish colonies had to pass) and the Americas grew seventeenfold between 1511–15 and 1606–10. The booming demand – and periodic downturns – were felt with particular force by the makers of cheap woollens and linens in the southern Netherlands and adjacent northern France: the rhythms of Lille's light drapery production, for instance, corresponded to those of Seville's shipments to the colonies. For most European industries, however, the world economy only became significant in the later seventeenth and eighteenth centuries.

The main determinants of Europe's industrial advance thus lay within Europe itself. Population grew from 61 million in 1500 to 78 million a century later, and the proportion of Europeans living in cities of 10,000 or more – and thus dependent on the market for what they consumed – expanded from less than 6 to nearly 8 percent across the same period. More important than sheer numbers, many Europeans' incomes rose. This was especially true among more fully employed urban groups, farmers benefiting from higher prices and intensifying agrarian commercialization and specialization (which also led them to shed much non-agricultural production in favor of purchased goods), and landlords and other property-owners who collected mounting rents (including in-kind payments) or sold demesne-raised produce. State-building, mainly through its perhaps inevitable concomitant war, stimulated numerous industries, most notably shipbuilding, textiles, and metallurgy. To cite just one example, France hastened to develop its own iron industry when the Habsburgs – with whom France fought repeatedly across the long sixteenth century – came to dominate arsenals in Germany, Liège, and Milan that boasted Europe's most advanced technology.

The supply of goods was also significantly modified. Migration had

6 Although using new technology, printing shops, like those in most other crafts, were mainly small. The printer and his journeymen performed a variety of tasks, whereas the compositors, shown by the window, were specialists. As this mid-sixteenth-century woodcut also reveals, printing from its inception was all but monopolized by men.

long been critical for the diffusion of knowledge that spawned new trades or revived somnolent ones. In this Age of Reformations a new force, religious persecution, caused the movement of thousands of skilled and unskilled workers, along with sizable amounts of capital. Calvinists fleeing repression in France and Italy galvanized nearly moribund woollens and silk crafts in Geneva. Their co-religionists from the southern Netherlands brought light drapery and other trades ranging from diamond cutting to oil pressing to England, the Dutch Republic, and western Germany. At the same time, new commodities appeared on the market, often broadening and deepening demand. Most were inexpensive items destined for individual consumers. Knitted stockings, ribbon and lace, buttons, starch, soap, vinegar brewed from beer, knives and tools, pots and ovens, and many more goods, formerly made only for local custom, now entered into channels of national or even international trade. The best known and most widely adopted new industry was printing with movable type, which spread swiftly throughout Europe after Johann Gutenberg perfected his innovation in 1453. Despite pockets of resistance – the scribes' guild delayed printing's introduction into Paris for twenty years – more than 380 working presses had sprung up by 1480, 1,000 (in nearly 250 towns) by 1500. Between 1453 and 1500, all the presses of Europe together turned out some 40,000 editions (known as *incunabula*). But from 1501 to 1600, the same quantity was produced in Lyon and Paris alone.

In metals and mining, technical improvements were available that saved substantially on raw materials and fuel, causing prices to drop. The construction of ever-larger furnaces capable of higher temperatures culminated in the blast furnace, which used cheaper ores and economized on scarce and expensive wood, cutting costs per ton by 20 percent while boosting output substantially. Again, roasting with lead to separate silver from copper (the "liquation" or *Saiger* method) allowed formerly worthless ores to be exploited, while better drainage channels, pumps, and other devices made it possible to tunnel more deeply into the earth as surface deposits began to be exhausted. In most established industries, however, technological change played little role; as in the past, new customers were sought by the development of novel products based on existing technology, a strategy of which changéants – woollens given the texture of silk – were a prime and hugely successful example.

Sharply declining "transactions costs" (the direct and indirect outlays associated with transporting, distributing, and marketing goods and services) were more influential. On a general level, the decrease was due to greater security thanks to the lessening – if never cessation – of wartime disruptions and to the economies of scale achieved when selling to large, concentrated urban populations. More specifically, it can be traced to transport innovations such as the carrack, a large ship that reduced rates for ocean-borne freight by up to 25 percent, and big four-wheeled Hesse carts for overland routes. The spread of specialized commission merchants and other efficient organizational forms – many of them pioneered in Renaissance Italy – further contributed to cutting costs, as did falling real interest rates, which dropped from 20 or 25 percent in the mid-fifteenth century to 10 percent a hundred years later. Symbolizing the interlocking and mutually reinforcing character of these changes, and their salutary effects on industry, was the rise of Antwerp as the greatest commercial and financial center of the age, lying at the confluence of overland and maritime routes and animating crafts throughout north-western Europe and on into Germany and Italy.

Yet also like agriculture, industry slowed, even reversed, as the sixteenth century drew to a close. This time, demand was crucial. Lagging agricultural productivity in a context of prolonged demographic and market growth had pushed up food prices; mounting imports of New World silver and gold also fed the continuing inflation. Despite rising in nominal terms, real wages fell increasingly behind: in most places they were cut at least in half over the long sixteenth century, often by two-thirds. Many city residents came to devote 75–80 percent of their incomes to food, a third to a half to bread alone. In the countryside, the burgeoning throngs of the landless, cottagers, and peasants with holdings too small for subsistence were equally dependent on food purchases. In the years around 1600, and continuing until the end of the long sixteenth century, many urban and rural folk faced rapidly rising taxes as well, on top of which the peasantry's rents and dues persisted in going up. Even in the best of times, these large groups of people spent only a small part of their earnings on manufactures; to survive when harsh inflation was coupled with growing state and seigniorial levies, they had little choice but to reduce even these outlays.

Admittedly, there were some who profited from the on-going price and rent rises and the concomitant redistribution of resources: commercial farmers, canny landlords, employers of labor, state officials. They could afford more and better manufactures: not just brightly colored woollens or soft French velvet but even superb Italian silks costing as much per ell as a journeyman mason earned in a month. But although their consumption could sustain some trades – and indeed kept the luxury goods sector prospering – they were too few to support the wide range of manufactures that had emerged during the previous secular expansion.

As a result, many industries went into a tailspin. Textiles were particularly hard hit, Mediterranean producers getting battered worst of all. The fate of Venice, where output tailed off after 1602 and averaged fewer than 10,000 cloths a year in the 1650s, was replicated throughout Italy; if anything, other cities saw their trades deteriorate earlier and faster. Florence's drapery dwindled to 14,000 pieces in the 1590s and 6,000 in the 1630s. Spanish data paint a correspondingly bleak picture. In Segovia, the only center to continue exporting beyond Iberia, just half of the 600 looms and 15 fulling mills that had worked in the early 1580s existed in the mid-seventeenth century, and they were silent much of the time as annual output dropped back to 3,000 pieces after 1635. Across Europe, too, mining and metallurgy were also severely affected. Alpine copper production, for instance, which fell off by two-thirds between 1526–50 and 1576–1600, decreased another 60 percent by 1626–50. Rural industry suffered along with urban: new drapery in Lys River valley villages collapsed in the later sixteenth century, just as in nearby Lille. Even though some industries rallied in the first two decades of the seventeenth century, most lost steam again even before the outbreak of the Thirty Years' War in 1618 and failed to revive thereafter.

Some bright spots shone amid the prevailing gloom, however. Most were in lands bordering the North Sea. A number of textile crafts in the southern Netherlands and northern France managed to prolong recovery beyond 1620; some even surpassed previous records. At Oudenaarde (Flanders), where linen sales had plummeted from 77,000 pieces in 1580 to 12,800 in 1590, they revived to 34,200 pieces in 1601, continuing upward to 103,900 in 1648. English industries also did well. Newcastle's coal exports continued to climb, reaching 529,000 tons in 1654, and textile crafts enjoyed restored health. The Dutch Republic wrote the most striking success story of all. During its "Golden Age," which stretched from the later 1580s to at least the 1670s, the recently prostrate Republic became the greatest industrial power in Europe.

The long sixteenth century issued, then, in a sharper differentiation among Europe's regions. Some became less industrialized than before, whereas others concentrated industrial activities. In particular, northwestern Europe took on a more preponderant and dynamic role at the expense of northern and central Italy most of all. Both in extent and in pace, the shift was as yet modest. But hand in hand with changes beginning to affect the agrarian sector it was laying the basis for the emergence of the lands bordering the North Sea as the core of the European economy. To understand this process in both its hesitations and its advances, we need first to survey the industrial histories of Europe's regions. What forces determined Europe's new industrial geography? How were the principal areas and crafts affected?

Redrawing the industrial map

The Mediterranean Basin

Italy

For at least a century, both established industries like cloth, mining, and ceramics and newer ones such as paper and printing registered impressive growth in Italy, carrying on the peninsula's previous preeminence. Textile trades ranging from Naples silk to Venetian woollens, in fact, attained their highest levels of output after 1600. For many decades, the peninsula's manufactures benefited greatly from demand generated by vibrant commercial, financial, and agricultural sectors, domestic demographic expansion, and continued high levels of urbanization. Thanks to the wide implantation abroad of Italian merchants and bankers, Italian industries also tapped expanding markets throughout Europe, while in the Middle East the Ottoman Empire became an important consumer of all kinds of Italian goods. At times, technical innovation played a positive supporting role. The spread of hydraulic silk throwing and reeling mills pioneered in Bologna significantly bolstered quality while at the same time appreciably reducing costs; new glazing methods that gave ceramics a more attractive and durable finish brought in many customers. Considerable government, ecclesiastical, and private building and reconstruction likewise stimulated Italian crafts, especially the luxury and artistic trades. Italian industry also adapted nicely to changing conditions. When American imports made silver mining unprofitable, iron and copper took its place and gave rise as well to increased production of knives, swords, scissors, and other metal goods. Again, the dynamism of the urban woollens crafts in Lombardy and Tuscany was largely due to their abandoning old drapery for less expensive new types.

Impressive as this performance was, by the end of the long sixteenth century most Italian industries not only shared in the downturn prevailing across Europe but fell out of the front rank that they had long occupied. Besides this relative decline that affected Italian industry as a whole, moreover, numerous trades – especially those located in the larger cities – lost ground in absolute terms. In Milan, for example, the number of silk looms dropped from 3,000 in 1605 to 600 twenty years later, and the 70 enterprises that turned out 15,000 pieces of woollen drapery in 1620 had by 1640 dwindled to just 15, making 3,000 cloths. As the information from Venice and Florence cited above suggests, similar histories could be related about many other towns and trades. What explains this reversal?

Slumping domestic demand provides one important answer to the question. Because of steeply rising taxes, heavier rents, dues, and other levies on the peasantry, high food prices, and the ebbing of their former commercial and financial supremacy, Italians had fewer resources to devote to manufactures. Not only poorer, their numbers were significantly fewer. By 1650, after several decades of severe and repeated plague epidemics, Italian population (11.3 million) had dropped back to its 1550 level, well below the 13.1 million counted around 1600. Nor did foreign demand step into the breach; although exports had fueled much industrial growth in the recent past, this option was now foreclosed. Dutch, English, and French producers made serious inroads into many markets long dominated by Italians; in particular, their light draperies won much of the lucrative Levant cloth trade and even penetrated the Italian home market. Papal-controlled mines had for several centuries been Europe's chief supplier of alum, essential for fixing dyes to cloth. But they lost that position once new mines opened near Liège (southern Netherlands), and in Yorkshire (England), Bohemia, Silesia, and Slovakia. Protective tariffs cut off access to the French market; war badly disrupted the German lands; state policy, repeated currency devaluations, and catastrophic inflation reduced once-copious sales in the Ottoman Empire to a trickle. Refocusing exports towards Iberia's still open markets – a strategy facilitated by Spanish political hegemony in Italy, a legacy of sixteenth-century wars – failed to make much difference. For as we have seen (chap. 3), Spain was itself caught up in increasingly severe economic problems, and these curtailed demand for manufactures.

As this last example indicates, Italian producers did not passively accept decline. Like their counterparts elsewhere, many urban enterprises concentrated on expensive goods, seeking to turn to their advantage the growing concentration of wealth throughout Europe (including Italy itself), Italy's still-abundant merchant capital, and the standards and skills for which the peninsula's goods were already famed. Instances of thriving luxury trades are not hard to find – expensive textiles, superb metalwork, handsome furniture, fine art. Even where the luxury sector flourished, however, it is doubtful whether it compensated for the industries that decayed. In Florence, the silk trades boomed; nevertheless, combined silk and woollens output in the mid-seventeenth century was a third lower than in the 1560s. Moreover, many industries specializing in the high end of the market did not prosper; outside Florence, employment among silkweavers dropped by half or more between 1620 and the end of the century, and the long-famous velvet and damask industry at Catanzaro in the Kingdom of Naples died out. With producers across Europe vying for the custom of what was, after all, a small group, Italian artisans often found themselves hampered by high taxes and wages, together with manifold government and corporate regulations. Hence comparable luxury goods could be made more cheaply abroad. Foreign artisans also became adept at fabricating less expensive yet good-looking imitations that even well-off consumers – Italian as well as foreign – came to prefer.

Another strategy to stem industrial decay – again part of a Europe-wide trend – was to decrease costs by shifting production to rural areas with lower wages and fewer rules to impede labor-saving innovation. As early as 1582, 70 percent of the silk looms in and around Genoa were located outside the city; by 1675, the proportion was up to four-fifths. In this case, however, ruralization did not spell success: only 2,560 looms were operating in 1675, as against 8,000 a century earlier. More fortunate were village trades producing for the lower end of the market, such as coarse fustians, woollens, and linens, as well as less expensive silks. Northern Italy was at the forefront of the movement. Urban elites in this region proved willing to invest capital in rural industry – as in agricultural improvement – and there was a large wage-earning labor force available for industrial employment during the winter and other slow seasons on the farm.

Yet over the rest of Italy it was the obstacles to the spread of rural industry that predominated during the long sixteenth century, and even in the North none became large enough to offset urban losses. Three principal reasons can be adduced. First, urban-based governments typically stood firmly in the way of industrial production in the contado both because they envisaged the countryside as a source of cheap foodstuffs and raw materials for city crafts and because they sought to protect politically and socially influential guild masters from lower-cost, less-regulated competitors. Second, most of those with the necessary capital preferred to keep it in trade or – as we have observed already – to invest it in land yielding rents and seigniorial dues, in various types of credit, or in conspicuous consumption. Third, the structures that characterized much of Italian agriculture effectively, if unwittingly, limited ruralization. Family farms, especially those exploited in mezzadria, kept peasants preponderantly occupied with agrarian activities. What little non-farming time they enjoyed was devoted to weaving cloth or fashioning tools for their own use – which of course also cut into purchases of artisanal products.

So if Italy boasted some vigorous and innovative areas and industries – if its decline was less severe and less sweeping than historians previously believed – nevertheless, by the end of the long sixteenth century a combination of internal constraints and external competition dethroned it from its former supremacy. And in many cases it lagged well behind Europe's emerging industrial leaders.

Spain

Although beginning from a much more modest level than Italy, Spanish industry expanded alongside agriculture from the later fifteenth century through the 1570s. The settlement of the Americas was of some importance. Spanish goods were sometimes granted monopolies in colonial markets (or managed without such help), seaborne trade with the New World – along with the defense requirements of a worldwide empire – busied Iberian shipbuilders, and raw materials such as hides from the Americas were processed by Spanish artisans. Yet even for Spain, which possessed the most extensive sixteenth-century colonial empire, Old World markets and materials were of greater consequence. Drawing on abundant domestic supplies of fine wool and raw silk, and well into the first half of the sixteenth century sheltered from foreign imports, the textile trades of Baeza, Córdoba, Cuenca, Granada, Segovia, and Toledo responded briskly to rising North African, Levant, Portuguese, and internal Spanish demand. Spanish trades adopted some new technologies as well. Water-powered forges and tilt hammers quickened the Catalan and Basque iron industries; the vast Almadén (Castile) mercury mine instituted the most advanced German methods. Integrated regional divisions of labor emerged, incorporating industry and agriculture, city and countryside. Around Córdoba, for example, villagers living south of the Guadalquivir River grew foodstuffs sold throughout the area; residents of a mountainous zone to the north herded sheep, spun wool, and wove good quality cloth for urban and export customers; Córdoba artisans finished rural cloth and made rough fabrics and other manufactures for sale to local peasants; and urban merchants provided capital, commercial services, and additional supplies to all three.

No more than its agriculture, however, was Iberian industry destined to stay healthy: the crisis that engulfed Spain sooner or later overwhelmed most of its leading crafts. The manufacture of woollens faltered after 1580 in all the major centers, with output plummeting as the seventeenth century progressed. Despite a more diverse industrial base, which boasted tanning and silkweaving as well as woollens, Toledo experienced severe decline. Shipbuilding slackened, Basque iron output slid from 300,000 quintals in 1545 to just 100,000 in 1658, and after 1645 the amount of mercury mined at Almadén sank back to early sixteenth-century levels.

Spanish industrial decline was, admittedly, part of a larger trend. But why was it of greater magnitude than in most other parts of Europe? Historians often point to severe demographic contraction. Already falling in the 1570s and 1580s, Spain's population dropped by a seventh between 1600 and 1650, that of towns by more than a quarter. Both were among the sharpest decreases in Europe. Still, the timing suggests that population decline, and especially deurbanization, were results as much as causes of industrial decay. More directly culpable were government policies and priorities that – in the industrial as in the agrarian sector – throttled development. Because export taxes on wool comprised an important part of Crown revenues, merchants served as the state's principal creditors, and landlord political power was robust, monarchs turned a deaf ear to pleas by cloth manufacturers to reserve half of Castilian wool for the kingdom's industry (up from the third on which it had first option since 1462). So even when the clip decreased after 1550, most of it continued to be exported to competitors abroad. Here, rather than in the agrarian sector, is where the Mesta's clout was most harmfully felt. Steps taken in 1548 to combat high prices likewise played havoc with industry. Existing protective tariffs on manufactures were lowered to encourage imports – which came flooding in – and then for nearly a decade Castilian producers lost access to European markets when the government forbade all exports of woollens, silks, and leather, save to the American colonies. Thereafter, monetary chaos – resulting from the increasingly desperate Crown's repeated devaluations, revaluations, and minting of copper coins that stoked inflation – was a further heavy blow. Catalan industry had already been badly harmed by royal policies that favored Castile, going so far as to banish Catalan cloth from the fairs and colonies of its sister kingdom.

But Spanish industrial difficulties went deeper, as is evidenced by the loss of markets that had once taken substantial amounts of Spanish manufactures. To be sure, the same problems within the Ottoman Empire that disturbed Italian exports to the Levant affected Spain's, too. But Iberian goods mainly suffered because they became uncompetitive – at home as well as abroad. In the Americas, more and more inexpensive wares were purchased from colonial artisans, whereas the elite was supplied by the Low Countries and France. Spanish textile producers also found it hard to sell to the Mediterranean consumers who had once made cloth Iberia's leading industrial export, and even Spaniards showed a marked proclivity for foreign fabrics. For example, the Court alone still bought an appreciable amount of Spanish silk, and it did so principally because Toledo, close to Madrid, could quickly respond to fashion changes. Other centers lost out to French and Florentine imports.

Waning competitiveness was rooted first of all in circumstances that drove Iberian production costs above those of rivals. Inflation seems to have struck Spain earlier than the rest of Europe. At the same time, for reasons that are as yet unclear but apparently included the presence of powerful guilds, Spanish artisans proved able to keep their wages abreast of prices better than their counterparts in other lands, whose tumbling real wages helped moderate industrial price rises. As the sixteenth century went on, the higher prices of Spanish goods also reflected soaring taxes (see chap. 3). These included national levies like the alcabala, assessed nearly every time an article changed hands during manufacture (a frequent occurrence when separate guilds controlled each stage of the production process), and the millones, which by boosting the cost of food inevitably pushed up wages. Numerous local imposts on various crafts also raised costs. And taxes remained high as the economy deteriorated, exacerbating and perpetuating difficulties – the more so because very little tax revenue (like the American treasure that was another potentially fruitful resource in the government's hands) was invested productively, even in roads or other infrastructure that might have helped cut transactions costs. Finally, in sharp contrast to their earlier taste for innovation, Spanish producers failed to keep up technologically with their rivals. Shipbuilders neglected to develop new designs or modernize procedures, while foundrymen took twice as long to fabricate goods as their competitors and used much more charcoal.

An economic environment characterized by adverse state policies, disrupted foreign markets, and excessive costs of production encouraged the redeployment of capital out of industry. Urban patricians were hardly immune to the lure of status and power, especially when these were coupled to sources of assured income. Much capital therefore flowed into land purchases; as in Italy, however, the goal was maximum rent income, not agrarian improvement. Substantial funds also found their way into usury, Crown juros and censos, municipal office, and conspicuous consumption, notably the acquisition of noble titles and seigniorial jurisdictions (available for purchase, as we have seen in chap. 3, thanks to the Crown's ongoing search for revenue and political support). Manufacturers likewise withdrew from production to try their hands at trade. Taking advantage of the skills and contacts they had accumulated over the years, most went into raw wool exporting and cloth importing, which of course only drove another nail into the coffin of the Spanish textile crafts.

Not everyone abandoned industry, to be sure, but none of the strategies the diehards pursued achieved much success in the face of their admittedly daunting problems. Many guild artisans – backed by monarchs eager as always for payments to the royal treasury and for help in keeping the urban peace – sought salvation in rigid adherence to regulations. They demanded strict enforcement of codes such as the Seville Ordinance with its 120 detailed rules for weaving, and, in the name of the tried and the true, denounced innovations such as techniques that yielded a glossy, colorful finish. Unhappily for them, many of their customers – who now wanted that finish – turned elsewhere, so the conservative approach was at best a rearguard action that protected only a dwindling band of masters. Nor, however, did a diametrically opposite plan work. Even though Valencia switched from expensive heavy silks in the early sixteenth century to cheaper satins by 1600, then again to much lighter taffetas by the 1630s, the Kingdom was no more than a minor center in 1650. Foreign manufacturers were also, in other words, able to make novel items less expensively than their Spanish counterparts.

What best resisted foreign products were cheap, low quality fabrics made by villagers or townspeople employed outside guilds in putting-out systems for sale to peasants and the urban lower classes. But a combination of agrarian and demographic reversals put even these crafts in a parlous state. Impoverishment and indebtedness curtailed the purchasing power of peasants and urban residents alike at the same time that their numbers were falling. If the Córdoba region is any gauge, the privatization of baldíos had an additional ill effect: the disappearance of small herds of sheep that had been critical sources of inexpensive wool for local weavers. As their output faded, wool prices rose, Córdoba's crafts languished, city merchants metamorphosed into rentiers, and the interrelated regional economy crumbled.

By the end of the long sixteenth century, Spanish industry was on the defensive. Those crafts that survived were small-scale and mainly oriented to domestic consumers, usually the least prosperous, who lived in the region of production. Very few Spanish manufactures were sold in foreign markets; on the contrary, a large proportion of the peninsula's industrial raw materials were exported for processing abroad, and they often returned as finished goods that undersold Iberian wares.

East central Europe

The east central lands strongly resembled Iberia in some crucial respects: industrial raw materials – notably minerals, hemp, and flax – were among their main exports; imports satisfied much of the demand of prosperous landlords, officials, and merchants; and many of their own manufactures were inexpensive goods consumed in the region. But the area was considerably less industrialized than Spain, not to mention most other parts of Europe. On the one hand, the growth of serfdom, which directed an increasing amount of labor towards agricultural tasks or towards the fabrication of many of the tools, textiles, and other goods used on the seigniorial estates, curbed the production of manufactures for the market. On the other hand, a puny urban market containing less than 2 percent of the region's population, rising poverty among the serfs, and the concentration of wealth in the hands of a landlord class that bought many luxuries from abroad all dampened demand for manufactures.

Pockets of industry had nevertheless long existed throughout the region, typically in upland districts endowed with flax, ores, and other raw materials, wood and water for energy, and peasant populations that welcomed non-agricultural work to supplement their incomes from small holdings. Extractive industries were particularly common. In the past, associations of artisans had operated most mining and metallurgy enterprises, leasing land and equipment from landowners. But in the long sixteenth century, feudal lords began to take an increasingly active role, opening new mines, glassworks, and iron foundries on their estates or taking over those previously leased out to free masters. Direct involvement in industry was, of course, part and parcel of lords' growing emphasis on manorially based production for the market as exemplified by demesne agriculture and rising in-kind levies on the peasantry. In the iron industry, the trend was strengthened by the adoption of technological changes, because the introduction of blast furnaces and continuous production required capital for equipment and labor beyond the reach of most artisans.

In the lordly enterprises, as in their late medieval predecessors, skilled work continued to be performed largely by free wage-earners, although now they owed money and in-kind payments to their employers. However, more and more auxiliary tasks, including cutting wood for fuel and hauling raw materials, were assigned to serfs as unpaid corvées, and even the less skilled types of production work were often carried out by serfs subjected to forced wage labor.

Some of these industries did not flourish. After an initial boom, Polish and Slovakian ironmaking, as well as Alpine copper and silver mining, dwindled after 1550. But a surprising number of extractive and fabricating trades proved successful over the long run. Poland and Silesia mined eight times as much lead in 1650 as in 1500. Over the same period, Bohemian and Austrian iron posted steady increases by making scythes, sickles, and knives. Initially, they were exported to western Europe, but from the mid-sixteenth century the competition became too keen, so they directed their goods to nearby Scandinavia, the Ottoman Empire, and east central Europe.

Textile industries also took hold. Hempen sail cloth from Poland and Prussia was sent to western Europe, along with linens from Silesia, Moravia, and Bohemia. Like metal wares, however, the bulk of textile output was sold in the region or further east, in Lithuania, the Ukraine, and Russia. As the increasingly enserfed population of all these areas became poorer in the seventeenth century, east central cloth displaced western stuffs. According to one estimate, west European fabrics, concentrated at the upper end of the market, filled only 20–30 percent of east central textile consumption by 1650. Like its agriculture, then, east central European industry specialized in goods exploiting cheap labor and local raw materials, factors of production in which it enjoyed a comparative advantage. But the region's possibilities for industrial expansion were cramped by the growing dominance of serf agriculture in its major markets, for this agrarian order restricted the supply and mobility of labor, employed most capital in land and trade, promoted estate autarky, and impoverished the majority of the population.

Western Europe

The most dynamic industrial areas were found in western Europe, but their experiences during the long sixteenth century were far from uniform. Western Germany, France, and the southern Low Countries housed some thriving trades and regions; overall, however, their industries were in a holding pattern. England boasted steady growth from a position of relative backwardness, while the Dutch Republic recovered from severe initial difficulties to emerge as the industrial flagship of the age.

Western Germany

The late medieval crisis persisted in many German lands until after 1500, but industry subsequently underwent sustained, if poorly documented, expansion. The manifold textile crafts formed the most widely found and probably the biggest industrial sector overall, but some of the mining and metal trades that dominated mountainous areas were substantial. In the Upper Palatinate, which alone turned out as much iron as all of France, that industry supported 20–25 percent of the population. Some German output was exported: woollens to the eastern Baltic and Scandinavia, linens to Spain whence they were shipped to the Americas, barchents to the Mediterranean and, in smaller quantities, to western Europe. But German consumers – both within the producing states and nearby – bought most manufactures. Prosperity in the countryside – where more than 95 percent of the population lived – thus strongly stimulated industrial growth. So did governments that decreed regional monopolies, guaranteed raw materials supplies, even sanctioned boycotts of competitors. In Hesse, for example, these policies aided the rise of large stove, pipe, and glassware manufactures. The technical changes already described were crucial for the important mining and metal trades; in addition, the growth in trade throughout Europe and wider afield spurred silver mining. Revitalized overland and riverine routes, which were especially thick in Germany, as well as the appearance of specialized carting firms and postal services, diminished transactions costs.

Despite all this, western German industry could not sustain growth. Like their peers further east, many mining districts went into a prolonged slump around 1550. The Upper Palatinate, which as late as 1609 boasted 182 forges with an output of 9,500 tons of iron, saw two-thirds of the forges close by 1618 and production drop by three-quarters. At the low point in 1665, 29 forges furnished less than 950 tons of iron. Textile trades prospered longer, in many places thanks to an influx of Protestant refugees with skills and capital. But recession became general throughout German industry after 1600. The Thirty Years' War, fought mainly on German soil, greatly exacerbated and drew out industry's difficulties. Population was decimated – in 1650 it was back at its 1500 level – trade disrupted, plant and equipment destroyed. But the decay clearly predated the outbreak of hostilities; it was rooted in both the state of the markets and the conditions of manufacture.

On the one side, consumption of German industrial goods simultaneously declined at home and abroad. Mounting burdens on the German smallholder majority (see chap. 3) cut into domestic demand, the even more dire condition of the enserfed peasantry further east obliged it to forgo German wares for local ones, and Mediterranean and Spanish American markets shrivelled. On the other side, German crafts lost their competitive edge due to rivals' greater success in cutting production and marketing costs, and, at home, to heavier tax burdens, changing government priorities, resource depletion, and increasingly rigid production structures. Not all of these conditions obtained in every instance. But they prevailed widely enough to cripple industry. Silver mines, undersold by New World producers using coerced Indian labor, could not justify the major investments required to maintain significant operations. Increasingly indebted states could no longer afford to aid local industry and in fact had to raise taxes; at the same time, the wood gobbled up by the fuel-intensive glass and metals crafts became scarcer and more expensive. The guilds that dominated urban industries sought to protect masters' jobs and incomes in a time of fierce inflation and dwindling sales by reasserting regulations and rejecting any form of cost-cutting innovation.

German industries were not entirely disarmed in the face of these problems. In particular, some entrepreneurs tried to reduce their outlays for labor and materials. In new urban crafts – most notably the light woollens established in Rhineland cities by Calvinists fleeing the southern Netherlands – they introduced products requiring fewer and simpler steps and indigenous wools. Elsewhere, processes that required less skill and capital migrated into the countryside to employ members of the growing proportion of farm households unable to maintain themselves solely by agriculture. Thus while dyeing and bleaching remained in cities, barchent weaving moved into rural districts, some of them east of the Elbe. By 1648, this transfer left Augsburg with only 500 barchent weavers, as against 3,000 in 1612. Cologne, too, became a center for putting out linen, barchent, and woollen textile work.

Nevertheless, implementation of cost-cutting strategies was a long, slow process. The pervasive destruction and insecurity occasioned by the repeated passage of marauding troops eroded the allure of village production, causing trades to move back into towns. Escalating seigniorial obligations left rural folk less time for industrial labor. Guilds remained politically potent in many cities, and – as in Italy – territorial governments were often anxious to support what they took to be the proper division of labor between agricultural countrysides and artisanal and commercial towns. In industry as in agriculture, traditional ways continued to dominate in Germany. Ruralization and other forms of innovation made their appearance, but on so limited a scale that they could not prevent widespread decay.

France

The cycle of expansion and retreat registered by French industry during the long sixteenth century closely paralleled the course of the country's agriculture outlined in chap. 3. From the end of the Hundred Years' War to the 1560s, output grew smartly in both existing and newly founded industries. Textiles reaffirmed and extended their primacy, as artisans across France turned out a profusion of fabrics for every taste and pocketbook. Inexpensive woollens came from Normandy, Picardy, Champagne, and Languedoc; Paris and Orléans became tapestry centers of the first rank; Tours and Lyon wove top-notch silks; fine as well as common linens poured from looms in northern and western provinces. Although never matching textiles in importance, mining and metallurgy throve in France's many upland areas, papermaking flourished in several districts, and Lyon and Paris took their places among Europe's foremost printing centers.

In industry as in agriculture, too, the Religious Wars ushered in a long period of torpor followed by decline. Robust resurgence – evident, for example, in the rebuilding of deserted iron foundries, the opening of new ones, and the extension of the iron-producing season – did not outlast the end of the first third of the seventeenth century. Both the revival and the subsequent difficulties struck virtually every industry. At Amiens, where say output had collapsed after 1585 – reaching a nadir in the later 1590s – the 1620s saw the highest levels ever recorded, only to fall off again thereafter. Even the metal trades, which at first benefited from France's entry into the Thirty Years' War – outlays on artillery, for instance, jumped from 600,000 livres in 1629 to 4 million in 1639 – suffered sharp reverses thereafter. By 1650, iron output was back to 1500 levels.

Both export and domestic markets, and luxury as well as more mundane goods, contributed to initial French industrial expansion. The silk trades diversified into brocades and damasks woven on the newly invented *grand-tire* loom and bested most Italian and Spanish producers in their homelands, not to mention elsewhere in Europe. Cheap French light drapery moved aggressively into Iberia, Italy, North Africa, and the Levant, while a large proportion of French linens was sold in Spain and its American empire. Demand within France – by far Europe's largest market – burgeoned, first of all by virtue of population growth from 16.4 million in 1500 to 19 million just a half century later. Because barely 4 percent of French people lived in cities of more than 10,000 residents at the latter date (just half the urbanization level in the rest of western Europe), rural consumption was crucial – and, up to the 1550s, was thriving, thanks to agriculture's healthy state and an easing of the tax burden. Commercial centers like Lyon, Rouen, and Toulouse participated in and helped to diffuse the commercial and financial advances of the age that helped develop markets at home and abroad.

Neither foreign nor internal demand proved able, however, to sustain French industrial prosperity on a broad scale. Luxury goods did best, as guild training and regulations, along with government support, helped them win and hold the custom of those Europeans who had gained from the consolidation of wealth. More ordinary goods, on the contrary, fared less well. Far and away their major export markets were in the Mediterranean – and these economies, we have seen, were atrophying well before the long sixteenth century came to a close. Trade in manufactures with the rising economies of England and the Dutch Republic was much more modest: France chiefly shipped them primary products like wine and salt.

On the home market, items of middling quality and price produced by urban artisans and increasingly protected by tariff and exclusionary barriers found a secure niche among the upper levels of the peasantry and moderately prosperous townspeople. But as a whole, domestic demand contracted. Unlike many other parts of Europe, France did not experience a demographic slump. Nonetheless, the country's population virtually stagnated for many decades, at best inching up to 20 million in 1600 and just 20.5 million in 1650. More important, much of the populace became considerably poorer. Taxes mounted exponentially (chap. 3): royal revenues went up fifteenfold in nominal terms between 1575 and 1635, eightfold in terms of grain prices. Concurrently, rents, dues, and food prices were climbing, real wages were tumbling, and the holdings of the peasant majority were shrinking. Under these conditions, even cheap manufactures perforce became luxuries – highly desirable and all but unattainable.

These circumstances did force many rural people to seek additional income from industrial employment, and neither serfdom nor, in most provinces, sharecropping stood in their way. Entrepreneurs responded in particular by initiating the transfer of the preparatory and weaving stages of both coarse and middling quality cloth fabrication into the countryside. This trend was strongly marked in linen manufacture, where peasants could use flax raised on their own holdings, but it also occurred in the woollens trades. At the end of the long sixteenth century, however, rural production remained embryonic. Like agriculture once again, industry in France showed promise of change that was as yet little realized. Guilds may have had something to do with this retardation, though despite them some merchants were able to organize rural putting-out systems. The state of the markets was an equally big problem. What was needed most of all was a revival of consumption both internally – which in turn depended to a great extent on agrarian transformation – and abroad, where new markets had to be opened and existing ones deepened. Both developments were slow in coming, and in the meantime Dutch and English competitors began making inroads – even with domestic French consumers.

The southern Netherlands

With the exception of new drapery, which like its Italian counterpart carved out a niche against keen English competition, southern Low Countries industries were in a parlous state during much of the fifteenth century. During the 1470s–90s, their problems were compounded by the political disruption, military destruction, and monetary disorder that attended the disintegration of the Burgundian state of which they formed the industrial heartland. From about 1500, however, conditions brightened markedly. Textiles in particular regained their health, and their premier position: around 1560, half of all exports through Antwerp, far and away the leading port in those parts, consisted of fabrics produced in the Netherlands. But traditional heavy drapery, which had long brought renown to Flanders and Brabant, accounted for a constantly shrinking share of output; it was supplanted by lighter woollens, linens, and mixed fabrics produced in town and village alike. The evidence from Lille already mentioned indicates the boom in light and new drapery; sales at Eeklo, the chief linen market of Flanders, surged from 6,000 pieces in 1509 to nearly 64,000 in 1565; and at Bruges, the weaving of fustians, unknown before 1492, soared to more than 30,000 pieces a year at mid-century. Using techniques that had yet to be mastered across the

Channel, Antwerp emerged as the leading center for finishing English woollens: these alone accounted for a fifth of exports from the port in 1560.

Important as cloth remained, the southern Netherlands industrial revival was broadly based. The eastern provinces, which laid claim to a proud mining and metallurgical history, saw these industries expand rapidly. In the Ardennes Mountains, 90 blast furnaces and iron foundries about 1500 became 220 in 1565. Around Liège, returns from the coal-mining tax grew thirtyfold over the first half of the sixteenth century. Output, first recorded in 1545, when 48,000 tons was mined, attained 90,000 tons in 1562. Finally, towns both encouraged long-established luxury and artistic crafts such as tapestry weaving, sculpting, and painting and welcomed a wide variety of new trades including printing, glass-blowing, diamond cutting, sugar refining, and silkworking.

Of primordial importance to southern Netherlands industrial growth was the revival of foreign demand, upon which the area's crafts had long depended heavily. This orientation, which took the provinces' goods throughout Europe, was greatly strengthened by the emergence of Antwerp as Europe's commercial and financial metropole, a development that, as we have seen, quickened industry throughout a broad hinterland linked by excellent riverine and overland transport. Lille, for instance, sold the lion's share of its textiles through Antwerp, even to consumers elsewhere in the southern Netherlands. From the end of the fifteenth century, when the Habsburgs succeeded the dukes of Burgundy as rulers of the Netherlands, industries also enjoyed easier access to Iberian and Spanish American markets. But Antwerp also developed close and profitable links with England, France, Italy, the Baltic area, and many other lands, thereby tapping the broadly spreading demand for manufactures and avoiding undue reliance on any single area.

Seconded by domestic urban prosperity and demographic growth, and by a richly productive agriculture, exports buoyed southern Low Countries industries until the 1560s. In that decade, however, foreign trade was disrupted first by commercial conflicts with England and then by disturbances in the Baltic; at the same time, Amsterdam took a growing share of business once monopolized by Antwerp. Fast upon the heels of these troubles, important markets in the Mediterranean entered on the long-term deterioration that also harmed Italian and Spanish industries, and the French Wars of Religion wrought years of havoc. At home, production was badly dislocated by the Dutch Revolt, which was most radical and violent precisely in southern industrial centers. From the later 1560s until the mid-1580s, cities, towns, and villages were repeatedly in rebellion or under siege; some – including Hondschoote, burned to the ground in 1582 – were physically destroyed. After their victory – achieved slowly across the 1580s – the Habsburgs sought to reimpose Catholicism on the rebel areas they had reconquered. But many artisans refused to reconvert and emigrated, and in their new homes abroad they implanted or reinvigorated industries – cloth and metals most of all – that competed with those they had left behind. Domestic consumption likewise slid in the aftermath of the Revolt, thanks to widespread deurbanization, joblessness, and price rises that were among the steepest in Europe. In these dark decades, output of many textile crafts tumbled three-fourths or more practically overnight (Hondschoote made 59,000 says in 1581; when records resume in 1585, 13,000); Antwerp's finishing trades withered as English cloth decamped to Amsterdam and Hamburg; Liège coal tonnage plummeted and Ardennes forges shut down.

Some industries never revived. Others hung on as shadows of their former greatness: as against 200 cloth finishing shops in 1580, just 40 were in business in Antwerp in the seventeenth century; the 4,000 silk weaving employees of 1585 had become 1,500 in 1650. Yet a number of trades recovered briskly once the fighting ceased. Urban luxury crafts, to begin with, both wooed customers from Italian goods and broadened their clientèle into the middling ranks of society. They did so in part by developing new products. Even more, they introduced specialized task work and a pronounced division of labor that, by allowing the employment of less skilled and therefore less expensive labor, enabled them to trim production costs and lower prices. As a result of these efforts, the number of embroidery masters at Antwerp doubled between 1603 and 1616 while the ranks of master diamond-cutters quintupled. The famed Plantin press won the exclusive right to supply Spain and its colonies with the breviaries and missals dear to the counter-Reformation Catholic Church. The making of majolica, jewelry, expensive furniture, tapestry, fine glassware, and mirrors also blossomed again in Antwerp and Brussels, fine linen in Ghent.

The iron industry likewise sought to cut costs while focusing on specific markets. In the Ardennes, production was concentrated around Habay, where in the first half of the seventeenth century twenty new furnaces and forges joined the fifteen or so already in existence. Other sites were abandoned, reducing the cost of transporting materials while increasing efficiency because the stages of production (smelting, casting, founding) could be more closely integrated. Moreover, Habay iron masters specialized in cast iron for the Liège region, which on its side relinquished smelting for the fabrication of arms, hardware, and – above all – nails directed primarily to the lively shipbuilding and construction trades in the neighboring Dutch Republic.

Just as they had been central to earlier growth, so textiles stood at the center of the revival. The resumption of regular trade with Iberia and the colonies once Habsburg rule returned was of greatest consequence, as sales in other markets continued to be mediocre; domestic demand, fueled by renewed urbanization, probably played a weightier role than before. Cheap fabric manufacture picked up in villages and small towns not only because peace returned but also because ongoing parcellization of holdings forced peasants to seek additional employment; thus the eightfold increase of rurally woven linen sold at Oudenaarde, cited above; and thus the rebirth of Hondschoote, which literally rose from the ashes to weave 61,000 says in 1630. In contrast to Italy and Germany, in the southern Netherlands neither cities nor guilds could stand in the way of the trend; nor did tenurial conditions restrict the mobility of rural labor. Urban producers, while focusing on standardized middle-market cloth, likewise managed to cut costs by relying on less skilled, lower wage workers, often artisans from failing industries. Once-mighty guilds, their power considerably diluted after the failure of corporate-led regimes during the Revolt, could present little opposition to entrepreneurial efforts even in towns. Outside their ken altogether were the thousands of urban women and children who took up the heretofore minor craft of lacemaking, enabling their hard-pressed families to survive, and the other women who labored in embroidery, ribbon and trimmings making, and allied clothing trades.

Although probably superior to what had been achieved in western Germany and France – not to mention the Mediterranean or east central lands – the success of southern Netherlands industry should not be exaggerated. By the end of the long sixteenth century, overall industrial output may have climbed back to its 1560s level but did not surpass it. Their abiding reliance on export markets made these provinces' manufactures peculiarly vulnerable both to the economic deterioration that spread across Europe and to more specific shocks like the Peace of Münster (1648), which opened Spain and its colonies to licit competition from goods made in Holland, England, and France, and to protectionist tariffs imposed abroad. In addition, the internal market, although rooted in a high degree of urbanization and a strongly commercialized agriculture, was not only small but limited by the marginal condition of much of the peasantry. Still, their focus on consumers abroad and the availability of cheap labor at home stimulated producers to reduce costs, adopt fresh products, and find new markets. These provinces confronted, then, both keen challenges and promising prospects. Specifically, they faced developing competition from England and the Dutch Republic.

England

At the beginning of the long sixteenth century, England's industrial employment and output ranked the country well below Europe's manufacturing heartlands. Apart from undyed and unfinished woollen old draperies, products of the country's only large-scale industry, England's major exports were raw materials such as wool, hides, tin, and lead. Imports satisfied much domestic demand for manufactures. By the end of the period, most of this had changed. Not only had resource exports tailed off – after many centuries, wool shipments to the Continent had virtually ceased by the 1570s – but foreign raw materials had become essential to some industries. Swedish iron bars, for example, were needed to fill a persistent shortage, even though English output quintupled between the 1550s and 1650s; and so much had English cloth output grown that imported Spanish wool was needed. Largely because of import substitution – which frequently depended on skills, technology, and capital from abroad – foreign manufactures no longer dominated English home markets. Thanks to investments by Antwerp merchants, for instance, the products of English glassworks ousted Continental window panes by the 1590s, bottles by the later 1620s, drinking glasses and mirrors during the next decade. Continental techniques were also copied when the first viable water-powered paper mill opened near the end of the sixteenth century; around 1650, as many as forty were in operation.

Iron output rose smartly – from 5,000 tons a year in the 1550s to 24,000 tons a century later – as did coal, although in this case reliable figures are unavailable. Nevertheless, cloth remained both England's leading industry and the only one that sent much output to foreign markets: as in the sixteenth century so in the 1640s textiles comprised 80 percent or more of exports. But the industry was significantly altered. For one thing, its volume was far greater. Per capita cloth output doubled or tripled and (corrected for inflation) sales abroad rose about fifteenfold in value between the later fifteenth century and the 1640s. Moreover, different types of textiles were being woven and they were sent to different markets. Up to the 1550s, nearly all the cloth England exported consisted of traditional broadcloth and kersey, a lighter and cheaper version, finished in Antwerp and re-exported to northern and east central Europe. But this arrangement was unsettled by commercial and political disputes even before the Dutch Revolt, which essentially destroyed it. Admittedly, commercial and finishing operations were transferred to Amsterdam and Hamburg, and kersey sparked a brief revival shortly after 1600. But the long-term trend of old drapery exports was unmistakably downward as fashions changed, the Thirty Years' War disrupted traditional markets, and Dutch, Prussian, and Silesian fabrics put up stiff competition.

Kerseys did, however, help to inaugurate new markets in the Mediterranean, which other producers rushed to fill with the textiles destined to regenerate the English industry: bays, says, serges, perpetuanas, and other light woollens (called new drapery in England), as well as mixed fabrics like fustians. Eventually, two-thirds of new draperies were sold in Spain (whence some went to the colonies even before these markets were legally opened in 1648), the rest elsewhere throughout the Mediterranean and, in small quantities, to Africa. In value, new-drapery exports rose nearly 75 percent between 1604/14 and 1640; by the latter date, exports of new varieties of textiles may already have rivaled the old. By the 1650s, fustian manufacture provided 20,000 jobs in Lancashire alone.

Foreign markets did not account for all of English industrial growth. Although poorly documented, domestic consumption was important: perhaps, as some historians have it, paramount. This is not surprising, given that English population rose rapidly and practically without interruption all across the long sixteenth century, from 2.3 million in 1500 to 5.5 million in 1650. The urbanization level tripled (from 3 to 9 percent), led by London. A medium-sized city of 40,000 residents in 1500, it was a great metropolis of 400,000 by 1650 – second in Europe only to Paris, which had 430,000 inhabitants.

As the long sixteenth century wore on, most of the swelling population heightened industrial demand by virtue of numbers rather than any gain in living standards: in fact, real wages were cut in half across the period. But some groups enjoyed buoyant real incomes. Prominent among them were yeomen and landowners, who undertook the so-called "Great Rebuilding" that endowed rural England with myriad new and improved country homes, farmhouses, and barns, and furnished them in an up-to-date manner; merchants and entrepreneurs were similarly active in cities and towns. Increasingly, too, such people wanted to dress fashionably, dine on pewter or ceramics, rest their weary heads on pillows and their bodies on sheets, and in general acquire more and better goods. New lifestyles and patterns of expenditure, once established in the upper echelons of society, were then emulated by many in the middling ranks, though instead of silk, a middle-class consumer would buy new drapery dyed a bold hue and given a glossy finish. London was singularly influential in this demonstration effect, developing and diffusing novel cultures of consumption among merchants, officeholders, lawyers, and prosperous artisans. As a result, according to some scholars, a "consumer society" was starting to emerge in England by the mid-seventeenth century. It was not, however, as yet a mass market, since the majority of people were too poor to buy manufactures more than occasionally.

England's prosperity supported the manufacture of luxuries from silks to crystal to coaches. Undeterred by high wages, high rents, and regulation, most were clustered in London, in close proximity to the bulk of their customers. But even in London, the majority of the nearly three-fifths of the labor force involved in manufacture made more ordinary goods. In the aggregate, crafts such as clothing, leather goods, beer, bricks, tiles, and metalwares destined for domestic consumers were most important; in terms of jobs, cloth finishing was probably the single largest London industry for much of the period. It too worked mainly for the internal market, because England lacked sufficient skilled artisans to finish cloth to the satisfaction of Continental buyers. In 1614, Alderman Cokayne of London joined with others to foster the industry (and line their own pockets) by persuading the Crown to forbid exports of undressed cloth. But Dutch importers retaliated by refusing to take cloth processed in England, so the scheme collapsed just three years later.

Many London industries operated outside corporate structures, cutting costs by disregarding some rules and employing poorly paid, often female, labor. To reduce expenses further, a number moved to the outskirts, where a continually renewed population of displaced rural folk lived just beyond the reach of municipal guilds and government. Some industries migrated to even more distant areas where the cost of living was lower and guilds had long since been greatly weakened or had vanished. By 1600, shoemakers were abandoning London for Northampton, silk throwers were relocating to north Essex, hosiers were leaving for Nottinghamshire. Independent of these movements, diverse industries sprouted in many parts of England outside the capital. A minority found towns congenial. Some of these, like fine broadcloth at Worcester, sought with some success (due largely to lower wages) to duplicate earlier trades with their carefully trained and regulated artisans. But most were like the new drapery at Norwich and Colchester, Sheffield's cutlery, or the small metal trades of Birmingham and Wolverhampton, governed by considerably looser structures. In any event, the great majority of English provincial towns remained centers of commerce and services rather than manufacturing; their main industrial tasks were to organize rural production and to trade its raw materials and finished goods.

For more and more industries were situated in the countryside. The growth of rural metallurgy in south Yorkshire and the West Midlands is a case in point. But principally it was a matter of textiles and related clothing trades. Although numerous towns retained textile crafts, English cloth-making seems to have become predominantly rural during the fifteenth and early sixteenth centuries – the heyday of old drapery – and remained so when new drapery took center stage. Spinning, weaving, and fulling were found in villages across England, and some country textile districts became heavily industrialized: in the Forest of Arden, 33 percent of households engaged in cloth production in 1530–69, 60 percent in 1570–1609. The availability of water power that permitted the building of more productive fulling mills probably played a role in the founding of rural clothmaking. A leading reason for its subsequent growth, however, was the presence of a large, constantly expanding, and little-regulated labor force. For even though no deep transformation of English agriculture occurred in this period, the changes that did transpire, together with steady demographic growth and falling real wages, engendered a swelling crowd of landpoor and landless in need of additional work for survival. Like their less numerous fellows who migrated to metropolitan areas, those who remained in the countryside supplied abundant cheap labor for the simplified (and thus requiring less skill) processes that came to prevail. Stocking-knitting was said to employ 100,000 countryfolk in the early seventeenth century.

Government enactments that helped keep down the price of raw materials enabled English industry – notably textiles – to reduce costs further. Wool exports were progressively forbidden, and colonial policies virtually forced Ireland's commercial agricultural sector to specialize in raw wool for English producers while blocking the development of an indigenous woollen cloth industry in Ireland. Before the mid-sixteenth century, England's close integration into Antwerp's orbit helped lower transactions costs, and thereafter England's developing transport, commercial, and financial sectors began to have similar effects. Technological advances, in contrast, were of little significance. In fact, where new methods were available, they met a good deal of resistance. This might emanate from guilds, which for instance actively hampered the diffusion of knitting frames (invented by William Lee in 1589) before the mid-seventeenth century. Equally important, new techniques were not necessarily cost-effective, even in more capital-intensive trades. Thus although charcoal-fired blast-furnaces raised their capacity from a ton or less before 1600 to two or occasionally three in 1650, they required a substantial initial investment and periodic costly relining, so many iron masters continued to use bloomeries.

The preferred – if traditional – way of pruning costs by means of innovation was to adopt manufactures made in fewer and simpler steps. So whereas turning out a Yorkshire broadcloth "dozen" of 21 square yards employed 15 people for a week, an 18 square-yard kersey could be made and dyed in the same amount of time by 8 or 9 workers, a productivity gain of 40–60 percent, even apart from savings on wages for less skilled labor. Finally, the substitution of coal for wood contributed materially to keeping costs down in industries like brewing, glassmaking, and salt boiling. In 1634, a traveler in northeastern England reported that at the Shields, near the mouth of the River Tyne, and thus accessible to "coals brought by water from Newcastle pits . . . are the largest salt works I have ever seen, and by reason of the conveniency of coal, and cheapness thereof . . ."[1] Trades like rural iron smelting that continued to use wood benefited, too, for they faced less competition and therefore less rapidly escalating prices for this scarce resource, particularly once urban home heating – by far the largest single consumer of fuel – switched massively to coal.

The pursuit of lower costs was not, as we have seen, confined to England. But ruralization proceeded further there, the country was blessed with abundant coal deposits cheaply accessible to the main population and industrial centers, and government policies either promoted or at least did not inhibit cost reduction. Nourished by nearly unbroken population growth, lagging prices, and new consumer goods, domestic demand kept expanding. England became, too, one of the most dynamic producers of cloth for export. In international markets, however, English manufactures faced vigorous contenders. The Dutch Republic presented a particularly strong challenge, for it not only had a wider variety of industries than England but relied to a much greater extent on labor-saving innovation.

The Dutch Republic

In the Middle Ages, the northern Netherlands had been overshadowed by the more populous, prosperous, and industrialized southern provinces. The industries that did exist in the north either, like herring packing and shipbuilding, serviced the maritime sector or, like brewing and most textiles, made goods that were sold mainly to consumers within the Low Countries. (Leiden's woollens formed the main exception, finding most of their customers in the Baltic region.) As we have noted above, moreover, industries in the area that became the Dutch Republic shriveled across most of the sixteenth century. Thus the dramatic growth in industrial output and the impressive diversification that marked the Dutch Golden Age were all the more remarkable because they came on the heels of prolonged industrial decline as well as at a time when most European industries were slipping.

Leiden's long-troubled drapery, which had nearly died in the wake of a 1574 siege, promptly mended once the turmoil of the Dutch Revolt was over. The city turned out 26,600 cloths in 1584, 102,000 in 1624, and hit

[1] William Brereton, *Travels*, in *Seventeenth-Century Economic Documents*, ed. J. Thirsk and J. P. Cooper (Oxford, 1972), pp. 235–6.

a peak of 144,700 pieces in 1664. Until the 1630s, the majority were light woollens and mixed cloths introduced by refugees from the southern Low Countries; but in that decade they were surpassed by expensive *lakens* made of fine Spanish wool and camlets woven of Turkish mohair. Besides weaving large amounts of fine linen, Haarlem emerged as the bleaching capital of the Continent. By 1628, it processed up to 100,000 pieces drawn from all over Europe, as against 20,000 mainly local linens in 1586. Delft specialized in ceramics, the number of potteries rising from two in 1600 to thirty-two seventy years later; Amsterdam developed silk weaving and dyeing, diamond cutting, glass blowing, leather working, and food processing: in 1661 the city boasted sixty sugar refineries, up from three in 1605. The Zaanstreek, a flat, watery district just north of Amsterdam, emerged as the most modern industrial zone in the Republic – probably in all of Europe. As against virtually none before 1600, by 1630 the region boasted 128 industrial windmills; three-quarters sawed lumber or pressed oil, the rest milled grain, made paper, or beat hemp. A handful of small shipyards repairing fishing boats around 1600 had in 1670 become sixty big yards making new ships, some of which hunted whales for the blubber-boiling industry that also grew up in the Zaan. How did this extraordinary turnaround occur?

Swelling domestic demand had something to do with it. The rate of Dutch demographic advance between 1500 and 1650, which brought population from 950,000 to 1.9 million, exceeded all but the English. The Republic also urbanized rapidly. The proportion of its people living in communities of 10,000 or more, one-sixth in 1500, had reached nearly one-third in 1650, far and away the highest in Europe. Dutch townspeople were, more momentously, prosperous as well as numerous. Their ranks included not only merchants, financiers, and entrepreneurs but also artisans and workers who enjoyed probably the highest real wages in Europe, thanks to both the century's most productive agriculture and a booming industrial sector that, by absorbing those forced off the land, made for a tight labor supply. Although the Delft baker who bought a painting from Johannes Vermeer was likely untypical, plenty of his fellows did acquire prints and small paintings, ceramics, furniture, all sorts of cloth, beer, gin, and many other manufactures. Then, too, the commercialized and increasingly affluent specialized agricultural sector that we have surveyed in chap. 3 consumed a broad range of manufactures. And to encourage domestic consumers to buy Dutch goods, from time to time the central government imposed steep import tariffs on rival manufactures like says and linen from the south.

But like their former countrymen to the south, the critical factor was expanding international trade. Low transactions costs flowing from their country's commercial hegemony were as crucial to the success of Dutch industry as to the flowering of the country's agriculture. As Dutch merchants opened new trade routes and reduced shipping rates with improved boats, superb commercial information, and cheap, readily available capital, the Republic won control of a substantial part of Europe's growing commerce and Amsterdam replaced Antwerp as Europe's greatest staple market and financial center. Dutch manufacturers thus came to enjoy progressively less expensive access to markets throughout Europe and across the world known to Europeans. We have seen that the Republic's textiles thrust into the Mediterranean basin, to the discomfiture of producers already established there. But they could also be found across the Continent and on into overseas colonies (including their own in North America, the Caribbean, and the East Indies), avoiding that dependence on one or a few markets that proved the Achilles' heel of many of their rivals. By virtue of their country's far-flung and superbly informed commercial networks, moreover, Dutch producers could stay closely attuned to evolving fashions and respond quickly and profitably to them. For this reason, Leiden alone eventually made at least 180 different fabrics.

Dutch industries did not rely, however, simply on adding new markets; they also widened their customer base in markets old and new. In so doing, they pursued strategies similar to those attempted elsewhere, but gave each a specifically Dutch inflection. For one, they took up high quality items such as cut diamonds, Chinese-inspired tiles, silks, and fine woollens, to cite but a few. Like their counterparts and competitors in the southern Netherlands, many Dutch manufactures of this type were offered at prices that put them within reach of upper middling strata. But whereas southern producers achieved this result by simplifying production, technical advances played a central role in the Republic. Lakens, for instance, caught the public's fancy due to their smooth texture, made possible by innovations in the finishing process.

Again, the Dutch were hardly unique in their efforts to develop new industries. But the Republic's superior commercial and transportation system gave it an edge in supplying the specialized trades known as "traffics" (*trafieken*) that grew up in or near ports to process imported raw materials, largely for re-export. Salt refining at Dordrecht, tobacco processing in Rotterdam, gin distilling in neighboring Schiedam, and sugar refining in Amsterdam are among the best known. Similarly, Holland became a major producer of copperware after its merchants took control of the Swedish copper trade in 1614. Many traffics (not to mention established industries like beer brewing, brickmaking, and linen bleaching) were energy-intensive, yet fuel costs, too, were kept low thanks to Europe's most highly developed network of internal water routes, which efficiently delivered cheap peat from the impoverished eastern provinces to the manufacturing centers in the west. Coal was not the only eagerly dug fuel of the day.

Like their rivals, of course, the Dutch also implemented practices to reduce labor costs whenever possible. In Leiden's light woollens industry, entrepreneurs divided and simplified processes so they could be performed by less skilled, less well paid workers, including women and children; Haarlem called on peasant women flax spinners living as far away as the southern provinces and western Germany. But the possibilities for ruralization, the preferred approach throughout Europe, were limited in the Dutch Republic. This was not so much because of opposition mounted by guilds, which since the Revolt had been firmly under the control of merchant-dominated municipal governments sympathetic to employers. Instead, the problem lay within the agrarian sector. Specialized agriculture quite fully employed the labor of the farm population, and in the populous western provinces impartible inheritance precluded the proliferation of smallholders and cottagers who might have provided the labor force for rural industry. What was sauce for the agricultural goose was not sauce for the industrial gander.

Once again, however, Dutch industry pursued a distinctive strategy to economize on labor in this context of tight labor supply and high wages: repeated and manifold recourse to new technology. Textile crafts were leaders in this respect. With a so-called "Dutch" loom, invented in 1604, a single worker could weave up to twenty-four ribbons at a time. Already by 1610 entrepreneurs had introduced forty-five of these looms in Leiden. More dramatic, the use of wind-powered fulling mills trimmed the workforce to just a fraction of its medieval total and reduced the once-powerful fullers' guild to impotence. Windmills also fostered the mechanization of many other industries from papermaking to rice husking. This approach was only viable, however, because Dutch entrepreneurs were able to mobilize large amounts of inexpensive capital to purchase the costly equipment needed. Commercial developments – it will come as no surprise to learn – blazed the path yet again. Originally established to amass funds for trading ventures, partnerships (*rederijen*) involving investors large and small, even artisans and farmers, were quickly adapted for industrial purposes. The funds thereby assembled paid for the mechanization of significant segments of Dutch production.

The shipyards of the Zaanstreek epitomize Dutch innovation. Large operations fitted out with cranes and other expensive equipment, these yards built ships quickly and cheaply. One turned out 20 vessels in 22 months; another constructed a ship in just 5 weeks. In 1669, a ship costing £1,300 in England was priced at £800 along the Zaan. An extensive division of labor, employment of subcontractors who specialized in a single item such as masts or blocks, and the proximity of auxiliary trades such as sailmaking, ropewalks, and anchor smithies further assisted cost-cutting efficiency. Then, too, the presence nearby of many sawmills allowed shipyards to carry limited inventories of lumber (their major raw materials cost) and make do with smaller and thus cheaper sites. Most yards enjoyed economies of scale by focusing on the high-volume production of a few types of ship, notably the *fluit* (flute), invented in the 1590s. Constructed of fir or pine cut in windmills rather than expensive hand-sawn oak, and more simply rigged than other merchant boats, flutes cut construction costs per ton by 40 percent. In addition, these long, shallow-hulled, flat-bottomed vessels were very economical to operate. Flutes required just half as many crew members as conventional ships transporting the same size load and carried no heavy, bulky weapons that displaced cargo. Not surprisingly, they soon proved enormously popular with shipowners and merchants across Europe.

The apex of prosperity for Dutch industry came in the third quarter of the seventeenth century. Still, an influx of capital, labor, and skills when Huguenots (French Calvinists) immigrated after the Revocation of the Edict of Nantes in 1685 formally ended religious toleration in France, hand in hand with renewed protective measures in the Republic, allowed many crafts to enjoy an Indian summer until about 1700. In its heyday, the Dutch achievement was the exception in a time of stagnation and decay. But together with the most advanced commerce and highly productive agriculture of its time, the Republic's industries brought economic leadership firmly to northwestern Europe.

Demand, supply, and industrial primacy

Even this brief survey reveals that many influences affected the fortunes of Europe's industrial areas during the long sixteenth century. Amid the welter of details, nevertheless, it is possible to identify crucial structures and conditions that time and again decisively shaped demand for manufactures and producers' ability to fulfill it, affording or refusing certain areas a comparative advantage in particular goods. Reviewing them helps elucidate the principal forces altering Europe's industrial geography across a turbulent period.

Not surprisingly, in economies still predominantly based on agriculture, the prevailing agrarian structures had primordial impact on industrial development, beginning with the consumption of manufactures.

Although even subsistence farmers had to purchase some industrial products – metalwares if nothing else – their resources were scanty, whereas specialized commercial farmers usually bought a variety of such goods. Rural demand was, moreover, strongly inflected by landlord levies. When moderate, as in the early part of the period, peasant demand for manufactures strengthened, most of all among the increasing body of market-oriented farmers. Conversely, subsequent landowner efforts to augment their incomes cut into peasant consumption, particularly as productivity stagnated or even fell. The upshot was most blatant in the serf agriculture of the east central lands where, thanks to very heavy lordly surplus appropriation, market-oriented farming had relatively weak stimulative effects on local industry. But throughout Europe, landlords concentrated a greater share of resources in their hands, influencing patterns of demand.

These trends in turn modified the supply environment, not only by encouraging production of expensive manufactures but also by prodding those trades aiming at more modest consumers to cut costs. In addition, the agrarian order bore upon the supply of industrial labor. It could allow or even encourage the release of rural labor for full-time or part-time industrial work, whether in the countryside among smallholders and the landless, or in towns bulging with immigrants from overcrowded farming regions or those practicing strict primogeniture. But agricultural arrangements could also block labor mobility advantageous to industry, as witness regions where sharecropping prevailed, lands under the dominion of neoserfdom, and districts where family farms fully occupied their tenants' time.

Commercial and financial structures were likewise salient to industrial development. Clear benefits accrued to industries linked to merchants able to quicken trade among Europe's regions, incorporate overseas areas into the Old World's trading orbit, and bring peripheral parts of individual lands more fully into the exchange economy, for beyond getting access to a larger market they typically benefited from concomitant reductions in transactions costs. Absence or loss of favorable commercial relations thus had severe and long-lasting ramifications on demand throughout the industrial sector. Financial and commercial arrangements also deeply concerned industry on the supply side, for they could ease – or complicate – access to and the cost of liquid capital. These were matters of especial importance to export-oriented production in an age when putting-out, the lifeblood of which was working capital, was steadily extending its reach.

Such initiatives were most likely to succeed where debilitated or non-existent corporate institutions accorded entrepreneurs greater flexibility, especially with respect to deploying labor and technology. Where guilds remained powerful, in contrast, recourse to cheaper labor – rural or urban – and adoption of innovative equipment were often hampered. But corporations did not always or even typically play a negative role regarding industrial development. For by training skilled artisans and sedulously enforcing quality controls, they helped create a comparative advantage for production of fine, higher priced goods.

Public authorities were involved as well. Their commitments could aid producers to adapt to new circumstances. Or they could thwart novel arrangements, as the history of Calvinist Geneva's textile trades trenchantly illustrates. After the Protestant Reformation, the city-state developed flourishing high-quality woollens and silk industries thanks largely to the highly skilled refugees who poured in. But after repeated visitations of the plague and a slowing stream of French exiles once the Edict of Nantes granted toleration in 1598, the labor pool shrank, driving up wages and prices. The Genevan government, however, was unwilling to attract immigrants from surrounding Catholic territories, opposed moving production into the countryside, and resisted the introduction of new methods. This stance sought to uphold urban monopolies, quality, and wages, but it succeeded mainly in overseeing industrial collapse.

Government policies could also mold demand. At certain junctures, states themselves weighed in with substantial orders for military equipment, public buildings, and luxury goods. Taxes had a much more consistently important – if less direct – influence. Declining real levies permitted greater consumption among the mass of the population; increases, particularly when sudden and steep, inevitably curbed their purchases, with manufactures first to be forgone. At the same time, of course, the profits of office, tax-farming, and outright gifts redistributed some of the resources gathered by the states to the upper levels of society, reinforcing consumption patterns rooted in structures of property relations.

Population trends also contributed to the state of industry, but the causal relationship was neither simple nor one-way. The generations born during the period of demographic advance that began in 1450/70 were at least potential consumers of clothing, housing, tools, and many other products; rising levels of urbanization magnified the effects of quantitative increase. Many among them, moreover, were available for industrial work; in the mainly labor-intensive manufacturing of the time, their numbers could keep the labor supply plentiful, conducing to wages, and thus the prices of manufactures, that lagged behind the cost of food, thereby promoting the further extension of the market. Hence the slowing or cessation of population growth that set in widely in the late sixteenth century has been associated with changes in patterns of supply as well as demand. But demography was not decisive; indeed, population movements could reflect as much as induce broader economic trends. Whether Europeans became industrial producers and consumers depended, that is, on complex interactions among agricultural, commercial, craft, governmental, and demographic institutions and circumstances.

Finally, it is worth recalling two factors that lent particular places and industries a comparative advantage even though they played minor roles overall in dictating industrial outcomes during the long sixteenth century. One was natural resource endowment. The presence of pure ores and seemingly limitless forests enabled Sweden to become Europe's largest single supplier of copper and iron and greatly expand its domestic iron trades; it should be noted, however, that these results had to await the arrival of capital and skilled artisans from abroad. Again, while English coal was principally used for home heating, it did allow some industries to reduce costs and boost output. The fate of the Spanish woollens industry testifies, however, that indigenous resources were no panacea in the face of otherwise unfavorable conditions. Nor were they essential: the great Dutch industries relied chiefly on imported raw materials. Second, the effects of technological innovations were beginning to be felt widely. Nonetheless, they were often rejected by artisans and officials alike or neglected because cheap labor was available. Their contribution was essential only in the northern Netherlands. In retrospect we know that recourse to technology – if not the specific technologies selected – pointed to the future. Yet at the time the Dutch Republic was in this respect, as in so many others, the exception.

The presence of at least some favorable conditions resulted in patches of industrial advance scattered across Europe. Even in the east central region, poor consumers could scrape together the wherewithal to acquire low-quality cloth fabricated from local wool, flax, or hemp by peasants impoverished but not fully tied up by seigniorial obligations. Conversely, every country had poor agricultural regions that participated weakly if at all in industrial activities. Nonetheless, it is possible to locate Europe's regions and countries on a continuum from least to most hospitable to industry, according to their peculiar mixes of demand and supply factors.

East central Europe's industrial development was hobbled throughout most of the long sixteenth century by an agrarian structure that simultaneously skewed consumption towards a restricted group (which in addition preferred foreign goods) and released few resources into production. As a result, industry was confined to a narrow range of products for equally limited markets. Initially, the Mediterranean lands' productive agriculture, broad commercial contacts, skilled labor forces, and sizable, prosperous urban populations encouraged manufacturing. But a baleful combination of production structures and government commitments that limited the supply and mobility of labor, steeply rising lordly and state exactions, loss of commercial hegemony, and deurbanization eventually overwhelmed these assets. By the end of the period, Italy had fallen far from its proud industrial leadership during the Renaissance; Spain had also seen promising early achievements come to naught.

At the outset, increasingly productive agriculture, mild lordly exactions, supportive government policies, and expansive urban and rural populations available for craft work propelled brisk industrial expansion in a middle band consisting of western Germany, France, and the southern Low Countries. Sooner or later, however, each was buffeted by agrarian slowdown, state and corporate policies that turned restrictive, and excessive levies, aggravated by sluggish or falling levels of urbanization. So although evidence of recovery could be discerned as the long sixteenth century drew to a close – most of all in the southern Netherlands – it remained precarious.

England and the Dutch Republic enjoyed the most propitious conditions for industrial progress: highly productive agricultures that spurred consumption of manufactures and supplied labor to the industrial sector, aggressive and efficient commercial and transport sectors, few corporate obstacles, moderate lordly rents and state taxes, and Europe's most rapid rates of urbanization. Their industrial economies were not identical. English trades were more often labor-intensive, employing rural workers to turn out standardized goods, an increasing proportion of which were commercialized versions of peasant handicrafts. For their part, the Dutch relied more heavily on an urban workforce and on labor-saving technology. Each in its own way, however, effectively mobilized productive resources in order to tap rising domestic demand and – in the teeth of fierce competition – to capture a robust share of foreign markets.

Much as these two countries profited from the changes in industrial leadership, their artisans and entrepreneurs were not alone in seeking productive arrangements that would best allow them to capitalize on good times and adjust with least distress to bad. Across Europe, existing relations of production were questioned and, in some instances, materially remodeled.

Artisans, merchants, Verlegers

Adjustment of output during the long sixteenth century was typically achieved by opening or closing additional production units replicating in size and technology the small handicraft businesses that had long predominated. Some big workplaces were established in specific favorable circumstances, but few survived long once conditions changed. Yet if neither the sophistication nor the scale of production altered much, capitalist relations significantly extended their reach at the expense of autonomous producers. What forces promoted this transformation? What were its manifestations and consequences? What problems did artisans confront and how did they react to them?

Artisans under pressure

In a few industries there appeared technological innovations that cost more to install and operate than artisans – even associations of artisans – could afford. As blast furnaces, tilt hammers, wire-drawing machines, and stamping, rolling, and slitting mills became more familiar components of the iron industry, for instance, fixed capital requirements soared. Besides the equipment and buildings, expensive in their own right, water impoundment, storage, and delivery facilities were needed. In addition, pig iron turned out by blast furnaces could not be forged until refined further in a new intermediate stage. In later sixteenth-century Antwerp, where a skilled worker earned 125–250 guilders a year, a large blast furnace alone cost 3,000 guilders, and other industrial plant was equally or more expensive.

Raw materials, not equipment, constituted artisans' major expense in most trades, however. Whereas, in 1583, an Antwerp silk weaver paid 12 guilders for a loom (and amortized that sum over the many years of the loom's useful life), every six weeks he or she had to lay out 24 guilders for the two pounds of raw silk required to make a piece of cloth. Thus access to cheap and plentiful primary materials was a constant preoccupation for independent producers. Using local materials might allow even the poorest among them to avoid reliance on merchant suppliers. The loss of such sources could therefore be devastating. As silk cultivation waned around Córdoba and Toledo, weavers in these cities were forced to become the employees of merchants who put out raw silk from Valencia and Murcia provinces. In the Dutch Republic, merchants who imported unprocessed salt from France, Portugal, and Spain gained control of the refining industry once exploitation of local salt marshes was halted for fear that dikes would be undermined.

We have seen, in chap. 2, that even artisans relying on imported raw materials could retain autonomy in a Kaufsystem so long as supplies were freely available for purchase on the market at a reasonable price. But should raw materials supplies somehow be engrossed, producers' independence could quickly be destroyed. Lille's light-cloth weavers repeatedly voiced the fear (echoed in municipal regulations) that a thread monopolist would reduce them to slave-like dependence. Their worst fears were realized in early seventeenth-century Antwerp, where a wealthy master bought up all the imported English tin at a cost of 100,000 guilders and forced most other pewterers to become his outworkers.

Credit undergirded production but created additional vulnerabilities. The lag of industrial prices behind those of raw materials and foodstuffs, coupled with rising taxes, made it difficult for many producers to repay creditors. Periodic downturns, when food prices shot up and demand for manufactures fell off, drove them further into debt or even bankruptcy, from which they might only emerge by agreeing to sell their products exclusively to merchants or fellow artisans who extended them loans. Frequent enough during periods of growth, such crises became deeper and lasted longer after about 1570, as did war-related disruptions of raw materials supplies and markets.

Artisans' autonomy was imperiled, too, by restrictions on their access to markets. During the long sixteenth century, a situation like this often resulted from the concentration of export trade in a few great entrepôts. The disappearance of regional markets where Flemish weavers had previously bought flax and sold linen left them at the mercy of big-city middlemen, who quickly turned them into domestic workers. In a similar fashion, formerly independent producers in southern Wiltshire (England), who had bought yarn from spinners or local brokers and sold their cloth to merchants in nearby Salisbury, became subject to London merchants who monopolized both wool supplies and woollens exports.

With good reason, finally, urban artisans feared the growth of industries in the countryside. For one thing, they worried that the spread of village crafts would reduce their supplies of raw materials, driving up prices. City producers also knew that rural locations enjoyed lower living costs, wages, and taxes, and often employed fewer or simplified processes. These advantages became a major preoccupation as competition intensified from the 1570s and 1580s.

In this threatening environment, many artisans – and political elites that championed them – understandably looked to institutions and rules for relief. The proliferation of guilds and restrictions noted in many parts of sixteenth-century Europe may have represented attempts – if often futile ones – to stop any change. This was not the only response, however. With the backing of municipal authorities concerned about undertakings deemed economically unwise, socially disruptive, and ethically reprehensible, some corporate trades recognized the impossibility of standing still but also sought to manage change for the benefit of autonomous masters. Lille's light drapery, for example, progressively implemented a small commodity production system, embodied in regulations that governed the thread market, mandated the separation of certain crafts, limited shop size, and essentially banned putting-out and non-guild labor. The goal was, in the words of corporate leaders, to ensure that "everyone can have the means of earning a living without the least being crushed and oppressed by the advance of the most powerful."[2]

More commonly, however, change was permitted, even encouraged, irrespective of artisan sentiment. In Louvain (southern Netherlands), all restrictions were lifted from the cloth industry in 1563 because, the town government averred, the best weavers ought to be allowed to garner the most business. Noble sheepowners in Hesse won permission to export wool by promising increased tax revenues for a hard-pressed state; only a year later, weavers, who had long enjoyed a near monopoly on local wool at favorable prices, could no longer afford enough to remain in business on their own and had to go to work for merchants putting out imported wool. And aside from all explicit permission, individuals chafing at the constraints imposed on their activities kept violating the rules. Some of their schemes were ingenious: forming companies in which each partner took charge of one stage of production to evade prohibitions against combining trades. Others were obvious: having work done in villages beyond the jurisdiction of urban corporations. But whether clever or plodding, whether acting within the rules of the game or in opposition to them, entrepreneurs increasingly seized the initiative.

Entrepreneurial initiatives

Putting-out

Attempts to reorganize production dated back, of course, far into the Middle Ages and in the long sixteenth century went forward during periods of both growth – already by 1520 enterprises owned and managed by urban traders had replaced almost all the syndicates of working miners in the coal basin around Liège – and retrenchment. Putting-out was widely preferred due to its low startup or entry costs and marked flexibility. An entrepreneur could initiate and expand production with a minimal outlay for plant and equipment, virtually all of which was the employees' responsibility; when demand slackened, simply reducing orders cut output quickly without immobilizing fixed capital.

Further encouraging the spread of putting-out was the appearance of an appropriate labor supply. It consisted not only of the many formerly autonomous artisans forced to the wall, but also of increasing numbers of

---

[2] Quoted in Robert DuPlessis, *Lille and the Dutch Revolt* (Cambridge, 1991), p. 108.

people who could afford the individually inexpensive tools of their trade but never possessed sufficient working capital to set up as independent producers. Many lived in the countryside, as we have seen. But a population suitable for domestic employment was also swelling in suburbs and even in towns among immigrants from villages, among journeymen excluded from mastership – a frequent by-product of corporate restrictions designed to help masters – among single women and widows, among artisans' wives and children seeking extra income during these decades of relentless inflation, and even among poor artisans.

Putting-out networks appeared in many trades. In some southern Netherlands villages, nearly every family made nails using cast iron rods that merchants brought them. Even luxury goods could be made in a Verlagssystem. At Antwerp, many sculptors, painters, engravers, and other artists in the Guild of St. Luke worked for merchants on contract. Similarly, highly skilled Lombard artisans organized in craft guilds that closely controlled entry to the trade and jealously guarded corporate privileges devised ornate suits of armor in their own small shops. Yet they were no longer autonomous producers but outworkers filling orders for merchant-manufacturers who alone had access to a dispersed and specialized market.

Still, putting-out was most firmly rooted in the textile industries – particularly the preparatory and weaving stages – because the same attributes that could bolster small producers also made these trades attractive to entrepreneurs. Manufacture was already or could readily be divided into separate processes that were relatively easy to learn, for the most part required little capital investment in equipment and thus were available to people with modest resources, and had traditionally been assigned to artisan family members (children carded, women spun, men wove).

Because early modern merchants – like their medieval predecessors – were particularly well positioned to become putting-out entrepreneurs, many scholars refer generically to Verleger as "merchant capitalists" or "merchant manufacturers." In fact, many were artisans, even if they often eventually engaged as well in commerce, where the largest profits were to be made. Sometimes fullers, shearer-pressers, dyers, and other finishers, who performed the most capital-intensive stages in the clothmaking process, assembled the resources to take control of poorer artisans in their craft or other stages of textile production; at Geneva, some even became creditors to small-scale merchant-entrepreneurs. Just before 1600, dyers introduced cloth manufacturing to the sheep-raising area around Calw in southwestern Germany; within a few years, 15 entrepreneurs employed 500–600 domestic weavers and many other artisans in town and country.

But nothing barred other artisans. In 1610, 2 Antwerp silk weavers with 15 looms (the legal limit) in their workplaces employed another 170 in putting-out arrangements. Some artisan entrepreneurs had sufficient assets to buy raw materials, extend credit during the production process, and market the finished goods. Others contracted to provide merchants with goods, hiring poorer masters and others to do the actual work but themselves organizing and supervising the production process. Guilds were often powerless to stop this form of subcontracting, and many seem not to have tried, probably because it was their more powerful members who took the lead.

As the preceding examples suggest, a Verlagssystem could be very large. Many Segovia merchants contracted with 200 to 300 people, the great English clothier John Ashe allegedly gave work to 1,000, and Silesian linen entrepreneurs are said to have employed several thousand. Substantial capital could be involved as well. Some big German merchant houses had up to one million florins invested in domestic linen production. Yet most were much smaller, because coordinating and supervising large numbers of people dispersed among many separate workplaces raised costs and reduced efficiency: scale could, that is, generate "diseconomies" rather than savings. A partnership formed in mid-sixteenth-century Florence by several members of the Medici family to manufacture woollen cloth at a time when the trade was booming dealt with only ten to fifteen outworkers at a time, the majority of them living in the city.

Occasionally, putters-out owned means of production that they rented to domestic workers. Frames for knitting ribbons or stockings, for example, were beyond the reach of the artisans who operated them. Equipment rentals amplified outworkers' dependence on the Verleger, a subordination already initiated by advances of raw materials and cash. Nevertheless, putting-out entrepreneurs remained outside the process of production, buying the output of labor – the finished items they contracted for – rather than the labor itself. But more capitalist methods also arose.

Centralized production

Problems intrinsic to the operation of a Verlagssystem encouraged some entrepreneurs to enter the sphere of production. In particular, they sought

7 The complicated machinery needed to drain deep mines was too expensive for the small miners' associations that had predominated in the Middle Ages and thus its adoption promoted concentration of ownership.

tighter supervision of the workforce in order to enhance coordination of labor-intensive production processes, assure better quality, or diminish opportunities for fraud. These goals did not mandate any increase in size. Nor did technology, since the same equipment was used in centralized as in dispersed shops. So in the main the workplaces established were modest, with a half dozen or so workers. Nevertheless, a few textile entrepreneurs ventured larger shops when their trades were booming. In the early sixteenth century, William Stumpe set up looms in the buildings of Malmesbury Abbey (England) that he had recently acquired; the extent of his legendary undertaking is in fact unknown, but it permitted him to buy vast landed properties, marry into the local gentry, and enter the governing oligarchy of the county. A few years later, four Antwerp cloth finishers had shops with between twenty and twenty-seven workers apiece, and some ribbonmakers assembled several dozen looms in one location.

Numerous city governments also established big workshops in existing hospices and newly founded workhouses to compel the poor to earn their keep and unlearn the alleged profligacy and laziness which, it was believed, gave rise to their condition. Most of these shops specialized in textile trades such as wool spinning, silk reeling, and dyestuff preparation that demanded little training, skill, or strength; used simple technology and were inexpensive to set up; had a ready market; had typically existed outside the corporate structure; and had traditionally employed large numbers of women, children, and the aged, all groups that loomed large among the poor.

No matter how sizable they were, big shops – like their smaller counterparts – usually focused on just one stage of production. Rarely is there evidence of big workplaces that combined trades. Still, one textile shop in Segovia performed every task from preparing raw wool to shearing woven cloth; by 1574, more than 100 people worked there, along with additional spinners living up to 15 leagues away. Amsterdam, too, had centralized shops in which dozens of women and children performed several stages of silk production, often using mechanical equipment. But these "proto-factories" were exceptional. Most Amsterdam silk was woven by domestic outworkers, and even in Segovia the great majority of cloth was made by scores of petty producers focusing on their separate crafts. Moreover, big cloth shops were only found during prosperous times and were dismantled when markets contracted. Thus the Segovia establishment had disappeared by the end of the sixteenth century.

In contrast to the divisions characteristic of the cloth trades, centralized workplaces had always been the norm in mining, peat-digging, salt boiling, and other types of resource extraction; in milling and other trades powered by wind and water, which could only be transmitted over very short distances; in metallurgy, soapmaking, tanning, glassmaking, beer brewing, and other industries in which several raw materials were brought together for processing; and in construction, shipbuilding, and other assembling work. Centralization also stamped new trades such as printing that integrated several tasks.

As in the Middle Ages, many of these workplaces remained small and worked in labor-intensive ways that required little capital and achieved low productivity. But in virtually all these industries, entrepreneurs attuned to the market were attempting to raise output by investing in expensive equipment. To be sure, highly capitalized businesses were not necessarily large employers of labor. At Antwerp, a blast furnace costing 3,000 guilders occupied ten or twelve artisans; a tannery priced at about 4,000 guilders had ten to fifteen full-time workers; breweries (6,000 guilders without implements) employed at most seven or eight men and two or three women; twenty to thirty people labored at a sugar refinery renowned for its size and worth 11,800 guilders. Even Christophe Plantin's printing office, Europe's largest and valued at 18,600 guilders in 1565, employed a maximum of fifty-six artisans, though usually the total was a dozen or so fewer. But in all these shops, ratios of capital to labor were high by the standards of the day. Fixed capital per worker in Antwerp tanning, for instance, was at least ten times as much as in silk weaving (which itself used expensive equipment compared to other weaving trades), perhaps twenty times in the big sugar refinery, and additional large sums were constantly needed to maintain machines built substantially of wood, leather, hemp, and other materials requiring frequent replacement.

At times, moreover, technological change made industrial plants both more capital intensive and bigger employers of labor than in the past. Producing salt by boiling brine drawn from springs used special coal-burning furnaces, massive but quickly worn out iron pans, watercourses, and numerous buildings, all of them quite expensive. And because the new equipment effected substantial economies of scale, saltworks with 50, 100, or even more workers began to appear. Mines grew even larger wherever the medieval pattern of multiple small, shallow, little-capitalized mines disseminated across a wide area yielded to the concentrated working of one big pit with the aid of imposing fixed investment, much of it in related crafts like founding and smelting. In 1581, the copper mine at Neusohl (Banská Bystrica) in Bohemia, which installed modernized gravitational draining pumps and the like, employed 607 people: 233 pickmen; 359 carpenters, orehaulers, and related helpers; 15 clerks and administrators. Even larger was the Almadén mercury mine in Spain, run by the Fuggers, renowned German merchants and financiers, under a very lucrative concession. In the early seventeenth century, it employed as many as 450 pitmen, 300 more in the drainage countermine, 270 in cartage, and 150 in the ovens and associated works.

In structurally concentrated trades, as in textiles, great workplaces were largely a phenomenon of periods when demand was swelling. Even then, however, such units remained exceptional because demand was neither big nor constant enough to justify continuous large-scale production. This explains the otherwise surprising fate of the large, vertically integrated capitalist building enterprise set up in the late 1540s by Gilbert van Schoonbeke, a rich self-made Antwerp entrepreneur. It boasted 15 brick-kilns, along with storage buildings and 60 houses for the 400–500 workers who operated the kilns; several chalk-burning ovens; and several hundred acres of fen with five dormitories for the 100 or more workers who dug peat to fuel the kilns and ovens. But once the new ramparts around Antwerp were completed – the raison d'être of the enterprise and one that yielded Schoonbeke a gross profit of 30–50 percent – the business was disbanded.

Admittedly, municipal workhouses opened during and persisted across boom and bust, even though they quickly proved industrial white elephants. Provided with inferior materials and incompetent supervisors, the cheap but essentially coerced labor of youthful, aged, infirm, or unwilling tenants in institutions from Amsterdam's *rasphuis* (a workhouse that specialized in scraped – rasped – brazilwood, a red or purple dyestuff) to York's hosiery knitting school turned out low-quality but expensive goods that very few consumers would buy. At best, like the poor sick women and children who reeled silk in Geneva's *Hôpital Général*, workhouses might serve in a pinch as auxiliary suppliers for manufacturers. But they survived because they obeyed not an economic but a welfare, fiscal, or correctional logic: busying otherwise idle hands, relieving – if only marginally – municipal welfare budgets, or, most often, disciplining populations from prostitutes to beggars.

Such anomalies aside, from Segovia to Wiltshire large-scale units of production collapsed or were abandoned in the later sixteenth and seventeenth centuries as entrepreneurs sought maximum flexibility to cope with increasingly uncertain markets. Only in those industries – the greatest cluster of which was located in the Dutch Republic – where concentration was a function of productivity-enhancing technological innovation could big workplaces find an economic justification. Elsewhere, concentration diminished as capitalists redeployed their investments. Who were the entrepreneurs making these decisions? How did they structure and manage the businesses in which they chose to invest?

Capitalists, finance, and organization

Industrial capital was drawn from many social strata, including artisans and peasants, but whether in town or country, in Verlagssystem or centralized workshop, merchants predominated among the more substantial financiers in all lines of business. In capital-intensive projects they often cooperated with wealthy landlords. Big peat-digging undertakings in fenland areas of the northeastern Netherlands, which employed hundreds of wage laborers, were jointly financed by merchants and nobles who invested tens of thousands of guilders in canals, bridges, locks, and other equipment needed both to prepare the land and to transport the peat to industries and households in Holland. On their own, moreover, landowners – including monasteries – had long made loans to small miners who dug on their property; now they started to finance expensive big mines as well. They also possessed industrial mills and were active in the metal trades, for besides capital (often raised by mortgaging their land) they controlled critical resources, notably water and timber. For their part, princes concerned to assure a secure supply of materials for weapons and to enhance revenues helped finance or even owned outright mines and foundries.

Very large putting-out systems might be assembled by a single person such as John Ashe, although the Medici company cited above indicates that several people could band together to form even modest networks. Nobles, sovereigns, and ecclesiastical institutions typically kept sole ownership of enterprises established on their estates. But other centralized manufactures were usually held by syndicates or partnerships. Whether Zaan windmills or Bohemian mines, such properties were divided into eighths, sixteenths, thirty-seconds, or even smaller parts; an individual might, however, own more than one share. In order to spread risks yet also control sizable output, entrepreneurs often bought shares in many large enterprises or owned outright a number of small ones.

As in the past, many owners of centralized workplaces were simply investors who leased plant and equipment to individuals or associations of artisans in return for cash payments and, usually, a percentage of output. But some, sensing opportunities for greater profit, became more closely involved in operating their properties. Evidence from ironmaking in the French-speaking ("Walloon") areas of the southern Netherlands shows that entrepreneurs employed several approaches, even in a single industry. At times, a collective of masters would own a forge, each master having the right to use it for a fixed number of days per month. When merchants bought up masters' holdings, they often continued this practice, but now they employed the previous artisan-owners for money wages to produce goods during their assigned periods. Merchant-owned slitting mills, rolling mills, and cannon works, however, were exploited by means of putting out: raw materials were distributed to journeymen and other artisans paid by the piece or by weight but working on their own or in small groups. Finally, a number of the leading entrepreneurs (men who owned up to five forges and five furnaces apiece) took on a yet more active executive role, engaging skilled artisans as salaried managers and as foremen who assembled and supervised a labor force of wage earners.

In the central German glass industry, it was masters who became capitalist entrepreneurs. During the sixteenth-century expansion, coal replaced wood for fuel and expensive glass-cutting machines were installed. Works became larger, employing twenty to thirty artisans as against ten before, and operated all year round rather than halting in winter. As in the Walloon iron industry, associations of masters had formerly owned or leased glassworks; each master had used the facility for just a few weeks, so each could only employ a few journeymen, who for their part could count on eventually attaining mastership. But the bigger, more heavily capitalized works belonged to just one or a very few masters. They ceased laboring to become full-time supervisors of their wage-earning journeyman employees, who now rarely entered the masters' ranks. As the market contracted in the seventeenth century, however, few masters any longer had sufficient resources to operate their own glass-works, so although the new technology and scale remained, ownership became increasingly dispersed once again. Their use of the works reduced, each small part-owner had to work alongside a few journeymen. Handicraft production was reborn, albeit in a technologically modified context.

A new entrepreneurial mentality?

Because capitalist control of production, whether in the form of central-ized units or, more commonly, putting-out systems, emerged with special vigor in Protestant lands and among Protestant minorities in predomi-nantly Catholic countries – and notably in areas and groups strongly influenced by the teachings of John Calvin – numerous scholars have posited a causal connection between reformed religion and entrepreneur-ial success. Of all the interpretations advanced, the one propounded by Max Weber (1864–1920) has proven the most compelling and controver-sial. To Weber, a systematic and relentless quest to maximize profits through continuous, rational enterprise combined with severe restrictions on consumption sharply distinguishes modern capitalism from traditional economic activity that sought only to earn enough for subsistence. This new spirit or "ethic" that both directed and legitimated business activities was not, he averred, the outgrowth of prior economic changes but appeared in the wake of the Protestant Reformation.

It was not, Weber asserted, that reformers deliberately promoted capitalism – most of them, he knew, abhorred economic and social change. But over time certain of their teachings about salvation were inadvertently elaborated in ways that fostered and sanctioned capitalists' behavior. In particular, Calvinist notions of predestination (the doctrine that God has already decided the fate of every soul) and God's utter transcendence, entirely beyond human experience and understanding, induced profound anxiety among believers who, after the repudiation of the Catholic Church, lacked traditional intermediaries and rituals for atonement. Ministers taught, however, that the faithful could attain some assurance of their own salvation ("election") while glorifying God by observing a code that Weber termed the "Protestant ethic." It comprised assiduous practice of a calling or vocation – a worldly occupation the performance of which also fulfilled divinely ordained tasks – and an ascetic, self-disciplined style of life.

Embraced by capitalists, this ethos had momentous effects, Weber believed, even after the initial religious impulses receded and it became a secular mentality. Continuous moneymaking, at first a means of honoring God, turned into an end in itself; systematic, rational planning and discipline, originally mandated to control sinful human nature, came to govern all relations; the drive to demonstrate election by ceaseless hard work and material success became the dynamic impelling the unceasing competition and innovation that distinguish capitalism. The new mentality alone did not, in Weber's view, cause the rise of capitalism, which also required the appearance of wage labor and the free market together with the legacy of Roman law, the European city, and the nascent bureaucratic state. But the capitalist spirit was central to the building of the new economic order.

Much of the "Weber thesis" has entered scholarly and even popular discourse. And because European thought about every type of secular matter had traditionally been permeated with spiritual values and couched in a religious idiom, religious convictions may well have played a role in directing economic attitudes and practices or at least in preparing a more receptive environment for new opinions about business activities. But that there was a positive correlation between Protestant faith and capitalist values turns out to be very difficult to demonstrate. For one thing, examination of specific cases suggests that Reformed businessmen may not have held the views ascribed to them. Whereas orthodox Dutch Calvinists stood resolutely against the new economic ideas and practices, the Republic's capitalists generally opposed the idea of predestination, indeed were barely Calvinist. Geneva's Calvinist capitalists did not live ascetically nor give any evidence of believing that their success demonstrated their merit: in their eyes, wealth was a trust confided to them by God for distribution to the poor, not a sign of election. Puritans were not disproportionately represented among English entrepreneurs, so no special ethos need be invoked to account for their ventures, while in Scotland, deeply marked by Calvinist teachings, there were few capitalist stirrings.

Even disentangling the effects of doctrine from other aspects of religious influence is problematic. Besides their beliefs, Protestant entrepreneurs often enjoyed training and capital resources that distinguished them from their fellows. Their marginal status as minorities or refugees freed many from the social and ideological constraints of the larger society while integrating them into close-knit communities and networks that supported their enterprises as well as their faith; in France, moreover, exclusion from other professions virtually channeled many Huguenots into business.

Finally, it is not clear that meaningful attitudinal contrasts distinguished capitalists of different faiths. Systematic moneymaking and thrifty husbanding of capital were already highly valued among advanced entrepreneurs well before the Reformation: many businessmen of the Italian Renaissance period inscribed their ledgers "to God and to profit," assiduously practiced double-entry bookkeeping to keep a close watch over their individual property, and praised thrift. Such views and behavior may well have become more widespread during the long sixteenth century. But the fact that they surfaced in Catholic Antwerp as well as in Protestant Amsterdam suggests that religious tenets specific to one faith were not the crucial factor shaping the process. Rather, a variety of novel ideas, opportunities, and constraints – material as well as spiritual – evoked an array of entrepreneurial efforts to rationalize business activities. So while the development of a new mentality governing economic behavior was a momentous historical transformation, it was, like the structural changes that it accompanied, neither homogeneous nor rapid.

Entrepreneurial capitalisms

The capitalists of the long sixteenth century favored putting-out, which melded centralized direction and dispersed production. At a time when demand was particularly volatile and largely a function of forces that lay outside entrepreneurial control, and when possible cost-cutting productivity gains of technology were explored in only a few trades and places, putting-out was a boon to capitalists in several critical respects.

Because output could quickly be adjusted simply by augmenting or reducing the flow of raw materials and credit by which the Verleger organized and funded production, putting-out improved responsiveness to market shifts. By allowing workers to be hired beyond the confines of specific localities or corporate bodies, moreover, the Verlagssystem facilitated the diminution of labor costs. In addition, by obliging hired hands to provide their own implements and workplaces, the domestic system ensured that a major share of the expenses of manufacturing fell on their shoulders. Then, too, it forced workers to bear much of the brunt of fluctuating demand: not only they but their fixed capital was used less or wholly idled during downturns. Finally, putting-out allowed capitalists to continue earning most of their profits from lucrative commercial and financial operations – selling raw materials and finished goods, and extending credit – while minimizing their costs and risks of production.

Some capitalists did invest in plant and equipment and become involved in managing production. But the record of such enterprises was mixed at best. Those based on concentrations of workers using existing methods proved ephemeral unless propped up for non-economic reasons. Those rooted in productivity-enhancing technological change had the greatest chances of success. Even they, however, proved vulnerable to the market disturbances that increasingly wracked the European economies, as central German glassmakers learned to their sorrow. Little wonder that established methods, labor- rather than capital-intensive, retained their appeal.

All across the long sixteenth century, alternative forms like small commodity production were tested, and many independent artisans survived. Some were fortunate enough to enjoy the protections afforded by skill or urban guild. Yet even in villages were to be found peasant families with access to local raw materials who took up craft work when farm tasks were light and, by using simple tools and their own dwellings, kept fixed costs to a minimum. Making small amounts of clay pots, wooden utensils, cheap cloth, shoes, and other simple leather goods that they sold themselves, they never became integrated into putting-out systems organized from nearby towns but retained their independent status in what has been called "peasant industry;" at times they even organized rural associations that secured local monopolies.

Yet if many Europeans continued to labor autonomously in modes both innovative and traditional, it is nevertheless true that the initiative lay with capitalist entrepreneurs. They were especially active in the countryside, as witness the fate of once-independent English rural spinners. Their ranks had included, according to a contemporary document, a great number of poor people that will not spin to the clothier for small wages; but have stock enough to set themselves on work, and do weekly buy their wool in the market by very small parcels according to their use and weekly return it in yarn, and make good profit thereof, having their benefit both of their labour and of the merchandise, and live exceedingly well.[3]

As late as 1615, these petty spinners manufactured the thread used in up to half the pieces woven in the export-oriented broadcloth industry of the West of England. But in the crisis and shakeup that overtook the craft soon thereafter, most were swallowed up into putting-out networks organized by powerful yarn "badgers" (brokers). It was not, moreover, only such "poor people" who were vulnerable. The power of capital to reorganize production relations extended even into highly skilled corporate trades such as the luxury crafts of Antwerp. Whether in the more common form of putting-out or the still unusual form of technologically advanced centralized production – yet again a Dutch hallmark – the potential for capitalist expansion was being avidly exploited in Europe during the long sixteenth century.

SUGGESTED READING

Many of the overviews cited at the end of chap. 2 contain valuable material on industry in the long sixteenth century. For studies that focus more directly on specific countries during this period, see R. van Uytven, "What is New Socially and Economically in the Sixteenth Century Netherlands," *Acta Historiae Neerlandica*, vol. 7 (1974); Violet Barbour, *Capitalism in Amsterdam in the Seventeenth Century* (Baltimore, 1950); *Dutch Capitalism and World Capitalism*, ed. M. Aymard (Cambridge, 1982); D. C. Coleman, *Industry in Tudor and Stuart England* (London, 1975); G. D. Ramsay, *The English Woollen Industry, 1500–1750* (London, 1982); Gaston Zeller, "Industry in France before Colbert," in *Essays in French Economic History*, ed. Rondo Cameron (Homewood, Ill., 1970); R. Ludloff, "Industrial Development in 16th and 17th Century Germany," *Past and Present*, no. 12 (1957); *The Rise and Decline of Urban Industries in Italy and in the Low Countries: Late Middle Ages–Early Modern Times*, ed. Herman Van der Wee (Leuven, 1988), which concentrates on the Flemish-speaking areas of the southern Netherlands and northern and central Italy; Richard Goldthwaite, *Wealth and the Demand for Art in Italy 1300–1600* (Baltimore, 1993), Part I; and *Crisis and Change in the Venetian Economy in the 16th and 17th Centuries*, ed. Brian Pullan (London, 1968).

Among many fine local studies, see Herman Van der Wee, *The Antwerp Market and the European Economy*, 3 vols. (The Hague, 1963); G. D. Ramsay, *The Wiltshire Woollen Industry in the Sixteenth and Seventeenth Centuries* (2nd edn, London, 1965); Herbert Heaton, *The Yorkshire Woollen and Worsted Industries From the Earliest Times up to the Industrial Revolution* (Oxford, 1920). Michael Zell,

---

[3] "The Organisation of the Woollen Industry," 1615, in *English Economic History. Select Documents*, ed A. Bland *et al.* (London, 1925), p. 355.

Industry in the Countryside. Wealden Society in the Sixteenth Century (Cambridge, 1994), David Rollison, *The Local Origins of Modern Society. Gloucestershire 1500–1800* (London, 1992), and Victor Skipp, *Crisis and Development: An Ecological Case Study of the Forest of Arden, 1570–1674* (Cambridge, 1978) focus on change in rural textile areas. Consult also Herman Kellenbenz, "The Fustian Industry of the Ulm Region in the Fifteenth and Early Sixteenth Centuries," and W. Endrei, "The Productivity of Weaving in Late Medieval Flanders," both in *Cloth and Clothing in Medieval Europe. Essays in Memory of E. M. Carus-Wilson*, ed. N. B. Harte and K. G. Ponting (London, 1983); and *The New Draperies*, ed. N. Harte (Oxford, 1997).

For mining and metallurgy, John U. Nef, "Silver Production in Central Europe, 1450–1618," *Journal of Political Economy*, vol. 49 (1941), remains fundamental. Ferrous trades are treated by D. W. Crossley, "The English Iron Industry 1500–1650: The Problem of New Techniques," and Domenico Sella, "The Iron Industry in Italy, 1500–1650," both in *Schwerpunkte des Eisengewinnung und Eisenverarbeitung in Europa 1500–1650*, ed. Hermann Kellenbenz (Cologne and Vienna, 1974), pp. 17–34, 91–105. (For those who can read languages other than English, the articles in this volume provide the best overview of the iron industry in virtually every part of Europe, east and west.) See also Philippe Braunstein, "Innovations in Mining and Metal Production in Europe in the Late Middle Ages," *Journal of European Economic History*, vol. 12 (1983), which continues into the early sixteenth century, and, for east central Europe, Milan Myska, "Pre-Industrial Iron-Making in the Czech Lands," *Past and Present*, no. 82 (1979). Far and away the best work on coal is John Hatcher, *The History of the British Coal Industry*. Vol. I. *Before 1700: Towards the Age of Coal* (Oxford, 1993), which confirms the quantitative magnitudes of growth asserted in John Nef, *The Rise of the British Coal Industry*, 2 vols. (London, 1932), while disputing its account of structural transformation.

For other industries, see Eleanor Godfrey, *The Development of English Glassmaking 1560–1640* (Chapel Hill, NC, 1975); Carla Rahn Phillips, *Six Galleons for the King of Spain. Imperial Defense in the Early Seventeenth Century* (Baltimore, 1986), which discusses shipbuilding at length; and R. W. Unger, *Dutch Shipbuilding before 1800. Ships and Guilds* (Assen, 1978). Joan Thirsk, *Economic Policy and Projects. The Development of a Consumer Society in Early Modern England* (Oxford, 1978), treats newly developed industries, while essays in *Consumption and the World of Goods*, ed. John Brewer and Roy Porter (London, 1993), look at the consumers who bought their goods.

Many of the works already cited also investigate changes in organization; for analyses more specifically concerned with this subject see Raymond De Roover, "A Florentine Firm of Cloth Manufacturers: Management and Organization of a 16th-Century Business," in his *Business, Banking and Economic Thought in Late Medieval and Early Modern Europe* (Chicago, 1974); D. W. Crossley, "The Management of a Sixteenth-Century Iron Works," *Economic History Review*, 2nd ser., vol. 19 (1966); John U. Nef, "The Progress of Technology and the Growth of Large-Scale Industry in Great Britain, 1540–1640," *Economic History Review*, vol. 5 (1934–35), which, in contrast to this chapter, sees capital-intensive industrialization as significant in the sixteenth century; and George Unwin's classic

Industrial Organisation in the 16th and 17th Centuries (Oxford, 1904). For an important but neglected craft, see L. A. Clarkson, "The Organization of the English Leather Industry in the Late Sixteenth and Seventeenth Centuries," *Economic History Review*, ser. 2, vol. 13 (1960), and Clarkson, "The Leather Crafts in Tudor and Stuart England," *Agricultural History Review*, vol. 14 (1966). See also D. M. Palliser, "The Trade Gilds of Tudor York," in *Crisis and Order in English Towns, 1500–1700*, ed. Peter Clark and Paul Slack (London, 1972), and R. W. Unger, "Technology and Industrial Organization. Dutch Shipbuilding to 1800," *Business History*, vol. 17 (1975). Joel Mokyr, *The Lever of Riches. Technological Creativity and Economic Progress* (New York, 1990), is a lively and up-to-date survey of technological innovations.

Max Weber's *The Protestant Ethic and the Spirit of Capitalism* (Engl. trans. New York, 1930), the most celebrated statement of his views, was originally published in a German sociological journal in 1904–5. Weber's *General Economic History* (1919–20; Engl. trans. New York, 1927), esp. chs. XXII, XXIII, XXVI, XXIX, XXX, outlines his broader interpretation. For a sampling of the enormous literature the "Weber thesis" has spawned, see R. H. Tawney, *Religion and the Rise of Capitalism* (London, 1926); Albert Hyma, "Calvinism and Capitalism in the Netherlands, 1555–1700," *Journal of Modern History*, vol. 10 (1938); Kurt Samuelson, *Religion and Economic Action. A Critique of Max Weber* (New York, 1961; orig. publ. 1957); H. M. Robertson, *Aspects of the Rise of Economic Individualism* (New York, 1959); Jelle C. Riemersma, *Religious Factors in Early Dutch Capitalism 1550–1650* (The Hague, 1967); Paul Seaver, "The Puritan Work Ethic Revisited," *Journal of British Studies*, vol. 19 (1979–80); Gordon Marshall, *Presbyteries and Profits: Calvinism and the Development of Capitalism in Scotland, 1560–1707* (Oxford, 1980); Marshall, *In Search of the Spirit of Capitalism* (New York, 1982). For a recent overview, see the essays in the volume *Weber's Protestant Ethic. Origins, Evidence, Contexts*, ed. H. Lehmann and G. Roth (Cambridge, 1993). A good source book is *The Weber Thesis Controversy*, ed. R. W. Green (Boston, 1973).

For primary sources, the volumes listed at the end of chap. 3 are recommended.

Part III

Introduction: Crisis and recovery: Towards capitalist industrialization

The hard times that marked the end of the long sixteenth century expansion persisted for many decades. Agricultural output shrank as yields diminished and the area under cultivation decreased; prices, land values, and in some areas rents and tithes stagnated or fell. Industrial production faltered; trade within Europe and overseas was in the doldrums. Demographic difficulties accompanied economic ones: population slumped from 78 million in 1600 to 75 million half a century later; recovery, to 81 million in 1700, was far from general, and English, French, and Polish population actually dipped. Problems had been evident before 1600, and distress lingered into the second quarter of the eighteenth century, but the so-called "seventeenth century crisis" reached its nadir between about 1660 and 1715. Although northwestern Europe was least affected, its economies did not escape unscathed, and the Dutch Republic saw its Golden Age come to an end.

The crisis was rooted in structures and practices, delineated in Part II, that cramped capital investment, popular consumption, labor mobility, and peasant, artisan, and entrepreneurial initiative. It was magnified and prolonged by warfare, epidemic disease, changing marriage and fecundity patterns, monetary disorder, and climatic mutations. From the Thirty Years' War (1618–48) to the War of the Spanish Succession (1701–14), the recurrent hostilities that unfolded across Europe and its colonies entailed considerable cost, disruption, and destruction. Standing armies and navies replaced mercenaries hired for (and released after) every campaign season, and during this period of nearly perpetual strife the forces' size continually grew. Countries as diverse as France, Sweden, and the Dutch Republic quintupled their armies between the 1590s and the early eighteenth century. New and bigger weapons from flintlock to cannon, along with vast networks of fortifications, were very expensive to acquire and maintain, and although the general price level was stable or dropping, even standard matériel shot up in cost. Financing such outlays by stiff and generally regressive taxation and massive borrowing cut into demand and investment.

On a wide scale, too, troops forcibly requisitioned supplies, compelled the payment of ransoms and other levies, burned and pillaged. Manpower shortages, disorganized domestic markets, and interrupted access to foreign consumers were superimposed upon ravaged crops, slaughtered livestock, and demolished shops and equipment. On top of all that, soldiers often brought epidemics, whose effects were heightened by food shortages. In 1659, for example, a Polish force occupied southern Jutland and northern Schleswig on the Danish–German border. It undertook little serious fighting but besides confiscating foodstuffs introduced typhus so virulent that in a triangular area measuring 30–40 miles on a side population losses averaged 80 percent, and in a few districts reached nearly 100 percent. Thirty years later, a fifth of the land still lay vacant in some parishes.

Epidemics also struck repeatedly apart from during wartime, causing deaths to soar while conceptions fell far beneath the usual level. Such mortality crises were hardly unknown prior to the seventeenth century, but now they became more frequent occurrences. Even in normal times, moreover, demographic growth was hampered by a rising age of marriage among women of all social classes for reasons that, although not fully understood, seem only partly related to economic conditions. Because nonmarital conception was uncommon, the delay in marriage translated into a lower birthrate, the critical variable determining population movements. Insofar as demographic expansion contributed to the health of European economies, sluggishness – or worse – could only have retardative consequences.

In nearly every state, recurrent clipping of gold and silver specie, minting of despised copper coinage, and multiple devaluations provoked monetary instability that was pivotal to a harsh downturn that gripped much of Europe in the early 1620s and powerfully influenced economic fluctuations during the next century. And, from the 1640s until about 1715, Europe experienced wetter summers and colder winters. Probably the result of reduced sunspot activity that diminished the amount of solar energy reaching the earth, this "Little Ice Age" shortened the growing season and helped cut yields. The resultant hardships emerge clearly from a diary entry by the Essex (England) minister Ralph Josselin: "The season cold and things hard, price[s] of corn and commodities rise and little or no work . . ."[1]

For all that, the seventeenth-century crisis was considerably less acute and uniform than the late medieval collapse of the fourteenth and early fifteenth centuries. Many historians, in fact, reject the term "crisis" as

---

[1] *The Diary of the Rev. Ralph Josselin*, entry for 2 March 1651, printed in *Seventeenth-Century Economic Documents*, ed. J. Thirsk and J. P. Cooper (Oxford, 1972), p. 51.

inaccurately capturing the reality of a phenomenon so protracted and disparate; it is retained here with the understanding that it denotes a time of structural adaptation and renewed initiatives as much as contraction. Thus although preparing for, fighting, and paying the debts consequent upon war absorbed great sums, military spending benefited industries such as armaments and shipbuilding, the regions – found in every state – that depended on them, and ports, whether existing ones like Plymouth in England, or wholly new foundations like Brest, Lorient, Rochefort, and Sète, established under Louis XIV. The larger military forces of the time also gave jobs to crowds of men. According to one estimate, 5 percent of all European males between sixteen and forty were in uniform during the 1680s, most of them from the poorer strata of the population. Armies may thus have absorbed under- or unemployed labor, enhancing aggregate demand.

Admittedly, wars devastated many districts, but as a rule property damage was rapidly repaired. Despite some glaring exceptions, moreover, demographic recovery was also much swifter than in the later Middle Ages. Germany lost at least a quarter of its people during the Thirty Years' War, yet by 1700 its population of 15 million was only one million below its 1600 apex, and European population as a whole was, albeit slowly, on the rise again. After the Black Death, in contrast, at least a century passed before broad demographic growth recommenced. The fact that seventeenth-century epidemics tended to be highly localized, unlike the fourteenth-century plague, which had touched nearly every corner of Europe, contributed to the brisk beginning of population revival.

Most of all, the seventeenth century was not simply an era of difficulties. For the laboring poor, in fact, it provided something of a respite after the long sixteenth century, when real wages had been cut in half due to food prices that rose twice as fast as rates of pay. Now, thanks both to moderating prices and a tighter labor market, real wages stabilized or, in some especially favored places, actually grew. In addition, structural changes seen during the long sixteenth century – specialized and commercialized agriculture, ruralized manufacture, capitalist production relations – were not reversed but consolidated during the troubled decades. In time, they interacted with novel conditions to touch off a new round of growth, and in the second half of the eighteenth century these set the stage for the advent of capitalist factory industrialization. During the crisis years, too, the pattern of regional differentiation that had arisen in the sixteenth century intensified; in the expansive period that followed, northwestern Europe increased its lead over its neighbors and rivals. There was as well a further reshuffling within this region, as the Dutch Republic lost its primacy both to the revitalized southern Netherlands and especially to England, poised to become "the first industrial nation." Led initially by the Dutch, too, but increasingly under English hegemony, this area also brought to fruition a world-economy centered on western Europe. Even in Spain – whose fate has long epitomized the seventeenth-century crisis – recent research has uncovered positive stirrings in several sectors of the economy. This was, in short, a period of adjustment as well as of retrenchment. The anatomy of these complex and momentous developments from the mid-seventeenth century to shortly before 1800 – a time that we might call "the long eighteenth century" – is the subject of Part III.

SUGGESTED READING

The classic interpretation of the seventeenth-century crisis is Eric J. Hobsbawm, "The Crisis of the Seventeenth Century" (1954), reprinted in *Crisis in Europe 1560–1660*, ed. Trevor Aston (London, 1965). It has sparked a good deal of debate, which can best be sampled in *The General Crisis of the Seventeenth Century*, ed. Geoffrey Parker and Lesley M. Smith (London, 1978). For a sharply critical view, see A. D. Lublinskaya, *French Absolutism: The Crucial Phase, 1620–29* (Cambridge, 1968), esp. ch. 1. For a world-systems perspective, consult Immanuel Wallerstein, "The 'Crisis of the Seventeenth Century'," *New Left Review*, no. 110 (1978). P. J. Coveney, "An Early Modern European Crisis?" *Renaissance and Modern Studies*, vol. 26 (1982) provides a general review of the scholarship.

A number of specific studies shed light on both the empirical and conceptual aspects of the crisis; many have already been mentioned in the suggested readings for chs. 3 and 4. For Spain, see (besides *The Castilian Crisis of the Seventeenth Century*, cited at the end of chap. 3) James Casey, *The Kingdom of Valencia in the Seventeenth Century* (Cambridge, 1979), and Michael Weisser, "The Agrarian Depression in Seventeenth-Century Spain," *Journal of Economic History*, vol. 42 (1982), which focuses on Segovia and Toledo. For Italy, consult Richard Rapp, *Industry and Economic Decline in Seventeenth-Century Venice* (Cambridge, Mass., 1976); Domenico Sella, *Crisis and Continuity: The Economy of Spanish Lombardy in the 17th Century* (Cambridge, Mass., 1979); Sella, "Industrial Production in Seventeenth-Century Italy. A Reappraisal," *Explorations in Entrepreneurial History*, vol. 6 (1969); and Antonio Calabria, *The Cost of Empire: The Finances of the Kingdom of Naples in the Time of Spanish Rule* (Cambridge, 1991). Concerning France and issues of fiscal burdens, James B. Collins, *Fiscal Limits of Absolutism. Direct Taxation in Early Seventeenth-Century France* (Berkeley, Calif., 1988), is excellent; for commercial issues, particularly as they impinge on England, see Barry Supple, *Commercial Crisis and Change in England, 1600–1642* (Cambridge, 1959).

Germany was particularly affected by the Thirty Years' War and subsequent conflicts. The best case study is Christopher R. Friedrichs, *Urban Society in an Age of War: Nördlingen, 1580–1720* (Princeton, N.J., 1979); the most up-to-date consideration of the issues is *The Thirty Years' War*, ed. Geoffrey Parker (rev. edn London, 1987). The region of Liège, a cynosure of both fighting and war production, is discussed in Myron P. Gutmann, *War and Rural Life in the Early Modern Low Countries* (Princeton, N.J., 1980).

5   Agricultural disparity and development

From depression to renewed growth

The onset and severity of the seventeenth-century crisis varied from region to region, but evidence from across Europe attests that agriculture was adversely affected for as much as a century. Yields of cereals dropped in many places, most sharply east of the Elbe. Large tracts went untilled. In the Soncino district of Lombardy, 18 percent of land was unplanted in 1668, as against 1 percent early in the century. Around 1660, just half of arable land was cultivated in Koscian county (Poland), less than a third in Gniezno county, barely 15 percent in Masovia province. Numerous regions saw agricultural output contract. Tithe data suggest that grain production in Mediterranean France dropped by a third in the last decades of the seventeenth century. Pastoral activities also suffered heavy reverses. Wool production sagged by a half in the kingdom of Naples between 1612 and 1686, while Spanish Mesta wool exports sank 40 percent from 1612–20 to 1662–70.

Around the mid-seventeenth century, prices began to decline; despite often violent short-term fluctuations, most remained low well into the next century, often at half their previous peak. This was a boon for consumers, including, of course, the throngs of rural landless and landpoor. Commercial farmers, on the contrary, faced falling incomes, although in recompense rents often dipped. Landowners found themselves hard pressed, as many agricultural properties became less remunerative. Between 1620 and 1660, land values throughout Lombardy shrank by up to 50 percent; land rents in Castile about as much. South of Rotterdam (Holland), prices for impoldered land plummeted from 400 to less than 100 guilders an acre over the course of the century after 1650. Between 1622 and 1641, the Hôtel-Dieu (main hospital) of Beauvais in northern France received 30 *muids* (about 340 U.S. bushels) of grain a year from its domain of Reuil-sur-Brèche, but just 17–18 (200 bushels) in 1713–26. Faced with tenants who simply could not pay, the Abbey of

Affligem in Brabant (Belgium) remitted 420,000 guilders' worth of rents in the years 1674–84.

Recovery began as early as the 1720s; by the mid-eighteenth century it was general over rural Europe. In the second half of the century, yields in northwestern Europe stood as much as 50 percent above their low points and the rest of the Continent also registered substantial, albeit lesser, gains. Land returned to cultivation. In Silesia, 15 percent more land was tilled in 1798 than in 1721; in the Breisgau (southwestern Germany), the area under the plow grew a remarkable 74 percent from 1699 and 1798. Agricultural production and trade rebounded smartly. In the Pays de Caux (Normandy), the years from 1713 to 1790 saw cereal output advance 60 percent and livestock herds expand more than 50 percent. Between 1686 and 1806, the number of Dogana sheep tripled from their low point in the previous period. Spanish Mesta exports doubled between 1692 and 1730, then doubled again by 1780.

Prices, already on the rise in southern and east central Europe in the 1730s, quickened their upward pace during the second half of the century. By the 1790s, they were double or even triple the low points reached in the crisis. Land became a lucrative investment once again. The Hôtel-Dieu of Amiens doubled its income from ground rents between the 1730s and the 1780s, while leases on pastures in the Auvergne (France) went up nearly three times. Land prices and rents in northern Germany about tripled between 1740–60 and 1801–5.

During this century and a half of crisis and recovery, the agrarian economies of Europe faced shifting constellations of pressures and opportunities. Some common traits continued to characterize rural Europe. But the diversity already present during the long sixteenth century among regions, countries, or even within a single country became even more pronounced. This chapter examines the significant forces impelling or thwarting change, the crucial innovations that occurred, and the distinctive outcomes of these processes. We shall be particularly attentive to the extent to which farming furnished commodities (food and raw materials), factors of production (particularly labor and capital), and consumer demand that could stimulate industrialization.

Patterns of agrarian change

Trends demarcating large agrarian regions within Europe had become evident during the long sixteenth century, in spite of the hesitancies of structural change. Most immediately apparent was the contrast between the neoserfdom engulfing east Elbia and the free peasantry elsewhere. If less pronounced, divisions were also evident within the rest of Europe, notably distinguishing the lagging agriculture of the Mediterranean lands on the one hand and the vibrant farming of the Low Countries and England on the other. During the seventeenth-century crisis, and even more during the subsequent upswing, these disparities became more strongly etched. The most productive agricultures, for instance, increased their average grain yields by nearly a half between the sixteenth and eighteenth centuries, whereas the least productive raised them barely a fifth. In this period, too, the cumulative effects of structural transformation became evident. They set apart dynamic areas like Catalonia, the duchy of Milan, and French Flanders within regions where overall agricultural development languished. Even more, they differentiated northwestern Europe as a whole.

East central Europe

Declining demand, the rise of new competitors, and numerous wars and their aftermath struck hard at the extensive arable and pastoral producers of seventeenth-century east central Europe. Impoverished by the ever greater burdens of neoserfdom, the rural majority could buy fewer agricultural products, while in the cities of the region, which in the long sixteenth century had absorbed increasing amounts of foodstuffs and raw materials, markets contracted as population dropped by a third, a half, or even more. Western consumption, too, fell steeply. Whereas 137,000 tons of Baltic rye and wheat passed through the Sound between Denmark and Sweden each year between 1600 and 1649, an average of only 112,000 tons was tallied from 1650 to 1699 and 64,400 in 1700–49. Annual exports of oxen from Hungary, 100,000 head a year between 1550 and 1600, fell to 60,000 during the next half-century. The appearance of dynamic new competitors had much to due with east Elbia's difficulties in western markets. English net exports of grains, flour, and malt rose from an average of 2.4 million bushels in the mid-1670s to more than 7.2 million bushels in 1745–54, most sent to the Low Countries and the Mediterranean basin, formerly the chief markets for Baltic grain. More and more of the livestock consumed in western cities came from breeders in Denmark, western Germany, and the Netherlands.

East Elbia was further disrupted by the Thirty Years' War, followed by a series of geographically more limited but equally destructive and costly conflicts that hobbled revival. A great deal of land became vacant and production decreased. On east Prussian estates, 58 percent of the area was under cultivation in 1600, 32 percent in 1683. In the district of Stargard in Mecklenburg, only a fourth of abandoned farmland had been reoccupied as late as 1708. Poland's cultivated area contracted 20 percent between

1620 and 1720, total output 25–30 percent. Landlords of all types saw their incomes dwindle. By 1700, revenues from Hohenzollern princely domains in Brandenburg and Prussia (after 1618 also under Hohenzollern rule) were half their 1600–24 level; smaller landowners, marginal even in good times, were often forced to sell out.

The prolonged crisis created some possibilities for agrarian change in east central Europe. Seigniorial authority frequently collapsed in wartime and peasants ceased to pay rents or dues and to render labor services, on occasion resorting to insurrection or less overt forms of resistance. Under duress, or to repopulate their lands, some lords made significant concessions. On the Stavenow estate in Brandenburg, average manorial robot service fell from 3 to 2.5 days per week between 1618–47 and 1694–1700, the yearly rent in rye from 7 to 3.6 bushels.

More often, however, lords seeking to restore their incomes used legal or other forms of coercion to revive or extend earlier claims over the peasantry's labor and surpluses. They were convinced – perhaps by peasant rebelliousness as much as by labor scarcity – that only the maintenance or indeed the strengthening of serfdom could assure them a sufficient, cheap labor force for the commercial agriculture that they continued to practice. Thus in the Korczyn district of Poland, where as we have seen (chap. 3) peasants were already burdened with heavier robot during the sixteenth century, the level of obligations rose further during the seventeenth century. Serfs owed 1,196 days of work on lords' estates in 1600/16 but 1,785 days in 1660. The proportion involving compulsory but unpaid manual work rose from 45 percent to 62 percent, whereas paid labor days fell from 15 percent to 5 percent. As corvée obligations grew, peasants were able to cultivate less land on their own. Output from peasant holdings plunged as much as 37 percent across the seventeenth century, as against just 6 percent on large estates. Whereas 80 percent of peasants on the estates of the Bishop of Chelm (Poland) farmed the 40 acres needed to support a family in 1614, only 50 percent did in 1676; on crown lands around Cracow, the figure decreased from 70 percent in 1564 to 44 percent in 1660.

The experience of the Polish peasantry was not unique. In Brandenburg-Prussia as a whole, peasant rents and labor services nearly quadrupled between 1614 and 1717, and after 1650 hereditary dependence was imposed on remaining free peasants in Prussia. In Bohemia, where much of the old nobility was wiped out early in the Thirty Years' War, the largely foreign conquerors who replaced them quickly dismantled remaining customary and legal protections for the peasantry. Lords enlarged their demesnes by seizing unoccupied holdings, then worked them by raising the robot owed by serfs to three or – at haymaking and harvest time – even more days per week; especially unlucky peasants (who formed as much as a fourth of the rural population) owed six days a week year-round. Admittedly, when a major rebellion erupted in 1680 against the heightened burdens, the Habsburg emperor Leopold I (ruled 1658–1705) issued a decree limiting labor services to three days a week, forbidding summary rent and fee raises, and freeing serfs from having to buy all goods from their lords at prices set by the lords. But the edict remained a dead letter, for lords uniformly ignored it – save for those who used it as an excuse to raise robot wherever it had previously been less than three days a week. In Hungary, too, corvées of three to six days per week became commonplace, as against one in the sixteenth century.

In the eighteenth century, east central agriculture rebounded with the return of peace. Yet market conditions had changed appreciably from those obtaining during the long sixteenth century. To be sure, pronounced demographic expansion – population in the region rose by two-thirds between 1700 and 1800, as against a half in the rest of Europe – boosted domestic demand for agricultural produce. Sales of east Elbian foodstuffs in western Europe, however, remained depressed, even when England's grain exports waned after about 1750. For substitutes had spread widely across Europe – rice, maize, and potatoes, which in the late eighteenth-century southern Netherlands supplied 40 percent of the nourishment formerly furnished by cereals, helping turn those provinces into grain exporters. Hence shipments from Gdansk continued to drop, to 20,000 tons by 1770, and even around 1800, after several decades of recovery, they totalled only 60,000 tons. Similarly, though by 1770 Hungarian cattle exports regained their 1570 high point, they had lost former markets in south Germany and Italy. Now breeders had to focus on nearby areas within the Habsburg Empire, notably Austria and Bohemia. In short, east central European agriculture had to rely less on traditional foreign markets and more on demand within the region, following – albeit with a century's delay – the reorientation pioneered by the region's industry (see chap. 4).

These circumstances evoked a variety of responses. Some east Elbian peasants and lords alike sought to profit from rising prices and commercial opportunities in nearby cities, often by promoting agrarian innovations like those we have already observed being introduced further west. There is evidence of peasants dividing common lands into individually farmed holdings; raising fruit, pigs, poultry, and other specialized crops; developing new products, such as the dessert wines for which Hungary became famous. A few landlords, too, hazarded productivity-enhancing innovations. The most notable was *Koppelwirtschaft*, in which grain was grown for several years, then the arable was converted to pasture for livestock for a period of three to six years, after which the rotation recommenced. "There is certainly no system of husbandry more regular, or more to be depended on," enthused one informed observer, adding that "everything is fixed in the most accurate manner. Every work has its proper time, and its regular succession . . . This system, therefore, is certainly the most eligible for the proprietors of extensive estates . . ."[1] As in the west, this type of convertible husbandry could have a significant impact on peasant life, since to institute the new rotation system, landlords reallocated holdings, expelling tenants in order to form large consolidated fields. Implementation of Koppelwirtschaft in the Stargard district of Mecklenburg, for instance, decreased the number of peasant holdings from 319 to just 140.

In some places, the eighteenth century also saw the bonds of serfdom loosened. Whereas traditionally they had lacked guarantees against expulsion or arbitrary changes in the charges they owed, and could not sell, lease, or mortgage their land (though custom usually allowed bequeathal to a son), now some peasants were able to purchase rights of inheritance, irremovability, and the like. Peasants in a few territories – notably the Hohenzollern lands – also benefited when rulers seeking to enhance their revenues and curb noble wealth and power while retaining a peasantry able to pay taxes introduced Bauernschutz policies modelled on those pioneered in western Germany (see chap. 3). On the Stavenow estate in Brandenburg, this resulted in a division of peasant surplus in which seigniorial rent took about 18 percent of a tenant's annual rye crop, the prince claimed another 16 percent – and the peasant kept nearly two-thirds. At the same time, Stavenow peasants won the right to substitute cash payments for performance of some labor services, reduced haulage obligations, and leases of seigniorial meadows on good terms. Serfdom was not, for all that, ended.

Demographic increase contributed to landlord willingness to make changes. Nobles who now enjoyed a surplus of labor services in excess of estate needs could see good reason to commute robot into cash payments; by 1750, this step had been taken on about a fifth of Bohemian estates. Again, the replacement of robot by wage labor – in 1800, hired laborers worked three-quarters of the land of the lordship of Boitzenburg (Brandenburg) – was encouraged by the parcelization of holdings, which in places multiplied the numbers of landless. In Prussian-controlled areas of Silesia, middling peasants and smallholders (respectively 57 and 38 percent of villagers) had vastly outnumbered cottagers (5 percent) in 1577; by 1787, cottagers (52 percent) had become more numerous than

---

[1] A. Thaer, letter to the Board of Agriculture (1794), printed in *Documents of European Economic History*, ed. S. Pollard and C. Holmes, vol. I (London, 1968), p. 11.

peasants (23 percent) and smallholders (25 percent) combined. In the late eighteenth century, too, just 35 percent of the inhabitants of the royal estates in Cracow province (Poland) were peasants with sufficient land for subsistence, whereas 56 percent were cottagers; in Bohemia, the landless comprised 40–60 percent of the rural population.

Even at the end of our period, however, Koppelwirtschaft and loosening serfdom remained straws in the wind. Faced with new conditions, the great majority of landowners responded in familiar ways. In order to expand output, many expropriated serf holdings and incorporated them into their existing demesnes; others transplanted the existing seigniorial system onto newly settled land. Rather than instituting novel tenurial arrangements, estate owners typically saw in growing land hunger a chance to intensify feudal levies and cancel reductions previously granted. Thus serfs on the Stavenow manors found their earlier gains erased: by 1727, they were obligated for 2.8 days of robot a week and their yearly rye rent had more than doubled to 7.4 bushels. In Poland, nobles established a remarkably lucrative trade in grain alcohol, the *propinacja*, which both consumed grain difficult to sell on international markets and absorbed – at times by mandating compulsory purchases – peasant cash that might otherwise have been spent off the estate. On royal properties, where revenues from agricultural products fell from 70 percent of total income in 1661 to 41 percent in 1764, *propinacja* grew from 6.4 percent to 37.6 percent. In Bohemia, estate-brewed beer – the only kind that serfs were permitted to buy – served similar purposes. Whereas in the early eighteenth century breweries supplied less than a quarter of lords' income, in 1757 they accounted for 43 percent.

Thus feudalism remained firmly rooted in east central Europe through both crisis and recovery. Commutation of labor services was often accompanied by increases in other obligations; moreover, it could be (and on occasion was) revoked when landlords' labor requirements changed. Even peasants buying rights to the land they tilled did not come to own the property, for they still owed charges, even robot, and could be deprived of the land for any number of reasons. Although in 1740 Prussian lords lost their customary right to expropriate peasant lands, until late in the eighteenth century peasants still regularly owed up to six days of labor.

Even the most powerful absolutist-minded monarchs proved powerless to effect much change in the seigniorial system. In the late eighteenth century Frederick the Great, who reigned over Prussia from 1740 to 1786, as well as the Habsburg monarchs Maria Theresa (ruled 1765–80) and Joseph II (1780–90), sought to modify peasant conditions as part of larger programs of enlightened centralizing reform. Beginning with their hereditary lands, they began to regulate peasant obligations to lords (again fixing labor services at a maximum of three days per week and converting some obligations into payments in cash or kind), strengthen peasants' right of occupancy on the land they tilled, tax all land equally, and curb the administrative and judicial power of the nobility. In part at the urging of native thinkers, and in part under the influence of the ideas of François Quesnay (1694–1774) and his fellow "Physiocrats," French reformers who argued that the creation of a class of thriving tenant farmers would spark broad economic growth, Maria Theresa and Joseph undertook further reforms on some Crown estates. They abolished personal bondage, commuted labor services to annual cash rentals, and divided demesnes into small farms worked by peasants with hereditary tenure. Finally, in a series of bold decrees in 1781–83, Joseph extended these changes to the peasantry throughout the majority of the Habsburg Empire.

It was all very largely in vain. Like their predecessors, most seigniors strenuously opposed the implementation of the crucial reform measures, overtly refused to obey them, and eventually rolled them back. The great nobles were the vanguard of obstruction. Having weathered the seventeenth-century storms, the magnates enhanced their wealth and power in the next century. Thus in 1700–50 the value of output coming to market from upper noble estates in Poland more than doubled, whereas from the lower nobility it remained stagnant and from the peasantry dropped by more than half. In the late eighteenth century, less than 10 percent of the land around Lublin belonged to nobles holding less than 4,000 acres, whereas in the mid-fifteenth century, their share had been nearly 50 percent. Across the same period, nobles with more than 22,000 acres increased their proportion from 13 percent to 42 percent. Against such concentrated wealth and power, monarchs had little choice but to back down. Thus Maria Theresa disbanded her own oversight commission rather than confront continued magnate violations of her reforming decrees. And thus Leopold II (Emperor 1790–92) reversed the abolition of robot.

East central European agriculture, already long oriented to the market, made food and industrial raw materials like wool and flax available to the non-farming population. The rapid growth of landpoor and landless strata engendered a potential labor supply for industry. Magnates concentrated control of wealth and other human and natural resources. At the same time, however, the persistence of neoserfdom not only limited the mobility of labor but depressed agricultural innovation, productivity, and incomes. Thus demand for manufactures remained low among the overwhelmingly peasant majority, and town populations, while expanding, remained tiny. These contradictions could only complicate east Elbian industrialization.

Mediterranean Europe

Italy

Across the period of crisis and recovery, the regional divisions that had emerged in Italian agriculture during the long sixteenth century were accentuated, with discrepant implications for economic growth and eventual industrialization. Pursuing their long-established pattern of diversification into new crops, the northern areas (Piedmont, Lombardy, the Veneto, and parts of Emilia-Romagna) boasted the most productive agrarian sectors; from the 1740s, if not earlier, they registered slow and regular improvement, albeit no dramatic breakthroughs. Mezzadria tightened its grip on the central states (Tuscany, Umbria, the Marches, and the rest of Emilia-Romagna), thereby assuring mediocre and stagnant levels of output outside scattered districts where peasants prospered by cultivating vines, olives, and especially mulberries. Although the southern half of the peninsula and Sicily had some impressively productive commercial farmers, particularly in the immediate vicinity of big cities, overall the *Mezzogiorno* continued to slide into the backwardness that has bedeviled it to this day. Here, in fact, agriculture underwent a process of despecialization as the region returned mainly to the extensive cultivation of grain and nomadic sheep and cattle herding.

The commercial agriculture of northern Italy proved most adaptable to new conditions. As grain consumption and prices fell in the later seventeenth century, farmers once again branched out into new specializations. Some planted artificial grasses and switched to dairying; the fame of Parma's cheeses dates from these years. Others introduced interculture, planting vines and other crop-bearing trees in grain fields, or, like the hemp growers of Emilia, cultivated profitable industrial crops. Rice, already widely grown, expanded its territory. Maize spread rapidly after the 1620s; by the mid-eighteenth century, it accounted for half the total cereals production in the Veneto. Compared to wheat, maize had a considerably higher yield per acre and consequent lower selling price, so it became a staple of the northern Italian popular diet. As a result, not only were the famines of previous centuries banished but more wheat – which maize rarely displaced elsewhere in Europe – could be exported.

These changes were facilitated by a renewed influx of urban capital, whether seeking more secure investments than trade or industry during the crisis years or, during the expansionary decades, aware that profits were again to be made from the land. Combined with a lightening fiscal burden, these funds overcame the shortage of resources that had played so critical a role in choking off sixteenth-century growth. A number of the new landlords, like their predecessors, supported innovations. These included new forms of tenancy in which substantial tenant farmers employed as day laborers some of the growing crowd of peasants dispossessed initially by agrarian depression and later by rising rents. Alongside them existed peasant-proprietors who also utilized capitalist methods of land management and employed wage earners. Assured of a supply of cheap labor, both groups responded ably to increasing demand and prices as the eighteenth century went on. They eliminated fallow, cultivated fodder crops, manured more frequently, invested in irrigation, improved tools, built better buildings, and plowed up wastes, marshes, and other previously uncultivated ground. None of these methods was new, but taken together they could result in agriculture as productive as any in Europe.

Still, adequately capitalized modern farms were the exception; intensive agriculture – like extensive – exhausts the soil without proper fertilizing, and too many northern Italian farms had insufficient livestock. So although very good, well manured land in mid-eighteenth-century Lombardy recorded wheat yield ratios of 15–20: 1, the average across northern Italy in that period seems to have been on the order of 6–7: 1 – just what it had been in the sixteenth century. These problems were exacerbated by the continuing propensity of too many landlords to neglect investment for peasant squeezing, a temptation hard to avoid when the number of peasants – and thus the demand for land – rose smartly from the later seventeenth century. In the Vercelli district (Piedmont), landowners demanded two-fifths of their tenants' wheat crop in 1670, half of it a century later; for rice, their share jumped from half to two-thirds. Capitalism had yet to triumph throughout the northern Italian countryside.

In central Italy, agriculture achieved stability through stalemate. Although sharecropping continued to give poor and propertyless peasants access to land, by and large it condemned agriculture to stagnation. Landlord investment to expand output customarily took the form of establishing new farms rather than upgrading those already in existence. Admittedly, during bad years landowners proved willing to extend additional credit and postpone payment, but that only locked peasant families into swelling, hereditary fetters of debt. On the Tuscan estate of Altopascio, peasant indebtedness burgeoned more than sixteenfold from 1624 to 1718 and kept growing until the estate was sold in 1783, at which point the great majority of peasants had no assets whatsoever. Under these conditions, second-rate methods were the norm, the more so because contracts often ran for only a year and sharecroppers had to leave behind any permanent improvements they had made. Because so much of any surplus went to the landlord, mezzadria also put a premium on achieving bare subsistence and on producing on the holding as much as possible of what the family consumed. Neither change nor growth was generated within the system. As many eighteenth-century travellers commented, indeed, an up-to-date, productive farmstead was a rarity in a mezzadria zone.

In the past, southern Italy had specialized in foodstuffs and raw materials exported most of all to northern and central Italian cities. During the long eighteenth century, these markets were gradually lost. Already in the later sixteenth century, the inefficiencies and excessive levies to which southern agriculture was subject had made Mezzogiorno grain costly and irregularly supplied; thereafter, cheaper competitors and substitutes like maize and rice effectively displaced it abroad. By 1710–20, exports were but a tenth of what they had been in the 1580s. In this period, too, northerners planted mulberry trees to satisfy their silk industry. Finally, the simultaneous decay of the north Italian woollens industry threw the Dogana into a profound slump, the number of sheep dropping by up to 75 percent. Even in the eighteenth century, when demand revived, southern agriculture never regained its earlier bloom, and exports had all but vanished for good. Cities in the region – especially the booming capitals of Naples, where population nearly doubled during the eighteenth century, and Palermo – absorbed most of the foodstuffs supplied by farms whose yields consistently fell; a small, locally oriented woollens industry around Naples and Salerno consumed the bulk of the Dogana's output.

Despite its dismal state, southern landlords made money from virtually every aspect of the agricultural economy. They collected seigniorial monopolies, excises, and judicial fees, and they engaged in tax-farming and money-lending; when prices were low, these activities constituted the largest part of their revenues. Few proprietors lived on the land, preferring city pleasures while leasing their latifundia in large blocs to substantial middlemen. The necessary labor was provided by permanent and migratory wage-earners drawn from the 60–70 percent of the farm population who were day laborers (*braccianti*). Possessing but wretched huts and tiny gardens planted with vegetables and a few trees or vines, braccianti only survived by foraging for wood, chestnuts, and other forest products, hunting (and poaching), and other expedients legal or not, for grain farmers needed significant amounts of labor for just 30 days a year, vineyard owners for 60–90 days.

On their side, the middlemen were nothing if not enterprising. So when population grew in the eighteenth century, they were often willing to subdivide their big holdings into small tenancies. These were sublet on short-term, insecure leases at high rents to tenants who also borrowed money, seed, and cattle at usurious rates and soon staggered under the weight of debts that encumbered increasingly meager and unproductive plots. Either way, much of the peasantry's surplus was skimmed off. What was done with it?

For the most part, it was channelled – as during the long sixteenth century – into various forms of conspicuous consumption (much of which further embellished cities) or into government bonds. Those who did put money into land bought additional estates from their spendthrift fellows or holdings from failing peasants, then leased them to the ubiquitous middlemen. But neither landlords nor middlemen invested in irrigation, drainage, tree planting, and fertilization, and peasants were too indebted and had too unsure a hold on their tenancies to undertake on their own these projects, urgent though they were. Consequently, southern Italian agriculture faced ever more pressing problems with malarial marsh formation, soil depletion, deforestation, erosion, and the spread of impenetrable brushland. An increasingly wretched peasantry engaged in, or were the victims of, endemic lawlessness and recurrent but fruitless rebellion. So although its agrarian order was founded on landlords' property rights over land rather than over people, southern Italy came to resemble east central Europe in its predominantly extensive arable and pastoral agriculture oriented, as foreign markets slipped away, more and more to regional consumers.

Across the eighteenth century, then, severe constraints continued to hobble Italian agriculture, but their weight was unevenly distributed among regions. Mezzadria could be found in most states, because many landlords sought assured – if modest – incomes whenever they leased family-sized holdings to peasants. But it was most oppressive in the central region. Increasingly a hindrance to either the accumulation or the investment of capital that might have boosted productivity and provided resources to urban population and industry, sharecropping could also hamstring rural industrialization. For even when family labor was underemployed on the *mezzadro*, many landlords actively opposed supplementary craft work for the market lest it cut into agricultural production, the basis of lords' income. (At best, such a family would receive additional land to till.) Municipal controls on grain supplies and prices – again most resolutely upheld in the states of central Italy – likewise shackled agriculture, depressing peasant revenues and discouraging farmers from specializing in other crops or introducing innovations.

The establishment of large properties also continued apace, now favored by the adoption of legal devices that transmitted estates undivided across generations. This concentration of property ownership could foster agrarian improvement, as when resident northern landlords pumped capital and innovations into their substantial farms. Even in the north, however, the lure of city and court promoted absenteeism, and with it interest in and commitment to improving the countryside waned. The problem was much worse elsewhere. It was compounded by the accumulation of land in the hands of the Catholic Church, which was forbidden to alienate it but lacked the liquid capital to develop it adequately. By the early eighteenth century, fully a third of Italian property was held in ecclesiastical mortmain (the perpetual ownership of real estate by institutions prohibited from selling or otherwise transferring it).

Finally, feudal levies were still collected all over Italy. Their burden was lightest in the north, where landowners received most of their income from farming and correspondingly less from seigniorial dues and rights, and where municipal and central governments had pruned feudal jurisdictions. Central and southern proprietors, in contrast, relied more on feudal revenues in the absence of agricultural progress – which therefore became that much more difficult to launch.

Northern Italian agriculture thus provided the most fertile soil for industrialization. Mainly by applying existing innovations more widely, its farms fed the population adequately – and even had a surplus available for export – and supplied important industrial raw materials. The rise of large capitalist holdings involved expropriating and expelling many peasants from the land; they were thereby "freed" – impelled – to seek jobs in urban or rural industries to supplement whatever farm work they could obtain. At the same time, however, the agrarian sector soaked up capital, rather than releasing it to other sectors of the economy, and the impoverishment of much of the peasantry – part and parcel of the process of capitalist modernization – restricted demand for manufactures. For all that, conditions were more propitious for industrial enterprise than in central and southern Italy, where agricultural productivity was low, labor was largely immobilized on the land, and capital was diverted away from productive investment.

Spain

Growing regional imbalances rooted in difficulties and differences already manifest by the end of the long sixteenth century, and aggravated during the subsequent period, marked Spanish agriculture as much as Italian. Castilian farming, weighed down by excessive state and seigniorial levies and the virtual absence of productive investment, faced additional troubles despite – in fact, partly because of – the Mesta's renascence across the eighteenth century. Several of the peripheral kingdoms initially showed great promise that was destined to remain unfulfilled. As in the past, Catalonia was the vanguard. Its peasants not only continued to develop the most productive agriculture in Iberia but provided an environment in which industrialization emerged.

After a long decline, Castilian pastoralism hit bottom in the 1670s: at that point, Mesta herders had as few as 500,000 sheep. Soon thereafter, however, foreign demand and wool prices picked up, and with them migratory and sedentary flocks and exports all revived. As early as 1708, the Mesta herded 2.1 million sheep, and the number grew to 3.5 million in 1765; the previous maximum had been 2.85 million (1511–19). Non-migratory flocks totaled another 2.1 million or so head in 1765, also a record. Wool exports averaged 5,140 tons a year in the 1770s, as against a high of 4,025 tons in the halcyon 1570s. At the outset, the growing flocks were accommodated without friction because of the widespread abandonment of land during the depths of the seventeenth-century crisis. But once population started to rise – there were 7.5 million Spaniards in 1700, 10.5 million in 1800 – competition for land ensued. This time, in contrast to the sixteenth century, the Mesta prevailed by virtue of the enhanced power in the central councils of state that landlords and merchant-financiers had acquired in the intervening years. So half or even two-thirds of land was kept in pasture, thereby hobbling the extension of arable, with the result that food prices began to soar, especially after 1750.

Problems that had long bedeviled Castilian agriculture likewise persisted. Most peasant holdings remained too small and undercapitalized either to provide adequate subsistence or fully to employ tenant families. Predominantly short-term leases gave tenants no security and thus discouraged their investment. During the years of low population that stretched across most of the seventeenth century, grain yields sometimes topped 5:1 as inferior land was vacated. But they soon dropped back to 4:1 or even lower because repeated cropping depleted the soil. Along with heavy rents and dues, onerous taxes oppressed rural society.

Out of these trials emerged a yet more polarized and impoverished countryside. The ranks of the middling peasantry, already hard pressed, became further depleted, while those of the impoverished lower strata ballooned. A census taken in 1797 found that 44 percent of the rural population consisted of practically destitute day laborers (jornaleros). Another 27 percent were tenants, 19 percent small landowners; many of these two groups were so overwhelmed with debt as to be on the edge of bankruptcy. Admittedly, a tiny stratum of of relatively well-to-do farmers had made its appearance in nearly every community, and in some places its members experimented with new crops and methods. But in general the financial, technical, and infrastructural obstacles to modernization were so great – Castilian road remained a synonym for wretched, and other transport facilities were little better – and the opportunities for profiting in time-honored if agriculturally pernicious ways so close at hand, that these farmers did not prove the leaven needed for agricultural progress. Instead, they turned to loan-sharking, tithe and tax farming, the subletting of inadequate plots at extortionate rents.

The concentration of landholding likewise proceeded apace. This trend served the Church, that 1 percent of the population whose share of Castilian wealth climbed from 9 percent in 1630 to 12 percent in the mid-eighteenth century. But most of all it helped the great nobles, whose wealth and numbers soared. An account written about 1600 named 180 aristocratic families that dominated the countryside; another, dating from the 1790s, listed more than 650. Among them, they possessed more than 4,900 villages, nearly 2,300 towns, and 15 cities. Their ascent was based partly on the acquisition of plots from failing peasants, partly on the losses suffered by poor hidalgos, forced to sell out by escalating indebtedness and rental income that had dropped by as much as half during the crisis.

Like their predecessors, of course, many great nobles also experienced severe financial problems due to their lavish style of life, huge dowries for their daughters, expensive government service, and, during the worst years of the seventeenth century, dwindling estate revenues. Even in troubled times, however, their holdings were shielded from sale by *mayorazgo* (entail: a legal device that restricted inheritance to a designated, immutable series of heirs) and served as collateral for loans. Most important of all, the grandees – again like their forebears – rarely failed to receive lavish aid from the Crown: alienated royal taxes, high government posts, protection against creditors, interest-free loans, or even outright gifts. Thanks largely to government largesse, the duchy of Infantado, in debt to the tune of nearly 900,000 ducats in 1637 (at a time when a jornalero felt lucky to earn 30–50 ducats a year), had redeemed nearly all its obligations by 1693. In this environment, landowners had little reason to spend on agricultural improvement, the more so as land remained primarily a social rather than an economic investment. The appearance of purchasers from the ranks of officialdom in the eighteenth century brought no change in values, for they too spent their income from the land on dowries, palace construction, and enlarging their estates.

Because of this structure of propertyholding, it was landowners – especially the greatest among them – who benefited from rising rents (which began to move upward as early as 1660) and the renewed agricultural growth that quickened after 1750. Swelling population did stimulate greater and more liberalized commercialization of agricultural products, a trend symbolized by the formal abolition of the long-ignored tasa in 1765. Far from changing production, however, landlords responded to expanding market opportunities by raising rents and fees, frequently dividing land into tiny holdings rented at extortionate rates. Some enclosure occurred, but rarely to introduce large-scale farming or intensive methods. On the contrary, enclosed land – often on marginal soil – was also rented on conventional terms and used for traditional crops. A superb chance for agricultural modernization was wasted. Landlords, grain merchants, tax and tithe farmers, and other middlemen – not peasants – captured the gains from enhanced commercialization. And because there was little investment, productivity remained low and high prices, subsistence crises, and reliance on imports continued until nearly the end of the Old Regime.

In recovery as in crisis, in sum, effective agrarian change was blocked by top-heavy social and political structures that concentrated property and power in the hands of landlords who drained capital away from the land while leaving peasants insufficient holdings, security, and incentives. The existing order was strengthened by the abiding vitality of feudal authority. To be sure, village communities strove to frustrate landowners who tried to claim exclusive rights over pastures and waste and to convert arable to pasture, and at times they succeeded. Nevertheless, seigniorial jurisdiction continued to provide landlords with significant revenues as well as political and social power.

Throughout the eighteenth century, heavy surplus extraction by landlord, church, and state hampered productivity gains, capital investment, and the efficient distribution of resources in Castilian agriculture. Most peasants found their only markets in nearby provincial capitals; these, however, were by and large both small and economically and demographically stagnant until the late eighteenth century. Madrid did extend its reach ever further into surrounding regions but failed to provoke transformation of customary forms of agricultural production and peasant-squeezing. Although the Mesta was thriving, aided by pasture rent ceilings imposed by the crown, it employed little labor. Olive cultivation was also developing widely, yet it too provided insufficient work for the crowds of underemployed and jobless found across the countryside. Nor would it be easy to redeploy that labor out of the agrarian sector, since foodstuff surpluses were negligible at best and most wool was sent abroad – including to Catalonia – for manufacture.

As early as the second half of the seventeenth century, the kingdoms along the Atlantic coast in northwestern Spain showed signs of agrarian advance. In particular, family farmers introduced maize and potatoes, often on fields converted from cattle pastures. Unfortunately, extending arable at the expense of pastoral reduced supplies of fertilizer, which in turn curtailed gains in foodstuff output just as population soared in the eighteenth century. As a result, virtually all raw wool raised in the area had to be exported in order to pay for now-vital grain imports from France. Pronounced demographic growth also brought about so great a division of holdings that most peasants could survive – and poorly at that – only by dint of taking on any available stop-gap, including going to sea to fish. Every year tens of thousands of rural folk had to trek to Portugal and other parts of Spain in quest of temporary agricultural work, and another large group emigrated permanently. Even the Basque provinces, although protected by privileges (*fueros*) against heavy state taxes and extortionate nobles, experienced alarming problems of peasant indebtedness, foreclosure, poverty, and vagrancy as swelling numbers outstripped productivity increases.

These circumstances did engender a potential labor force for industry, especially in the countryside, and the northwestern provinces also had mineral deposits. Yet like Castile, the great majority of the population was extremely poor, forced to dedicate nearly all their paltry incomes to food – which constantly became even more expensive, further limiting demand for manufactures. Here, too, merchants and landowners had a vested interest in exporting raw materials and, like their counterparts in east central Europe, a preference for imported goods. All in all, the agrarian sector of northwestern Spain would find it difficult to furnish significant factors of production for industrialization.

Catalonia alone – yet again – could boast an agriculture that both increased its productivity and released important resources to industry. No striking innovations were recorded, although maize, potatoes, and root vegetables were added to an already impressive array of crops. But along with some larger proprietors who employed day laborers, the many Catalan peasants secure on family farms with long-term leases, customary rights to inheritance, and moderate rents and taxes faced bright commercial prospects. Not only did Catalonia's population more than double across the eighteenth century, the fastest rate of increase recorded in Spain, but Barcelona's numbers grew from 43,000 to 115,000, and the city's merchants shipped much produce abroad. As before, Catalan farmers responded briskly to the market, investing in irrigation systems, abundant fertilizer, and other methods characteristic of advanced agriculture throughout Europe even if uncommon elsewhere in Spain.

Catalan agriculture was therefore able to supply foodstuffs in sufficient quantities and at satisfactory prices to industrial producers, to consume substantial amounts of the goods they made, and even to furnish some of the capital they required. The kingdom's day laborers – if few of its family farmers – were also recruited for the industrial labor force. These agrarian assets helped Catalonia to become the cradle of Spanish industrialization.

Western Europe

Western Germany

Agriculture suffered badly from the long decades of war that devastated Germany west of the Elbe during most of the seventeenth-century crisis. Yet although production plummeted, and for years remained at very depressed levels, vigorous recovery set in during the eighteenth century, picking up speed from the 1740s. As in the later sixteenth century, some northwestern states forged ahead by emulating progressive areas in the neighboring Low Countries. Overall, however, western Germany's agriculture left an ambiguous legacy for industrialization.

The Thirty Years' War, prolonged by conflicts in the second half of the seventeenth century which in many places were even more destructive, hammered western Germany. By the 1680s, noble estates in Bavaria had sunk to as little as one-quarter of their value in 1600. Landowners, forced to forgive loans, lower rents, and reduce seigniorial dues while also serving princes on the battlefield and at court, were deeply in debt. Throngs of peasants, too, had been forced to the wall. Innovations previously attempted were frequently abandoned. More intensive methods, adopted when labor was abundant and cheap, became impracticable when depopulation reduced the labor force, pushing up wages, and irrelevant when demand slackened. Rotation cycles had to be shortened because long-neglected land required more frequent rest when put back under the plow. Total output fell, although productivity may have been less adversely affected since it is likely that the least good land was taken out of cultivation.

Taking a page from their east Elbian brethren, during the seventeenth century some landlords, hoping to exploit wartime dislocation and demoralization, tried to form large estates worked by enserfed peasants owing labor services. But the mainly free-peasant farming that had arisen across the later Middle Ages and sixteenth century survived. By means of flight and violence, most of the rural population successfully resisted reenserfment; in fact, corvées and other existing feudal obligations were generally mitigated if not abolished. Even in Bavaria, where nobles were more powerful and big estates more plentiful than elsewhere in western Germany, many peasants managed to win commutation of labor services into monetary payments.

Noble attempts to turn back the clock also ran up against state-building princes who redoubled their efforts to centralize power, secure their tax base, and curb aristocratic authority. As a result, not only was the landlords' offensive blunted but by the eighteenth century up to 90 percent of the land in western Germany was owned by peasants or (more commonly) held by them on hereditary leases with fixed rents whose weight lightened as inflation quickened. The peasantry's total burden was not alleviated, however. It remained at a quarter or a third of gross output, since princes continued to raise their levies as landlords' exactions abated.

The peasant elite that had begun to take shape during the sixteenth century consolidated its primacy during the long eighteenth century. Inheritance laws, another aspect of Bauernschutz policies, helped the process, for in myriad states governments sanctioned or even mandated that holdings be passed on undivided to heirs. Substantial farmers were also able to buy land vacated during one or another war, another measure actively championed by many princes. Because of these developments, the number of farmers with holdings adequate for the practice of commercial agriculture remained constant or even expanded modestly.

Compared to their pre-crisis predecessors, these farmers were more welcoming of innovations such as new fodder crops and stall feeding, and they were more firmly – but also more flexibly – oriented to production for the market. Thus when agricultural wages were high and grain prices were depressed in the seventeenth century, many abandoned cereals for cattle and oxen breeding, since prices for meat and leather stayed healthier and livestock could be tended by family members. Others, their land less suitable for pasture or located close to cities, planted vines or horticultural crops. Then, during the eighteenth century, as grain prices rebounded and those of meat lagged, and demographic increase helped moderate wages, west German commercial farmers switched back to cereals.

Concomitantly, the number of smallholders, cottagers, and laborers dependent on wage work, whose ranks had thinned during the seventeenth-century crisis, underwent massive expansion in the course of the eighteenth century as population doubled between 1650 and 1800 (a pace equaled by no other sizable area in Europe), most of the expansion occurring in the countryside. Areas where impartible inheritance was not practiced were most strongly affected. In the 1780s, of the 2,900 peasant families in the Hochberg district of Baden, in crowded southwestern Germany, where holdings were divided equally among heirs, 45 percent were landless or had 1.8 acres or less; 39 percent held between 1.9 and 7.2 acres; and just 16 percent had 7.3 acres or more. But even in Electoral Saxony, which virtually outlawed parcelization, rapid population growth vastly expanded both the numbers and proportions of peasants with holdings that could not provide subsistence (Table 5.1).

Throughout western Germany, then, but most extensively in the

Table 5.1. *Non-noble rural population in Saxony in 1550 and 1750*

	1550		1750	
Group	Number	Percent	Number	Percent
Farmers (subsistence and above)	215,000	74	250,000	39
Cottars, gardeners	20,000	7	310,000	48
Village laborers	55,000	19	82,000	13
Total	290,000	100	642,000	100

northwestern area, advances inaugurated in the sixteenth century were revived once again and more heartily pursued from the early 1700s. They helped feed a rapidly expanding population and furnished wool, leather, flax, hemp, and other important industrial raw materials. In most rural areas, too, a large multitude of landpoor and landless folk eager for employment came into existence. At the same time, however, heavy state, landlord, and, in some places, church levies pruned the disposable income of even the most substantial farmers, while food prices that escalated from the 1730s, leaving wages far behind, reduced mass demand for manufactures. Western German agriculture could hamper as well as promote industrial development.

France
The ultimately disappointing performance of French agriculture during the long sixteenth century was recapitulated during the subsequent period. French farming, more adaptable than usually conceded, participated in trends and exhibited traits associated with agricultural improvement. But it fell short of matching the gains registered by the pacesetters. Thus the seventeenth-century crisis brought rural France falling yields, prices, farm incomes, and rents, along with rising taxes, wartime destruction, massive debt, and land abandonment. Even many rich laboureurs suffered from these trends, and many smaller peasants were prostrated. During the worst years, stretching from about 1660 to the 1720s, output tumbled 10 percent or more, rents by at least 25 percent. From the second quarter of the eighteenth century, marked recovery set in, characterized by fewer and less damaging wars, relatively lighter taxes, reviving output, yields, and prices, rents that as much as doubled, renewed cultivation of vacant holdings, and large-scale land clearance. In all these respects, however, the situation in France differed little from that obtaining over much of Europe.

No less in tune with currents flowing across Europe – or with its own prior development – was the spreading commercialization of French agriculture. As in the sixteenth century, big tenants leasing large, compact holdings from noble, clerical, and bourgeois landowners were most common in the open-field districts of northern France. There they grew grain for the many towns and cities, Paris most of all (its population, 220,000 in 1600, was 510,000 in 1700, 576,000 just half a century later). Substantial farms producing for the market emerged in other regions as well, and by the end of the eighteenth century they occupied perhaps a third of French land. More small and middling peasants, too, were drawn into specialized commercial farming. They engaged in stockbreeding and dairying, tended vines and olive trees, grew tobacco, and much more. French peasants of all kinds showed themselves willing, moreover, to alter their crop mix in response to changing demand and competition. Thus, to take just one example, when pastel lost customers to imported tropical indigo, farmers in the southwest phased it out in favor of maize. Large-scale land clearance and drainage, along with enclosure and engrossment of holdings, also occurred in France as in other parts of Europe.

The evolution of the agrarian social structure likewise took a similar path in France to that followed elsewhere. The process of polarization, which had already begun to mark the countryside during the long sixteenth century, advanced apace. Many peasants were ruined during the crisis decades, and others were displaced as landowners began to enclose and reorganize their estates during the eighteenth century. These developments, together with resurgent population (the 22 million French people of 1700 were 27–28 million in 1800, less than a tenth of whom lived, at either date, in towns with more than 10,000 inhabitants), and the prevalence of partible inheritance, helped expand the bottom of French rural society. By 1789, a sizable proportion of country residents – a majority in many areas – were impoverished, underemployed cottars and landless laborers. At the same time, a small minority of well-off plowmen who both owned and leased large holdings dominated across France. "They are really agricultural entrepreneurs," wrote A. R. J. Turgot (1727–81), the famous French economist and reform-minded official, "who possess, like the entrepreneurs in all other branches of commerce, considerable funds, which they employ in the cultivation of land."[2]

Yet for all that developments in French agriculture bore many resemblances to those occurring throughout Europe, its achievements were limited. Admittedly, in the provinces that had been conquered from the southern Netherlands in the late seventeenth century yields were as high

---

[2] Turgot, *Oeuvres*, excerpted in *Documents of European Economic History*, ed. S. Pollard and C. Holmes, vol. I (London, 1968), p. 38.

as in the districts that had remained under Habsburg rule, and there were pockets of high productivity elsewhere in France. On the whole, however, yields averaged just half to two-thirds as much, having improved little and slowly from the 4–6 : 1 reported in the sixteenth century. Again, although farms in the Paris basin and in scattered areas elsewhere could achieve rates of output growth close to those attained in the leading English counties, they could not sustain the advance. Whereas farmers in the English Midlands boasted steady productivity gains of 0.2–0.3 percent a year for 200 years, the annual average increment of their counterparts in the top French regions over the same period was just 0.13 percent. Not only, as a result, did the best French farming areas continually stumble. In addition, total French agricultural output increased, by most estimates, just 25 to 40 percent between the depth of the crisis and the late eighteenth century, at best barely matching population growth, and even that minimal expansion all but ceased after about 1770. All across the period, agricultural problems provoked subsistence crises and attendant food riots, including those that helped usher in the French Revolution. What explains France's sluggishness?

In some places, communal agriculture, backed by villages opposed to alienating or enclosing collective property, entrenched inefficient practices, discouraged investment, and hobbled innovation by landlords and tenants alike. Nevertheless, the force of these constraints should not be exaggerated. Collective regulations were far more limited in extent and flexible in practice than is often claimed, so change could and did take place even where they operated. Common gleaning rights usually did not interfere with individual farmers' ability to use their fields as they wished, for instance, and common rotations co-existed with initiatives entailing new crops and other innovations. Many peasant communities, moreover, had never owned collective property, and numerous villages that had enjoyed it in the past had been forced to sell it in order to pay ruinous tax increases imposed during the seventeenth century. The process of dispossession persisted across the eighteenth century. Farmers big and small repeatedly usurped remaining common land, and even when the Crown tried to stop these seizures (mainly to ensure that villages would have sufficient revenues to meet their tax bills), its remedy was to require the leasing of commons, not their retention for collective use.

Did, then, time-honored values and practices widely accepted by the rural classes play a more important role in hampering agricultural change? According to many historians, hidebound French peasants valued security over growth, a customary standard of living over change, self-sufficiency over marketable surpluses. They clung tenaciously to fragmented holdings that were too small and dispersed to justify modernizing investment or effort. Even large properties, which landowners commonly pieced together over many generations, frequently consisted of widely scattered plots in numerous villages. So instead of being worked as sizable, efficient, innovative farms, they were rented out as smallholdings exploited in customary ways. French peasants were slower than their fellows elsewhere in Europe to accept potatoes, maize, and buckwheat, considering them symbols of degradation rather than resources for economic advance. They also clung to traditional rotations even though these allegedly reduced productivity. Near the end of the eighteenth century, a third of the arable land on even the largest and most heavily capitalized farms around Pont-St-Pierre (Normandy) was dormant at any given time; as late as 1840, 27 percent of all France's cultivated land lay fallow. And many villages, when forced to lease their common lands, chopped them up into small farms, often thought to be less efficient than larger ones.

On their side, many owners – both noble and bourgeois – are said to have prized land especially for the social status and tax exemptions it imparted. Therefore they tended to buy more property rather than improving what they already possessed; treating their estates as means for indulging in lavish consumption, they minimized agricultural expenditures – even the maintenance of essential buildings like barns – instead of investing for returns over the long term. The profit motive often took second place to other considerations: instances of landlords who refused to enclose due to paternalistic ideas of their obligations to tenants, or because they wanted to maintain unobstructed courses for the hunt, are legion. Many nobles had, moreover, little reason to fear that failure to improve their estates would jeopardize their way of life. As in Spain, rich grandees in particular could count on state aid to maintain their lavish standard of living: the Condé family, for instance, one of the largest and wealthiest landowning clans in France, received half its enormous income from kingly largesse.

That such mentalities and practices existed cannot be denied, but recently their significance, extent, and effects on agricultural development have all been reassessed. They were not, to begin with, incomprehensible, archaic survivals, but had a logic within the context of constraints and opportunities found in later seventeenth- and eighteenth-century France. In the numerous regions suffering from poor communications – like the Vivarais, where roads were so inadequate that near-starvation existed a few dozen miles from plentiful grain supplies – the cultivation of a variety of produce by traditional methods, while inefficient in terms of productivity measures, was a rational decision rather than a matter of blind adherence to superannuated ideals of self-sufficiency. Throughout France, moreover, values and practices were firmly rooted in property rights and resulting landholding patterns. By lawsuit, passive resistance, and occasional overt violence, supported intermittently by royal protective policies, many peasants had gained de facto control of their holdings at fixed rents. Understandably, they were loath to tinker with arrangements that at least allowed them to subsist, especially in places where the likelihood for benefiting from change was, by any reasonable calculation, tenuous. Landlords' unwillingness to reorganize and invest – to exchange, in short, an assured income for a very speculative future gain – is also hard to criticize in such circumstances.

Second, some historians now believe that emphasis on traditionalistic and retardative attributes has concealed many instances of more progressive behavior and mentality. According to this new interpretation, more peasants than once suspected undertook specialized commercial farming, began improving their land, tried out novel crops and farm implements, even favored enclosure and tenurial reorganization. In the ranks of landlords, too, were to be found resolute improvers. More and more, for instance, converted once-hereditary leases to six- or nine-year adjustable terms. These not only gave property owners a greater degree of control over the land – in particular enabling them to expel tenants more easily and quickly – but encouraged them to invest in improvements, now that they could recoup their outlays within a reasonable time.

Finally, French agriculture was not immutable. Despite enjoying secure leases, peasants lost land due to debt or expropriation, and sometimes these vacated holdings were consolidated into big farms. Then, too, although division of holdings picked up steam during the eighteenth century, existing big commercial farms appear to have been substantially exempt from the trend. At least in the Paris basin, in fact, where fields remained dispersed, some tenants undertook on their own to rent numerous adjacent parcels in order to assemble compact farms of up to several hundred acres. Consolidation was also to be found in other regions where the availability of accessible markets, satisfactory transportation facilities, and cheap labor made large-scale commercial agriculture profitable. And even where conditions did not favor the emergence of big farms, agriculture was not necessarily stagnant: highly productive vineyards were but one instance of dynamic small holdings. French agriculture was influenced by contradictory trends, in short, but some did move in directions that favored innovative peasants and landlords.

Their initiatives were destined to bear disappointingly little fruit, however. Over too much of France, too many levies and too little investment limited or even throttled the positive consequences of forward-looking farmers and property-owners. Just as in the long sixteenth century, the excessive appropriation of the peasant surplus that drained

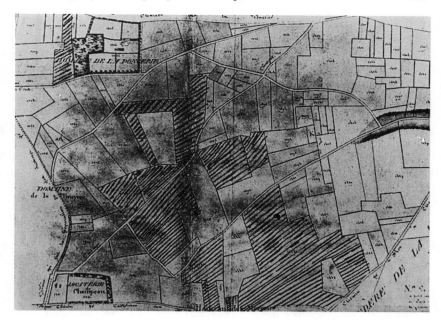

8 The ambiguities of French agriculture are vividly illustrated in this cadastral map from Charost (Département of Cher, central France): the shaded properties had been bought up by one individual but he continued leasing them separately.

resources out of the agrarian sector crucially impeded the transformation of French farming. Among landlords, improvers continued to be outnumbered by traditionalists, as too many owners directed their capital and energies towards exploiting the peasantry rather than improving their properties.

In addition, peasants in some regions continued to pay onerous seigniorial dues, for these could constitute a large part of landowners' income: up to a fifth in Normandy, more than a quarter in the Auvergne. Far from reducing these charges, in fact, numerous landlords embarked on a feudal offensive during the second half of the eighteenth century, raising fees that had long been collected and dusting off claims for many that had fallen into disuse. In 1780, for instance, seigniors in Burgundy claimed a panoply of fees including "the twelfth part of the price of each and every acquisition, due upon all goods without exception . . . a manual corvée for each laborer at harvest time . . . an annual corvée of plowing or cartage at grape-harvesting or seed-time . . . a tithe on all the lands of the seigniory at a rate of one in every fourteen sheaves," not to mention free maintenance of waterways leading to castle moats, levies on wine-sellers, and yet others.[3] At the same time, they sought to take advantage of stepped-up demographic growth – most of which occurred in the countryside – by sharply raising rents.

The mounting weight of state levies probably did the most mischief. The tax system continued to lay the burden of war and state-building most heavily on peasants, those in the grain-growing regions most of all. Annual crown imposts – 60–70 million livres in the early 1630s – had perhaps doubled by the end of the Thirty Years' War and then soared again in the 1690s. The load on the peasantry apparently lightened in the eighteenth century, whereas levies on noble landowners increased (although they never approached the rates paid by non-nobles), thus contributing to the cessation of the great anti-fiscal revolts that had shaken much of rural France in the previous century. But the increased reliance on consumption taxes kept up the pressure on the peasantry, as did church tithes (about 9 percent of gross output, though not levied on all products). Moreover, the fact that peasants' taxes invariably grew when they invested in improvements very likely discouraged many from doing so. Worse, the government's failure went deeper than the reach of the tax collector's hand into the peasant's pocket. For not only did the state bleed the countryside, it insufficiently invested in the kinds of improvements – notably roads, canals, and other means of transport – that it could best finance and implement and that would have made a world of difference in promoting the commercialization of agriculture, the growth of specialization, and the enhancement of efficiency.

During the later seventeenth century, a time of generally low prices, even a tenant on a good-sized farm of 100 acres in the rich grain-growing region north of Paris found it all but impossible, thanks to the exactions of landlord, monarch, and priest, to assemble the funds needed for investment. Often, indeed, such tenants were forced to borrow at high interest rates or alienate property. As prices and output improved in the eighteenth century, farm revenues increased, yet the small and middling peasants whose holdings occupied some 70 percent of the land still found it very difficult to accumulate capital to invest. After about 1760, spiraling rents and dues once again cut into the surpluses of all farmers, helping to abort a promising agricultural spurt that had begun to make itself felt throughout France.

By the end of the eighteenth century, then, the majority of French peasants cultivated undercapitalized plots, used low-yield farming methods, and furnished modest amounts of produce to the market. Unable to accumulate sufficient capital to undertake new departures, and

---

[3] Quoted from a "Manual of Rights," in Pierre Goubert, *The Ancien Régime* (New York, 1973), pp. 96–7.

cognizant that a large part of the profits of improvement would be pocketed by outsiders, they were locked into a system where change was very slow to occur and likely to be broken off. With holdings much in demand, landlords had little reason to invest; many of the funds they did provide took the form of loans that hastened peasants' impoverishment and ultimate dispossession. As we have seen, however, some farmers big and small worked units that engaged in specialized commercial agriculture. Yet this sector, too, encountered serious obstacles to agrarian modernization. For one thing, market orientation was no guarantee of prosperity. In Languedoc, for example, viticulture proved viable even on tiny parcels but provided a marginal existence, and the same was true of the small farmers in French Flanders. Again, some commercial holdings enjoyed productivity-enhancing innovations financed by tenants and lords linked by flexible and mutually beneficial contracts. Many, on the contrary, were just expanded versions of traditional farms that might even be occupied on sharecropping tenure. And numerous substantial tenants found irresistible the lure of financially exploiting their poorer neighbors; like many landlords, they extracted peasant surplus rather than innovating in agriculture. Forsaking farming for rent-collecting, tithe-farming, dividing and subleasing their holdings, and making usurious loans, they acquired a vested interest in perpetuating an abusive and underperforming system.

Low productivity and heavy surplus extraction also left most of the peasantry with insufficient income to consume substantial amounts of manufactures. As in many other corners of Europe, however, poor underemployed peasants in France were also seeking work. Ironically, the presence of this cheap, abundant throng may have checked the introduction of labor-saving innovation on some large farms. Industry also began to employ these peasants. By the end of the eighteenth century, spinners and weavers comprised more than half of the working population in the villages of the Pays de Caux (Normandy), and this was far from being an exceptional case.

The Low Countries

During the long sixteenth century, Europe's most specialized, commercialized, and highly productive agriculture had contributed pivotally not only to the signal vitality of the southern Netherlands economy, including its notable convalescence after the Dutch Revolt, but even more impressively to the blossoming of the Dutch Republic's Golden Age. This progressive agriculture was not sufficient to exempt the countryside in either part of the Low Countries from experiencing the seventeenth-century crisis. But when diffused into previously laggard areas it did promote strong and sustained recovery throughout the southern Netherlands and the inland provinces of the north. In the maritime provinces of the Dutch Republic, however, agrarian advance came virtually to a standstill as the economy entered a long period of decline.

Agricultural downturn took hold first in the southern Netherlands, touched off by renewed warfare starting in the 1630s. In the 1680s, grain output stood at its lowest level since the later Middle Ages, and rents had dropped by up to two-thirds. No later than 1720, however, the rural economy rallied vigorously, aided by the onset of prolonged peace. By 1750–70, grain output was 30–35 percent above the level of a century before. Rents surged, doubling or tripling in some cases.

Two complementary types of agriculture evolved, each with its characteristic production and social structure. One revolved around substantial farms. It was found especially in west Flanders, where in the eighteenth century up to three-quarters of all holdings were 25 acres or larger, and in a band extending from Hainaut across southern Brabant into the Namurois, where big farms occupied 50–60 percent of the cultivated surface. These farms specialized in mixed grain and livestock agriculture, mainly for urban markets; horticultural and industrial crops, although never of major importance, now all but disappeared. These holdings were owned largely by nobles and urban bourgeois who shunned direct involvement in farming but encouraged agricultural improvement. Thus they sought tenants with sufficient financial resources to exploit the holdings capably and then sustained good relations in order to keep them and their descendants on the farms. For this reason, landlords reduced rents during the seventeenth century, and both then and during more propitious times provided credit, seed, and cattle, and invested in drainage systems, better buildings, and other expensive projects.

All this enabled their tenants to introduce innovations as well. Most – including forage crops that supported additional livestock, making possible more intensive manuring, and rotations that sharply cut the amount of land left fallow or dispensed with it altogether – were copied from areas where they had been established in previous centuries. Others, such as the "Brabant" plow (easier to maneuver, thanks to a curved moldboard), were new inventions. Together, they helped improve productivity. Not that the high grain yields recorded by medieval Flemish and Brabantine peasants were often surpassed. But they came to prevail more widely, and where adopted they doubled yields between the first half of the seventeenth century and the end of the eighteenth.

These advances came at a price, however, which was paid by middling peasants. Unable to afford costly improvements, and thus increasingly uncompetitive, they lost much or all of their land. Their downward mobility further enlarged the ranks of smallholders with unviable plots, the landpoor, and the landless. The numbers of pauperized peasants also expanded as a consequence of demographic revival centered in the countryside. The southern Netherlands population of 1.9 million in 1700 climbed to 2.9 million in 1800, while the proportion of people living in towns dropped from a quarter to less than a fifth.

The other dominant form of southern Netherlands agriculture – the one, indeed, that had distinguished the most highly urbanized areas since the thirteenth and fourteenth centuries – was the labor-intensive small peasant holding. Found above all in the densely populated vicinity of big towns, these farms raised a little grain for their own consumption. They specialized, however, in dairying, gardening, and industrial raw materials like flax and dyestuffs. This agriculture remained highly productive, but as in the past, most peasants' holdings were too diminutive to provide them real prosperity. As the eighteenth century proceeded, moreover, they came under intensifying pressure as population increased – ironic testimony to their success. Land hunger pushed up rents – by the 1790s, tenants on tiny parcels paid up to 40 percent of their gross revenues in rent – and accelerated the division of holdings. Some peasants sought salvation in the potato, which gave yields up to five times higher than wheat. Nearly a sixth of the arable surface of east Flanders (where average farm size was smallest) was planted in potatoes in 1800. But even with potato-growing up to two-thirds of peasant households could no longer wring a livelihood from their plots and sought supplementary wage labor.

The Dutch Republic also boasted two distinctive kinds of agriculture, but they differed from those in the southern Low Countries. In the maritime provinces that were the heartland of the Golden Age, the major investments and crucial structural changes that accompanied rapid development had been completed by the 1660s. After that point, the great wave of agricultural expansion came to an end. Output stagnated or even fell slightly until at least 1750, and even then revival was feebler and shorter lived than anywhere else in Europe. Poldering activity – an indirect index of the demand for agricultural goods – had been at its height between 1615 and 1639. By 1665–89, it had fallen nearly 75 percent, and it remained depressed for nearly a century thereafter. Many owners, in fact, sold land or simply abandoned it; large fields lay vacant in numerous villages.

Until the middle of the eighteenth century, these problems can be traced in part to at best sluggish population growth and thus demand in the Dutch Republic itself and in its leading nearby markets – the southern Netherlands, western Germany, and France. The most damaging aspect of the demographic trend was urban population decline of at least 10 percent in both parts of the Low Countries between 1700 and 1750. The emergence abroad of competing producers of specialty farm goods was likewise detrimental. Agriculture in the maritime provinces faced some important specific complications as well. For one thing, the absolutely vital drainage systems reached the point where they required costly large-scale renovation and replacement just as demand and prices fell. In addition, decades of warfare with England and then with France forced the government to raise taxes steeply, and the burden fell heavily on the countryside. Dutch landlords, who had always viewed land nearly exclusively with an eye to its profitability, pulled out when returns were unsatisfactory. So capital for new investment – or even for routine maintenance – became difficult to obtain. Finally, livestock virus epidemics ravaged herds – a singularly devastating blow to a region so heavily oriented to dairying. In 1714, and again in 1745, 80 percent of Friesland's cattle died within just twelve months.

As the maritime provinces experienced agricultural stagnation or, more often, decay, the farming sector in the traditionally backward inland areas perked up thanks to specialization, innovation, and deeper involvement in the market economy: thanks, that is, to the belated acceptance of agrarian practices pioneered earlier in the advanced Netherlands provinces. Peasants in once desperately poor Drenthe, for instance, sloughed off many non-agricultural activities onto artisans and shopkeepers. They also abandoned mixed cattle, horse, and grain farming for – now in contrast to their counterparts to the west – sheep and especially cereals, consuming buckwheat (and later potatoes) while selling more profitable rye. Abolishing common grazing after harvest in favor of temporary sheepfolds, plowing and weeding more frequently, and using turf-manuring (in which sod, cut from waste lands, was spread in sheep pens and then dug into fields), they boosted yields from a miserable 3:1 in 1600 to a quite respectable 7:1 in 1800.

Other strategies were pursued elsewhere. On the sandy soils around Den Bosc, for instance, peasants gave up cereals for dairying and stockraising; rather than rely on imported grain, too expensive when hauled overland, they planted potatoes for their own consumption. Farmers in districts of Utrecht and Gelderland bordering the Rhine river took up another specialty altogether: tobacco sold to Amsterdam merchants. Output mounted across the seventeenth century, cresting around 1710, and although competition increased from areas with lower labor costs – the American slave colonies, of course, and east central Europe as well – stayed high until about 1750 and perked up again in the 1770s.

Smallholders dominated tobacco growing, in part because it used horticultural techniques with which they were familiar, and in part because it required no expensive investments. Most important of all, the labor-intensive crop would support a heretofore underemployed family –

women and young children performed much of the work – on as little as an acre and a half. So much labor was lavished on Netherlands tobacco, in fact, that although per capita output was lower than in the American colonies, the yield per acre was two to three times higher. In consequence, even peasants with minute plots could preserve their autonomy within long-accepted norms emphasizing joint effort, security for all, self-employment, and the maintenance of the family as a production, consumption, and social unit. Yet in contrast to earlier periods, this goal was achieved not through diversified subsistence agriculture but by specializing in a cash crop.

By the eighteenth century, rural households in every part of the Low Countries were deeply involved in the market as producers and consumers. But the diverse structures within which they worked had distinct ramifications for the process of industrialization. The interrelated agrarian sectors of the southern Netherlands afforded the most auspicious context. The big mixed farmers, blessed with secure tenures and aided by prices that, as the eighteenth century went on, rose faster than rents and wages, supplied basic foodstuffs and robust demand for manufactures for both personal and farm use. Small peasants and day laborers, although their consumption was limited by poverty, did provide additional food crops and vital industrial raw materials. They also constituted a proliferating mass of inexpensive labor that was only partly employed on either their own holdings or the large farms.

In the maritime provinces of the Dutch Republic, farmers' wealth and their high rates of market participation had, since the sixteenth century, stimulated non-agricultural employment and goods production. But the long agrarian slowdown across the later seventeenth and eighteenth centuries, rising output abroad of specialized agricultural products that took away customers from Netherlands exports, and, at home, high taxes and prices for imported grain, colluded to blunt that impact as time went on. Prosperous Dutch farmers seem, moreover, to have been partial to traditional artisanal goods. Much as this preference aided largely urban crafts, it inhibited purchases of factory-made items. In some zones of the inland provinces, peasants managed to develop labor-intensive agricultural specialties that kept them and their families fully occupied. Many more were pauperized, unable to achieve subsistence on their puny holdings. Like their fellows across the border in the southern Netherlands, they could be tapped for industrial work.

England

In the course of the seventeenth and eighteenth centuries, English agriculture became Europe's most productive. Roughly equal, on a countrywide comparison, to French farming around 1600, by 1700 it outdistanced its rival across the Channel, and the gap continued to widen thereafter. At the same time, moreover, English yields and productivity caught up with, and very likely surpassed, those registered in the foremost provinces of the Low Countries. No more than during the long sixteenth century did a dramatic agricultural revolution occur. But vital and durable innovations first introduced in the earlier period were greatly extended and consolidated. What had previously been experimental and circumscribed became normal practice throughout much of the country. Landlords, who already by 1700 controlled three-quarters of England's farmland, contributed to the process, most notably by enclosing more land and providing capital during a crucial period. Even more than in the sixteenth century, however, it was working farmers – both tenants and independent owner-occupiers – who created and implanted the new husbandry.

Slumping grain prices, falling rents, and substantial arrears were common features in mid- and later seventeenth-century rural England. But in sharp contrast to virtually every other corner of Europe, these were not the signs of unrelieved agrarian distress. For despite them, from about 1660 to the 1740s English farm production grew smartly. Some output gains came, as in the past, simply from expanding the area under cultivation or used for pasture. Qualitative improvements were more important, however, as indicated by grain yields that jumped by between a third and a half. For the first several decades, population dipped slightly, but even when demographic advance resumed, output exceeded it. Between 1700 and 1760, according to one recent estimate, agricultural output rose 0.7 percent a year, population 0.44 percent, allowing per capita consumption to increase. Wool production rose, while the advance in wheat yields and output was so decided that after 1700 England became a major cereals exporter. In 1750, it shipped abroad nearly 7 percent of domestic grain production, and this represented nearly one-fifth of all domestic exports. To be sure, from this point expansion of agricultural output failed to keep up with rapid population growth, as English numbers swelled by 50 percent between 1750 and 1800 (far and away the fastest rate of increase in any major European country). So food prices mounted sharply and by the 1770s England became a substantial importer of grain. Still, wheat yields, productivity, and aggregate output also continued to mount by up to 30 percent in the second half of the eighteenth century.

More important, changes that first appeared in the last decades of the long sixteenth century were not only widely diffused during the subsequent century of expansion but maintained afterwards. Initially, they represented attempts by farmers to profit during a time of weak demand, sliding prices, and rising wages, but they proved equally well suited to a period of ebullient demand, resurgent prices, and falling labor costs. To begin with, commercial agriculture became dominant, furnishing a greater variety of produce. Farmers added new crops ranging from vegetables and dyestuffs to wheat and rye substitutes such as buckwheat, maize, and potatoes. Crop rotations that included roots and artificial grasses, floated water meadows, convertible husbandry, more frequent manuring and liming of fields, drainage systems, more rational farm layout, careful selection of seed and breeding animals – these and many other practices, most of them pioneered before 1650, were now extensively and efficiently implemented. Norfolk and Suffolk formed an especially active center for innovation, but initiatives percolated into other regions; they were even taken up in the northwest, long a byword for backwardness.

Facilitated by improved riverine, road, and coastal transport, specialization progressed as well, fostering interregional and international trade in agricultural commodities. The upland west and north became more thoroughly pastoral. Within the eastern and southern counties, three zones took shape. Quickly deploying the latest innovations, light-soil areas concentrated on mixed grain and cattle farming. Heavy-soil valleys, on the contrary, found many aspects of the new husbandry expensive and unsatisfactory; having become, in consequence, less competitive as cereal producers, they expanded pastoralism at the expense of arable. Finally, horticultural and industrial crops blossomed in ever-expanding regions around urban centers – most notably London, where population soared from 400,000 in 1650 to 575,000 in 1700 (when it had become Europe's biggest city), 675,000 half a century later, and 865,000 in 1800.

Progressive landlords were once seen as central to England's process of agricultural modernization in the eighteenth as in the sixteenth century. In sharp contrast to their blasé, penurious Continental counterparts, it was held, these forward-looking owners eagerly read the latest farming manuals and, concerned to modernize farming, enclosed, engrossed, and invested in all manner of innovation to enhance the efficiency of their increasingly large estates. Current scholarship has appreciably diminished their role in the later as in the earlier age. Certainly, the profile of landlords changed somewhat as large proprietors boosted their share of land thanks to agrarian depression, a more active land market at all levels, and the rise of mortgage finance. According to one estimate, owners of more than 3,000 acres held at least 25 percent of land in 1790, up from 15–20 percent in 1690 (and often had holdings spread across England, which minimized the effects of localized problems), whereas those with less than 300 acres – usually in one place – had dropped from between a quarter and a third to less than a sixth. Larger owners proved best able to survive low prices and rents during the seventeenth-century agrarian depression, to absorb the land tax introduced to pay for the wars against Louis XIV's France later in that century, and then to profit from subsequent agricultural recovery.

What is considerably less clear is whether concentration of landed property had much to do with elevated levels of investment or the introduction of modern farming methods. Doubtless landlords such as Charles "Turnip" Townshend (1674–1738) actively promoted agricultural improvement. But most seem to have been concerned primarily to maximize prestige, not profit. They were anxious to preserve and if possible to enlarge their estates, and they had sufficiently deep pockets to tide over these great holdings when times were hard. When prospects brightened, moreover, they were equally anxious to fatten their rent rolls, and in the brief 1750–90 period managed to double many and even to triple some. Not to invest in their farms, however: less than 10 percent of their revenues was plowed back into farm improvements – approximately the same amount as their French peers. Instead, they sought enhanced incomes in order to pay hefty marriage portions for their daughters, settle younger (non-inheriting) sons in suitably genteel careers, and spend lavishly on country houses, the London social "season," prolonged visits to Bath and other resorts, and innumerable other modes of conspicuous consumption little different in kind from those in which their fellows abroad indulged. The risk-taking, "improving" English landlord has, in short, gone the way of the rapid, thorough agricultural revolution.

This is not to say that landowners added nothing to the process of change, but rather to note that their participation was concentrated in a few realms – and even there their contributions should not be overstated. First, they continued to enclose a great deal of farmland by means of negotiated agreement, force, and – increasingly from the 1750s – Act of Parliament. As before, areas like the south and east Midlands, blessed with good soil and vigorous nearby urban demand, and peopled by customary tenants enjoying little legal security and lacking documentation to support their claims, were most affected.

In some locations, enclosure freed farmers from restraints imposed by communal regulations, allowing them to keep more livestock for animal products and manure, enlarge the arable by regularly cultivating marginal land, reduce or eliminate fallows, and experiment with the crop mix that best suited their specific fields and current market conditions. When enclosure did encourage tenants to adopt all available technical, cropping, and stocking innovations – and, farmers working enclosed units seem to have been more prone to do so than their fellows who had open-field holdings – the gains could be significant, particularly in the numbers and size of livestock.

For all that, the effects of enclosure need to be kept in perspective. Although open-field districts lagged behind enclosed, their yields also grew impressively. This is not surprising. Enclosed areas may generally have been the first to adopt new methods and crops, but in a competitive commercialized setting – which England was fast becoming – innovations soon spread to open-field farms. As in France, the rigidity of the old system has been exaggerated, especially its purported inability to manage communal resources for efficient use. Recent research suggests, on the contrary, that peasants sitting on manorial courts and parish committees or "vestries" actively promoted the adoption of fodder crops and new fallow practices, encouraged improved methods of cultivation, and effectively established stints to maintain common pastures.

Conversely, enclosure did not inevitably portend new practices. If it promoted conversion from arable to pastoral on heavy Leicestershire soils, in County Durham it entrenched a traditional three-course rotation. This stability came about in part because landlords usually enclosed not to stimulate improvements but, by terminating existing leases, more sharply to raise rents – which indeed commonly went up twice as much on enclosed as on open-field holdings. Landlords clearly benefited from enclosure and its usual companion engrossment. But enclosure seems to have been no more critical for advances in productivity and output in the eighteenth than in the sixteenth century. Indeed, instances when change did not ensue in the wake of enclosure reflect the fact that agricultural methods that had evolved over the centuries were often the most appropriate ones for the districts where they were found. In these cases, enclosure did not represent the replacement of an agricultural system on its last legs, but the redistribution of profits of a still vital one from farmers to landlords.

Many scholars now believe, in fact, that the major output gains realized on enclosed farms stemmed from extending the land area under regular cultivation by plowing up wastes rather than from strictly technical innovations that were found more widely. And alongside this privatization of formerly communal assets has to be set the loss of village solidarity and community and of individual peasant households' independence that had been sustained by communal agriculture. According to a recent study, widely held grazing rights on common wastes were worth the equivalent of a sixth of an agricultural day laborer's wage, and gleaning rights in common fields were likewise of considerable economic value to numerous peasants. Thus to abolish these rights was to knock a critical prop out from under marginal smallholders, cottagers, and the like; female heads of households, who were concentrated in the lower strata of the peasantry, were hardest hit.

Less ambiguous was the role that landlords played in getting agricultural advance off the ground in the later seventeenth century. In the aftermath of the Civil War, many owners were forced to rehabilitate neglected or damaged estates, and they lowered rents, advanced credit, and made improvements both to attract new tenants to vacant holdings and to help existing tenants hang on. It appears that landlords invested more capital in farming in the final third of the seventeenth century than in any period of comparable length in that or any preceding century. Falling interest rates (from 10 percent before 1625 to 6 percent in 1651 and 5 percent after about 1680) and the advent of long-term mortgages eased the financing of improvements. So did landlords' growing ability to draw on mercantile and other nonagricultural resources, including appointed office.

Government policies seconded landlord initiatives. Legislation enacted during the Civil War and Interregnum (1640–60) had abolished royal courts that had enforced feudal tenures and, however intermittently, obstructed enclosure. As a result, landowners came to possess nearly full ownership of their properties, allowing them to proceed with tenurial restructuring more smoothly and speedily. After the Restoration of the monarchy in 1660, parliaments controlled by aristocratic oligarchies responsive to landlord interests passed numerous acts that effectively shielded the agrarian sector from the potentially ruinous consequences of falling grain prices and rising output, while supporting the expansion of new crops and pastoralism. The Corn Law of 1670 imposed variable duties on wheat imports according to domestic selling prices, and in succeeding years additional statutes subsidized cereal exports, encouraged the use of grain in beer and whiskey and the growing of industrial crops like flax, hemp, and madder, and protected cattle, apples, and other crops from foreign competition.

It was working farmers, however, whose efforts were again decisive for English agricultural development. Although some were independent owner-occupiers, an increasing number were capitalist tenants employing wage labor on big farms. These might well be enclosed units, but there was no necessary correlation between farm size and enclosure. While land was often leased in small holdings after enclosure, over England as a whole the average farm was becoming bigger, even where enclosure did not occur. In the south Midlands, for instance, 85 percent of open-field farms had 100 acres or more in 1800, as against 32 percent in the early seventeenth century.

The indefatigable traveller and publicist Arthur Young (1741–1820) waxed rhapsodic about big farms:

. . . no small farmers could effect such great things as have been done in Norfolk. Inclosing, marling, and keeping a flock of sheep large enough for folding, belong absolutely and exclusively to great farmers . . . Nor should it be forgotten that the best husbandry in Norfolk is that of the largest farmers . . . Great farms have been the soul of the Norfolk culture: split them into tenures of an hundreds pounds a year, you will find nothing but beggars and weeds in the whole county.[4]

Yet despite Young's encomia, many contemporaries were uncertain about the advantages of big farms, especially because suitable tenants were thought to be hard to find. Scholars, too, while acknowledging that large holdings may have reduced fixed costs for implements, draft animals, and labor on a per-acre basis by distributing them over larger areas, have questioned whether they were more innovative, invested more capital per acre, or realized higher yields than small holdings. After all, numerous middling and small proprietors relying principally on family labor participated successfully in commercial agriculture.

What mattered, after all, was that farmers with access to markets exploited that opportunity by embracing new crops that were in demand and more efficient techniques of raising them. Many did. They utilized family members and other workers more fully by introducing labor-intensive market gardening and industrial crops, and they switched from oxen to horses and, in the late eighteenth century, to novel plows; between them, these changes more than doubled the amount of land that a plowman could turn over in a day. Farmers are now also credited with devising many of the innovations once ascribed to improving landlords like Townshend and inventors such as Jethro Tull (1674–1741) of seed-drill fame.

The second half of the seventeenth century was as critical for farmers as for landowners. In the one case as in the other, much of the achievement was inadvertent. Like landlords' investments, farmers' innovations were responses to an immediate crisis of stagnant demand and falling grain prices, not the fulfillment of a program of agricultural improvement. Yet as they planted more artificial grasses and clover and turnips for fodder, constructed more water meadows, or improved their breeding stock, farmers not only managed to pasture cattle and sheep more densely and therefore secure more animal products for sale in the market. They also obtained additional fertilizer and, thanks to the nitrogen fixed by their

[4] Arthur Young, *The Farmer's Tour*, 1771, printed in *English Economic History. Select Documents*, ed. A. Bland *et al.* (London, 1925), p. 531.

fodder crops, reinvigorated the soil. Both raised arable yields, thereby intensifying the downward movement of prices and hastening the diffusion of new techniques and crops to compensate for lost income. Both likewise enhanced labor productivity. For although many innovative crops and practices were labor-intensive, they were mainly implemented by using previously underemployed farm labor more consistently, thus more efficiently, since the number of workers per acre fell.

The slow but real transformation of English agriculture reinforced changes in the rural social structure that had been incipient during the long sixteenth century. Especially in mixed-farming and grain-growing areas, large farmers became dominant; in fact, it was during the long eighteenth century that in these regions the relations of production often considered characteristic of English agriculture across the entire early modern era finally became dominant: landlord, big tenant farmer, landless laborer. The holdings they farmed proved best able to marshal the resources required to weather periods of depressed prices, to enclose and engross farms, to build sheepfolds and water meadows, to purchase horses and new plows. For sowing, harvesting, and other seasonal jobs, they had access to a growing crowd of villagers created both by the renewal of pressures already familiar in the previous period – such as rack-renting, excessive entry fines, and, of course, enclosure – and by the fragmentation of holdings once demographic growth restarted. As on the Continent, the rural lower strata also burgeoned because indebted small peasants found it more and more difficult to compete with modernizing farmers. The growth experienced by English agriculture provided work for many of those reduced to the status of cottagers and the landless, but not all. Adult males were favored, the proportion of men in the ranks of agricultural laborers rising across the eighteenth century at the expense of women and children. Yet even men saw their security of employment deteriorate as hiring by the day supplanted year-long contracts and a sizable minority was engaged only at harvest-time.

Admittedly, some small family farmers survived in arable areas, notably in the vicinity of towns with their demand for horticultural and industrial crops. But pastoral and forest zones provided much more benign environments, because common and waste land was more plentiful, partible inheritance more accepted, industrial work more available, and prices for the items they produced remained healthier. Throughout pastoral and woodland districts, in fact, viable plots of up to 16 or 20 acres multiplied at the expense of both larger and smaller holdings; even many of the formerly landless were able to acquire land. Most hospitable were so-called "open" settlements, where weak village and manorial institutions allowed peasants displaced from holdings elsewhere to immigrate.

Initially occupying land as squatters, they later acquitted a small fee to regularize their status and agreed to pay modest rents for their new tenancies.

Open villages sometimes existed in mixed-farming and grain areas, serving as refuges for tenants ejected from enclosed manors. Much more prevalent in these districts, however, were "closed" settlements, where strong landlord control, limited wastes and commons, and the practice of impartible inheritance minimized the growth of both population and the number of farms. Frequently, indeed, holdings declined in number, while the remaining ones grew bigger. In any case, not only were new arrivals unwelcome, but most children of existing tenants had to emigrate. Nonetheless, a degree of economic integration might obtain between neighboring open and closed villages, whereby the former provided casual labor to the large farms in the latter, while each consumed some of the other's produce.

The repercussions of all these developments on industrialization remain a matter of controversy. Some historians argue that agriculture contributed little or nothing. Far from supplying cheap commodities, they note, English farm output fell behind demand as the pace of industrialization and demographic growth picked up during the second half of the eighteenth century, pushing up food and raw material prices. Only massive imports from Ireland and the Continent, which together furnished nearly a sixth of English grain consumption by the early nineteenth century, filled the growing cereals deficit. Nor, according to this school of thought, did the agrarian sector furnish much demand for domestic manufactures. The real wages of agricultural laborers sank after 1750, while landowners bought many imports, luxury handicrafts, and personal services. In addition, farmers became a smaller proportion of the English population: although in absolute numbers the agricultural labor force increased some 10 percent in the eighteenth century, population as a whole jumped at least 70 percent. So whereas farm consumption of manufactures rose by a third between 1700 and 1800, this took only a small proportion of the threefold growth of industrial output. Agriculture was also not a major source of industrial capital. Landlords invested little in manufacturing (or in trade, for that matter), and the amounts they spent on improvements made on farms may have resulted in a net inflow of capital into the agrarian sector.

Yet English agriculture did serve industry in several important respects. For one thing, cheaper food and raw materials were made available in the 1660–1740 period. So for nearly a century – a time when, it should be remembered, the outlook on the Continent was far bleaker – most English people enjoyed rising real per-capita income. Mounting industrial output and prices indicate that this enhanced purchasing power translated into broadening domestic demand for manufactures. It also shaped new consumer expectations that sustained increases in per-capita consumption of industrial goods even when agricultural prices rose again and real incomes stagnated in the second half of the eighteenth century. Across the entire span of crisis and recovery, too, widespread and continuous agricultural innovation released labor to the extent that by the end of the eighteenth century less than one-third of the population in the country as a whole worked the land, as compared with 60 percent around 1700. Some of those displaced migrated to towns: the level of English urbanization climbed from less than 9 percent in 1650 to 20 percent in 1800, when in all Europe England ranked second only to the deurbanizing Low Countries. Others stayed in the countryside, frequently moving to open villages, where over time repeatedly divided holdings became too small for subsistence. In either case, increasing numbers of workers were at hand for industrial work, thereby helping to keep wages low, profits and rates of capital formation high.

Agricultural development and industrialization

Across Europe, agriculture underwent important changes across the period of crisis and recovery. New methods of cultivation, rotation systems, and crops spread widely: it is telling that maize and potatoes, although known since the sixteenth century, were commonly planted only in the eighteenth. If for no other reason than to pay rents, dues, tithes, and taxes, nearly all villagers – even east Elbian serfs – had to sell at least some of their produce or labor. More positively, expanding commercial opportunities, most of all in the neighborhood of the large cities emerging all over Europe, and a broader array of consumer goods drew many farmers into the market. Specialization typically accompanied the expansion of commercial agriculture, as competition forced farmers to focus on crops and livestock for which comparative advantage in the form of soil, climate, or transport facilities best equipped – or least handicapped – their holdings. Practices and communities grounded in subsistence agriculture, already under severe pressure during the long sixteenth century, became increasingly untenable. Rural society polarized more sharply. Property and wealth concentrated among minorities of landlords and peasants; some tenants operated big capitalist farms characterized by considerable and continual investment and the employment of wage labor. The landpoor and landless, their numbers augmented by accelerating demographic growth, found it hard to make ends meet and sought work wherever they could find it.

These trends helped change the face of European farming. The results were far from uniform in speed or extent. Because diverse systems of property and tenurial relations, levels and types of surplus appropriation, and political regimes prevailed across Europe, peasants and lords were disparately willing and able to undertake and sustain innovations that would achieve development as well as growth. In east central Europe, where the personal and property rights of peasants were severely circumscribed, lords' power to extract surplus in a variety of ways from hauling services to leisure-time drinking was correspondingly greater. Under these circumstances, increasing productivity was a priority for neither rural class. Growth that did occur remained as in the past predominantly extensive, whether it involved cultivating heretofore unused land on existing estates or opening virgin soil on new manors with forcibly relocated serfs.

Peasants in western and southern Europe were legally free and generally enjoyed tenurial rights that allowed, indeed spurred, innovation. Yet most of them also encountered fiscally exacting states and powerful landowners who skimmed off many of the resources needed to support agrarian change while returning little to the land. In these respects, there was little to choose among the Mediterranean lands, western Germany, or France. In each, initiatives of all kinds that had begun during the sixteenth century were perpetuated or resumed. But outside a few provinces – generally those already bell-wethers in the previous period – development advanced little. Not only were family farmers chronically short of funds. Large tenants who might have played a strategic role similar to that of their peers in England constantly and unhelpfully hived off into peasant-squeezing.

Agricultural growth and development proceeded furthest in the Low Countries and England. Little shielded – and, by the same token, little trammeled – by village communities or government policies, farmers on adjustable cash leases felt keenly the competitive pressures of the market and thus had every incentive to improve. On their side, landlords possessing full property rights in the land collected tidy rents, although with generally weak seigniorial dues and jurisdictions their levies were rarely so onerous as to stifle their tenants' enterprise. In England and the southern Netherlands, in fact, landowners provided timely assistance in the depths of the seventeenth-century crisis. Different agrarian structures emerged on each side of the North Sea, however, each representing a distinct path to agricultural progress. Large, enclosed capitalist tenancies predominated in England, family farms in the Low Countries. Both were highly productive, but the former was notable for its labor productivity, the latter for the productivity of its land.

Drawing up a balance sheet of agriculture's contributions to industrial-

9 The commercialization of agriculture affected even modest peasants. As the men set off for the fields with spade and (in the background) flock of sheep, the women and children depart for market with milk, eggs, and vegetables.

ization highlights the significance of these disparities, but it also reveals distinct ambiguities within and limits to those contributions in every part of Europe. In the east central region, low productivity combined with formidable impositions to curb incomes and demand for manufactures among the enserfed masses, which the emergence of a thin layer of wealthier peasants could do little to offset. These same factors made for meager food surpluses, curbed the production of raw materials, and – along with neoserfdom – kept a very large proportion of the population on the land. Simultaneously, the declining competitiveness of the region's produce in western and southern European markets cut into many landlords' consumption, which even in palmier days had benefited domestic artisans little because a taste for imported goods was a hallmark of the east central elite style of life.

Peasant consumption was greater in the more productive agricultures of France, Italy, Spain, and western Germany. Still, exploitative states, landlords, and peasant intermediaries checked its expansion. The appropriating governments and classes themselves created pockets of demand, but they were insufficient in amount and kind to spur broad industrialization. The farm sector did supply numerous raw materials – but, as the Mesta demonstrated all too well to Castile, these alone did not necessarily create a sufficient comparative advantage for domestic producers. Sizable districts within these lands boasted levels of agrarian productivity and prosperity equal to the best found anywhere in Europe; in this period, however, they had only faint influence on even their closest domestic neighbors.

Much of the farm population in northwestern Europe was undeniably prosperous, and its agricultures yielded abundant foodstuffs and raw materials. Yet all was not rosy. In the maritime provinces of the Dutch Republic, agricultural specialization led to dependence on increasingly expensive imported grain and oriented demand more towards handicrafts than industrial products. Fragmentation of already small holdings was taking a heavy toll on many family farmers in the southern Netherlands. The English agrarian sector proved unable to keep up with growing demand for cheap food, coming to rely increasingly on grain and cattle from Ireland and Scotland, and as English farmers' share of the population decreased sharply so did their potential to affect consumption strongly. Even the supply of capital to industry, long thought to have distinguished English from Continental agriculture, turns out to have been neither large in scale nor distinctive in nature. English landlords did invest modest amounts in mining ventures, and they helped to finance canals, turnpikes, and other transport improvements. But so did landowners across western and eastern Europe. And in England as on the Continent, the vast majority of capital that flowed out of the agrarian economy streamed into credit instruments, officialdom, and social display.

What every European agriculture proved best at furnishing was labor. This was as true in areas where family holdings remained dominant as in those coming under the sway of capitalist farming. Agrarian commercialization and specialization, burdensome surplus appropriation, subdivision and concentration of land, expulsion in consequence of tenurial restructuring or impartible inheritance, rural population growth – singly or together, these created a growing throng that needed work. Most could not find it, or could not find enough, on farms, whether their own or anyone else's, and therefore sought it in non-agricultural activities, whether fishing, carting, or – most of all – manufacturing. But not every agrarian regime provided a hospitable environment for non-farm employment. Neoserfdom was most restrictive, although sharecropping also constrained labor mobility. Closed English villages, like Holland's specialized agriculture, harried away those not needed to till the soil or tend the livestock. Yet over Europe as a whole – if not in every village – there existed multitudes of under- and unemployed men, women, and children. Would they find jobs? In what areas and industries? Subject to what kinds of production relations? And for what markets?

SUGGESTED READING

Many of the works listed at the end of chap. 3 contain material relevant to this period. For east central Europe, see also E.M. Link, *The Emancipation of the Austrian Peasant, 1740–98* (New York, 1949); W. E. Wright, *Serf, Seigneur and Sovereign. Agrarian Reform in Eighteenth Century Bohemia* (Minneapolis, 1966); L. Zytkowicz, "The Peasant's Farm and the Landlord's Farm in Poland from the Sixteenth Century to the Middle of the Eighteenth Century," *Journal of European Economic History*, vol. 1 (1972); A. Klima, "Agrarian Class Structure and Economic Development in Pre-Industrial Bohemia," *Past and Present*, no. 85 (1979); Witold Kula, "Money and Serfs in Eighteenth Century Poland," in *Peasants in History*, ed. E. J. Hobsbawm (Calcutta, 1980); and Helen Liebel-Weckowicz and F. J. Szabo, "Modernization Forces in Maria Theresa's Peasant Policies, 1740–80," *Histoire Sociale/Social History*, vol. 15 (1982).

R. Zangheri, "The Historical Relationship between Agricultural and Economic Development in Italy," in *Agricultural Change and Economic Development. The Historical Problems*, ed. E. L. Jones and S. J. Woolf (London, 1969), remains valuable for Italy. For a fine case study, see Frank McArdle, *Altopascio* (Cambridge, 1978). Dino Carpanetto and Guiseppe Ricuperati, *Italy in the Age of Reason 1685–1789* (London and New York, Longman, 1987), ch. 2, contains some useful material. Peter Musgrave, *Land and Economy in Baroque Italy: Valpolicella, 1630–1797* (Leicester, 1992), is a polemical work that questions the nature and severity of the rural crisis; it also contains a useful discussion of sources for agrarian history as well as their limits and problems.

The Castilian Crisis of the Seventeenth Century (cited in ch. 3) is especially useful for Spain's time of troubles. See also Pierre Vilar, "Agricultural Progress and the Economic Background in Eighteenth-Century Catalonia," *Economic History Review*, 2nd ser., vol. 11 (1958–59). In addition to general histories cited in previous chapters, the early sections of David Sabean, *Property, Production, and Family in Neckerhausen, 1700–1870* (Cambridge, 1990) help explain one region in western Germany.

M. Morineau, "Was there an Agricultural Revolution in Eighteenth Century France?" in *Essays in French Economic History*, ed. R. Cameron (Homewood, Ill., 1970), continues to provide a provocative starting point for France. For an important case study, see Jonathan Dewald, *Pont-St-Pierre 1398–1789. Lordship, Community, and Capitalism in Early Modern France* (Berkeley, 1987). The works of Robert Forster argue that nobles were active, careful, and enterprising landlords rather than impoverished rentiers; see his "The Provincial Noble. A Reappraisal," *American Historical Review*, vol. 68 (1963), and "Obstacles to Economic Growth in Eighteenth Century France," *American Historical Review*, vol. 75 (1969–70). P. M. Jones, "Rural Bourgeoisie of the Southern Massif Central. A Contribution to the Study of the Social Structure of Ancien Régime France," *Social History*, vol. 4 (1979), focuses on intermediaries between lords and peasants. E. Labrousse, "A View of the Allocation of Agricultural Expansion among Social Classes," *Review*, vol. 2 (1978), examines property ownership and wages in the eighteenth century.

Two important essays in *European Peasants and their Markets*, ed. W. N. Parker and E. L. Jones (Princeton, 1975): Franklin Mendels, "Agriculture and Peasant Industry in Eighteenth Century Flanders," and Jan de Vries, "Peasant Demand Patterns and Economic Development. Friesland 1550–1750," focus on the Low Countries. H. K. Roessingh, "Tobacco Growing in Holland in the Seventeenth and Eighteenth Centuries," *Acta Historiae Neerlandica*, vol. 11 (1978), and J. Bieleman, "Rural Change in the Dutch Province of Drenthe in the Seventeenth and Eighteenth Centuries," *Agricultural History Review*, vol. 33 (1985), summarize their authors' longer books published in Dutch.

The literature on England is immense and constantly growing. To begin, consult *The Agrarian History of England and Wales*. Vol. V, *1640–1750*, ed. Joan Thirsk, 2 vols. (Cambridge, 1985), and Vol. VI, *1750–1850*, ed. G. E. Mingay (Cambridge, 1989). For the best brief account, see J. V. Beckett, *The Agricultural Revolution* (Oxford, 1990). For a sampling of recent works, see C. E. Searle, "Custom, Class Conflict and Agrarian Capitalism: the Cumbrian Customary Economy in the Eighteenth Century," *Past and Present*, no. 110 (1986); George R. Boyer, "England's Two Agricultural Revolutions," *Journal of Economic History*, vol. 53 (1993); J. M. Neeson, *Commoners: Common Right, Enclosure and Social Change in England, 1700–1820* (Cambridge, 1993). Good overviews have been written by P. K. O'Brien, "Agriculture and the Industrial Revolution," *Economic History Review*, 2nd ser., vol. 30 (1977), and Robert Allen, "Agriculture during the Industrial Revolution," in *The Economic History of Britain since 1700*, ed. R. Floud and D. McCloskey, second edn (Cambridge, 1994), vol. I.

Finally, some representative contemporary documents are to be found in *Documents of European Economic History*. Vol. I. *The Process of Industrialization 1750–1870*, ed. S. Pollard and C. Holmes (London, 1968), chs. 1 and 7.

Europe's industrial evolution in the later seventeenth and eighteenth centuries built largely on existing foundations, but in the process many were quantitatively and qualitatively transformed. The agrarian sector continued to impinge strongly on manufacturing, both in terms of demand for and, because the rural population increasingly provided the industrial labor force, in terms of the supply of goods. Governments that had long influenced industry now took up more conscious and aggressive policies. The expanding colonial empires established by the Atlantic powers were subsumed into a functioning world economy centered on northwestern Europe. While textiles remained the major European industry, within it linens, mixed fabrics, and cottons burgeoned, unleashing far-reaching change throughout the entire economy. In tandem with new consumption habits and expectations – many the outgrowth of distinctive types of urbanization – a rising stream of less expensive consumer goods from straw hats to cuckoo clocks became a flood that swept onto domestic and foreign markets. Rural manufacturing expanded massively: the countryside assumed industrial primacy in many parts of Europe, and nowhere more than in the northwestern lands.

The impressive industrial advance of the age came about mainly because existing technologies and modes of organization were more intensively exploited. By the end of the period, however, a few industries in a few areas were about to embark upon the process of restructuring and mechanizing factory production that we know as the Industrial Revolution. This chapter tells how, within an ever more capitalist Europe, rejuvenated and novel sources of demand now felt on a global scale, state regulations and programs, and vastly extended rural industrialization laid the groundwork for – and the boundaries to – this watershed.

Consumers, capitals, constraints, and colonies

European manufactures spread spatially and socially both at home and around the world during the long eighteenth century. Old World demand remained preponderant in scale and scope. But in contrast to the long sixteenth century, overseas sales helped overcome limits on consumption within Europe. Not only did the world economy prevent the return of crisis, it also provided signal impetus to industrialization.

Both because food remained the largest category of expenditure in popular budgets, and because farming remained far and away Europeans' single biggest occupation, the state of agriculture significantly shaped the state of industry. Well into the first half of the eighteenth century, stagnant or falling foodstuff prices – of cereals most of all – in a context of sticky or even slightly rising pay levels boosted real wages and, in particular, enhanced the share of urban and rural wage-earners' income available for discretionary spending. It appears that they disbursed about half the gain on manufactures. At the same time, the ongoing expansion of market-oriented agriculture obliged more farmers to buy items they previously had made or which they now needed to stay abreast of their fellows.

Urbanization disproportionately boosted demand. Although the proportion of citydwellers in the population as a whole only inched up from 8 percent (1650) to 10 percent (1800), their absolute numbers nearly doubled in a time of accelerating demographic advance that saw the 75 million Europeans of 1650 become 123 million by 1800. Even more important, the number of cities with 80,000 or more people, and the number of people living in them, increased more than twofold over that century and a half; Atlantic ports, naval stations, capitals, and new industrial centers also burgeoned. These large cities required heavy infrastructural investment, providing extra stimulus to iron and other metallurgical trades. They also fostered the improvement of commercial structures and means of transportation, and even though these were constructed primarily to move grain and bulky energy sources more efficiently, they widely lowered industry's transactions costs. Spreading networks of canals and canalized rivers brought the advantages of cheap internal transport that the Dutch Republic had long enjoyed to other areas, for example, helping to integrate regional and inter-regional markets.

Capital cities also attracted fashion-conscious elites that consumed disproportionate amounts of luxury goods. On a bigger scale than in the long sixteenth century, the level of demand often became great enough to warrant introducing cost-reducing specializations and divisions of labor that by lowering prices contributed to ongoing market growth. Correlatively, the diffusion of urban styles powerfully molded demand over broad areas. London remained the extreme example of this kind of cultural authority. By the early eighteenth century, 11 percent of all English people lived there and many more directly experienced London life, whether as temporary migrants or as visitors on political, commercial, legal, or social business. Their exposure to the great city helped dissolve traditional consumption patterns and generate new ones as former luxuries became necessities. No other city was nearly so dominant demographically. Yet Continental capitals, too, tended to serve as tastemakers once the consumer society pioneered in England began to appear elsewhere in Europe. Paris housed at most 3 percent of French people, yet it boasted numerous artisans who made fine goods or put the finishing touches to merchandise that provincial workers had roughed out. Specializing in ornamentation, the Paris clothing trades depended on and thus strongly encouraged constant fashion changes and their widespread adoption well beyond its borders. Paris also turned out a proliferating array of cheap knockoffs of upper-class luxury items – umbrellas, canes, watches, fans, and other "populuxe" goods, as one historian has termed them.

Some of the most influential consumption innovations travelled upward rather than percolating down. In later seventeenth-century England, the rage for clothing made of calico emerged first in the urban middling strata, who used it as a cheap substitute for brocade and silk. Only after the directors of the East India Company consciously mounted a publicity campaign – among other things, they gave King Charles II large monetary "gifts" so he would wear a calico waistcoat – was aristocratic disdain overcome. Once it was, a more casual upper-class style that originated in England became a foundation of the calico industry throughout Europe.

New means of cultural diffusion nurtured new habits of consumption. Printed advertisements were being posted in London in the seventeenth century; by the eighteenth, they had appeared in Paris and elsewhere on the Continent. Newspapers, which from the start prominently featured advertisements for all sorts of commodities, were founded first in metropolitan centers and then, beginning in the early eighteenth century, in the provinces and colonies. Around 1753, when Europe's population was no more than 100 million, annual newspaper circulation is thought to have surpassed 7 million. An increasing number of magazines that prominently featured fashion plates and reports also appeared. Printed matter circulated more expeditiously thanks to the organization of regular postal services among many more cities than ever before. From 1660, for instance, mail boats shuttled between Amsterdam and London twice a week and riders joined Amsterdam with Hamburg, while Paris already had a semi-weekly service to several major provincial towns. Ideas and goods were sped on their way by road improvements that on main routes cut travel time in half between the later seventeenth and later eighteenth centuries.

The desires thereby conveyed could more readily be satisfied now that itinerant pedlars were being supplemented by a thickening network of retail shops: in England they trebled in number across the first half of the eighteenth century. Making an ever-widening range of goods available on a permanent basis – and providing an even more sublime abundance by special order to their wholesalers in the big cities – and engaging in competitive pricing, they were critical to both the quantitative and qualitative growth of consumption.

Constituted and diffused in these ways, aspirations for increasing amounts of material possessions spread among many Europeans, perhaps inducing what Jan de Vries has called an "industrious revolution." According to this interpretation, in the long eighteenth century house-holds began to reject the typical pre-industrial pattern of aiming for a customary standard of living (which entailed making many of the textiles, eating utensils, furniture, and other goods that they used) and, once having attained it, opting for leisure rather than further toil. Instead, they sought additional income in order to satisfy rising expectations for manufactures that they bought, and they maintained this new preference even when real wages began to dip in the second half of the eighteenth century. Thus they raised the intensity of their labor by slogging away for longer hours and during previously slack periods, and they set to work family members not heretofore employed in industry. Some of the households thus motivated to augment their purchasing power were those of city artisans. But many more were found in the countryside, preemi-nently among smallholders, cottagers, and landless laborers. Such con-sumers seldom bought clocks and china, of course. The market for non-essential goods developed most among the urban middle classes and substantial commercial farmers. Poorer families did, however, buy a greater variety of clothing and household items, thereby ensuring that the manufacture of cheap fabrics, metalwares, pottery, and the like would be major growth sectors within European industry. In every group, it appears, women were frequently the pacesetters in developing and accepting new consumption patterns.

Finally, government spending – most of it, as in the past, devoted to the military – enhanced demand for a parade of goods from bricks to boots. Navies had particularly important effects in this era of colonial empire-building. Employment at English naval shipyards rose at least fourfold from 1650 to 1750, while the complete overhaul of the Spanish navy in the eighteenth century led to the opening of new armaments plants and encouraged Basque iron founders to adopt improved bloomeries that raised output and quality.

Despite all these stimuli, growth of domestic European markets was slowed by several substantial obstacles. On much of the Continent, to begin with, interstate and internal levies impeded the movement of goods, increasing costs and prices. Products travelling on the Rhine, for instance, owed numerous tolls to the many states lining the riverbanks. At several sovereign cities they had to be unloaded and offered for sale; only then could they be shipped on, and only in boats operated by members of the towns' guilds. Again, several of France's peripheral provinces, including rich industrialized parts of Flanders conquered in the later seventeenth century, were deemed "foreign" for fiscal purposes. Upon entering the central "Five Great Farms" provinces, goods made in these reputedly foreign parts had to pay duties similar to those imposed on manufactures from lands outside His Majesty's dominions. To be sure, in some lands internal tolls were reduced or eliminated in the course of the eighteenth century. At almost the same stroke, however, high tariffs or outright prohibitions were instituted on interstate imports of manufactures. Although customs duties between Hungary and the rest of the Habsburg Empire were cut drastically in 1754, for example, and two decades later nearly all internal duties were abolished among the various Austrian provinces, tariffs on foreign manufactures jumped so much that many items were effectively excluded.

In the second half of the eighteenth century, moreover, the limits of agricultural growth began to be felt once again. Even in England, farm output began to trail behind demographic increase, pushing up prices and thus dampening demand among wage-earners and others dependent on food purchases; this was only partly offset by healthier incomes among landlords and market-oriented farmers able to stay ahead of rent increases. For the most important crimp on demand across Europe as a whole remained the levies on the majority of the population that tilled the land. Albeit in varying proportions, taxes, rents, dues, and tithes encumbered popular consumption. The weakness of "mass" demand was a persistent problem in eighteenth-century Europe, threatening to abort eighteenth-century expansion just as it had in the long sixteenth century. But this time another factor was at play – substantial overseas demand – that helped sustain European producers. So although Europeans remained the paramount customers for each other's manufactures – as late as the 1790s, three-quarters of all European exports went to other Europeans – non-European markets were becoming ever more significant to European industry.

During the long sixteenth century, European trade with other continents had been principally speculative in nature, except for textiles sold in Spanish America and the Levant. The demand it generated had been peripheral to industry in all but a few areas, and in no instance was it substantial enough to take up the slack when European markets contracted in the seventeenth century. In those dark decades, however, many European states sought to find and colonize overseas markets that would jump-start their own depressed economies. Even the tiny duchy of Kurland in the eastern Baltic briefly planted its flag on the West Indian island of Tobago and in the Gambia (West Africa).

In the event, only a few European states were to build colonial empires. But from the later seventeenth century many more profited as trade along previously established overseas routes intensified. This build-up was facilitated by – and further stimulated – commercial advances such as cheaper shipping, superior information, and the supplanting of bullion transfers by bills of exchange. America, Africa, and Asia took 55 percent of English manufacturing exports in 1772–74, as against 16 percent around 1700, a more than sevenfold rise in value, whereas Europe absorbed just 13 percent more. The same overseas regions accounted for 40 percent of France's manufacturing exports in 1787–89, up from 6 percent in 1716–20; the Caribbean alone bought thirteen times more. Although such statistics have been compiled only for England and France, which gained the most from this trade, we know that mounting quantities of Silesian linens, Bohemian glass, Valencian silks, and much else also went abroad.

The most important sphere of the European-directed world economy encompassed both sides of the Atlantic. A sharply delineated division of labor emerged among Europe, Africa, and the New World, which became knit together by one or another variant of the so-called "triangular trade." In the most highly developed version, initially a Dutch creation of the second third of the seventeenth century, European merchants exchanged cloth, metal goods, weapons, and other manufactures in West Africa for slaves, who were dispatched across the Atlantic to work on West Indian and mainland American plantations. There they grew sugar, tobacco, cotton, rice, and other agricultural products that were carried to Europe for processing in newly developed industries; at the same time, many New World colonies, forced to specialize in commercial agriculture, depended on Europe for manufactures. Secondary triangular systems also emerged, involving the European colonies in northern North America. They supplied both foodstuffs (notably grain, meat, and fish) to southern and island plantations, and fur, wood, and fish to Europe, while consuming European industrial goods. Some New England merchants took the further step of shipping rum to West Africa, exchanging it for slaves who were taken to West Indian sugar plantations, and then sending molasses back to New England where it was distilled into rum. Because this trading network diverted sugar from processors in the mother country and also cut into sales of British manufactures in

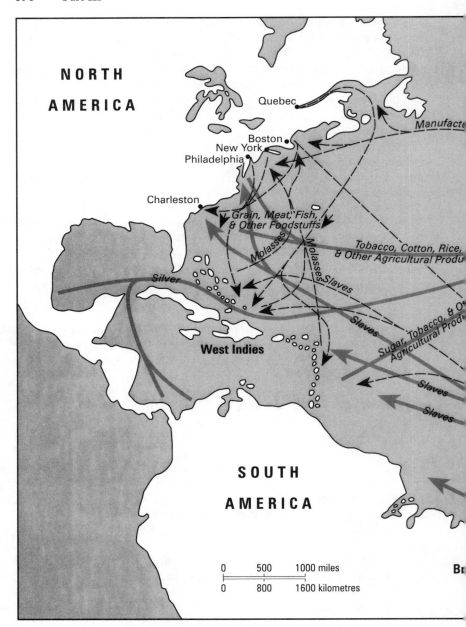

3 Triangular trades

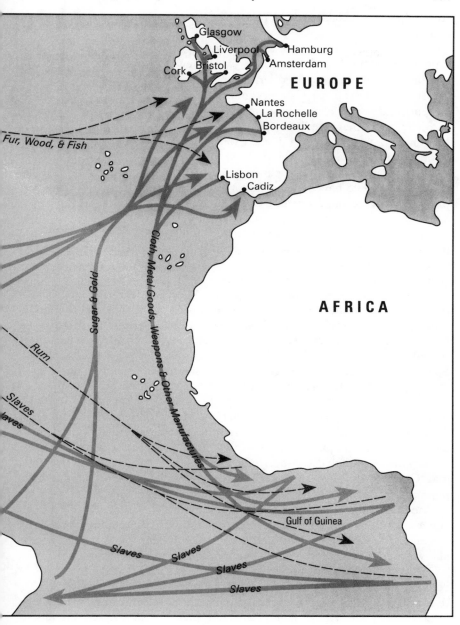

Glasgow
Liverpool
Hamburg
Cork
Bristol
Amsterdam

EUROPE

Nantes
La Rochelle
Bordeaux

Fur, Wood, & Fish

Lisbon
Cadiz

Cloth, Metal Goods, Weapons & Other Manufactures

AFRICA

Sugar & Gold

Rum

Slaves

Slaves

Gulf of Guinea

Slaves   *Slaves*

Slaves

Slaves

Africa, British officials tried to break it up, but their success was far from complete.

Central to all versions of the triangular trade – and thus to the functioning of the Atlantic economy – were New World plantations. First established in the eastern Mediterranean, where it was further elaborated (most likely on the basis of slavery) in the Crusader kingdoms during the eleventh and twelfth centuries, plantation agriculture was later transferred to Sicily and other Mediterranean islands. In the later Middle Ages, Iberian conquerors carried it further west, to newly settled Madeira, the Azores, and the Canary Islands, and thereafter to the New World. Practicing labor-intensive methods of cultivation that underwent little change that would have raised productivity, plantations increased output primarily by extension, opening up fresh land and taking on additional workers.

Both to clear land taken by violence, guile, and – occasionally – purchase, and then to cultivate it profitably, planters needed a large and inexpensive labor force. Securing one involved experimentation; African slaves did not predominate until well after 1650. Free wage labor proved too costly and recalcitrant, so it quickly became clear that onerous plantation toil would require some degree of coercion. Originally, Iberian settlers turned to Amerindians. From the beginning, Portuguese colonists favored bondage, at first using native slaves; then, when labor demands soared while Indian numbers dropped, Africans. With few exceptions, Spaniards preferred a tributary system known as *encomienda* – another import from the Old World where it had been imposed on the Moors during the *Reconquista*. By its terms, the Spanish crown granted settlers land and rights to exact both material goods (encomienda) and labor (*repartimiento*) from Indians; in return, the grantees were supposed to protect and Christianize the Indians and allow them to cultivate subsistence plots. Although the system long survived in modified form in South and Central America, in the Caribbean harshly overworked native populations quickly died off and encomienda was scrapped.

One alternative, which found favor mainly in the West Indies and North America, was to employ indentured servants from Europe; they bulked largest in the labor force during the seventeenth century. Although not all were destined for agriculture, much less plantations, some 350,000–375,000 white bound servants entered the British American colonies alone between 1580 and 1775; they represented almost two-thirds of the total white immigration during those two centuries. Perhaps a tenth as many left France, mainly for the Antilles. Yet indentured servants (known in French as *engagés*) also fell short of meeting plantation labor demands. Many died before their terms were up – according to one

French royal official, more than eleven of every twelve engagés perished while under indenture – and the survivors had to be replaced when their contracts were finished after three to seven years. Most important of all, the pool of recruits shrank as the European economies revived.

That same revival also quickened demand for colonial agricultural staples or "groceries," as customs accounts classified them. Across the long eighteenth century, they became central to Europeans' new consumption expectations, at first among the well-to-do, then more widely. As Europeans developed a collective sweet tooth and a liking for rum, sugar consumption soared: British purchases rose an astounding 2,500 percent between 1650 and 1800. The use of tobacco likewise expanded by leaps and bounds thanks both to dropping prices and to its acceptance as the mark of a new and desirable sociability. Industrial raw materials – notably indigo and cotton – also became important plantation crops. It was to meet growing demand that planters across the Americas turned ever more completely to slaves from Africa. There had been some slaves in New World colonies since they were founded. But from the late seventeenth century the plantation colonies became slave societies. The proportion of free farmers in the population, and their share of farm output, decreased dramatically, and agricultural labor became closely identified with black slaves. Admittedly, in the eighteenth century Chesapeake Bay planters also bought transported white English convict laborers: for just one-third the price of an African slave, the labor of a felon could be purchased for seven or fourteen years, depending upon the seriousness of the crime committed. Yet the 20,000 men and women thus supplied were just a drop in the bucket compared to soaring plantation demand for workers.

Between 1450, when they first became active on a large scale, and 1600, European slavers took many Africans to Europe. But thereafter their destinations were overwhelmingly New World colonies from Brazil (which alone received 2.5 million slaves in the seventeenth and eighteenth centuries) north to the Chesapeake Bay area on the North American mainland. From 1450 to 1800 the Americas received at least 7.5 million slaves from Africa, three-quarters of whom arrived during the eighteenth century. Taking into account deaths during the ocean crossing, the infamous "Middle Passage" when up to a quarter of the human cargoes perished, slavers actually bought and shipped as many as 10 million Africans.

Swedes, Brandenburgers, Danes, and (increasingly) North Americans participated in the trade, but at least in the eighteenth century the chief slave merchants were from Atlantic Europe: the English (who accounted for two-fifths of the total), Portuguese (about 30 percent), French (one-fifth), and Dutch (6 percent). England's preponderance was based both on its extensive and expanding colonial empire and on its possession, after 1713, of the lucrative *asiento*. This was a contract by which the Spanish government leased to an important person – usually, and unsurprisingly, a Castilian aristocrat – the right to sell licenses allowing merchants of a given country to import slaves into Spanish colonies. Previously, the asiento had been held briefly by French and, for much longer, by Portuguese slavers, who even after losing it remained prominent because of their extensive network of African trading posts.

The slave agriculture of the Americas resembled east central European neoserfdom in that both fused the raising of commodities for the market with coercive production relations, resulting in economic systems that were neither fully capitalist nor wholly seigniorial. Just as the owners of serf estates sought to augment the marketable surplus they controlled by boosting labor services, moreover, so did plantation owners attempt to raise output by reducing slaves' free time, lengthening the workday, and abridging or eliminating midday breaks even in the hottest weather. Nevertheless, slave agriculture was more completely integrated into the developing western European economies than neoserfdom was. In the latter, after all, peasants made many of their own craft goods and saw their agricultural output become increasingly less vital to western consumers as the eighteenth century went on. New World plantations, in contrast, sold the greater part of their mounting output of groceries to and bought many consumption goods from the Old World. Thus they at once relied on and nourished the emergent capitalism of western Europe.

But just what and how much did they contribute? More generally, how valuable were colonial empires to European industrialization? According to one prominent view, rooted ultimately in Marx, gains from exploitative slave-based agriculture and colonial trade were central to the process of original accumulation that provided the funds needed for the triumph of capitalism and, eventually, mechanized factories within Europe.

Although this interpretation has sustained heavy attack, much evidence can be adduced to support it. Admittedly, voyages often ended in shipwreck or capture by pirates or privateers, and plantation agriculture proved risky enough to bankrupt many owners. But English slavers, at least, averaged profits of 8–10 percent, and booming European demand for colonial products created additional opportunities for ample gain by merchants and plantation owners. As always, much of their revenue found its way into landed estates, conspicuous consumption, and government debt, or, among traders, was plowed back into commerce and allied activities like marine insurance. Nevertheless, some colonial merchants, at least, did put funds into many types of manufacturing, often encouraged by the so-called "store system," in which manufactures were traded directly for colonial raw materials. Around Glasgow, the tobacco entrepôt of Europe, they invested substantially in tanneries, slitting mills, forges, sugar refining, sailcloth making, coal and copper mining, linens, and eventually cottons. Merchants themselves, however, did not become industrialists. Rather, they put money into industry at the behest of entrepreneurs but usually had little to do with the operation of the businesses in which they had invested.

The bulk of industrial capital came, nevertheless, not from colonial but from domestic sources. Even in Great Britain, which captured the lion's share of overseas trade profits, less than a fifth of capital for all types of investment came from gains realized in intercontinental trade. The Atlantic economy mattered most for European industries because of markets and raw materials rather than capital. Africa alone took more than 10 percent of total French exports in the later eighteenth century, and nearly 5 percent of British. Dutch and English records indicate that textiles comprised about half the goods sent to Africa, along with appreciable amounts of metal wares, weapons, and distilled spirits. In the Americas, despite the growth of colonial textile, shipbuilding, and other industries (at times in defiance of laws designed to protect home producers), slaves, Amerindians, and especially free colonists consumed much larger and growing amounts of European manufactures. English exports of manufactures grew ninefold between 1699–1701 and 1772–74. France's exports to her West Indian and North American colonies expanded eightfold across the eighteenth century: in 1787, a third of French manufacturing exports went to the New World, including sizable amounts destined for Spanish colonies.

Colonial demand had a salutary effect on woollens, silk, and cotton trades across Europe. Europe's linen industries were particularly oriented to the colonies. To cite just one example, nine of every ten *bretañas* (linens) from Brittany went to Spain, whence most were re-exported to Spanish America. But the colonies bought much else besides cloth: everything from hats to hoes, paint to pewter, brass buckles to mirrors. The trade with Africa that increasingly accompanied colonial commerce likewise benefited European industries, especially metallurgy and textiles. Already in the early sixteenth century, Portugal had made cheap woollens for sale to African slavers, and from about 1700, on a much larger scale, England wove cottons and other light fabrics for the same market.

For their part, the colonies produced raw materials for extremely profitable and rapidly growing processing industries within Europe, particularly its northwestern quadrant: in England, their value quadrupled between 1699–1701 and 1772–74. By the 1770s, sugar accounted for 60 percent of England's imports from America, perhaps half of France's. The 9 million pounds of tobacco sent to Europe in the 1660s had become at least 220 million pounds in 1775; each year around 1750, English hatters alone took at least 80,000 beaver furs, double the 1700 figure; and from the 1760s, New World cotton output boomed, soon surpassing the Levant and Asia as Europe's main suppliers.

Asia, too, became a market for European goods, albeit never on the scale of the Atlantic. Around 1700, only 3 percent of English exports went to Asia, as against 12 percent to the Americas and Africa; in the early 1770s, the shares were 8 percent and 43 percent, and England ranked ahead of any other European nation. Still, Asia took on the average four and a half times as many English manufactures after 1763 as during the preceding half century. Moreover, the composition of exports dramatically altered. Whereas before 72 percent had consisted of bullion, 28 percent of manufactures, now the proportions were reversed: 27 percent bullion, 73 percent goods.

By the late eighteenth century, European manufactures had penetrated heretofore peripheral or recently created markets from domestic popular strata to overseas colonies. This increasingly broad and global reach lent a growing dynamism to European industries both old and new – to Lyon silk, Flemish linens, and Bohemian glass, as well as to Zurich cottons, Ghent-refined sugar, Swedish iron, and Stockport hats. Not all existing crafts were reborn nor did all new foundations bloom. But across Europe, industrial activity quickened, encouraging experiments with new methods and structures of production. Governments figured prominently among the progenitors of these attempts.

State and industry

For centuries, political authorities throughout Europe had intervened in many aspects of industry to regulate quality, assure raw materials supplies, help control labor, and occasionally – in strategic sectors – to direct production in state-owned workplaces like the Venetian Arsenal. Before about 1650, most of these activities were undertaken by municipalities (or, in Italy and Germany, by city-states) and the guilds located within them. Central governments might step in with general directives on, say, wages or guild organization, but their attention was sporadic at best. From the mid-seventeenth century, however, states intruded much more systematically. Sometimes they were responding to depressed economic conditions; at times, they acted for reasons of prestige. But with increasing frequency and determination, monarchs and statesmen took on an activist economic role in order to build up the military and financial strength of their regimes. Convinced that national wealth and power were intimately and mutually connected, they sought to promote both by means of economic development. In so doing, they borrowed from – and helped to elaborate – a body of ideas, assumptions, and practices labeled, since the time of Adam Smith (who castigated them for obstructing the free play of market forces), "the mercantile system" or "mercantilism."

Mercantilist measures were designed to help a state capture a larger share of international trade and augment bullion supplies at the expense of its competitors, notably by expanding exports and reducing imports of manufactures. In pursuit of these goals, governments not only raised barriers against foreign finished goods, but aided the development of domestic industries and the formation of protected markets for their products. In these ways, they attempted to create comparative advantages for their own industries or, if nothing else, hinder those of rivals. States also championed industrialization to provide jobs for what elites considered dangerously disorderly throngs of the underemployed – who to boot allegedly wasted, by receiving charity, resources that could better be used for the ends of power and plenty.

Tariffs and outright bans that kept out manufactures from abroad while attempting to enhance the inflow of raw materials and to create captive markets were the most effective and widely adopted mercantilist steps; what constrained inter-European trade fostered industrialization within the market units thereby constituted. England pioneered such policies to the advantage of its own woollens industry (see chap. 4); with the Navigation Acts of 1651 and 1660 and subsequent laws it extended a system of monopolies across industries and across the Atlantic. The empire became an enormous free-trade zone for English manufactures and their prime source of raw materials.

Scotland's experience after its union with England in 1707 gave it equal access to protected markets and raw materials demonstrates the powerful impact of the empire on industries in the metropoles. Previously limited by the poverty and small size (just over 1 million inhabitants) of the domestic market, in the eighteenth century Scottish textile industries throve as the rapidly expanding American colonies became their chief overseas customers. Similarly, the Navigation Acts helped to funnel tobacco to Glasgow, which soon became the tobacco entrepôt and a leading processing center for all Europe. But even on the smaller scale available to other countries, barriers against imports of competing goods proved helpful to home industries. In the mid-eighteenth-century southern Netherlands, for example, duties on Dutch, French, and Prussian goods were instrumental to the flowering of trades such as sugar refining, flannel making, and the weaving of mixed cotton–linen fabrics.

The most successful example of protectionist industrial development was the result of ramparts directed not against other European goods but against an Asian import. In the later seventeenth and early eighteenth centuries, Indian calicoes took European markets by storm: from only a few thousand pieces around 1650, English imports surged to 860,000 pieces in the early eighteenth century, Dutch to 100,000. In the face of this deluge, pressure from European textile producers struck a sympathetic chord among mercantilist-inspired officials concerned by the outflow of silver, since at that time Europe bought much more in Asia (including spices, pepper, tea, and coffee as well as textiles) than it sold there. In response, many countries progressively restricted, or banned outright, imports of calicoes.

The linen industry was a major beneficiary of these acts: shipments of Irish linen rose from virtually nothing in 1700 to 40 million pieces a century later; Scottish output grew from 2 million yards (1728) to 13 million (1770); Galician linen output doubled between 1750 and 1800. Textile printing also blossomed: by the 1760s, Barcelona was the largest center in Europe. Initially, printers used imported plain calicoes, but increasingly they switched to mixed fabrics or pure cottons woven within Europe, for cotton manufacturing throve as an import substitution industry once Indian calicoes had been debarred. Annual imports of raw cotton woven within England grew slowly from 1.1 million pounds around 1700 to 4.2 million in 1772, then exploded to 41.8 million by 1800. French cotton and cotton–linen output rose by an average of 3.8 percent a year between 1700–10 and 1780–89; by 1790, more than 170 places in France made these fabrics. By that date, in fact, few countries in Europe were without a cotton industry.

Through empire-building and market protections, the English state created an auspicious environment for industry, but it left development essentially to private initiative. On the Continent, however, the advance of industry often entailed a more direct and active government role. This might take the form of monetary subsidies, tax concessions, prizes and monopolies for inventors, payments to immigrant skilled artisans, abolition of restrictive guild practices, or on occasion state ownership and operation of enterprises. France under Jean-Baptiste Colbert (1619–83), minister and advisor to King Louis XIV (reigned 1643–1715), and Sweden under Charles XI (ruled 1660–97) were particularly energetic in the later seventeenth century; Frederick the Great's Prussia (1740–86) and the Habsburg Empire of Maria Theresa, her husband Francis I, and their son Joseph II, whose reigns extended from 1740 to 1790, in the eighteenth.

Numerous trades received benefits, but military, prestige, and luxury industries were most favored. They compiled a mixed record, but probably fared better than most subsequent commentators have been willing to concede. It is not, admittedly, hard to discover such industries that made overpriced, poor quality, or superfluous goods. Although a contemporary claimed that "experts prefer Berlin porcelain to all others" because Frederick the Great "put everything in train for making it [the Prussian royal porcelain works] more perfect,"[1] the enterprise had to resort to bizarre expedients to get rid of its stock. Among other things, all Jews were required to pay a sum to the factory when they were wed; in return, they received whatever surplus goods the factory wished to unload. Moses Mendelssohn (1729–86), silk merchant turned noted philosopher, thereby acquired twenty life-sized porcelain apes. Again, Swedish woollens and silk employment dropped by half between 1756–60 and 1771–75 after state subsidies were reduced, for the cloth was so badly made that few would buy it.

It is equally easy, however, to find striking success stories: the St-Gobain (France) glassworks that employed 230 workers at its foundation in 1665 but had 1,500 in 1700 and has continued to this day; or Berlin's silk and velvet industry, another pet project of Frederick the Great, which had 460 looms in 1767, 835 in 1771, 1,750 in 1778. In many German states, too, it was only by dint of partial or complete government ownership that mines gained access to the capital needed to sink deep shafts. Thus the failure of some assisted industries is not necessarily an indictment of aid, but may indicate that it was undiscriminating or insufficient. Numerous industrial initiatives, in fact, came to grief when needed funds were diverted to warfare. Others foundered because they clung to outmoded products or production structures.

Most often, such enterprises are faulted for wastefully diverting resources that could have been employed more efficiently elsewhere. It is not, however, evident that other opportunities went begging for lack of the capital, labor, or raw materials dedicated to the state-assisted enterprises. Nor is it clear that losses outweighed gains in the industries that were established or reinvigorated. Even in England, industries benefited significantly from an imperial framework set up, enlarged, and defended by the state. In the heavily agrarian societies on the Continent, most of which not only lacked comparable empires but were burdened by narrow consumer demand, real or perceived shortages of capital, insufficient technical skills, and a paucity of entrepreneurship, nascent industrial enterprise seems often to have needed assistance on a scale that govern-

[1] Friedrich Nicolai, *Beschreibung der königlichen Residenzstädte Berlin und Potsdam* (1769), in *Documents of European Economic History*, ed. S. Pollard and C. Holmes (London, 1968), vol. I, p. 61.

ments alone could provide. Those who made government economic policy sought primarily to enhance the military, financial, and political standing of their states. Yet in so doing, they helped to expand the scope of European industrialization beyond what market forces alone could have achieved.

Proto-industry and proto-factory

As villagers from Castile to Silesia, the Orkneys to Sicily, were drawn into industrial production, a large and increasing proportion of the commodity cornucopia was made in the countryside: the trend already dominant in England now spread to the rest of Europe. But in contrast to the long sixteenth century, when the rhythms of Continental urban and rural crafts strongly correlated, rural industries during the long eighteenth century typically outdistanced their urban counterparts, often at the latter's expense. Milan had 600 silk reeling and twisting looms in 1635 but just 95 in 1781; in the countryside, their numbers shot up from 142 to 1,448. Linen production in villages around Valenciennes (northern France) doubled between 1730 and 1780, while the industry effectively disappeared from the city; whereas Lille's light drapery output fell five-sixths between 1700 and the 1770s, nearby Roubaix's rose sevenfold.

At least since Marx, for whom putting-out trades in the countryside during the period of what he called "manufactures" were essential to capitalist industrialization, scholars have recognized the significance of this golden age of rural industry. But during the past several decades, the approach known as "proto-industrialization" has generated a wealth of new insights and interpretations. As initially formulated by the economic historian Franklin Mendels, proto-industrialization was characterized by the production of goods for distant, often international, markets by peasant-manufacturers; it grew out of but was distinct from traditional cottage industries for local consumption. Pursuing agricultural activities that did not fully occupy their time, rural folk formed a cheap and elastic labor supply because they could combine farming with the working up of raw materials put out by merchant entrepreneurs; as economists would say, the "opportunity cost" of their labor was low, for they did not have to abandon other remunerative work to take on industrial employment. As proto-industries spread, some districts came to specialize in manufacturing; others nearby focused on commercial agriculture. Thus developed dynamic and symbiotic regional economies, organized and financed from towns, where rurally made proto-industrial goods were finished and sold. Eventually, rising labor, distribution, and supervisory costs brought growth to a halt, but by then proto-industries had provided capital, technical knowledge, a proletarianized and expanding labor force, entrepreneurs with marketing and managerial skills, and some of the consumer demand required for mechanized factory industrialization.

Every aspect of Mendels' theory has been subject to searching critique, elaboration, and reformulation, from which little has emerged unscathed. Some commentators object to the evolutionary models and teleological premises underlying the concept: proto-industrialization is to be understood, Mendels proclaimed in the subtitle of his germinal 1972 essay, as "the first phase of the industrialization process." More frequently, the hypothesis is faulted for trying to squeeze diverse if related phenomena into too narrow a conceptual mold. It is now clear that while a new departure in many places, rural industrialization elsewhere was the renewal of a centuries-old cycle, albeit on a much bigger scale that drew the populations of entire districts into industrial work. Although the growth of international and interregional trade in manufactures is best documented, proto-industries often produced for nearby consumers as well: the critical issue was not the location of demand but the fact that it was supplied by market-oriented putting-out producers. Similarly, although more pronounced in the countryside, proto-industrialization could be urban, too, for the underlying dynamic was the search for cheap and docile labor, wherever it might be found. Nor did proto-industries reign alone: in countryside as well as in town they co-existed with a variety of industrial structures, including the Kaufsystem and proto-factories. Finally, proto-industrialization bore a contingent rather than a necessary relationship with later industrial development; any specific region was as likely to return to an agricultural vocation as to see the rise of mechanized factories.

Despite these criticisms, the concept of proto-industrialization has gained general intellectual currency; more important, the hypothesis has unleashed a torrent of research and reassessment that crucially informs our understanding of industrial change during the long eighteenth century. We can now see more clearly the reasons for and extent of the efflorescence of industry in the countryside, its specific structural characteristics, and the ways it articulated with urban crafts, themselves undergoing important and often similar forms of development.

The ruralization of industry was driven first and foremost by entrepreneurs' efforts to cut labor costs. Often they could realize dramatic savings on wages by employing villagers. Weavers around Tilburg (Dutch Republic) were paid 45 percent less than their peers in Leiden, wages for silk reelers outside Milan were said to be as much as two-thirds below those prevailing in the city, and around Amiens rates up to 73 percent lower were cited. Wages were, of course, just one component of total costs; even so, evidence from the Cambrésis (northern France) suggests

10 One of the principal reasons for locating industry in the countryside was to take advantage of cheaper labor, which was often female and usually outside guilds, like these women in the Highlands of Scotland, who "waulked" (fulled) cloth with their feet while singing tunes that measured the length of the task.

that lower pay alone made rural linen weaving 10–20 percent cheaper than urban. This was a powerful incentive to initiate production in or relocate it to the countryside, particularly as prices for manufactures drifted lower until the mid-eighteenth century. In addition, the supply of village labor was abundant. So as demand picked up, output could be raised by incorporating new individuals, settlements, or entire districts, without pushing up pay rates, at least for some time.

Not all the countryside proved equally hospitable to industry, however. Logic – not to mention examples from every corner of Europe – indicates that pastoral zones would be decidedly welcoming, since labor-extensive animal husbandry provided little work for many family members. But stock-raising areas did not enjoy a clearcut comparative advantage in terms of labor supply, for arable regions – even grain-exporting districts like the Pays de Caux or the Alentejo in Portugal – also turn out to have supported widespread proto-industrialization. Part of the explanation lies in the seasonality of most farm work in arable as well as pastoral areas, which allowed industrial production in slack periods. Soil quality also played an indirect role: less fertile and thus poorer parts of even predominantly arable regions tended to take up industry. The availability of local wool, flax, straw, iron, or wood could likewise stimulate industrialization, but even in locations that were so blessed growth in output might necessitate imports of raw materials. The linens of the Minho (Portugal) were initially made of flax from the region, but when the supply proved insufficient, Baltic flax was used. And in many villages – just as in towns – imported raw materials, whether from Europe or, like cotton, from further away, were crucial from the start.

Although agrarian environments created propensities, political or economic power and social institutions were likely to be decisive – albeit often in a negative way. As far as possible, the Swedish state crushed rural weaving that threatened textile industries backed by the state, and fiscal dependence on urban crafts led the authorities in the duchy of Württemberg (Germany) to obstruct the development of rural manufactures. Conversely, changed political circumstances could allow rural industry to blossom. Until 1638, residents of Gross Schönau in Saxony, ruled by the nearby city of Zittau, could make cloth only for local exchange. But when urban guild power waned during the Thirty Years' War, villagers quickly began to weave for markets in Dresden, Hamburg, even France and England. By 1729, 782 looms were in operation, up from just 16 in 1647.

Many landlords discouraged rural industrialization in order to maintain a large and inexpensive pool of agricultural laborers or, as in Italy, to maximize their sharecropping income. In closed English villages, landlord prohibitions against dividing holdings, along with strict limitations on cottage building, effectively thwarted industrial development both by assuring that holdings were large enough fully to employ tenants and by excluding the landpoor and landless who would need proto-industrial work. The landowners' main intent, however, was to preserve large-scale commercial farming.

Other landlords, in contrast, actively promoted village industrialization. In Ulster (Ireland), for example, they not only permitted fragmentation of tenancies but established markets where flax and linens were sold. Scottish landowners favored rural linen production because it both allowed them to raise rents and helped keep on the land the additional labor needed for sowing, harvesting, and other seasonal agricultural work. To feudal lords in Silesia and Bohemia, industry brought new revenues in the form of permission fees owed by entrepreneurs and workers alike and compulsory purchases of food, beer, and raw materials from the estates at stipulated prices. Rural crafts could also provide a lucrative outlet for the flax, wool, and yarn that many east central lords collected as in-kind payments, and serfs who had additional income from industrial jobs could pay higher seigniorial levies. So some feudal lords themselves developed rural industries, employing serfs not needed in the fields. And even some Italian landowners encouraged women in mezzadria households to reel silk (extract filaments from cocoons, twist several together, and wind them on cylinders), since this work made the cultivation of mulberry trees more lucrative for sharecropper and landlord alike.

Finally, tenurial structures and communal regulations strongly influenced the implantation of industry in the countryside. England was not alone in harboring open villages, where fragmented tenancies and immigration furnished recruits for industry, nor closed settlements that limited their appearance. In the canton of Zürich, for example, proto-industry flourished in the uplands, which had few constraints on settlement or on splitting up plots. It was virtually absent, however, from areas near Zürich, despite transportation and communication advantages. There, rules originally established to safeguard the livelihood of peasants practicing traditional three-field cultivation effectively barred entry to newcomers and restricted population growth among villagers by blocking the division of holdings. Consequently, no surplus labor pool formed and the countryside never industrialized; much the same held true in Holland, where family farms predominated.

Within villages, the poor and the landless of course often sought industrial jobs: in the Pays de Herve east of Liège (southern Netherlands), families holding as little as two and a half acres of land kept alive by joining nailmaking, weaving, spinning, and coal mining to dairying. Peasants in many places took up more remunerative proto-industrial work rather than farm additional land from which only limited returns could be expected or even entirely stopped cultivating inadequate holdings. Prosperous peasants also took on proto-industrial employment: linen weaving around Osnabrück (Germany), in fact, was dominated by the largest farmers, while in the Tierra de Campos (Castile), independent peasants enjoying high grain yields and farming income wove using wool from their own herds. They may have aspired to a higher standard of living, to fuller participation in the budding consumer society. Or, like peasants in the Achterhoek district of Gelderland province (Dutch Republic), they may have sought to hold on to their land during periods of agrarian downturn.

Men and women, old people and children, were all drawn into rural manufacturing. Whole families might participate, as members of both genders and every age spun and wove or, as in the Dalnarna region of Sweden, forged iron tools and implements. But divisions of labor based on gender and age were common. They were not uniform, however; local customs and opportunities determined the specific allotment of tasks. In the Pays de Herve, for instance, industry was a male preserve, dairying that of women and children. In Castile, on the contrary, wives wove and husbands undertook dry-farming; in parts of the Alentejo, women and children made cloth while men cultivated grapes. In Italian mixed farming areas, where male laborers found continuous agricultural employment, women and children made lace and plaited straw. On small independent farms in Switzerland, men cultivated the land and women made textiles; yet not far away, in districts where such holdings were rare and entire families labored in proto-industries (as well as on tiny plots), gender distinctions were muted as men, women, and children all spun cotton. The forces determining the type and degree of involvement in proto-industry existed, in other words, not only at the levels of state, region, or village, but even within households.

Urban merchants are usually seen as the catalysts for proto-industrialization, and many a time this was indeed the case, for they had capital, commercial contacts, and expertise, and were attuned to market conditions. Research has demonstrated, nevertheless, that they were far from the only city-based entrepreneurs. Despite guild taboos, artisans seeking to raise output might hire rural producers, as the Lille light woollens weaver Jean-Baptiste Desruelles put out thread to village weavers (and, because this was illegal, paid a heavy penalty for doing so). It would be a mistake, however, to envisage the countryside as passively submitting to urban initiatives: rural entrepreneurs were also active on their own behalf. Their numbers included pedlars, carters, and innkeepers, as well as commercial farmers who were knowledgeable about markets: in the Mora

(Sweden), prosperous peasants sold the clocks made by their poorer neighbors. In the linen industries of the Zürich uplands and the Cambrésis, village merchants were prominent. Some were former weavers who had accumulated a little capital; others were peasants who raised the necessary funds by mortgaging their holdings. In the English stocking trade could be found small-town tradesmen, farmers, even thrifty servants. Each bought up a handful of knitting frames and, by leasing them out, became a petty capitalist.

No matter what their origins, entrepreneurs most frequently hired villagers on a putting-out basis, although, as in the past, many variations existed (see chap. 2). In some parts of Sweden, for instance, capitalists granted artisan iron fabricators monetary advances in return for all their output of cutlery, files, locks, scissors, hammers, and guns. Yet at Eskilstuna, also in Sweden, entrepreneurs (among them the crown) supplied all raw materials and paid piece-rates on receipt of the finished goods. Bohemian linen putting-out included three approaches: cash advances to weavers who bought their own raw materials, the distribution of flax to wage-earners, and a much simpler method whereby merchants' agents placed orders with domestic weavers.

More often than is usually imagined, corporate rules dictated rural industries' output, quality, terms of competition, and labor discipline; as in towns, regulations sometimes were the result of initiatives by the producers themselves, sometimes were imposed by merchant-entrepreneurs, and sometimes were established by states for fiscal reasons. But for the most part, proto-industrial workers carried out actual production without any form of oversight save final delivery to – and acceptance or rejection by – the entrepreneur. Once a Verlagssystem became large or business conditions deteriorated, however, entrepreneurs often found it expedient to hire supervisors. Southern Netherlands merchants, for instance, employed inspectors to oversee their very numerous rural nailmakers – by 1764, one of these capitalists had 100 employees, another 310, a third 640 – as cutthroat competition and tiny profit margins pushed wages so low that workers embezzled as much iron as they could get away with.

In the Verviers area, also in the southern Netherlands, the greatest merchant-manufacturers – in 1745, just 12 out of 204 accounted for half of all output – developed a more complex arrangement. They employed agents (*façonnaires*), giving these men, who organized all stages of production, both the necessary wool and instructions about the type of cloth they were to deliver. Entrepreneurs liked the scheme because they could calculate price and quality ahead of time – the façonnaires had to absorb all losses should production prove too costly or the goods unsatisfactory – yet without themselves having to hire or manage workers. On their side, the agents were able to increase their profits by extending their putting-out networks deep into the countryside.

As in earlier centuries, then, but now on a European-wide canvas, it was not technological change but the incorporation of dependent, inexpensive, ample – and therefore largely rural – labor into some form of Verlagssystem that accounted for output growth in most industries during the long eighteenth century. Proto-industry was a form of extensive growth with many continuities with the past. Remarkably enough, however, in rural trades from Castilian wool weaving to Finnish furniture making, numerous village producers remained independent artisans, owning their implements and working up raw materials that they raised on their farms or bought in local markets. How was this possible? What determined which relations of production – putting-out or Kaufsystem (see chap. 2) – would prevail?

Not surprisingly, wealth favored independence. Within a given community, the better-off peasant-artisans were more likely to be autonomous, the poorer employed in putting-out. The availability of credit also mattered: thanks to a small-scale but functioning capital market, modest but independent peasant papermakers in the rural Veluwe district in the eastern Dutch Republic drew upon the resources of functionaries, professionals, widows, merchants, and other people from nearby towns. Location also played a role. Isolated areas were more likely to work on a putting-out basis for merchants who linked them to distant markets than were districts with direct access to a variety of suppliers and buyers. Thus in the countryside around Bielefeld in western Germany, an old Kaufsystem persisted in the linen crafts into the nineteenth century. Every stage remained the bailiwick of an independent producer. Spinners bought flax that growers had already steeped, bleached, crushed, and broken. Then they completed the preparatory process, and spun the flax into yarn, selling each week's output as soon as it was ready. Weavers who typically owned just a loom or two bought yarn directly from these spinners or from small dealers in local yarn markets, and after weaving a piece brought it to Bielefeld where numerous merchants awaited.

But whether rural producers worked in a Kaufsystem or in putting-out depended most of all on the structure of their local agrarian economy. In Ulster, for example, tenants on even very small holdings had the resources to set up on their own as autonomous petty producers both because they enjoyed secure tenures and reasonable rents, and, because they grew much of their own flax or could buy direct from other peasants, were not dependent on merchants for supplies. The impact of specific agricultural arrangements was even clearer in the West Riding of Yorkshire, where the two production systems coexisted in adjacent districts: independent farmer-weavers manufactured traditional heavy woollens, whereas dependent landless or landpoor domestic workers employed by substantial merchant capitalists made lighter worsteds. Woollens producers practiced arable husbandry on viable middling-sized holdings in better soil areas and, with the aid of family members and perhaps a few journeymen, used their own tools and raw materials to turn out good-quality cloth that they themselves often marketed. Worsteds, on the contrary, were woven in pastoral and infertile upland districts. There, weak landlord control, early enclosure, and partible inheritance resulted in polarization between a few big stockbreeders who also organized the putting-out systems and a mass of underemployed, impoverished cottagers who barely scraped by even with the aid of industrial outwork.

As in the Middle Ages, some rural trades never integrated agricultural with industrial work. Ironmaking in Vizcaya, one of the Spanish Basque provinces, although organized on a putting-out basis until the later eighteenth century, employed full-time workers and seasonal migrants rather than local farmers because here the grain harvest – when most agricultural labor was needed – coincided with the period when water to operate bellows and forges was most abundant. But even where agriculture and crafts had once been combined, the link typically grew more tenuous over time, and increasing numbers of villagers came to work only at industrial jobs. From Ulster to Austria, the weaving, tanning, smithery, mining, tile-making, and a multitude of other trades that previously had provided by-employments for peasants had become the full-time occupations of landless artisans.

Where did these full-time village craft workers come from? In some instances, their divorce from the soil was a consequence of the success of proto-industrialization. Permanent full-time industrial work could be more remunerative than stitching together an income from part-time craft employment and a hardscrabble farm. Proto-industry's demographic dynamic also helped generate its own labor force in some places. Because the availability of industrial jobs meant that they no longer had to delay marriage until they inherited agricultural holdings that could support families, youths in proto-industrial areas might wed younger than their peers in purely farming districts. In the absence of effective birth control, a lower marriage age and its corollary, a longer span of fertile years for married women in a context of relatively low illegitimacy rates, inevitably raised the birth rate. Fewer and fewer offspring could obtain viable plots, yet they remained in the villages – now as permanent industrial workers. Elsewhere, however, dense population and landlessness – perhaps, as in English open villages, due to weak controls on immigration – preceded proto-industrialization and in fact were major reasons for its implantation. Then, too, the presence of industries could heighten demographic growth both by attracting immigrants from and by discouraging emigration to places with fewer work opportunities.

Proto-industrialization was rooted in small, dispersed, usually household units, even when technological innovations were introduced. The frame for knitting stockings fitted easily into cottages, while Kay's flying shuttle (1733) perpetuated domestic weaving by enhancing the productivity of handlooms. Even such apparently archetypal cotton factory machines as Hargreaves' spinning jenny (1764), Arkwright's water frame (1769), and Crompton's mule (1779) were initially placed in the dwellings of domestic workers. Yet the cost of machines made it difficult for autonomous artisans to maintain their independence and allowed the extension of capitalist control. Sometimes entrepreneurs also sought to enhance efficiency by clustering several stages of production in close geographic proximity. In the woollen drapery of Gloucestershire (England), for example, substantial capitalist clothiers began by moving finishing trades into the same villages as weaving; over time, some parishes came to house all production processes, and in their routinized discipline strikingly resembled later factories.

Occasionally, proto-industrial entrepreneurs grouped together numerous workers in buildings specifically designed for industrial production. They might take these steps to try to reduce embezzlement of raw materials or other types of fraud to which domestic workers resorted to raise their earnings. Or they sought to respond flexibly to consumer demand at a time when fashions were starting to change more frequently. Clothiers specializing in fine textiles in particular found it hard to supply customers with up-to-the-minute fabrics by relying on a dispersed labor force that to boot had the disconcerting habit of leaving wheel or loom whenever agricultural duties beckoned. The solution was to hire landless men and women. But because they usually lacked both homes wherein they could work and necessary tools, fully equipped workrooms had to be supplied.

Concern to control the labor force and the production process more closely than was possible in dispersed proto-industry accounts, then, for the emergence of many of the centralized worksites that historians term "manufactories" or "proto-factories." Others were established for technological reasons. In the textile trades, where proto-factories were most common, entrepreneurs often sought to introduce water-powered machines to perform specific individual operations, usually those involved with preparing the raw materials or finishing the woven fabric. Among the earliest, largest, and most advanced were the "Bolognese" or "Piedmon-

11 This aerial view of the Waldstein proto-factory places it firmly within its manorial setting. At the left are the manor farm buildings and fields, including sheep pasturage, from which wool was obtained (it was also imported from as far away as Spain). In the center is the main factory complex, which included separate dye and spinning houses, fulling mills, and shearing building. Most of the buildings are arrayed around an enclosed yard with tentering frames on which cloth was stretched for drying. The village, with church, school, and marketplace, is on the right side of the picture; along the streets are located cottages for German weavers, with attached loom sheds. Ten Dutch weavers and their families lived and worked in the largest building of the complex around the tentering yard.

tese" silk-throwing mills of northern Italy. Combining the previously distinct processes of winding, twisting, and doubling, they employed an average of 98 workers; the biggest provided 300 jobs. Mainly the property of merchant-artisans who had their own supplies of raw silk, these enterprises supplanted small hand-driven mills owned and operated by individual families. In England, the water frame moved into sizable water-powered factories after Arkwright, the inventor and patentee, decided to license only units containing 1,000 or more spindles, thereby abruptly ending a promising domestic craft. Technological change also encouraged the emergence of proto-factories in the metallurgical trades. At Matthew Boulton's Soho works outside Birmingham, 600 men in five large buildings operated the most technologically advanced water-powered machines of the day (the 1760s) to make a sweeping array of small metalwares.

In the absence of managerial or technological imperatives, the great majority of entrepreneurs saw no compelling reason to tie up their capital in fixed plant; the minority that did found their profits on average below those of their competitors who concentrated on putting-out, and as a result numerous early manufactories soon closed. And even when some operations were performed in manufactories, the labor-intensive stages of the production process usually remained in the hands of domestic workers. In the Vesdre district of the bishopric of Liège (southern Netherlands), for example, a Verleger would have raw wool machine-carded in his proto-factory, then put it out for spinning and weaving before taking back the woven fabric for fulling in a different part of his mill. Similarly, despite the presence of Bolognese and Piedmontese throwing mills, Italian silk weaving and finishing remained handicrafts. Even in English cotton manufacturing, where a striking series of inventions mechanized spinning and increasingly concentrated it in factories, domestic handlooms remained dominant well into the nineteenth century.

A few manufactories housed several stages of production, including some that did not use a centralized source of energy. Such establishments were most common on estates in east central Europe, perhaps because the necessary physical plant could be built or converted at low cost using corvée labor. But even in these manufactories the majority of the workforce, if not the majority of the production processes, remained outside the mill. The Osek (Bohemia) woollen company, which belonged to a Cistercian monastery, prepared wool and wove, fulled, dyed, and dressed cloth in proto-factory buildings. Yet of its 766 employees, 656 were women who spun at home. The light drapery manufactory opened in 1715 by Count Johann von Waldstein in the tiny village of Horní Litvinov

(Bohemia) went so far as to bring some spinners into the mill, although most continued to work in their homes. This establishment was noteworthy, too, for its far-reaching division of labor, designed to exploit the economies of scale possible even in the unmechanized operations of a large manufactory. Divided into forty-five distinct procedures, production was carried on in separate workshops by several hundred specialized workers, among them even artisans who fashioned tools used by the clothmakers. In retrospect, we know that the Waldstein mill presaged the future. But in its own time it was an anomaly. The typical manufactory was simply one element in a production system largely organized on a putting-out basis.

Neither putting-out nor manufactories were exclusively rural phenomena. Urban domestic systems which, as we have seen, had existed since the Middle Ages, proliferated in the eighteenth century. New industries that developed outside corporate frameworks accounted for an increasing share of Verlagssystem production. And even in established trades guild privileges and protests were ignored; more and more often, in fact, it was rich guild masters who themselves engaged in putting-out, although corporate rules usually did prevent them from opening sizable workshops. For entrepreneurs could find cheap labor in towns. Subsidized grain prices and organized urban provisioning moderated living costs, while improved charity systems – the urban equivalent of cottagers' small plots in the countryside – provided wage supplements. The thousands of male and female linen spinners working in Ghent, it was reported in 1738, relied on poor relief as much as their own labor. An urban Verleger could keep wages especially low by tapping the female labor pool, constantly fed by an inflow of single and widowed village women. In 1789, there were said to be some 13,600 poorly paid women and girls employed as domestic lace-makers in Lille, then a city of approximately 60,000 people.

A scattering of proto-factories likewise made their appearance in the urban industrial landscape. Even before the mid-seventeenth century, some merchants and finishers in Leiden had begun to assemble weavers, shearers, and other artisans in single workplaces in order to supervise the production process more closely, obtain lower prices for raw materials bought in bulk, and speed up the turnover of working capital. These shops had seldom contained more than a couple of different trades, but in the eighteenth century, the scale of manufactories grew. On occasion, this was due to the introduction of new technology. The five-story Derby (England) silk mill, built in 1718, where a single enormous water-wheel drove all the machines (78 winding mills, 8 spinning mills, 4 twisting mills), employed 200–300 workers. Mainly to enhance managerial control, a few manufactures also developed in luxury crafts that involved numerous intricate operations performed by highly skilled artisans using costly raw materials. But most made more mundane goods, usually standardized textiles and metalwares.

As in the past, repeated attempts were made during the long eighteenth century to employ orphans, prisoners, vagabonds, and workhouse inmates in order to defray their maintenance costs while also teaching them work habits if not skills. On occasion these schemes gave rise to large and elaborate manufactories, nearly all of which turned out textiles. One in Cadiz (Spain) provided jobs to 850 workhouse residents, some of whom operated a spinning jenny, looms, and stocking frames. But even when tending machines, coerced workers proved unwilling and insubordinate. So for reasons of low productivity and poor quality, most of these manufactories soon closed or saw their goods, spurned by every buyer, pile up in storerooms.

Like its rural counterpart, the urban manufactory was typically integrated into a Verlagssystem that mainly employed country folk. Jacob de Heyder and Co. employed 100 weavers in their Lier (southern Netherlands) flannel mill, another 100 in the weavers' own homes in that town and in Antwerp, 2,000 spinners in villages, and an unknown number of workers in their fully-equipped Lier calendaring mill and dye works. In the late 1780s, the "Calwer Zeughandlungskompanie" of Augsburg provided work to up to 4,000 combers and spinners and nearly 1,000 other workers performing every stage in woollens production, but only 168 of them – dyers, bleachers, pressers, and other finishers whose tasks were thought to require rigorous oversight – worked in central shops; the rest labored in their own cottages.

In the eighteenth century, in fact, age-old contrasts between urban and rural production – already long blurred in England – were losing force across the Continent as trades escaped city monopolies, as village entrepreneurs took their place alongside their urban fellows, as unregulated trades proliferated in bucolic and inner-city settings, as the countryside came to harbor more and more full-time industrial workers: as, in short, proto-industrial enterprises engendered similar – often linked – work units and relations of production in town and country. The upshot of the golden age of rural industry was the superseding of old dichotomies. Much more widely and successfully than in such sixteenth-century precursors as Córdoba, neither town nor country but the region became the paramount industrial space.

Varieties of uneven industrialization

Each area of Europe enjoyed differential access to the new sources of demand, and each proved disparately receptive to new industries, forms of organization, and techniques, so each developed distinctive patterns and levels of industrialization. Eighteenth-century industrial development did not entirely bypass Mediterranean Europe. On the whole, however, it confirmed that region's subordination to more advanced western lands – a trend that had become evident by the end of the long sixteenth century. The movement of Europe's economic center of gravity to the Atlantic coast states was consolidated. Within that area, too, was reaffirmed the primacy of the northwestern quadrant, those lands around the Channel and North Sea encompassing the Rhineland, the Low Countries, Britain, and northern France. Yet even there not all territories progressed in equal measure. The Dutch Republic lost its commanding position, whereas the southern Netherlands recovered smartly. Britain's performance was strongest overall, but France's was comparable or even superior in some important respects. And even in the more laggard regions there were conspicuous bright spots, districts and industries that ranked among the foremost in Europe. If anything, industrialization in the eighteenth century was a more uneven process than in the past.

East central Europe

Several areas east of the Elbe shared in eighteenth-century industrial advance. Some continued to find customers mainly in the region or further east, but others recaptured markets in western Europe or developed new ones in the colonies of the Atlantic nations. Textiles most of all, but also metals and glass – industries that dated back to the Middle Ages – remained the premier trades across the eighteenth century; during this period, too, the regions that prospered the most were those with already established industrial vocations, frequently because of rich endowments in raw materials such as flax, wool, ores, and glass sand. In these respects, east central industrialization represented an intensification of existing trends rather than new departures.

Low-priced linens destined largely for western Europe and its colonies were the leading manufacturing export of Bohemia, Saxony, and Silesia; in the latter region, 230,000 flax spinners were employed in 1772. Woollens ranging from fine fabrics worn by nobles to cheap stuffs used for peasant clothes and feed sacks were woven in Austria, Bohemia, Moravia, Little Poland, and Silesia for customers in Russia and the Near East as well as within east central Europe. Beginning in the 1720s, cotton production advanced smartly around Vienna and in the west Austrian province of Vorarlberg. A few other industries also looked abroad. Bohemia exported glass throughout Europe, the Near East, and the New World. The mining and metallurgical trades of Austria's Alpine provinces ranked among Europe's leaders: in 1767, Styria alone turned out as much pig iron as England.

Mining, metallurgy, and glassmaking had been essentially rural all along; alongside them developed several significant proto-industries. Woollens, linens, nails, locks, leather goods, and wooden articles were fabricated from abundant local raw materials; imported cotton and other primary products were also used. Inexpensive textiles, which secured a firm hold not only among domestic consumers but also on export markets both in eastern and southeastern Europe and in the Americas, comprised the largest proto-industrial sector. As a result, a few east central areas had become industrialized on a scale comparable to regions in northwestern Europe. By 1798, textiles occupied 17.5 percent of Bohemia's population, and in some villages in the mountainous northern districts the proportion reached four-fifths. But not all industry was rural. At Brno (Moravia), cloth industries had been founded that in the nineteenth century would make it the "Manchester of Central Europe," and some version of its experience was duplicated in several other towns.

At least in Bohemia, British factors, who sent their output to merchants in London for export to the New World, were critical to the rise of rural textiles. From the time of his arrival in 1713 to his death in 1724, Robert Allason, for example, helped transform Rumburk from a sleepy village with 30 looms to a bustling linen center with 580 looms, not to mention Allason's two bleaching plants and a mill housing a flax-crushing shed, dyeworks, and starching shop. Indigenous entrepreneurs were active elsewhere, such as in the Polish village of Andrychów, where at the end of the eighteenth century perhaps 1,000 looms wove 20,000 pieces of linen a year. With capital accumulated in agriculture, peasant merchants organized putting-out systems that employed their neighbors, some of whom eventually abandoned farming entirely for full-time industrial work. Most Verleger operated on a very modest scale, carrying their petty output on their backs from village to village within a restricted area. But a few better-off peasants constructed extensive networks of domestic producers, formed companies with others of their stature to export to distant areas, and even opened finishing shops. So while foreign capital accounts for some east central proto-industry, the region also had resources of its own that could be mobilized; it was not solely dependent upon outside funds for industrial development.

The great majority of those – employers as well as workers – who engaged in the rural cloth industry remained serfs. But their lords (like other seigniors, noted in chap. 5, whose estates remained wholly agrarian) were willing to accept cash payments in lieu of corvées because rapid demographic growth had given rise to an excess of peasant labor obligations relative to estate needs or because soil quality or inaccessibility to market made demesne-based commercial agriculture impracticable. But this was not the only way that feudal lords sought through industry to exploit surplus peasant labor profitably: a number set up both putting-out operations and centralized workshops on their manors or leased out the privilege to merchants. Lords apparently did not force serfs to work in these manufactories, but in places where feudal obligations were heavy, many peasants were glad to find extra employment. Most of these enterprises, which made everything from glass to fine fabrics, were short-lived, falling victim to inadequate demand as well as inferior quality supply. But a few flourished; the Waldstein light drapery manufactory was probably the best known, but several other lordly domains in Bohemia received 10–15 percent of their total revenues from textile and iron enterprises.

East Elbian industry also received encouragement from princes seeking to strengthen their states; as in agriculture, the Hohenzollern monarchs of Prussia and the Habsburg emperors were the most active. As early as the reign of Frederick William, the Great Elector (1640–88), Prussia banned both imports of numerous foreign manufactures and exports of vital raw materials. In this way, trades manufacturing a broad range of everyday and luxury items were to be assured of having protected material supplies and markets for finished goods. Some of these industries were subsidized or otherwise supported by the War Commissars who ran the armed forces. In the eighteenth century, as the country became increasingly militarized (the army absorbed two-thirds of all government revenues, giving rise to the quip that Prussia was "not a country with an army but an army with a country"), the military took on a widening role in industrial development. A textile trade that included early factories was established to supply army uniforms, and to furnish weaponry the state owned and operated numerous armaments works, mines, and ironworks, as well as closely supervising private ones. The army was a much less important spur to industrialization in the Habsburg lands, and state assistance was therefore directed much more to private entrepreneurs. They were lent capital and equipment (much of it imported from western Europe), their businesses were exempted from guild regulations and privileges, state-sponsored spinning and weaving schools trained employees for them. And beginning as early as the reign of Emperor Charles VI (1711–40), the government took a strong interest in improving transport throughout the far-flung Habsburg territories, so rivers were dredged, canals dug, roads rebuilt.

Government aid doubtless helped jumpstart certain industries. The most impressive instance was in Austria, where in the late eighteenth century the state-owned Linz woollen manufacture provided some 35,000 jobs. Four-fifths of them were held by domestic spinners, most of whom lived in Bohemia, hundreds of miles distant. If not so spectacular,

Prussian support was also significant. Not only did the Hohenzollerns sustain a range of manufactures for prestige and mercantilist reasons, but the army, which quintupled in size between 1713 and 1786 to become one of Europe's greatest, provided a big, continually growing, and sheltered market.

Yet despite state and private initiative and rapid population growth, industrialization remained spatially and quantitatively limited in east central Europe. For one thing, restrictive institutions, practices, and policies remained in place. Serfdom, of course, was the primary obstacle. Most landlords did not have, or did not perceive that they had, labor above their agricultural needs and thus could not envisage permitting, much less encouraging, industrialization on their estates. Although the Imperial government attempted to erode guild monopolies, they survived in many places in the vast Habsburg empire, slowing the development of village putting-out, elsewhere the most dynamic form of industrialization. The Prussian state, too, helped keep corporate institutions powerful so that they could control and police the urban populace. Much more restrictive was the Hohenzollern policy of confining industry to towns to ease collection of the Excise, the sales tax that was fundamental to state finances, and to maintain adequate supplies of foodstuffs from full-time farmers. In practice, these goals were never fully realized, but the scheme did hamper ruralization and the benefits that, as we have seen, accrued from it.

East central producers also faced increasingly difficult access to foreign markets as tariffs and duties were widely introduced, often in retaliation for those erected by east Elbian states to protect nascent industries. Given the importance of exports for such leading industries as linen, woollens, iron, and glass, the loss of customers abroad was a sharp blow. Their greatest problem, however, was the condition of the domestic market. To be sure, tariff walls were raised against imports, and internal barriers lowered to create larger, more integrated home markets. Even so, home demand was modest and therefore could not compensate for the loss of foreign customers. The high taxes that paid for the enormous Prussian army depressed consumption in that realm, and heavy seigniorial levies, combined with low agricultural productivity, had the same effect more generally. So in these still overwhelmingly rural lands – even in 1800, the urbanization level of barely 4 percent was less than half the European average – the mass of the population not only remained poor but continued to make many of the textiles, household utensils, and farm implements they used. Cottage crafts were widely practiced. But most were not integrated into market production and thus held back, rather than fostering, industrial development.

Italy

Entrepreneurs in Italian states attempted few new departures. Instead, they expanded several promising initiatives previously undertaken. In many towns, where guilds continued to dominate production, luxury goods such as glass, furniture, artworks, and clothing, many of them sold abroad, were the only prosperous crafts. As woollen crafts continued to shrink in Florence and several other cities, moreover, resources were redeployed into silkmaking, which rebounded nicely from depressed seventeenth-century levels thanks to bountiful supplies of indigenous raw silk and newly opened markets in Germany and the Ottoman Empire. But the dynamic industries were increasingly found in the countryside; this held true even for silkmaking, which during the eighteenth century was Italy's leader. Venice saw the weaving of silk *ormesini bassi* move to Alpine valleys, and the majority of the 6,000 looms turning out silk braid in the Padua area were to be found in the city's hinterland. Rural districts also assumed much of the production of other expensive goods: Lombard peasants took up fine felt hatmaking, for example, as the craft disappeared from Milan. The manufacture of cheaper items that used mainly local raw materials, were organized on a putting-out basis, and were destined chiefly for local and regional markets likewise multiplied in villages and small towns. Newly implanted crafts as diverse as leather, glass, and printing joined existing mining, metallurgy, and textile trades. By the end of the seventeenth century, the Bergamo area alone already wove more woollen cloth than Venice ever had, while Venice's own craft was near extinction. Some rural crafts found customers abroad: by the mid-eighteenth century, hats and other straw items ranked second only to silks among Tuscany's exports. Finally, many of the aristocratic landowners who backed agricultural innovation in Lombardy invested as well in deep mines and rural manufactories, including water-powered mills for silk and paper.

Yet if Italy was involved in trends common throughout Europe, the peninsula's industrial development remained sluggish. For one thing, competition intensified, even in silks, Italy's flagship export – often, ironically enough, because foreign manufacturers equipped themselves with the superior technology that had once been an Italian monopoly. More important, the protective measures that multiplied across the period excluded Italian manufactures from markets abroad, including the dynamic colonial and overseas trade of the Atlantic states.

Italian industries were thrust back, therefore, onto home markets. Already by 1700, only one-third of Venice's labor force worked in export-oriented trades, as against one-half a century earlier. But there, too, problems abounded. Urbanization stalled at levels little above – and in the north below – those attained during the long sixteenth century. Further, the political divisions of the peninsula kept domestic markets restricted, while tolls, tariffs, and different currencies hampered trade among them, and even in the north important segments of the peasantry were becoming too impoverished to generate much demand. Ruralization also encountered labor supply problems. Admittedly, guilds were losing strength as urban trades withered and agrarian structures were changing, and together these trends allowed proto-industry to expand. In mountainous districts of Lombardy, poor peasants were able to cling to their tiny plots by having women and children take on silk reeling and throwing or, less often, cotton and woollen weaving. Similarly, in central Italy, women from landless agricultural laborer families plaited straw or willow. But most sharecroppers were still hindered from participating in domestic industrial production and commercial farmers remained fully engaged in arable activities.

It remains a matter of debate whether the growth registered in towns and rural areas compensated for the decay experienced by industries in the major cities. In the countryside around Vicenza, on the Venetian Terraferma, the number of silk looms rose from 100 in 1675 to more than 1,100 in 1781, for example, whereas in Venice itself the 800 looms present as late as 1750 had dwindled to just 60 in 1792. Moreover, the environment in which they operated made many Italian entrepreneurs cautious. So although Florence's silk output went up 50 percent in value between 1650 and the 1760s, its manufacturers, their eyes firmly fixed on repeated fluctuations in demand, declined to install expensive Bolognese and Piedmontese mills. Even in the late eighteenth century, nine-tenths of Florentine silk was still spun by hand.

Their wariness is understandable, for the products of Italian industry were of decreasing consequence outside the peninsula and often distinctly secondary even in their own states. As in agriculture, structural transformation was still in its early stages. It would be an exaggeration to characterize Italy, as some scholars have, as converted into an underdeveloped area that only exported primary articles in return for foreign manufactures. But – as symbolized by the rising quantities of silk thread that its mills sent to be woven in France and England – Italians increasingly supplied semi-processed goods to industries abroad that performed the most skilled and profitable final stages. Although crisis in Lyon and changes in fiscal and customs policies set off a boom in Lombard and Piedmont silk in the 1780s, and a handful of innovative enterprises were to be found, on the whole Italian industries lagged behind – and often served – their competitors in more dynamic economies.

Iberia

By focusing on domestic and colonial markets, Spanish industrial output not only revived from a state of near collapse at the end of the sixteenth century but expanded across the eighteenth. Villagers and inhabitants of small towns working up local raw materials made a variety of cheap and medium-priced woollens and linens. In a few cases, protective tariffs and restrictions on primary product exports contributed to the development of higher quality import substitutes. Using raw silk that previously had been exported, artisans in Valencia and its environs busied 800 looms in 1721, 4,000 by the end of the century. Sizable military purchases aided trades from shipbuilding to textiles, and government-assisted entrepreneurs produced not only fine woollens, tapestries, porcelains, and other luxury items for the elite but less expensive manufactures as well. As the concessions granted to the Royal Cloth Works of Segovia make clear, the goal of state-subsidized enterprises was to supplant imports: the Works was to produce shirting, baize, serge, and "any other kinds of woollen cloth that come from foreign countries or that are manufactured in those realms."[2]

Nevertheless, Spain's industrialization remained modest in scope and success. Even the liveliest trades lagged far – and increasingly – behind the European leaders, and in most cases behind their own sixteenth-century levels. At its height in the 1780s, Segovia's woollens output, for instance, was not even half of what it had been two centuries before. Although raw wool output quadrupled during the long eighteenth century, by far the greatest part continued to be shipped abroad. The few industries that exported to European markets faced sharpening competition. England cut its imports of Spanish bar iron 94 percent between the 1730s and the 1780s in favor of Russian, more cheaply produced thanks to serf labor. Although Spain retained political control over a vast and costly colonial empire, it was unable to enforce trade monopolies. So Dutch, French, and especially English interlopers and their home industries derived most of the economic benefits; what is more, even Spanish merchants carried large amounts of foreign manufactures to the colonies.

Nor did home demand remain healthy. As the state's chronic fiscal crisis deepened, government industrial orders and aid ebbed. In any event, the value of crown-backed import-substitute manufacturing was hardly self-evident. Admittedly, in a country where industrial jobs were scarce, the Guadalajara woollens enterprise did have some 2,000 urban employees in the 1780s, along with 15,000 spinners working at home. Yet big annual subsidies and the provision of inexpensive raw materials

---

[2] Quoted in Angel García Sanz, *Desarrollo y crisis del Antiguo Régimen en Castilla la Vieja* (Madrid, 1986), p. 232.

notwithstanding, it turned out cloth that was so expensive and of such poor quality that the army had to be forced to take it. The financial crisis also led to the imposition of higher levies on industry, which both aggravated market-based difficulties and sustained the long-established but ruinous diversion of capital into tax-exempt land, offices, and loans. Despite the monarchy's desire to promote industry, moreover, the state was not strong enough to resist accepting treaties that left most trades without protection against imports, although high transport costs (in part the result of a still very inadequate infrastructure) provided a kind of de facto protection for cheap, low-profit goods. Unfortunately, demand for these was also narrow: the lamentable situation of the peasant and urban masses restricted Spanish industrialization in the eighteenth century, just as it had in the sixteenth. Between 1680 and 1730, falling grain prices may have helped stimulate demand, although tax rises seem to have eaten up much of the extra purchasing power. Thereafter, the cost of food mounted again, along with rents and seigniorial levies, inevitably curbing sales of manufactures. Landlords and urban elites benefited, but they retained their ingrained preference for foreign goods. Middling strata were too small to take up much of the slack.

Weak markets discouraged investment and innovation. As the price of charcoal mounted, for example, fuel accounted for up to three-quarters of the cost of producing iron. Yet although more efficient blast furnaces would have cut costs and made their iron more competitive, most iron founders rejected the new equipment as too costly given the modest levels of demand. For the same reason, few installed slitting mills, thus foreclosing the possibility of crafting high-profit wares. On their side, merchants saw little reason to invest in cloth production or to assemble large textile putting-out networks. They deemed it safer and more lucrative to export wool and other raw materials or semi-finished products like iron bars in return for cloth and other manufactures, even if the resulting trade deficit had to be paid for by transferring funds that might otherwise have helped to animate Spanish industry.

The textiles of the Córdoba area epitomize the difficulties facing Spanish industry. From the later sixteenth century, its products had progressively lost ground to cheaper foreign cloth. Finally, in the years around 1700, private entrepreneurs received government help to revive both the woollen and silk crafts. Foreign artisans were brought in to instruct apprentices in innovative techniques, new equipment (including special presses that gave the brilliant finish that customers wanted) was purchased, privileges and protections were decreed. Several centralized factories opened: a representative one contained twenty-four woollen looms, warping frames, dye boilers, presses, and other machines.

Yet in contrast to similar establishments elsewhere in Europe, Córdoba factories employed few if any rural workers, even in labor-intensive processes like spinning. A perceived need to supervise manufacture closely in order to assure sufficient quality lay behind the decision to concentrate all stages in one location. But it saddled the businesses with high fixed costs while making them unable to respond to downturns by shedding outworkers. It also did not, in fact, result in cloth equal in quality to imports. Unsurprisingly, the enterprises failed to survive for long; the only thriving branch of Córdoba textiles was the one specializing in ribbon and trimmings fabricated according to traditional artisanal techniques.

Portugal, which attempted to industrialize in the late seventeenth and eighteenth centuries, fared no better. Despite government funding, monopoly grants, and initial preferential tariffs, its textile, glass, iron, leather, soap, and other industries remained uncompetitive in price and quality with long imported and widely preferred English goods, especially after the Methuen Treaty (1703) opened up Portugal and Brazil to English woollens without tariff. Thus an eighteenth-century commercial boom founded on the discovery of vast gold fields in Brazil redounded to England's benefit: her exports to Portugal and its colonies jumped 266 percent between 1698–1702 and 1756–60, whereas Portugal retreated to her role as exporter of olive oil and wine, into the cultivation of which available investment flowed. Admittedly, Portuguese cottons and silks scored some successes on home and colonial markets in the 1780s–90s, after the gold flood dropped off sharply and it became difficult to pay for imports. But these industries were supplying a contracting market, and in any event they proved short-lived, succumbing to the upheavals of the Peninsular War (1808–14) and imports of cheap machine-made English cloth.

Catalonia was the one Iberian region that consistently bucked the tide, for in industry as in agriculture the province – particularly the eastern districts – more nearly resembled northwestern Europe than the rest of Iberia. The numerous family farmers and substantial urban middle classes had the means to purchase manufactures, and day laborers were available for supplementary industrial work. In sharp contrast to their counterparts elsewhere in the peninsula, Catalan industries enjoyed a constant inflow of capital from merchants, landlords, commercial farmers, the urban bourgeoisie, and artisans. By switching to new fabrics and a proto-industrial form of organization, Catalan woollens pulled through the seventeenth-century crisis and then recovered remarkably well. Rural putting-out workers made a wide variety of inexpensive, light, and colorful cloth for the buoyant regional market, whereas those in towns focused on more costly and elegant types sold throughout Iberia. Despite fierce foreign competition and weak restraints on imports, the woollens industry quadrupled the number of looms producing for the market across the eighteenth century.

Newly introduced trades – hardware, paper, leather, and above all printed cottons – were particularly dynamic in Catalonia; the latter industry owed its existence to substantial infusions of commercial capital and to a series of laws that between 1717 and 1728 choked off imports of Asian fabrics. By the 1780s, thousands of mainly urban workers were employed in or as outworkers for more than 100 cotton spinning mills and printed calico factories; already English spinning jennies and water frames had been introduced, and steam power was soon to follow. Despite having to contend with similar fabrics from Britain and elsewhere, Catalan cottons succeeded with customers throughout Spanish America, and substantial amounts were sold in every corner of Spain.

Their growth and innovation put Catalan industries at the forefront in Iberia. More than any others they were able to supply predominantly poor markets in Spain and its colonies with appropriately inexpensive goods, as well as to turn out good-quality manufactures for the thin stratum of prosperous consumers. They did so in part by importing technology and skills from the more advanced countries of northwestern Europe, by closely attending to changing fashions and structures of demand, and by cutting shipping, trading, and other transactions costs. Most of all, Catalonia's trades succeeded because they flexibly adopted both proto-industrial and proto-factory forms of production that allowed them to match their competitors' costs and prices. But if Catalonia was becoming a more industrialized region, the rest of the peninsula was not, apart from scattered, small, and often technically retrograde enclaves. To a greater degree than Italy, then, Iberia took its place in the new international division of labor as a source of primary products and a consumer of manufactures from abroad.

Western Germany

Because of the fragmentation and diversity that persisted in Germany throughout the eighteenth century, industries existed in a great variety of institutional, fiscal, and political environments that make generalizations hazardous. Nevertheless, two interlocked common trends can be discerned, although they held least true in the northwestern and Rhineland regions. First, urban industries both survived and stagnated behind corporate walls; second, rural trades – already present in many states from the later Middle Ages – spread widely yet faced powerful obstacles to their full development. Consequently, the ravages of decades of warfare were repaired, yet in most of western Germany industries never managed to get up a full head of steam.

Guilds that remained considerably more powerful than elsewhere in Europe continued to control a great deal of production (half of output in 1800), limit competition, obstruct innovation. Their force was felt in the countryside as well as in towns. To be sure, imperial ordinances in 1731 and 1772 gave individual states the right to end corporate monopolies and to open up crafts to all who wanted to practice them. But many governments – even absolutist ones – failed to implement or enforce the legislation; some, in fact, strongly defended corporate producers against rural competitors or imposed guilds on village producers. Not only were guilds rich and privileged institutions that sat in the halls of power in many states and controlled financial resources needed by government treasuries. Most policymakers still deemed them essential to a proper social and economic order as well as valuable instruments of social policing and discipline, and thus never seriously contemplated abolishing them despite their harmful effects. Thus at Augsburg any changes that threatened the position of independent master weavers were stubbornly spurned, even though this cost craft and city dearly: from one-quarter of all taxpayers in a city of 48,000 in 1600, weavers dropped to just 6 percent of 28,000 people in 1800. Thus, too, guilds blocked all attempts at organizational and technological innovation in the Württemberg worsted industry, the introduction of ribbon factories in Alsace, and many other new departures.

The fragmentation of markets among the myriad states, each with its own heavy tariffs, customs, and transit tolls, also continued to hamper industrialization. The trades that developed behind these protective barriers, usually with one or another form of government backing, loomed large in the economies of specific states. Yet with rare exceptions their traditional production structures and small markets made them prime examples of misallocated resources: inefficient producers that survived only because of repeated infusions of public funds. Finally, private consumption remained quite circumscribed. Apart from the states – particularly their armies – only nobles, upper clergy, and merchants, professionals and other members of the tiny urban elites (even in 1800 barely 5 percent of Germans were townspeople) generated much demand for manufactures. Most of the peasantry was poor and burdened with heavy rents and state levies; low income levels compelled the rural masses to seek industrial work but restrained their purchases.

In a few areas, however, innovations did appear. Most involved manufacture outside guilds, whether by so-called "free masters" in towns or – most commonly – by domestic workers, who were predominantly though not exclusively country folk. These developments were particularly marked in the Rhineland and Westphalia, where proto-industrial towns and villages tripled or quadrupled their populations. The trades that in the nineteenth century would make the Ruhr Europe's leading mining and metallurgy district were already making their appearance, but textiles were the major growth industry. Some fabrics were sold in nearby German states, Holland, and Scandinavia: others were shipped via Amsterdam and Hamburg to the Americas, the Levant, and Russia.

These regions were, of course, the heartland of agricultural change in western Germany (see chap. 5). They benefited as well from the presence of a talented cadre of entrepreneurs, many of them immigrant Mennonites or other Protestants excluded from the sclerotic urban trades. At Krefeld in the Rhineland, for instance, they developed a flourishing silk and velvet industry; by 1791, 46 percent of the town's population specialized in ribbons and light fabrics. It was the capitalists of this area, too, who pioneered the use of new technology. In the 1770s, water-powered ribbon looms were installed in Barmen; in the next decade, a five-story spinning mill equipped with water frames, jennies, and mules modeled on English prototypes was built near Düsseldorf; and soon thereafter mechanized knitting frames were in operation. So although the great majority of German states was barely touched by industrialization, the Rhine and northwestern districts began to display many of the characteristics of the nearby Low Countries, northern France, and England.

The Dutch Republic

During the eighteenth century, as in the past, Dutch industrial trends ran counter to those prevailing generally in Europe; this time they turned down just when others began to prosper. Weak spots had already become apparent in the later seventeenth century, but decline spread rapidly from the 1720s. The decay appeared first in the textile crafts of Holland's cities – the very trades that had initiated the Republic's industrial expansion. By 1700, Leiden's output had fallen to 85,000 cloths, well below the 1664 peak (144,700 pieces), but because an increasing proportion consisted of expensive lakens, the drop in value was less steep. From that point, however, output of every type of cloth dwindled: the number of lakens was off by two-thirds between 1700 and the late 1730s. Even going back to cheap, rough fabrics such as bays and warps did not halt the inexorable slide: 54,000 cloths in 1750, and just 29,000 in 1795 – not many more than in 1584, at the dawn of the Golden Age. Statistics from Haarlem's linen weaving and bleaching, Amsterdam's silkmaking, and virtually every other urban textile trade tell the same story.

Other industries held up longer, but from the 1720s/30s the rot spread widely. Zaan shipyards launched 306 ships in 1708, barely 5 in 1790, and if not quite so catastrophic, conditions were bad enough in related crafts like sawmilling – the number of Zaan mills shrank from 256 in 1731 to 144 in 1795 – and the manufacture of sailcloth, where Dutch production was halved between 1730 and 1770. Delft pottery, which supported thirty large businesses between 1670 and 1720, barely kept ten afloat in 1795. Beer brewing, in the Middle Ages and again in the Golden Age one of Holland's major employers and export industries, experienced a three-quarters drop in output across the eighteenth century. Tobacco processing, sugar refining, Gouda clay pipes – it is very hard to find an urban industry that did not founder, save a handful of luxury trades like Amsterdam diamonds, Utrecht and Naarden velvets, and Hilversum carpets, and even they attained modest prosperity at best. Rural industries in the interior provinces fared little better, whether linens in the Twente district of Overijssel, in the Achterhoek (Gelderland), and in Friesland, or the mixed linens and cottons of North Brabant that held out until the 1740s before joining the common slump. There were rare success stories such as gin distilling at Schiedam and Zaan papermaking – where output of 20,000 reams a year about 1650 had grown to 160,000 in 1780. But these were now the exception rather than the rule, and neither in quantity nor in value did any of these industries match those that had decayed.

Depressed domestic demand and the loss of markets abroad were the primary causes of Dutch industrial decline. At home, a prosperous agriculture and high disposable incomes of a rapidly growing urban population had together fostered the Republic's trades during the Golden Age. These foundations crumbled during the eighteenth century. A somnolent agrarian sector no longer provided the dynamic demand of earlier years; in a period of consolidation or, in some districts, retrenchment, no large-scale investments were made and even routine maintenance and re-equipping were often deferred. While the rest of Europe was undergoing ever more pronounced urbanization, the proportion of the Dutch population living in towns contracted after 1700, and many cities actually lost inhabitants. As a consequence of wars with Britain and France, the country amassed an enormous debt that was serviced mainly by raising sales taxes that cut into popular consumption. Per capita incomes stopped growing sometime after 1650. Finally, industrial decline led to widespread under- and unemployment, including in crafts that had served the once more numerous and prosperous urban classes, as well as exerting downward pressure on the wages of those who still had jobs.

The Republic could not turn to its colonies to rekindle demand. Dutch possessions in the Americas were modest in size and population, and the much larger East Indies bought few European manufactures. In contrast to those of England or France, moreover, Dutch domestic and colonial markets were easily accessible to imported wares. Customs duties were quite low except when it came to goods from the southern Netherlands. The few protective measures on the books were poorly enforced, because the Holland merchants who controlled the Republic's commerce and government generally opposed restrictions that might have limited their business. Identifying their interests with those of the country as a whole, merchants and their publicists argued that tariffs on imports would ruin the Dutch economy, founded as it was on trade. Thus, for example, calicoes from the Indies were allowed free entry into the Republic, notwithstanding the pleas of Haarlem and Leiden textile entrepreneurs.

Despite the merchants' obstinate defense of free trade, in the first half of the eighteenth century the Republic lost the European commercial primacy established during the Golden Age. The causes of this loss were many, but chief among them was the rising tide of protectionism, which proved especially harmful to Dutch industry, long heavily dependent on sales abroad. As other countries slapped export duties or prohibitions on raw materials vital to many industries in the resource-poor Republic, as well as high tariffs on Dutch manufactures, these became uncompetitive; at times, too, Dutch goods were subject to outright exclusion from European and colonial markets. Smuggling, at which Dutch merchants excelled, provided some relief but also inevitably raised prices. Amsterdam's calico-printing industry clearly demonstrates the impact of mounting barriers. The first shop opened in 1678, and by the early eighteenth century eighty were in operation. But the subsequent closing of foreign markets – including those in Spain, once a leading customer – caused most to fail. By 1770, only twenty-one workshops remained, whereas in Barcelona (which took over the Spanish market) calico printing was, as we have seen, flourishing.

Whether state-assisted or not, indeed, the industrialization of other lands was as detrimental to the Dutch in the eighteenth century as it had been to the Italians in the sixteenth, since both had achieved much of their industrial growth by selling goods that less advanced countries did not produce. In both instances, too, the diffusion of techniques from the earlier leader allowed once-backward lands to catch up. As the southern Netherlands and Westphalia developed their own Dutch-style bleaching crafts, for example, they sent Haarlem less of their massive output of unfinished linen. Foreign glassblowing, sugar refining, papermaking, and other trades similarly adopted Dutch procedures – often, as in Guadalajara, under the tutelage of Dutch artisans – and then used them to build competing industries.

In the Republic, however, technical innovation ceased. Many merchants shifted their capital into finance and real estate. But even those who kept funds in industry invested in existing technology. Very likely, they were reacting to weak demand. Yet they also seem to have been heavily committed, attitudinally as well as in terms of capital, to Golden Age technology – and for good reason. Compared to a labor-intensive strategy such as putting-out, after all, Dutch technology saved on labor in a high-wage country, and it made excellent use of wind and peat, the country's most abundant energy sources. The advantages of Dutch technology were not lost on producers abroad, who often imitated it. But they also turned massively to putting-out, water power, and eventually steam, and these gave them the edge.

Like their counterparts elsewhere, to be sure, Dutch entrepreneurs did, in the later seventeenth century, try to cut costs by relocating production to the countryside, especially to the interior provinces where agrarian change was generating a surplus labor pool. Whereas earlier village spinners and weavers had worked for the booming crafts of Leiden, Haarlem, and other cloth cities, now all stages of production including finishing were carried out in the countryside and small towns, and this process of ruralization probably contributed to the initial downturn of the urban textile industries. But as we have seen, the bloom was also quickly off rural textiles. Excluded along with their urban rivals from markets abroad, and unable to find compensation in shrinking colonial and domestic demand, by the mid-eighteenth century they, too, were part of the downward spiral.

According to some historians, the Dutch economy overall remained stable across the eighteenth century; it may even have grown modestly after about 1750. But if this was accomplished – and other scholars strongly disagree – it resulted from the growing strength of the country's financial sector, the extension of commercial agriculture into the interior provinces, and the ability of some branches of commerce (notably imports and re-exports of colonial groceries) to hold their own. Now Dutch merchants were selling fewer domestically made goods, however, for both relatively and absolutely Dutch industry was in a state of decay – if not of collapse. By 1800, the value of manufactures imported into the Republic was nine times that of industrial exports. A new transformation of the Dutch economy led it away from industrialization as its days of dynamism and technological primacy faded from memory.

The southern Netherlands

By the mid-seventeenth century, many industries of the southern Nether-lands had overcome the severe disruption attendant upon the Dutch Revolt and recovered their enviable position of a century earlier, only to face harsh conditions once again, when warfare and foreign occupation ravaged much of the country between the 1670s and 1713. During this period, and lasting well into the eighteenth century, the trades of these provinces labored under significant handicaps. In particular, as in the Dutch Republic – although for reasons of military weakness rather than commercial strength – the domestic market long remained accessible to competitors. High duties and outright bans abroad excluded many southern Netherlands products, while the Dutch Republic, England, and France prevented Spain, which ruled the provinces until 1713, from instituting effective retaliatory measures and insisted on free entry for their manufactures. Whereas Britain cut imports of southern Netherlands linen from 30,000 pieces in 1660 to 2,000 in 1711, for example, English cloth could enter Flanders and Brabant upon paying duties of just 4–6 percent. Then the Peace of Utrecht (1713–15), which transferred the provinces to the Austrian Habsburgs, forbade them to set their own tariffs and thereby kept their doors open to foreign goods.

Little wonder that many industries sought refuge in established practices. But these were of little avail. Antwerp ribbon and passement makers, for instance, clung to hand manufacture, refusing to accept ribbon mills; nevertheless, their numbers plummeted from 4,800 in 1650 to fewer than 300 in 1738. Other urban luxury trades likewise all but disappeared, including tapestry weaving, gold- and silversmithing, and diamond cutting. Some rural trades also declined: the woollens of Hondschoote, for example, slid into final oblivion and the village's remaining residents became full-time farmers. From the 1720s, however, numerous proto-industries fabricating low-cost goods of modest quality began to revive in country and (on a smaller scale) city, thanks to both supply and demand factors. Population growth concentrated in the already crowded country-side of central and southern Flanders created ever less viable small-holdings and a more numerous class of landless laborers, while in towns the collapse of corporate crafts threw many workers onto the labor market. At the same time, highly productive agriculture and the wide adoption of the potato kept food prices low and, together with abundant labor, wages as well. As a result, entrepreneurs could produce manufactures – linen most of all – to sell at very competitive prices. Flemish linen output rose by nearly two-thirds between 1700 and 1785, and up to half of all Flemings came to engage at least part-time in making it; even the bleaching was now performed at home rather than in the Dutch Republic. The great majority of the linen was sold in Spain and Spanish America, markets to which southern Netherlands goods continued to enjoy ready access across the period. In addition, tens of thousands of people in nearly every province turned out woollens destined for consumers at home as well as abroad, particularly Germany and the east central lands. And as before, large mining and metals industries centered around Liège and Namur produced mainly for export to the Dutch Republic, Germany, Spain, Portugal, even the Ottoman Empire.

When the political and diplomatic climate changed, moreover, the interventionist governments of the emperors Maria Theresa and Joseph II were prepared to act and entrepreneurs to respond. After the 1748 Peace of Aachen at the end of the War of the Austrian Succession failed to restate the injurious Utrecht clauses, and France and Austria entered into closer relations, protective tariffs were introduced, subsidies and monopolies granted to a variety of industries, and the transportation infrastructure improved, all to quick effect. Sugar refineries opened in Brussels and Ghent and grew considerably once favorable excise treatment arrogated by the Dutch in 1715 was revoked in 1749, and other processing industries like salt and tobacco likewise displaced Dutch products. Linked to the rest of the country by new roads, and assisted by higher tariffs, Charleroi coal supplanted previously large-scale imports of English coal; it also promoted the growth of metallurgical industries in surrounding districts. Fine woollens, woven in and around the eastern towns of Verviers and Eupen, not only took away business from Leiden but soon became European leaders in quality and levels of output.

The fastest growth was to be found in import-substitute light fabrics that now enjoyed protections similar to those of their English and French rivals. Initially copied from Rouen in the late 1720s, the fabrication of very cheap, multi-hued cotton–linen *siamoises* flourished at Antwerp, where by 1764 no fewer than 1,250 looms were engaged in weaving them. Elsewhere, Prussian-style linen–woollen flannels, developed from the mid-1750s after very heavy taxes on wool exports caused an upsurge in domestic supplies and a considerable fall in prices, eventually reduced imports from Germany 90 percent. Armed with a twenty-five-year monopoly, in 1753 the entrepreneur Jan Beerenbroek initiated calico printing at Dambrugge outside Antwerp, employing nearly 600 workers to turn out 74,000 pieces a year. After 1778, additional works sprang up; soon there were eight in Ghent, six in Bruges, four in Antwerp, and others elsewhere. Finally, cotton spinning began in the 1780s in many Flemish and Brabant towns. Already in 1789 Antwerp alone boasted 4,000 male, female, and child spinners; their numbers had grown to 6,000 in 1800. Although by that date mechanization had barely begun – and, ironically, Antwerp long remained on the sidelines – the southern Netherlands had reaffirmed their industrial vocation in the branches that proved the springboards to mechanized factory industrialization. Little wonder that in the early nineteenth century they should be the first on the Continent to experience the Industrial Revolution.

France

Across the long eighteenth century, France became the Continent's foremost industrial power. Rural manufacturing, previously rudimentary, expanded greatly after 1650, finally taking advantage of the masses of village poor engendered by agrarian change and (especially after about 1740) rapid demographic growth. As throughout Europe, woollen and linen proto-industries proliferated across village France. Equally striking was the rise of regional specialties, not only textiles like stocking knitting in Languedoc or silkmaking in the countryside around Lyon, but also crafts producing such disparate goods as nails, verdigris, and straw hats. As elsewhere, too, many established urban crafts faded as village manufacturing extended. At the same time, vigorous new urban industries appeared, even in cities with dying traditional crafts. Rouen's decline as a drapery producer, for example, was offset by its emergence as a great cotton center; output soared 700 percent between 1715 and 1743. Similarly, Lille (annexed to France in 1667) turned to thread twisting, linen weaving and bleaching, and calico printing as light woollens tapered off. Regional shifts also occurred within a context of overall expansion, so slow growth in marginal eastern and western textile districts was more than made up for by pronounced advances in the north, center, and southwest.

France's comparative advantage is often said to have lain in high-quality goods made by skilled labor, and many of these did flourish. Take silk. Employment in Lyon climbed from 3,000 in 1660 to 14,000 in 1739 (and continued to advance, albeit less dramatically, across the century), while production quadrupled between 1730 and 1767 in the Dauphiné and grew 5.7 percent annually in Nîmes from 1730 to 1789. Overall, French textile output increased by about three-quarters in terms of square yardage, but two and a half times in value, indicating a shift to more expensive fabrics. Still, French industries made much greater quantities of cheaper goods. Long-established woollens and linens advanced steadily across the century, but output of newer fabrics like cottons and cotton–linens grew most rapidly, owing to ebullient West African, colonial, and home market demand. Heavy industry likewise progressed nicely. Coal production was up seven- or eightfold between 1700 and 1789, and output of iron rose from 40,000 tons in 1740 to perhaps 140,000 tons in 1789.

Most determinedly in the ministry of Colbert, but continuing long after, the government intervened deeply in French industrial development. To build up domestic production, officials deployed the full panoply of mercantilist measures, including preferential tariffs, import prohibitions, monopolies, financial inducements to immigrant artisans, exemptions from guild rules, loans and grants of money, buildings, equipment, and raw materials. Like contemporary critics, present-day historians have often condemned these policies for misallocating resources and creating obsolete, excessively regulated production structures that – once the initial stimulus dissipated – raised costs, prevented industry from adjusting quickly to changing consumer tastes and market opportunities, and blocked the inflow of fresh talent, capital, and energy. Is this assessment valid?

Assuredly, on the basis of some evidence. Many of the enterprises Colbert favored came to grief even before his death. But his departure did not mark the end of the problems faced by such businesses. As the eighteenth century went on, increasingly numerous and rigid rules confined drapery from the royal manufacture of Clermont-de-Lodève (Languedoc) to the Levant market at a time when Atlantic trade was swelling. A big cotton proto-factory that opened at Darnétal outside Rouen in the 1750s blessed with royal privileges, tax exemptions, a large state subvention, and the patronage of Madame de Pompadour (mistress and then confidante of King Louis XV), who went so far as to distribute the firm's handkerchiefs to influential people in Paris, was never more than second-rate.

Yet while recognizing the shortcomings in the manner in which mercantilist policies were often conceptualized and implemented, it would be unwise to overlook their considerable achievements in specific periods and places. Many were critical to the beginnings of enterprises, particularly in the troubled later seventeenth century. Government-mandated inspections – central to the French mercantilist project – helped Languedoc woollens to conquer the Levant market, the most rapidly growing one in which French goods were then sold. They helped Breton linens to win back Iberian consumers, who had begun to take their business elsewhere as standards slipped in the seventeenth century. State enterprises like Sèvres porcelain (also promoted by Mme. de Pompadour) and Gobelins tapestries earned healthy profits, employed sizable workforces, and set the tone for luxury trades throughout Europe. Moreover, it was royal manufactures – repeatedly subsidized by financiers' and tax farmers' investments ordered by the king's ministers – that first introduced technological innovations like spinning jennies, water frames, and coke furnaces to France. Against Darnétal must be set the royal manufacture established at Sens in the same years: by 1776, two-thirds of its yarn was spun on jennies. Government policies also played a crucial role in furthering capitalist reorganization of industry. In Languedoc drapery, for example, state-mandated regulations, fees, and inspections favored substantial merchant-manufacturers who built up putting-out systems at the expense of autonomous producers. State involvement was no guarantee of French industrial development, but neither did it preclude important change and growth.

Reevaluation has likewise substantially modified the common view that guilds or *jurandes* – which remained important institutions in French urban trades until the Revolution – uniformly obstructed technological and organizational innovation, held obdurately to overpriced, outmoded products beyond the reach of most customers, and drove up transactions costs, depressing profits and investment throughout the industrial sector. Of course, numerous guilds resisted change of any sort. But in contrast to Germany, many – perhaps the majority – proved increasingly flexible in accommodating change, often because the larger masters sought to take part in entrepreneurial initiatives. Thus jurandes permitted employers to subcontract even across guild boundaries, hire free (non-corporate) laborers to work alongside guild artisans, and redefine hours, workplace conditions, and methods of production at the expense of privileges long considered sacrosanct. All of these innovations cut costs; at the same time, they concentrated control in the hands of narrow groups. Whereas there were no woollens masters in Amiens owning six or more looms in 1662, by 1733 they constituted a sixth of the total and held 40 percent of all looms. Finally, guilds thwarted neither the proliferation of new products made entirely outside the jurandes nor the development of rural industry. Already under Colbert big cloth entrepreneurs in Rouen and Amiens had been exempted from guild rules so they could put out work to villagers. Around many other towns, too, industry spread far into the countryside long before receiving explicit authorization in 1762: as early as 1708, a government inspector in Burgundy wrote that "unauthorized workers" made "many textiles in villages, localities, and small towns where there is no [corporate] mastership."[3]

During the eighteenth century, in fact, many merchant capitalists championed guilds as effective institutions for monitoring quality as well as for disciplining labor. These same considerations likewise recommended corporations to municipal and royal authorities. The Colbertian ideal, which also guided his successors, envisaged a strictly regulated economy supervised by guilds, which in turn would be overseen by the state. Entrepreneurs also found guilds helpful in enforcing strict divisions of labor that enhanced productivity and permitted profitable economies of scale. More than ever before, in short, guild privilege simultaneously masked and facilitated the power of capitalist employers, allowing them to reorganize production. So when Turgot attempted to suppress guilds in

[3] Quoted in Paul Butel, *L'économie française au XVIIIe siècle* (Paris, 1993), p. 206.

1776 – alleging that their "arbitrary and selfish rules . . . ensure an incalculable reduction of commercial and industrial activity"[4] – the resulting uproar from masters, entrepreneurs, and local authorities forced their reestablishment just six months later.

Both luxury and inexpensive standardized products of French industry did well on foreign markets. Overseas trade expanded most rapidly of all, growing eightfold in value across the eighteenth century, whereas all foreign trade tripled in value. Already taking nearly 20 percent of French exports in 1716, the colonies absorbed almost a third in 1787, for these markets remained buoyant when exchanges between France and the rest of Europe slowed down after 1750. In addition, France was the leading supplier of manufactures for Spanish America, and considerable amounts of blue-dyed "Guinea cloth" from the Nantes region and printed cottons from Rouen were exchanged for slaves in West Africa. Thanks to concerted initiatives by the government, manufacturers, and enterprising Marseille merchants, the Levant consumed more industrial goods from France than from any other European country. Finally, French exports were dominant in Italy and Spain, and her silks were preferred by Germans and east central Europeans.

For all that, the internal market absorbed at least three-quarters of French goods. The growing commercialization of agriculture was especially important in enlarging demand for inexpensive and moderately priced manufactures, now including a variety of metal tools and implements. Urban middle-class and popular consumption swelled, too, with the cloth and clothing trades the main beneficiaries. Continual fashion changes required new purchases, lighter and brighter fabrics gained in popularity, and novelties such as undergarments, handkerchiefs, and window curtains came to be considered necessities. Whereas fewer than a tenth of Paris artisans owned cotton clothing in the early eighteenth century, for example, two-fifths did in 1789. French luxury trades continued to monopolize the large internal market for high-quality goods as well. Taken together, foreign and internal demand promoted perhaps fourfold growth in gross industrial output over the eighteenth century.

These gains were achieved in the face of some major problems. For one thing, the demand for manufactures by France's American empire was always restricted. Even before the loss of Canada in 1763, substantially fewer than 100,000 French settlers lived in mainland North America, which held the largest concentrations, as compared to well over a million in comparable British colonies; the number of French colonists in the

---

[4] From the edict of 1776, printed in *Documents of European Economic History*, ed. S. Pollard and C. Holmes (London, 1968), vol. I, p. 61.

West Indies was no more than 35,000. The great majority of the colonial population consisted of slaves, and their already reduced consumption needs were increasingly filled by yet cheaper goods from lower-wage producers on the peripheries of Europe: Silesian, eastern German, and Irish linens, for instance. And even where French goods continued to dominate, colonial sales provided little stimulus to industrialization in the mother country. Because of their close links with the slave trade, for example, Nantes cotton manufacturers failed to develop any market besides west Africa or to diversify into other types of fabric. A substantial amount of French industrial exports thus came from abroad; at the same time, much of the country's growing reexport trade with the rest of Europe (it rose from 18 to 33 percent of all exports between 1716 and 1787) consisted of colonial produce to pay for manufactures.

Other foreign markets also proved disappointing. Growing disorder in the Ottoman Empire, as well as its government's attempts to develop import-substitute industries, curbed exports there. Spain and its American possessions, long the leading outlets abroad for linens, France's biggest textile craft, took fewer as the income of the Spanish peasantry stagnated or fell and less expensive cloth entered the markets. Across Europe, a later eighteenth-century shift in fashion to simpler English designs cut into sales of elaborate and luxurious French goods. Little wonder that growth in foreign trade decelerated after mid-century.

Weaknesses were apparent in the home market as well. Poor transportation and internal tolls continued to keep final prices high. Much of French agriculture remained unproductive and much of the rural populace poor. After about 1770, peasants faced rents and taxes that rose faster than output, thereby reducing their purchasing power. With only about 9 percent of French people living in towns, and a preponderance of marginal small farmers, these unfavorable agricultural conditions, in conjunction with difficulties in foreign trade, did not bode well for continued industrial growth, and in fact output in many industries stagnated from the 1760s and 1770s.

Worst of all, in the late 1780s French industry was hammered by a quick succession of heavy blows. First, in 1786 the Anglo–French Eden Treaty, which sharply lowered tariffs, resulted in a surge of textiles, hardware, and pottery imports. Over the long run, this free-trade treaty might have strengthened industry by weeding out inefficient producers and stimulating competition: after all, fine cottons manufacturers learned to imitate English goods and make them more cheaply. But it was widely disruptive in the short run, especially to the many industries already facing stagnant or closing markets at home and abroad. Fast on its heels, moreover, arrived very high grain prices in 1788–89, which further depressed consumption, and then a decade and a half of revolution and war, which badly disturbed foreign trade of all sorts.

Up to these final years, however, eighteenth-century France had experienced remarkable growth. On an annual basis, French industrial output grew 1.9 percent between 1701–10 and 1781–90, as against 1.1 percent in Britain. So while at the beginning of the century industry accounted for only about a quarter of France's total output, in comparison to a third in Britain, in the 1780s the figure was up to two-fifths in both countries, perhaps even a little higher in France. Fixed capital was becoming more important in industries like cotton weaving and printing, shipbuilding, metallurgy, and glassmaking. By 1789, the French iron industry was considerably larger than the British, turning out nearly two and a half times the tonnage.

But if this suggests that the differences between eighteenth-century France and England are best understood in terms of degrees rather than of absolutes, we should be careful not to minimize the significant distinctions that did obtain. Despite the gains registered, by the eve of the Revolution only a fifth of France's working population was employed in industry, as against more than two-fifths in England, and whereas manufactures made up two-thirds of English trade, they accounted for just two-fifths of French. Because of the generally lower standard of living prevailing among the French peasantry, the fact that the great majority of French people worked the land put limits on domestic demand for consumer goods. France's smaller industrial sector and lower rates of urbanization were also reflected in the modest size of its coal industry: 600,000 tons of coal were hewn in 1789, whereas England already mined 5 million in 1750 and hit the 15 million ton level about 1800; on a per capita basis, English output was seventy times that of the French. Again, perhaps because of the country's huge pool of underemployed labor, technological innovations were introduced at a much slower pace in France than on the other side of the Channel. In 1789 there were 900 spinning jennies in France, as against 20,000 in England, and although considerably larger than the English, the French iron industry relied much more on traditional charcoal-fueled, low-capacity furnaces.

Much of French industry thus continued to employ time-honored technologies and remained within existing organizational structures. But within them, sustained, substantial secular growth took place and capitalist relations developed apace. France was home to some proto-factories, notably in cotton spinning and calico printing. But its entrepreneurs made much greater use of one of the kingdom's leading resources: the vast, under-employed farm population that could be paid very low wages for industrial by-employments. Although much was to change under the

impact of more mechanized competitors, France long retained a pronounced bias towards small-scale, labor-intensive industry along with a
strong high-quality sector.

England

Throughout most of the eighteenth century, English industry was
distinguished neither by uniquely high rates of growth – in many respects,
we have seen, the performance of France, the only other country for which
estimates exist, was superior – nor by dramatic structural change. Even in
1780, most English products, equipment, and workplaces greatly resembled both their predecessors in 1700 or even 1600 and their contemporaries across the Channel. Only from the 1770s did a few industries begin
both to grow very rapidly and – more significantly – to introduce radically
new machines into the production process on a large scale. Understandably, in light of subsequent developments, the eighteenth century has
been repeatedly analyzed to uncover the roots of the complex transformation summarized in the term "Industrial Revolution." Yet in order to
avoid anachronism it behooves us to try to understand eighteenth-century
English industries in their own right.

Much of the industrial development of this period represented an
extension of trends already evident in the long sixteenth century: dominance of woollen textiles as the country's major industry and far and away
its leading export; diversification of manufactures, seen not only in
woollens, where new and revised varieties appeared yet again, but also in
the rise of new trades, many of which supplanted imports; the centrality of
rural industry. But there were also crucial new departures involving
markets, products, technology, and forms of state intervention that
affected demand as well as supply.

English exports of manufactures more than doubled in value between
1700 and 1780. Only to a limited extent was this due to expansion of the
European market, traditionally by far the leading destination for English
goods. Exports of manufactures to the Continent increased barely an
eighth as lower-wage domestic producers and rising trade barriers took
their toll; Continental producers captured most of the growth in demand
within Europe itself. England's dynamic markets lay elsewhere, in regions
barely tapped before the mid-seventeenth century: colonies in North
America and the West Indies, which in the early 1770s took manufactures
worth eight times as much as in 1700, and in Ireland (a sextupling of
exports), as well as Africa and Asia (exports to both regions also registered
sixfold gains). So whereas in the early eighteenth century Continental
Europe took 84 percent of all exported manufactures, on the eve of the
American Revolution it took less than half. Conversely, North America

and the West Indies' share jumped from 10 percent to about 47 percent, Ireland's from 2 to 6 percent, Africa, Asia, the Levant, and Latin America's from 3 to 8 percent.

Territorial expansion through conquest, and demographic increase founded in large part on forced as well as voluntary immigration, made for much bigger colonial markets. British America had nearly four times as many people in 1700 as in 1650, and their numbers multiplied another tenfold by the early 1770s; Ireland's population at least doubled between 1650 and the 1770s. Mercantilist tariffs, bounties, monopolies, and prohibitions, backed by naval force, restricted these consumers as far as possible to British products. Although these measures were never wholly effective, they directed a great deal of demand into British channels, and the Staple Act of 1663 priced many foreign goods out of the market by requiring that they be reexported via England before going to the colonies. English industries also gained lucrative privileged access to the colonies of both Portugal, through the Methuen Treaty, and Spain, by the Peace of Utrecht. Between 1698–1702 and 1756–60, for instance, British exports to Portugal, largely textiles, rose 266 percent, and most were sent on to Brazil.

Overseas markets proved especially valuable to the textile industry. Before the early eighteenth century, England sold woollens essentially to Europeans, but when these markets began to close up, sales in North America took up the slack, allowing English output of woollen cloth to increase two and a half times across the eighteenth century. Despite this growth, however, woollens – both old and new draperies – finally lost the preeminence in English exports that they had held since the later Middle Ages. Whereas woollens were 85 percent of manufactures exported around 1700, they were only a half in 1770, a fifth in 1800. Linens and later cottons not only supplanted woollens but, thanks to vibrant New World demand, greatly expanded English textile export totals. Sales abroad of English linen, which were about 180,000 yards in 1730, jumped to 1.7 million yards a decade later, and reached almost 9.6 million in 1760. Well into the 1780s, linens from Ireland and Scotland also sold splendidly in the colonies, to which they were exported under the same terms as English goods. After 1750, consumption of cottons rose meteorically: barely 1 percent of manufacturing exports in the mid-eighteenth century, they were at least 35 percent fifty years later. More prosperous people bought muslins and other fine cottons, while cheap varieties were within reach of those who could not afford woollens or even linens. Cottons were initially most popular in America, which took four-fifths of those exported into the early 1770s. But subsequent developments showed that Continental demand could still have a significant impact, for Europe – even as it was taking a smaller share of British manufactures in general – bought nearly half of the kingdom's cottons in 1800.

The other sector of English industry experiencing rapidly growing foreign demand was metalwares, notably a wide variety of brass, steel, and iron objects referred to as "toys." This category included instruments and tools used in the workplace, along with jewelry, small weapons, locks, buckles, buttons, and similar items for the home or personal adornment. By 1800, metalwares accounted for 15 percent of exports of manufactures, as against 3 percent a century earlier.

Because output and trade statistics are very incomplete, it is difficult to discover the shares of export and domestic demand and thus their relative contributions to industrial advance. According to careful recent estimates, exports took about a quarter of total industrial output in 1700, a third in 1801. Besides indicating that export growth was significant across the eighteenth century (despite a dip between 1760 and 1780), these figures demonstrate that the great majority of industrial goods was consumed at home, even if certain industries – most notably cottons and woollens – were always more dependent on foreign markets. What mattered most for English industries, however, were the interactions of foreign and domestic demand: they were not rigidly separate spheres but were linked, formally and informally. In the second half of the eighteenth century, for example, as simple linen and cotton dresses became all the rage for women and unadorned woollens for men – thereby helping English textiles at the expense of French – books, magazines, and samples disseminated the fashions not only throughout provincial England but across the Continent and far into the New World.

Markets abroad and at home also spelled one another: when export growth slowed in 1710–30, and again during the 1760s and 1770s, domestic demand took up the slack. Continued growth meant that productive capacity did not sit idle for long. As a result, producers, especially in smaller trades such as metals, paper, glass, and even cotton in its early years, felt confident enough to embark on specializations, divisions of labor, and individually minor but cumulatively important technical innovations – such as the stamps, molds, and simple machines for rolling and boring devised by metal artisans – that cheapened their wares and allowed them to attract yet more customers. Particularly after about 1750, when grain prices rose more than wages, the fact that prices for industrial products dropped kept demand from being choked off. Middle-income households, whose numbers rose from 15 to 20 or even 25 percent of the population between 1750 and 1780, bought more and more everyday wares from pottery to iron pots to linens and printed goods

– precisely the goods in which British industry specialized. Artisans, workers, and farmers also began to wear manufactured stockings, tell time on clocks, deck their hats with ribbons.

These industries – and others – were increasingly affected by techno-logical innovation in the form of improved or novel machines. Already in the later seventeenth century, tape and ribbons started being woven on Dutch (or double) engine looms and stockings on knitting frames; reverberatory furnaces burned coal to smelt lead, tin, copper, and brass; innovative techniques drastically cut clockmaking costs. Soon after the dawn of the new century, Abraham Darby devised the coke-fired blast furnace for smelting iron and Thomas Newcomen constructed a usable steam engine for draining mines and otherwise pumping water. Across the century, the flow of inventions sped up, including crucibles for steel, Watt's steam engine, cotton stocking-knitting frames, the iron puddling furnace, and the cluster that helped revolutionize textile production – the flying shuttle, spinning jenny, water frame, spinning mule, and power loom. Adoption of new technology, to be sure, was typically a slow process before the final decades of the century and even by the 1790s accounted for only a small fraction of total output. But the habit of developing and applying mechanical innovation was becoming ingrained in English industries, particularly in textiles and metals, and this tendency both fed on and contributed to their dynamism.

Private enterprises housed these machines, for England had few Continental-style state businesses. Nevertheless, many of its industries were nurtured by a multitude of mercantilist measures: no more on the supply than on the demand side did Britain have a free-market economy. As in most of Europe, Asian calicoes were barred once they had created a domestic market for lighter and brighter fabrics; English-woven cottons took their place. Linens, too, owed much of their success to government assistance. This included duties of up to 150 percent of value levied on linens imported from the Continent; the removal of previously heavy import duties on flax from the Continent, whence England got most of its supplies, in 1731; and a 1742 Act of Parliament that gave bounties to exports of the coarse linens most in demand in the colonies. Abolishing all tariffs on Irish and Scottish linen, thereby granting them equal access to overseas markets, likewise set off a boom in these two trades. Shipments of Irish linens to England (whence many were re-exported) grew nearly twenty-two times between 1705 and 1750, and Scottish output went up eighteenfold from 1728 to 1815; many were rough "osnabrugs" that imitated – and then supplanted among New World consumers – linens from Osnabrück, Germany. Protective duties were also decisive for other industries, such as white paper, where output quadrupled between 1710 and 1800 as increasingly high tariffs reduced imports nearly to zero.

As in the long sixteenth century, the most dynamic industries were primarily to be found in the countryside. Already in the early 1720s, Daniel Defoe wrote of districts in Yorkshire that were "one continued village . . . [where] almost at every house there was a tenter [a frame on which fulled cloth was stretched to dry], and almost on every tenter a piece of cloth . . ."[5] Some crafts had long been predominantly rural, but even vigorous urban trades were subject to relocation. London's fine-cloth and clothing trades, for instance, were continuing to transfer less skilled aspects of production such as silk twisting, framework knitting, or cheap hat and shoe fabrication to the lower-wage provinces.

The simultaneous transformation of England's industrial geography assisted the growth of rural production. The north and west, where once little but farming had been practiced, became the center of the country's textile making, mining, and metallurgy, whereas the south and east deindustrialized. In part, the switch was the work of flexible entrepreneurs not wedded to traditional goods, organizations of production, and London-centered commercial networks. It also reflected the rising importance of always essentially rural mining and metallurgy, which now needed new sources of energy (water and coal) and, with the exhaustion of southern deposits, of raw materials (iron, lead, and copper ores). Most of all, the change rested on the concurrent agrarian reorganization, in the course of which cereals areas in the south and east came mainly to employ full-time male labor (leaving women and children to work in dispersed cottage trades like straw-plaiting, lace-making, button fabrication, and the like). The increasingly pastoral north and west, in contrast, had surplus labor of both genders, a very large proportion of which came to work in non-agricultural trades. In some Lancashire districts, 85 percent of male heads of household worked in textiles around 1750; women's and children's participation rates were not calculated but from all accounts were comparably high.

Still, some industrial expansion occurred in towns and cities. New drapery revived at Colchester, Exeter, and Norwich during the 1660–1700 period, a time that also saw the development of urban sugar refining and tobacco processing, along with the clock, watch, and fine-silk and linen trades brought by Huguenots who arrived in sizable numbers after 1685. Though the woollens towns in the south and east encountered rough seas as the eighteenth century went on, new urban industrial centers grew up, notably places like Birmingham, Leeds, Manchester, and Sheffield in the Midlands and the West Riding of Yorkshire. There they

[5] Daniel Defoe, *A Tour Through the Whole Island of Great Britain* [1724–26], 2 vols. (London, 1962), vol. II, p. 194.

stood at the center of and helped direct booming and increasingly specialized industrial districts. In addition, many small "country towns" were born or reborn throughout the country, their prosperous artisans serving well-to-do local gentry and merchants. And of course many luxury trades remained in London, close to an enormous clientèle and – critical for those based on responsiveness to fashion changes – on the spot when a new style suddenly swept the capital's trend-setting scene. Little wonder, in light of all this, that England became more and more urbanized, the proportion of towndwellers rising (by a conservative estimate) from 9 percent in 1650 to 20 percent in 1800.

Calculations of the extent of English industrial growth are as subject to controversy and constant revision as any eighteenth-century statistics. But estimates now suggest that output accelerated regularly, growing 0.7 percent annually between 1710 and 1760, 1.3 percent in 1760–80, at least 2.0 percent from 1780 to 1800. Woollens, leather, soap, and other more traditional trades lagged behind the average, whereas coal, nonferrous metals, and especially cotton and iron grew faster, particularly after 1770.

In terms of the overall pace of growth, Britain long lagged behind France. But Britain enjoyed advantages that quickened expansion as the century went on. A more productive agriculture and more efficient commercial system kept a smaller proportion of the population devoted to raising food. Hence even though industry boasted neither growth rates nor levels of productivity that were exceptional in a European context, the fact that more people were working in industry meant that many more manufactures were produced. Industrial goods, like agricultural produce, also benefited from savings in transactions costs due to improvements in marketing – notably thickening clusters of retail shops – and transport – not only canals, especially in the Midlands, but even more a network of turnpikes that extended exponentially between 1720 and 1770, setting off a burst of advances in carting and related services. In addition, English manufactures were less focused than their French counterparts on troubled southern Europe and the Levant: the Mediterranean demand that had been crucial to English industrial growth from the long sixteenth until the early eighteenth century thereafter played a much reduced part. Instead, England's industrial exports were oriented much more to rapidly growing and highly protected colonial markets. Understandably, then, manufactures comprised 54 percent of England's foreign trade in the early 1770s as against just one-third in France in 1787.

Across the long eighteenth century, England replaced the Dutch Republic as Europe's commercial leader. Sales in a multitude of markets meant that downturn in one could be offset by advance elsewhere. England also enjoyed larger, more dynamic, and more protected domestic and colonial (many, after 1783, ex-colonial) markets than the Dutch. At home and in North America, which loomed ever larger in British exports, consumption of the standardized, good-quality goods in which English industries specialized expanded among both enlarged middling strata and some segments of the laboring classes. English industry gained, moreover, not only from healthy demand but also from advantageous supply conditions. Once again supplanting the Dutch, England won European technological primacy; equally important – and here in sharp contrast to its rival across the North Sea – it reorganized and cheapened production by extensive ruralization. That England would first experience capitalist factory industrialization was far from inevitable during the greater part of the early modern period, but by 1780, we can now see, it had become likely.

The eighteenth-century extension of rural industry was of so great a magnitude as to represent a new departure. Even in the least industrialized and least prosperous areas, the variety of processes perhaps inadequately characterized as proto-industrialization finally opened up the agrarian sector's potential, while also speeding changes in urban production. The activities, workplaces, and production relations of industrialized country districts and manufacturing towns came to resemble one another. Among Europe's fastest growing cities in the eighteenth century were proto-industrial centers from Birmingham to Brno, Linz to Lokeren, Saint-Etienne to Sheffield, all of them previously little more than villages.

The most dynamic industrial regions were those favored by mutually supportive domestic and export markets providing strong and consistent demand. But the character of these markets was different than in the long sixteenth century. At home, the critical demand now came from expanding, if amorphous, middling groups – commercial farmers, small entrepreneurs, shopkeepers, affluent artisans. Abroad, overseas markets were most spirited, especially those North American and West Indies colonies that had few industries of their own. Within Europe, on the contrary, trade grew slowly, for Europe's own industrialization was accompanied, and fostered, by rising interstate barriers.

An open-ended transition

Industrial production fell more firmly under capitalist control across the eighteenth century. On the one hand, spreading proto-industry made a greater proportion of producers dependent on entrepreneurs for their raw materials, access to markets, wages – for, indeed, their entire livelihood. Although entrepreneurs generally contracted with individual workers, on occasion they organized putting-out systems on the basis of *Zunftkauf* or "guild purchase," by which a guild agreed to sell its members' entire output to a single merchant. On the other hand, capitalists concentrated control of the means of production, occasionally in big centralized workplaces but much more often through domestic systems that linked together numerous individually small units. And not merely were entrepreneurs coming to dominate industry; productive property was accumulating in the hands of a smaller number of entrepreneurs. Whereas Segovia's 173 woollen masters in 1691 owned an average of 1.5 looms (none had more than 5), the 58 masters in 1778 had an average of 3.9, and the four biggest averaged 13 apiece.

At the same time, more of Europe's areas, and a greater proportion of its people, had been brought into industrial work, at least part-time. This trend extended even beyond Europe's boundaries – onto its fishing boats and into its slave colonies. For several months each year, thousands of men and boys from struggling farms along the European littoral labored on North Atlantic cod ships, catching and processing fish according to a specialized division of labor that resembled nothing more than the proto-factories at home. In the later eighteenth century, the system changed – this time to a version of putting-out, whereby European merchants extended credit to fishers settled in isolated hamlets along the New World coast and were repaid in processed fish. On the plantations, the labor of the great majority of slaves was tightly integrated into the needs of industries in the metropoles. The very raison d'être of the plantation, after all, was not the cultivation of foodstuffs but the provision of groceries that were raw materials for European industries. The union of agriculture and manufacturing went yet further on many West Indian estates specializing in sugar. During the processing season, plantation owners and overseers put large numbers of slaves to work for long hours in crushing mills, boiling and curing houses, and distilleries. Regularly each year, then, slaves undertook skilled industrial labor, even though they continued to spend most of their time working the land.

Yet the trend toward increasing involvement in industry was far from irreversible: some individuals abandoned manufacturing, and whole areas deindustrialized. Often this fate was imposed by entrepreneurs who transferred their capital to lower-cost areas: thus worsted making, present in East Anglia since at least the mid-thirteenth century, was moved to Lancashire and the West Riding of Yorkshire. But it was also a decision taken by producers themselves, particularly peasant-workers. In the Achterhoek, for example, weaving had allowed small farmers to keep their land during a century of agricultural depression. Even so, when farming activity picked up after about 1750, many people left their looms and returned to the fields full-time.

Production structures, too, were not fixed once and for all; instead, a shifting constellation of market conditions, product type, entrepreneurial objectives, and artisanal resources repeatedly rearranged organizational forms. When Russian and Swedish competitors pushed iron from Vizcaya out of its main English market, Vizcayan merchants pulled their capital out of putting-out systems, leaving remaining production to small masters who could eke out a living using simple technology. Similarly, as urban employers prudently reduced their activities during the late seventeenth century depression, rural weavers around Clermont-de-Lodève in France became independent producers specializing in lower quality fabrics that used less skilled labor and cheaper materials. When recovery subsequently took hold, however, many a Clermont capitalist rebuilt his Verlagssystem. By the 1720s, the town's clothiers each controlled an average of 11–12 looms and employed some 300 workers, many of them formerly autonomous producers; blessed with the capital to buy expensive raw materials in bulk and to pay specialized workers, as well as the best access to international markets, they focused on high-quality cloth. Changes in demand in the later eighteenth century resulted in another turn of the cycle, for petty artisans weaving rough fabrics once again became preponderant. In Antwerp silkweaving, in contrast, small masters proliferated in prosperous times, when merchants were eager to buy their goods, whereas in downturns large artisan entrepreneurs got control of impoverished petty producers unable to sell what they had manufactured.

Not even centralized proto-factories proved necessarily permanent. In 1756, Count Joseph von Kinsky set up a manufactory for linen cloth on his Bohemian estate, later adding one for barchent and another for cotton. By 1764, the barchent mill alone employed some 400 people. Soon after, however, he closed the manufactories and put out the looms previously housed there to domestic weavers, after calculating that the overhead associated with buildings cut into rather than contributing to his profits. The Count's artificial-pearl business was also conducted on a putting-out basis, the workers (trained in a special school) using tools that he sold to them. But he kept open a large glassworks, having decided that it was more efficient than smaller ones previously used.

The proto-industrial era was thus one of open-ended transition, when mobile capital experimented with several modes of organization, forging and reforging structures and relations to profit best from shifts in labor supply, markets, prices, government policies, consumer demand, and raw material availability. These constant and complex changes had profound effects on workers and capitalists alike, transforming some roles, rules, and practices while consolidating others. Like industrial structures themselves, the experiences of labor in the age of manufacture shared some significant attributes but also became more diverse.

SUGGESTED READING

Many of the works cited in chap. 4 have relevance for the subjects treated here. For additional materials about consumer demand, see Daniel Roche, *The Culture of Clothing. Dress and Fashion in the "Ancien Regime"* (Cambridge, 1994; orig. publ. 1989); Beverly Lemire, *Fashion's Favourite: The Cotton Trade and the Consumer in Britain, 1660–1800* (Oxford, 1991); Lorna Weatherill, *Consumer Behaviour and Material Culture in Britain 1660–1760* (London, 1988); Neil McKendrick, John Brewer, and J. H. Plumb, *The Birth of a Consumer Society: The Commercialization of Eighteenth-Century England* (Bloomington, Ind., 1982). For developments in retailing, consult Hoh-Cheung Mui and Lorna Mui, *Shops and Shopkeeping in Eighteenth-Century England* (Kingston, Ont. and Montreal, 1989), and Margaret Spufford, *The Great Reclothing of Rural England: Petty Chapmen and their Wares in the Seventeenth Century* (London, 1984). Jan de Vries' discussion of the "industrious revolution" can be found in "The Industrial Revolution and the Industrious Revolution," *Journal of Economic History*, vol. 54 (1994).

The significance of the products of the Atlantic basin for European industries can be traced in Sidney Mintz, *Sweetness and Power: The Place of Sugar in Modern History* (New York, 1985), and Robert L. Stein, *The French Sugar Business in the Eighteenth Century* (Baton Rouge, 1988). For labor systems in the New World, see *Colonialism and Migration: Indentured Labour Before and After Slavery*, ed. P. C. Emmer (Dordrecht, 1986); *Work and Labor in Early America*, ed. S. Innes (Chapel Hill, NC, 1988); Richard S. Dunn, "Servants and Slaves: The Recruitment and Employment of Labor," in *Colonial British America*, eds. J. P. Greene and J. R. Pole (Baltimore, 1984); and Lesley Simpson, *The Encomienda in New Spain* (Berkeley, Calif., 1966). On the relationship between slavery and capitalist industrialization, see Eric Williams, *Capitalism and Slavery* (Chapel Hill, NC, 1944); Seymour Drescher, "Eric Williams: British Capitalism and British Slavery," *History and Theory*, vol. 26 (1987); *Journal of Interdisciplinary History*, vol. 17 (1987), a special issue entitled "Caribbean Slavery and British Capitalism," reprinted as *British Capitalism and Caribbean Slavery*, ed. B. Solow and S. Engerman (Cambridge, 1987); several clusters of articles in *Social Science History*, vols. 13 (1989) and 14 (1990); *Slavery and the Rise of the Atlantic System*, ed. Barbara Solow (Cambridge, 1991); Pierre Boulle, "Slave Trade, Commercial Organization and Industrial Growth in Eighteenth-Century Nantes," *Revue française d'histoire d'outre-mer*, vol. 59 (1972). Articles in *The European Discovery of the World and its Economic Effects on Pre-Industrial Society, 1500–1800*, ed. H. Pohl (Stuttgart, 1990) discuss aspects of the impact of the New World on the Old.

Adam Smith both conceptualized and condemned mercantilism in *The Wealth of Nations*, Book IV. Eli Heckscher, *Mercantilism* rev. edn (London, 1955), 2 vols., has long been the standard work. *Revisions in Mercantilism*, ed. D. C. Coleman (London, 1969), reprints excerpts from the most important articles and books published up to that time. D. C. Coleman, "Mercantilism Revisited," *Historical*

Journal, vol. 23 (1980), is an updating. Joyce Appleby, *Economic Thought and Ideology in Seventeenth-Century England* (Princeton, 1980) examines mercantilist thinkers and their critics; Leonard Gomes, *Foreign Trade and the National Economy* (New York, 1987) is a recent introduction to mercantilist thought. For the failure of mercantilist attempts at industrialization in late seventeenth-century Portugal, see Carl Hanson, *Economy and Society in Baroque Portugal, 1668–1703* (Minneapolis, 1981).

For background studies that contributed empirically and conceptually to the proto-industry debate, see Joan Thirsk, "Industries in the Countryside," in *Essays in the Economic and Social History of Tudor and Stuart England*, ed. F. J. Fisher (Cambridge, 1961) and E. L. Jones, "The Agricultural Origins of Industry," *Past and Present*, no. 40 (1958). Hermann Kellenbenz, "Rural Industries in the West from the End of the Middle Ages to the Eighteenth Century," in *Essays in European Economic History 1500–1800*, ed. P. Earle (Oxford, 1974), shows how widespread such trades were. For Franklin Mendels' position, see "Proto-Industrialization: The First Phase of the Industrialization Process," *Journal of Economic History*, vol. 32 (1972); another classic statement is Peter Kriedte, Hans Medick, and Jürgen Schlumbohm, *Industrialization before Industrialization* (Cambridge, 1981; orig. publ. 1977). The best overview is *European Proto-Industrialization*, ed. S. Ogilvie and M. Cerman (Cambridge, 1996). See also *Continuity and Change*, vol. 8, no. 2 (1993), a special issue devoted to the subject.

For historiographical evaluations of proto-industry, see L. A. Clarkson, *Proto-Industrialization. The First Phase of Industrialization?* (Basingstoke, 1985), which is also the best short introduction; D. C. Coleman, "Proto-Industrialization: a Concept Too Many," *Economic History Review*, 2nd ser., vol. 36 (1983); R. Houston and K. Snell, "Proto-Industrialization? Cottage Industry, Social Change, and Industrial Revolution," *Historical Journal*, vol. 27 (1984); and *Manufacture in Town and Country before the Factory*, ed. M. Berg, P. Hudson, and M. Sonenscher (Cambridge, 1983). These are largely critical; for more sympathetic accounts, see *Regions and Industries: A Perspective on the Industrial Revolution in Britain*, ed. P. Hudson (Cambridge, 1989). Paul Hohenberg and Lynn Lees, *The Making of Urban Europe 1000–1950* (Cambridge, Mass., 1985), Part II, and Carlo Poni, "Proto-Industrialization, Rural and Urban," *Review*, vol. 9 (1985), are good introductions to urban proto-industry.

For only a few of the many studies of particular industries and regions, see Maths Isacson and Lars Magnusson, *Proto-Industrialisation in Scandinavia* (Leamington Spa, 1987); Gay Gullickson, *Spinners and Weavers of Auffay: Rural Industry and the Sexual Division of Labor in a French Village, 1750–1850* (Cambridge, 1986); Pat Hudson, "Proto-Industrialization: the Case of the West Riding Wool Textile Industry," *History Workshop Journal*, no. 12 (1981); Liana Vardi, *The Land and the Loom. Peasants and Profit in Northern France 1680–1800.* (Durham, NC, 1993). For early factories, consult Stanley Chapman, "The Textile Factory Before Arkwright," *Business History Review*, vol. 48 (1974).

Studies of industries in particular areas vary considerably both in quantity and in value. For east central Europe, see Herman Freudenberger, *The Waldstein Woollen Mill* (Cambridge, Mass., 1963); Arnost Klíma, "Industrial Development in Bohemia 1648–1781," *Past and Present*, no. 11 (1957); Klíma, "Glassmaking

Industry and Trade in Bohemia in the XVIIth and XVIIIth Centuries," *Journal of European Economic History*, vol. 13 (1984); Klíma, "Domestic Industry, Manufactory and Early Industrialization in Bohemia," *Journal of European Economic History*, vol. 18 (1989). For brief overviews of Italian industry, see Dino Carpanetto and Giuseppe Ricuperati, *Italy in the Age of Reason 1685–1789* (London, 1987), chs. 1, 3. J. K. J. Thomson's excellent *A Distinctive Industrialization. Cotton in Barcelona, 1728–1832* (Cambridge, 1992) is one of the few English-language works on Spanish industry.

Scholarship in English on Germany is also thin, but see R. Ludloff, "Industrial Development in 17th and 18th Century Germany," *Past and Present*, no. 12 (1957); Herbert Kisch, *From Domestic Manufacture to Industrial Revolution. The Case of the Rhineland Textile Districts* (Oxford, 1989); Max Barkhausen, "Government Control and Free Enterprise in Western Germany and the Low Countries in the Eighteenth Century," in *Essays in European Economic History 1500–1800*, ed. P. Earle (Oxford, 1974); Peter Kriedte, "Demographic and Economic Rhythms: the Rise of the Silk Industry in Krefeld in the Eighteenth Century," *Journal of European Economic History*, vol. 15 (1986).

Dutch industry is usually considered in studies of the overall state of the Republic's economy. The best of the recent English-language works are Jan de Vries and Ad van der Woude, *The First Modern Economy: Growth, Decline, and Perseverance of the Dutch Economy, 1500–1815* (Cambridge, 1996), which appeared too late for its findings to be integrated into this book; J. L. van Zanden, *The Rise and Decline of Holland's Economy: Merchant Capitalism and the Labour Market* (Manchester University Press, 1993); James Riley, "The Dutch Economy after 1650: Decline or Growth?" *Journal of European Economic History*, vol. 13 (1984); and Jan de Vries, "The Decline and Rise of the Dutch Economy, 1675–1900," in *Technique, Spirit, and Form in the Making of the Modern Economies*, ed. G. Saxonhouse and G. Wright (Greenwich, Conn., 1984). Jonathan Israel, *Dutch Primacy in World Trade 1585–1740* (Oxford, 1989) emphasizes industrial decline. J. A. Van Houtte, *An Economic History of the Low Countries 800–1800* (New York, 1977), chs. 3, 5, and Joel Mokyr, *Industrialization in the Low Countries 1795–1850* (New Haven, 1976), ch. 1, also discuss the southern Netherlands. For the latter area, see also Myron Gutmann, *Toward the Modern Economy. Early Industry in Europe, 1500–1800* (New York, 1988); Christian Vandenbroeke, "The Regional Economy of Flanders and Industrial Modernization in the Eighteenth Century," *Journal of European Economic History*, vol. 16 (1987); and *Textiles of the Low Countries in European Economic History*, ed. E. Aerts and J. Munro (Leuven, 1990).

France is the best served of the Continental countries. For two excellent case studies, see J. K. J. Thomson, *Clermont-de-Lodève 1633–1789. Fluctuations in the Prosperity of a Languedocian Cloth-Making Town* (Cambridge, 1982), and T. J. A. Le Goff, *Vannes and its Region. A Study of Town and Country in Eighteenth Century France* (Oxford, 1981). On guilds, consult Hilton Root, "Privilege and the Regulation of the Eighteenth-Century French Trades," *Journal of European Economic History*, vol. 20 (1991); Emile Coornaert, "French Guilds under the Old Regime," in *Essays in French Economic History*, ed. Rondo Cameron (Homewood, Ill., 1970); Michael Sonenscher, *The Hatters of Eighteenth-Century France* (Berkeley, Cal., 1987); Sonenscher, *Work and Wages: Natural Law, Politics and the Eighteenth-Century French Trades* (Cambridge, 1989); and Gail Bossenga, "Protecting Merchants: Guilds and Commercial Capitalism in Eighteenth-Century France," *French Historical Studies*, vol. 15 (1988). Pierre Deyon and Philippe Guignet, "The Royal Manufactures and Economic and Technological Progress in France before the Industrial Revolution," *Journal of European Economic History*, vol. 9 (1980), is a favorable reinterpretation of the effects of mercantilism. For divergent interpretations of French growth, see Henri Hauser, "The Characteristic Features of French Economic History from the Middle of the Sixteenth to the Middle of the Eighteenth Century," *Economic History Review*, vol. 4 (1933); Denis Richet, "Economic Growth and its Setbacks in France from the Fifteenth to the Eighteenth Century," in *Social Historians in Contemporary France* (New York, 1972); and the classic comparison by François Crouzet, "England and France in the Eighteenth Century: A Comparative Analysis of Two Economic Growths," in *The Causes of the Industrial Revolution in England*, ed. R. Hartwell (London, 1967). John Clark, *La Rochelle and the Atlantic Economy during the Eighteenth Century* (Baltimore, 1981), notes the weak effects of colonial trade on French industries and the general economy.

For Britain, there are two fine recent overviews: Maxine Berg, *The Age of Manufactures 1700–1820* (London, 1985), and M.J. Daunton, *Progress and Poverty. An Economic and Social History of Britain 1700–1850* (Oxford, 1995). Paul Mantoux, *The Industrial Revolution in the Eighteenth Century: An Outline of the Beginnings of the Modern Factory System in England* (New York, 1928; orig. publ. 1906) can still be consulted with profit. *The Economic History of Britain since 1700*, 2nd edn, ed. R. Floud and D. McCloskey, vol. I (Cambridge, 1994) contains the most up-to-date summaries.

There are countless studies of individual English industries, the best of which concern the textile trades. For a small sampling, see *Textile History and Economic History. Essays in Honor of Miss Julia de Lacy Mann*, ed. N.B. Harte and K.G. Ponting (Manchester, 1973); David Corner, "The Tyranny of Fashion: The Case of the Felt-Hatting Trade in the Late Seventeenth and Eighteenth Centuries," *Textile History*, vol. 22 (1991); S.D. Chapman, *The Cotton Industry in the Industrial Revolution*, 2nd edn (Basingstoke, 1987); ch. 1; A.P. Wadsworth and J. de L. Mann, *The Cotton Trade and Industrial Lancashire 1600–1780* (Manchester, 1931). For some other important industries, consult D.C. Coleman, *The British Paper Industry, 1495–1860* (Oxford, 1958); W.H.B. Court, *The Rise of the Midland Industries* (London 1938); Roger Burt, "The International Diffusion of Technology in the Early Modern Period: The Case of the British Non-Ferrous Mining Industry," *Economic History Review*, 2nd ser., vol. 44 (1991).

Foreign trade is well surveyed by Ralph Davis, *The Industrial Revolution and British Overseas Trade* (Leicester, 1979). For Scotland, see S.G.E. Lythe and J. Butt, *An Economic History of Scotland 1100–1939* (Glasgow and London, 1975); *Scottish Capitalism*, ed. Tony Dickson (London, 1980), a collective effort with some excellent chapters; and Gil Schrank, "Crossroad of the North: Proto-Industrialization in the Orkney Islands, 1730–1840," *Journal of European Economic History*, vol. 21 (1992). Conrad Gill, *The Rise of the Irish Linen Industry* (Oxford, 1925) is superb.

Documents of European Economic History. Vol. I. *The Process of Industrialization 1750–1870*, ed. S. Pollard and C. Holmes (London, 1968), ch. 2, prints many relevant selections.

Part IV

7　Experiences of labor in the era of transitions

During the three centuries of the early modern period, capitalists increasingly concentrated control of the means of production without gathering much of the laboring population in large productive units. How this process of change within continuity impinged upon workers is the subject of this chapter. In it, we will examine arrangements of labor, work practices, structures of income, systems of payment, collective organization and action, understandings of workshop relations, and the particular ways in which women and children were incorporated into the workforce. The interactions of customs and innovations, institutions and ideas, led on occasion to open conflict. But like the attendant structural change, much proceeded quietly and gradually.

Labor systems and work practices

During the early modern period, east central Europe became chiefly an area of coerced labor as numerous aristocrats organized not only commercial grain growing, stock raising, pisciculture, and other activities related to the land, but also mining, glass and iron fabrication, and textiles. Neoserfdom originated and was most extensively elaborated in agriculture, but, as we have seen, serfs also came to be employed in industry. Just as the free peasantry had been subjugated, so free artisans were displaced. This process was hastened by the adoption of expensive innovations such as blast furnaces and the opening of large enterprises, both of which considerably increased the level of capital investment above that available to petty entrepreneurs.

Coerced industrial work had several guises. Entrepreneurs mainly used unpaid corvée labor to cut the costs associated with labor-intensive auxiliary tasks such as felling trees and making charcoal for blast furnaces or the transport of ore, sand, and other raw materials. Most positions at the actual workplaces used paid labor, though with wage rates determined not by contract or in the labor market but by employer fiat. Finally, much smaller numbers of wage-earning workers who were hired competitively would occupy the most skilled jobs. But unless they were foreign recruits (employed mainly as technicians and supervisors, and in decreasing numbers as time went on), they typically were subject to the aristocratic industrialists' feudal authority. The Bohemian Count von Kinsky could therefore dissolve his centralized workshops (see ch. 6), secure in the knowledge that no rival entrepreneur could lure away his domestic workers, since he remained their Grundherr.

In Europe west of the Elbe and its overseas extensions, labor systems varied from free to temporarily bound to permanently constrained. Free workers predominated, whether they sold the product of their labor, like artisans in handicraft shops and small family farmers, or the labor itself, like workers in proto-industry and manufactories, and "servants in husbandry" on commercial farms. Once they acquired shops or holdings, masters and peasants tended to stay put, although opportunities to improve their economic position, help establish purified religions, or escape persecution lured even solid artisans and farmers across European borders and as far as the New World. Laborers were considerably more mobile, even those working on the land: year in and year out, some three-quarters of English agricultural laborers changed employers when their annual contracts came to an end.

Industrial workers could and many did change employers even more frequently. Although a small core of workers remained in the same shop for years, the great majority did not. On the average, eighteenth-century journeyman tailors in Rouen stayed with a master for just 34 days, journeyman wigmakers for 118 days. At the Société typographique de Neuchâtel, a Swiss publishing firm that specialized in French-language books, workers arrived and departed every day, to the extent that half the labor force turned over within any given six months. The glazier Jacques Ménétra worked for six different Parisian employers in less than two years, while during three years, a journeyman joiner found jobs in at least ten distinct shops in and around Paris, Rouen, and Vernon. Schemes like the French *billet de congé*, which in principle prevented workers from leaving a job without the employer's express written consent, had little effect on turnover, since they were simply ignored by workers and masters alike.

Among young workers in particular, a period of repeated job changes seems to have been a common if unwritten expectation, perhaps in order to find an acceptable employer, or maybe just to postpone settling down and its attendant responsibilities. But in some trades, mobility was mandatory, since journeymen were required to complete their training by undertaking a national tour in the years after apprenticeship. Their movement was aided by linked semi-clandestine journeymen's associations that operated in many towns. Ménétra's autobiography gives a vivid, if somewhat fictionalized, sense of his time on the road, when for seven years his association, the *compagnonnage du Devoir*, helped him to find jobs and lodging in cities around France. Not that all movement was voluntary or part of a recognized cycle. Employers, too, had a hand in the matter, for they hired many workers by the week or the job. Printers, for example, often engaged a fresh staff for each book, firing everyone when the press run was completed.

Many free workers passed through stages when they voluntarily contracted away control over their labor. Chief among them were apprentices and indentured servants. In return for several years of work for little or no pay, both were promised significant rewards – the training needed for a coveted mastership or passage to and land in the New World – although the promise might remain unfulfilled or the term of service turn into a nightmare of harsh discipline, inadequate food, clothing, and lodging, or even be dishonestly prolonged. Other ostensibly free workers were caught up in coercive labor arrangements that lacked any semblance of consent, contract, or future recompense. The most notorious was the so-called "truck system," perpetrated mainly on isolated groups of laborers such as foundrymen and miners employed in remote mountain districts. Workers enmeshed in it were paid part or even all of their wages in goods or claims on goods redeemable only at "truck shops" (company stores), to which they were continually in arrears because their employers shamelessly manipulated prices and wages. By law, indebted workers were forbidden to quit their jobs, but many simply absconded.

Escape was impossible for all but a handful of the throngs of slaves (and sprinkling of transported convicts) who constituted the greatest concentrations of coerced labor under western European purview. Both groups toiled principally on New World plantations. Where delicate crops such as tobacco were raised, or timing was critical, as with sugarcane cultivation, slaves and convicts alike worked row to row in regimented gangs under a driver's watchful eye and frequently wielded lash. The many planters who grew hardy crops or wanted to save on supervisory costs, in contrast, assigned their laborers individually or in small groups to specific tasks. Yet for all that their labor was similar, and their private lives were equally subject to constant and intrusive policing, felons and slaves eventually parted ways. Should they survive, convicts could look forward to emancipation once they had finished their sentences. With rare exceptions, however, slaves could expect to slog away at the same burdensome, monotonous jobs twelve hours a day, six days a week, all year round until they died or became too old or sick to continue.

Pockets of coerced labor were also found within western Europe itself. Sugar plantations on Mediterranean islands, as well as latifundia in southern Spain and Portugal, sometimes used slaves. To assure themselves a sufficient cheap labor force, starting in 1606 Scottish noble mineowners promoted Acts of Parliament that progressively enserfed miners. Although the original laws only required colliers, salters, or lead miners to obtain written releases before changing employment, judicial interpretations gradually equated all mine and saltpan jobs with lifetime enserfment, and eventually the status was extended to workers' children, turning entire families into mine owners' property. Not until the end of the eighteenth century did Acts of Parliament end the colliers' legal servitude (and also abolish the surprisingly effective collective associations that the miners had managed to form).

Workhouses for paupers and criminals were more prevalent sites of compulsory labor. They were based on the assumption that those without jobs who became wards of the state lost their right to the free disposal of their persons and therefore could legitimately be forced to work. The Amsterdam rasphuis, where every inmate was obligated to grate the brazilwood dyestuff, was considered a model institution, despite never managing to become self-sufficient. The Dutch Republic also opened colonies run according to strict military discipline in the rural northeastern provinces to force the poor and beggars to farm. English workhouses began in the late sixteenth century as places from which raw materials were put out to the unemployed who worked at home, then returned their products to the same site for payment at rates set by the government. This arrangement proved unfeasible, however, for the authorities could not sufficiently supervise workmanship. To remedy this shortcoming and curb expenses, in the eighteenth century paupers were enclosed in institutions where in return for support they worked (in principle, for ten hours a day) without wages, training, control over their work conditions, or any say in the kind of work they were compelled to perform.

Rather than to teach specific industrial skills, in other words, workhouses were built to inculcate diligence, order, and routine. Many contemporaries thought, moreover, that these were values and habits that the entire laboring population needed to learn. Commons, open fields, and rights to gather fuel, glean, and pasture a cow on the waste were frequently condemned for allowing the survival of lazy, inefficient, insubordinate rural folk; as the *Gentleman's Magazine* avowed in 1766, Scottish peasants "would rather suffer poverty than work."[1] For their part, artisans were upbraided for laboring only a few days at a stretch or,

---

[1] Cited from Peter Mathias, "Leisure and Wages in Theory and Practice," in his *The Transformation of England* (London, 1979), p. 151.

after frittering away "Saint Monday" in the taverns, toiling furiously at the end of the week. Thus higher wages, it was believed, encouraged workers not to more regular or diligent exertions but to more loafing and imbibing. In his *Northern Tour* (1770), Arthur Young (the commentator whom we have met before) declared, "Great earnings have a strong effect on all who remain the least inclined to idleness or other ill courses by causing them to work but four or five days to maintain themselves the seven."[2]

Although often viewing them more positively, scholars have likewise attributed such work patterns to laborers' values and aspirations. According to Max Weber, who termed such behavior "traditionalism," to economists, who refer to a "backward-bending labor supply curve," and to sociologists, who identify a "leisure preference," pre-industrial workers sought to earn only enough to sustain an expected standard of living, so they simply laid down their tools once it had been attained. From another perspective, the historian E. P. Thompson argues that different notions of time and different work rhythms, in which periods of concentrated exertion alternated with indolence, obtained before clocks and machines enforced steady application. Are these interpretations well-founded?

Certainly, in a little-mechanized economy workers' muscle power and skills endowed them with a substantial degree of control over the length, pace, and intensity of the production process. Thus in the early seventeenth century artisans could stay away from the Venetian Arsenal nearly every Monday, knowing how empty were bosses' threats of fines or dismissal. Work tempos were affected, too, by rituals and revelries marking important occasions. An apprentice's successful completion of a masterpiece was joyously celebrated. Upon the arrival of a new journeyman at a French papermill, everyone stopped work to raise a glass of wine – and often the drinking did not end until days later.

But much more than workers' predilections determined the rhythms of production. The fact that many people worked at home meant that domestic concerns were critical – particularly, but not exclusively, to women with children to mind. Nature also played an important part in setting work cadences. Besides the usual seasonal variations in the amount of daylight and the flow of water, a sudden freeze or drought could bring work abruptly to a halt. In addition, the production system itself was so constructed as virtually to guarantee sharp oscillations in the demand for labor. Arrivals of raw materials were notoriously irregular, and entrepreneurs repeatedly overproduced during good times, creating gluts that just as recurrently threw laborers out of work. Sickness, injury, and age also enforced periodic joblessness. One Ralph Crawhall earned the most of

[2] Quoted from Mathias, "Leisure and Wages," p. 150.

any miner in the Whickham (England) colliery in May 1742, but by 1764, when he was older and often too ill to wield a pick, his impoverished family was on the edge of starvation.

From week to week, then, or even month to month, early modern work patterns were often remarkably erratic. Yet by the eighteenth century, at least, there is mounting evidence that the duration, regularity, and intensity of labor were on the rise. Cornish tin miners spent four hours a day underground at the start of the seventeenth century but six to eight in the eighteenth. By the middle of the century, the average Whickham pitman worked 239 out of 259 possible days, the man with the worst record only 16 fewer.

Laboring habits changed for a variety of reasons. In Protestant lands, the abolition of saints' days eliminated as many as fifty occasions upon which workers had enjoyed a day off, and the Catholic Church also simplified its liturgical calendar. Decades of inflation that outpaced wages – a condition that prevailed ever more widely across Europe as the eighteenth century progressed – meant that many people had to toil longer and harder just to maintain their existing standard of living. Among those employed in favored industries, locations, or jobs, in contrast, new work habits may indicate attempts to raise their levels of consumption or acquire new goods. The change can be seen with special clarity among coal miners. In the seventeenth century, English hewers – far and away the best-paid pitmen – worked only three and a half days a week, as against the five or six that were the norm for other employees, and they seem not to have had or sought more or different material possessions than their poorer fellows. But in eighteenth-century Whickham, hewers labored the most days of any mine employees – hardly the expected response if they still aimed only to fulfill customary needs or were expressing an option for leisure. Conversely, the refusal of hewers in isolated Scottish pits to work six-day weeks, despite considerable prodding by their employers, appears linked to their region's notorious shortage of desirable goods to buy.

Besides religious reform, the whiplash of necessity, and the lure of consumer goods, workers encountered entrepreneurial initiatives to boost both the quantity and the quality of their employees' labor by modifying the organization and the culture of work. As centralized workplaces that involved some coordination of the labor force, manufactories were the most logical sites for such attempts, so it is not surprising that the Venetian Arsenal was a pioneer in this respect. Already in the second third of the seventeenth century it had put in place an enlarged, hierarchic management force and imposed regimented work practices and quasi-military discipline to curb absenteeism, drunkenness, and the like. Along with these sticks, workers were offered carrots. Some were of a material nature:

tax exemptions, grants of money, wine rations, loans for buying tools, bonuses, and – most popular of all – guaranteed lifetime employment. Others were psychological and symbolic: militia, firefighting, and other civic duties that bestowed special status and bred an ethos of *arsenalotti* as members of a distinctive and honored community. Under the new order, work habits became more regular, workers more quiescent, and – the point of the whole exercise, at least for the Venetian government – yearly output of standardized galleys rose from seven galleys a year in the 1630s to ten in the 1640s.

State-imposed discipline (backed by a liberal dose of religious precept) was more singlemindedly emphasized in attempts to mold a compliant and conscientious labor force in Rhineland coal pits. All miners had to "swear an oath by Almighty God to remain loyal to our gracious King of Prussia . . . and to show obedience to the Mining Office set above them;" had to "live honourably and respectably, and appear on all working days at the mine at the proper time for the morning [religious] service;" and then had to "make ready for the work to which they are ordered by managers, overmen or deputies, and perform it loyally and diligently . . ." All violations of these rules, or those that forbade leaving without permission, refusing to accept mandated wages, hours, and worksites, engaging in "invective, swearing, blasphemy, fighting or brawling," or even failing to wear "miners' habit," were punishable by a system of graduated fines or dismissal.[3]

The most far-reaching initiatives were undertaken in eighteenth-century England. At his ironworks near Newcastle, Abraham Crowley built a factory village, school, and chapel, employed teachers, ministers, and doctors, established a grievance court and private poor-relief scheme. These paternalistic benefits were accompanied by – indeed, were integrated into – a harshly authoritarian, if moralistic, discipline that extended over every aspect of the employees' lives in order to mold them into submissive, industrious, loyal model workers.

More subtle and thorough was the system elaborated by Josiah Wedgwood at his "Etruria" pottery works in Staffordshire in the 1770s. To succeed in the increasingly competitive consumer market, Wedgwood emphasized both cost-cutting and the clever marketing of new wares manufactured more efficiently with the aid of a revamped production process, to which a well-trained and tractable labor force was central. Carefully designed apprenticeship programs sought to impart both technical knowledge and correct attitudes. On the job, a far-reaching division of labor helped raise standards but also sharply limited the range

---

[3] Regulations of 1768, printed in *Documents of European Economic History*, ed. S. Pollard and C. Holmes, vol. I (London, 1968), pp. 157–8.

of individual workers' skills: some employees, for example, spent their entire lives only scouring colored pieces, while others performed the identical operation on jasper ware. The new order did not rely, however, simply on reformed workers: above them stood an enlarged cadre of managers and foremen endowed with greater authority than their predecessors and the power to evaluate and if necessary fine workers for infractions of the detailed regulations that embodied Wedgwood's vision. And in order to wrest control of the duration of work from his laborers, Wedgwood replaced piece-rates by money wages, a portion of which was docked when a worker violated the hours rung by a bell at the beginning and end of the workday and at mealtimes.

At least by his own account, Wedgwood increased output, improved quality, and cut prices. At the same time, he boasted, he transformed a group of worthless, drunken malingerers into careful, sober, diligent laborers blessed with higher wages, better living conditions, and superior morality – even if, he had to admit, they persisted in quitting their posts each summer to go to riotous wakes (parish festivals) and fairs. Wedgwood was not representative of entrepreneurs of his time, nor was Etruria a typical workplace. But like the experiments at the Arsenal, the German mines, and Crowley's ironworks – and similar attempts at the Montgolfier paper mill in France and elsewhere – it does indicate that the introduction of new work patterns was not dependent on the advent of the mechanized power-driven factory.

Earnings

Some workers were their own sole support. Of these, the most numerous were the widowed and the never married; in addition, certain categories of workers – journeymen, indentured servants, domestic servants – were often required to remain single as a condition of keeping their jobs. Then, too, prosperous masters might maintain their families just on their income alone. But for most people, urban and rural, the household remained the earnings unit across the early modern era, as it had been in the Middle Ages. Family income was not stable, however, but cyclical. Relatively poor upon marriage, when establishing an independent household, a couple's income rose as long as the wife could be fully employed. This was unlikely to be a long period since, in the absence of birth control, children began to be born a year or so after the wedding, arriving every two and a half to three years thereafter (although the interval between births lengthened as the woman aged). As the wife gave birth to and raised children themselves still too young to labor, she was able to work less and family income fell, but it recovered as the maturing children began to work and the wife started helping again on the family holding or in the family shop or returned to the labor market. Best off were those families – a minority at any one time – in which the parents were in their physical prime and the children of an age when they added to the family income. Once the children left to go into domestic service, enter apprenticeship, or form their own families, household income began to drop again, touching a very low point – virtual destitution – if the aged parents became unable to work. Besides the ever-present dangers caused by nature, injury, illness, or economic fluctuations, then, household earnings were at the mercy of the family cycle.

Incomes were frequently derived from several professions as well as several earners. Numerous individuals worked at more than one pursuit, and family incomes could represent the pooling of resources derived from a range of activities. Just as many farming families engaged in crafts, so many rural industrial households realized part – at times a substantial part – of their income from pastoralism, gardening, or cultivating raw materials. In town and country alike, several household members might practice the same trade, or interdependent trades such as spinning and weaving, while others had wholly distinct occupations.

Forms of payment were equally complex. If independent producers or engaged in a Kaufsystem, artisans and households sold the products of their labor and received not a wage but a price for a good. If employed in a Verlagssystem, they received the difference between the entrepreneur's charge for the raw materials put out (and the credit extended) to them and the price that he or she subsequently paid them for the finished product.

In jobs paying wages, piece-rates generally prevailed: an individual or a work gang was paid per bolt of cloth, thousand pins, harvested acre. Enterpreneurs preferred the piece-rate (despite the constant temptation by workers to cut corners), since it obviated the need for much supervision and was thought to encourage hard work. On much the same grounds, workers, too, often favored piece-rate payment: by leaving them free to set their own tempo it gave them greater latitude to determine their own earnings. Piece-rate scales were not permanently fixed but were subject to constant negotiation. Igualada (Catalonia) weavers struck in 1757 against entrepreneurs who demanded wider fabrics for the same pay; six years later, their counterparts in Rouen successfully agitated for payment by the ell rather than by the bolt, since employers had been lengthening the bolts without raising rates. They also won the right to be paid before bleaching and washing had shrunk the cloth but got no satisfaction when they demanded remuneration for tying threads and other time-consuming ancillary tasks.

Time wages were most commonly paid in two situations. One obtained when many workers not of the same household were engaged collaboratively in a multi-stage process, such as construction, large-scale mining, or cloth finishing, so that calculating individual contributions was difficult or impossible. The other occurred when the period required to complete a single process or product had been standardized and was embodied in formal rules, as in textile fulling and some forms of tailoring. Time wages also became associated with more innovative branches of industry. In Tuscan ironmaking, they were paid in the more technologically advanced, capital-intensive branches, like blast-furnace smelting, dominated by larger entrepreneurs. Piece-work, in contrast, prevailed in nailmaking, general smithery, or other trades characterized by backward technology and artisanal control of the production process.

Whether time or piece, wages were likely to be only partly paid in cash. Because much business was seasonal and bills were paid slowly, employers with insufficient cash turned over goods (or allowed employees to keep a portion of the goods they produced) for the workers to use or to sell for themselves. Entitlements were another part of pay packets. Some workers received food or, like coal hewers and workers in industries that burned coal, received a stipulated quantity to use for domestic fuel; other laborers were furnished housing or were given grants or low-cost loans to buy or rent accommodations. Although affecting a decreasing number of industrial workers, these kinds of entitlements could significantly mitigate the ravages of inflation, especially among agricultural workers, for whom they persisted longest. The fact that the bulk of their income consisted of in-kind payments (including food, dwellings, gardens, and grazing rights) enabled manorial laborers in eastern Germany to maintain an essentially stable living standard between the late sixteenth and the early nineteenth centuries, a period that saw real monetary wages fall by half.

Many more workers enjoyed rights to a predetermined value or amount of materials defined as "waste" (although not all was literally such), which they either used to produce goods they marketed themselves or sold to or exchanged with merchants or other artisans. Pickers, spinners, and weavers took wool; tailors got scraps of cloth and trimming; shipwrights carried off wood scraps or "chips" – as much as one man could take one day a week, according to the English Navy Board, what they and their family members could take three times a day, according to shipyard workers. Some employers balked at the practice. The Navy Board tried repeatedly to end chip-taking in return for an increase in money wages; the workers accepted the raise but continued taking the chips, which they burned as fuel, used to build their houses, or sold. Geneva silk merchant-entrepreneurs insisted on the return of all waste. It was not only the cost that they objected to, for after all piece-rates could have been adjusted to take it into account. More worrisome was the possibility that artisans would use the substantial waste generated – a quarter or even a third of what was put out – to set up production free of merchant control.

Entitlement could shade off into or be supplemented by embezzlement, as workers sought to enhance earnings – a spinner's income could be raised by up to 20 percent in this way – by one of the few means under their control. Pilferage was an evident danger in putting-out but was equally possible in dockyards, coalmines, even small shops. Domestic workers also defrauded employers by substituting less good materials for those put out to them, and this problem seems to have grown larger as the typical Verlagssystem expanded in size, for it was usually too expensive and time-consuming to check completed goods carefully.

During periods when labor markets were tight, employers were often willing to tolerate a measure of what they privately deemed stealing, lest workers be driven away by the loss of what they considered legitimate income. And even in more normal times, many campaigns against filching were short-term attempts to cut costs and were soon abandoned. In the second half of the eighteenth century, however, employers and governments redefined many traditional forms of entitlement – long-recognized claims or rights – as bonuses (and thus revocable) or even criminalized them. Whereas Scottish miners considered free coal part of their regular pay, their bosses now argued that it was a reward only for workers who toiled for a full six days a week – significantly more than the established industry norm. In 1757, Staffordshire colliers' customary right to two weekly portions of coal, which comprised a third to a half of their wages, was reinterpreted as theft and abruptly cut off – or was supposed to be, since for the next fifty years, miners apparently received a daily payment in compensation. Similarly, during the 1760s entrepreneurs in Sedan (France) claimed that workers' appropriation of waste wool generated during weaving was a crime against property; the workers saw it differently and continued to take scraps despite the risk of being sent to the galleys. At a time when prices were rising and wages falling behind, workers were as loath to give up in-kind payments as employers were eager to end them.

In all, then, a wage earner's income might consist of five components, although any given worker might not receive all of them; typically, the core of workers whose services employers wanted to assure over the long term received the greatest range of emoluments. (1) Cash or in-kind advances repaid either by working a set period of time or by producing a prescribed quantity of goods. (2) Cash payments, disbursed at the completion of the product or – if a time wage – weekly, biweekly, or monthly, although normally calculated by the day. (3) Either a portion of the goods made or the cash equivalent. (4) Food, housing, and assorted other "customary" payments: these might be of recent vintage but once obtained were viewed by workers as traditional rights and were fiercely defended. (5) Raw materials left over from the production process or conventionally interpreted as scraps.

Neither money wages nor perquisites – the value of which was set by reference to prevailing wage rates – varied markedly or frequently, but they were not immobile. Their level was determined by the interaction of norms (considered "custom," but not necessarily longstanding), regulations, and market forces (more specifically, the supply of and demand for workers as played out in labor markets compartmentalized by trade, status, and gender). The specific role that custom played was most apparent during the long sixteenth century, when population expanded more rapidly than employment, creating a growing pool of under- and unemployed labor. Nevertheless, nominal wages were not reduced, thanks especially to norms that had become widely accepted during the labor shortages that accompanied the late medieval crisis. At the same time, however, custom was not taken to mandate that wages had to retain constant purchasing power, so sixteenth-century workers could not appeal to its authority to secure increases that kept up with the rising cost of living. Custom had, in sum, a mainly defensive function with respect to the play of market forces.

On their side, regulations had their most evident influence on the timing and magnitude of specific wage adjustments, particularly in state enterprises or in places where governments were substantial employers. Rules could not, however, singlehandedly override market forces to control general wage movements. This was clear, for instance, in the mid-sixteenth century, when pay scales increased across western Europe (although never as much as prices) after a bout of especially sharp inflation at a time that concurrent plague and influenza epidemics temporarily tightened the labor supply. To try to limit the spiral, many governments legislated statutory pay maxima. Yet even the authorities were soon obliged to violate the ceilings, both to comply with customary notions of fair wages and to be able to hire workers in the actual labor market. At most, a decreed maximum might slow the movement of wages by placing an additional obstacle in the way of laborers and employers, who risked fines for exceeding the published scales. The same was true in trades where organized groups of workers or employers convinced authorities to dictate wage rates: although the scales provided reference points – and often occasions for further agitation to have them obeyed (as custom) or revoked (as violating custom) – rarely did they alone prescribe the actual wages paid.

Wage hierarchies, which persisted despite changes in wage levels, likewise resulted from the interplay of custom, regulation, and segmented labor markets. Journeymen, who possessed all the skills necessary to become masters but lacked the requisite capital, were paid less than masters for exactly the same work: in the Toulouse and Geneva wool trades, for example, they received four-fifths of masters' pay. Laborers, who lacked specialized training even if they were not necessarily unskilled, got even less. Those working with master masons in Lille were paid about half as much; in England, a 3:2 ratio between craftsmen's and laborers' pay was the norm. Women continued to be most severely discriminated against, receiving just two-fifths to three-fifths of what men were paid for the same work. The differential was based largely on traditional secular and religious assumptions about the purported physical, mental, and moral inferiority of females and thus their inherent ineligibility for equal treatment. But it was enshrined in all manner of statute and reinforced by the segregation of women workers into a limited number of trades and types of jobs, thereby swelling those labor pools while shrinking others.

None of the wage determinants existed in a vacuum, of course; both employers and workers struggled to influence them in their favor. In this give-and-take process, employers enjoyed some important advantages. They hired and fired and could move or threaten to move to new locations, especially in the lower-wage countryside. Beyond that, they could call on public authorities to intervene, whether to forbid employers to attract workers with offers of higher pay, to open up guilds to "free" workers – and thus enlarge the labor supply – when shortages loomed, or to override craft privileges dictating work practices that drove up wages. Employers also resorted to underhanded measures. They used false weights when putting out raw materials or accepting finished goods, paid for labor with debased coinage, unilaterally reduced piece rates, charged abusively high prices for supplies, imposed fines for bad work as defined by the boss alone. All too often, employers set excessive rent levels for dwellings or equipment that workers were forced to take. Nottingham hosiers, for example, compelled workers either to rent frames or, if they used their own frames, to pay a "half-rent" for the privilege. Schemes of this kind were essayed repeatedly, although never more than at times when trade was depressed and workers had little choice but to acquiesce if they wanted to keep their jobs. But even in good times regular deductions quickly added up. English domestic hosiery workers owed 4 shillings of their nominal wage of 13 shillings $3\frac{1}{4}$ pence for such things as needles, oil, candles, coals, frame rent, and a host of other charges petty in themselves but significant in the aggregate.

Workers were not defenseless. Many had resort to the law courts, although these became less friendly to claims based on custom as time went on. Others resorted to political pressure. Even when employed in subcontracting or putting-out, guild masters could turn to corporations and through them to city fathers or even princely governments. Whether to redress inequities, or just to keep the peace, these authorities might order wage increases, mandate fairer payment, outlaw sharp practices. Less formal if more direct means were never neglected. Through journeymen's associations, confraternities, or word of mouth, workers circulated information about good and bad employers, boycotting the latter until they mended their abusive ways. If nothing else availed, they could ignore corporate or government decrees and leave in the middle of a job, or threaten to. Skill provided the greatest leverage. Because accomplished hewers were scarce, even enserfed Scottish miners enjoyed high wages as employers bid for their services. Least likely to benefit from any of these modes of pressure or protection were women, the less skilled, and those excluded from guilds. These were precisely the groups that were increasingly drawn into wage labor as production moved to the countryside, as forms of domestic work, subcontracting, and the like proliferated, and as corporations closed up. As a result, power in the labor market shifted in favor of employers. But they were far from having a free hand, since workers could draw upon a long history of combination and common effort.

Collective association and action

Work-related organizations and conflicts reflected the fact that the great majority of craft and industrial producers worked in small, dispersed units. Labor relations were often matters for face-to-face negotiation between masters and journeymen, putting-out entrepreneurs and domestic workers, mine "overmen" (supervisors) and the four or five members of a pit-face crew. This is not to say, of course, either that these workplaces were conflict-free or that the disputes were minor. On the contrary, both laboring conditions and attempts to modify them ensured frequent disputes. Moreover, the very directness of contact could make for great bitterness, and the issues involved were critical matters: work practices, wages, authority, and discipline. Because divisions among tasks tended to be vaguely delineated, journeymen were often told to do jobs they considered not theirs but apprentices' or found apprentices doing their work. Subcontractors typically earned their profits by cutting corners on journeymen's wages, hours, and working conditions, or by employing unfree workers and women. Apprentice complaints about not receiving the training specified in their contracts caused many clashes, and these disputes could quickly heat up, since most youths were apprenticed in their own town, so parents and other relatives were close at hand.

Employers repeatedly complained of their workers' insolence and insubordination. Some charges doubtless resulted from personality clashes, but others reflected attempts by journeymen in particular to claim a recognized and honorable place within the shop hierarchy. Bosses were not the only objects of what they considered worker misbehavior. Masters' wives were recurrently at the center of conflict. In part, this focus was an outgrowth of their responsibility, in many urban trades, for housing, feeding, and supervising much of the conduct of journeymen and apprentices. Rather than taking on the husband – and boss – it was easier to confront the wife, especially as women were widely considered inferior and, because excluded from male guilds, could be derided as untrained and as exercising improper authority. The strife also had a strong sexual component, as young males opposed a woman who, in a reversal of accepted gender roles, wielded power over them.

The small scale of worksites and the kinds of personalized labor relations therein did not, however, rule out collective association – at least among male workers, for women were nearly always barred from all but confraternities, some of which admitted journeymen's wives. Best known, and probably most common, were the associations (frequently referred to generically as "brotherhoods") formed in many countries among urban journeymen. They were nourished by cooperative work experiences that fostered a strong sense of common identity, reinforced in some trades by rising capital requirements and restrictive guild practices that were making it difficult for journeymen to attain mastership. Many associations grew out of religious confraternities, but they were essentially secular in nature and purpose; in various places, in fact, church, state, and employers cooperated to found new confraternities focused on pious exercises and designed to put workers under tighter control. Yet neither these competing bodies nor repeated legal prohibitions ended the existence of journeymen's own societies.

One of the earliest documented was the *Compagnie des Griffarins* ("Company of Gluttons") founded in the early sixteenth century by Lyon printing journeymen. Like masters' corporations but with a unique inflection, the Griffarins had elected officers, entrance fees, banquets, sworn oaths, and elaborate rituals; instead of devotion to a patron saint, however, there was an annual feast honoring Minerva, extolled as "the Mother of Printing and the Goddess of Knowledge." More famous were the loose national federations of locally based brotherhoods that emerged to manage the journeymen's tour – compulsory in many trades before one settled down – and the "tramping system," in which journeymen in need of jobs received tickets (claims for assistance by fellow practitioners of their craft in other towns) and money to enable them to seek work elsewhere. In France there were three of these *compagnonnages*, each

FV FATTO L ANNO 1517 SOTTO MISIER ZACHARIA D ANTONIO GASTALDO DE MARANGONI D NAVE D L ARSENAL.
FV RINOVATO D L ANNO 1773 SOTTO LA GASTALDIA DI FRANCESCO ZANOT TO GASTALDO E COMPAGNI

12 The chamberlain (*gastaldo*) of the carpenters' association of the Venetian Arsenal had this sign painted in 1517. It shows the group's patron saint, the shields of its patrons, and the stages of ship construction in which the carpenters participated.

claiming to have descended from workers who had helped build Solomon's Temple: the *Enfants de Salomon*, the *Enfants de maître Jacques*, and the *Enfants du père Soubise* (respectively, the children of Solomon, of the apocryphal Master James, and of the equally mythical Father Soubise). Each association also had more colloquial names of unknown derivation, the most commonly used of which were *gavots*, journeymen of the *devoir*, and *drilles*. In principle, each comprised just one trade, but in fact all were coalitions of separate crafts, their precise composition differing by town and period. At least in Paris – and perhaps in other cities with substantial populations of resident journeymen – the compagnonn-ages for young, itinerant men were paralleled by associations for older workers who had settled down permanently. Despite their different memberships, however, both groupings shared organizational forms, purposes, and modes of action.

Journeymen belonging to the various societies often quarreled with one another. Many disputes concerned honor, but even these were often interlaced with economic issues, notably the defense of jobs against younger aspirants, newcomers, or those practicing a similar but compet-ing trade. The Griffarins considered "Forfants," their term for journey-men who would not join the company, morally debased, but it is clear that concern to control the labor supply had a lot to do with their disdain. Journeymen hatters from Paris, Lyon, and Marseille found their once secure hold on fine-hat manufacture threatened when in the eighteenth century rabbit and hare fur – long the dominant raw materials elsewhere in France – became more popular than the beaver they worked. To maintain their positions and their wages, they undertook numerous and lengthy court cases and appeals, which rehearsed in tedious detail all the privileges and distinctions that in their eyes forever set apart the journeymen hatters of these three cities from any others.

Brotherhoods were no less vigilant about defending journeymen's interests against their employers, whether undertaking a boycott to force the master glaziers of Nantes (France) to improve job conditions, hauling masters into court over alleged unfair labor practices, or simply negotiat-ing about countless quotidian shop-floor matters. To press their de-mands, they rarely shrank from confrontation: the Griffarins often called walkouts from a single shop and struck the entire Lyon printing industry in 1539 and again in 1570. At the same time, many journeymen were as firmly rooted within the corporate economy as their masters and valued the status, benefits, and resources it bestowed. This orientation could lead associations to insist that masters fulfill their traditional roles and obligations so that disrupted craft communities could be mended and could function again like harmonious families or fraternities, as the

Griffarins were wont to put it. But even journeymen working in large
capitalist shops or putting-out arrangements, for whom the guild order
was barely a memory, emphasized the rights, dignity, and honor of their
status. To preserve these attributes, their brotherhoods undertook responsibility for maintaining good order in their ranks, whether by settling
disputes among their members or by judging and penalizing those charged
with misdeeds in the workplace. And virtually every workers' society
collected funds to distribute to ill, retired, or unemployed journeymen, as
well as to provide proper burials.

Because of these services, because of the vital support brotherhoods
provided in conflicts with other trades, and because masters themselves
had often once belonged to and retained links with such associations,
employers usually found it useful to establish a modus vivendi with them.
If imitation be the sincerest form of flattery, then printers' journeymen
were indeed honored. For Plantin, the great Antwerp printers, as well as
their counterparts in London, successfully coopted the brotherhood
structure, encouraging or even instituting single-shop organizations
(usually called "chapels") with a full panoply of rites, ceremonies, and
mutual aid. But chapels were so firmly under the employers' thumb as
virtually to preclude contestatory action, their main functions being to
apportion tasks, police the workplace, deliver assistance, and even grant
credit.

Not all trades boasted established, enduring workers' societies, but
other organizations – variously termed unions or clubs or committees –
did emerge, although it is difficult to discover much about them. Many,
probably most, had considerably less elaborate structures and rituals than
brotherhoods and a less continuous existence, materializing when collective action seemed called for, then fading from sight. From the late
fourteenth century, for example, fullers in several Holland cities engaged
in repeated and largely successful walkouts. Very little information has
survived, although it seems clear that brotherhoods did not emerge.
Nevertheless, both fullers' references to their long history of collective
action and the fact that their walkouts were preceded by large preparatory
gatherings in which demands and plans were formulated bespeak some
degree of continuity and organization.

Even if dormant much of the time – or perhaps just invisible to the
historian – worker associations could draw sustenance from several other
institutions. The charitable "box," while statutorily restricted to gathering and disbursing sickness and burial funds, provided some workers with
financial and administrative experience, as well as an on-going structure.
Frequently the governing council of a box met in what the English termed
a "house of call," a tavern that functioned as a hiring hall for a specific

trade. Weekly if not more frequent social meetings of artisans – also in taverns – likewise served to support collective memory, identity, and association.

Some assemblies were both more organized and more directly concerned with workplace matters. Such "court meetings," as the Dutch named them, were usually held in call houses or in squares, on bridges, or in other public places that served as open-air labor markets. They were designed first of all to settle informally conflicts between workers and bosses and among workers, from which judicial function they derived their name. Representatives chosen by each side negotiated a settlement and then presented their decision to the assembled workers – often numbering in the hundreds – who were authorized by clearly established rules to affirm fines of up to three weeks' pay or other penalties. Magistrates, who tended to consider the meetings illegal usurpations of their authority, forbade employers to participate and the gatherings to levy fines. But these prohibitions were ignored, for the assemblies served an invaluable conciliatory role that neither guilds nor government institutions were able to fulfill. When, however, the courts debated, voted on, and set in motion collective action, employers were as hostile as officials.

Employers, too, had organizations of their own, and these associations enjoyed a substantial advantage over workers' associations in that they were legal and in showdowns were usually supported by state authorities, whereas laborers' groups were likely to be outlawed and broken up as conspiracies. Guilds, increasingly exclusive and concerned with promoting only masters' interests, became the most common type of employer associations. But as the ranks of masters became more sharply differentiated, guilds proved less able to promote their divergent concerns. The corporation of cabinetmakers in Dijon (France), for example, was bitterly divided once wealthier masters won permission to enlarge their businesses as much as they wished and offered higher wages to attract workers. Small employers, who wanted to maintain stringent limits on the number of journeymen per shop, worker mobility, and wages, denounced and overtly tried to sabotage the change, paralyzing the guild.

In the face of such problems, specific groups of employers tended to ignore corporations and form separate bodies. Most were designed with a single purpose in mind – typically to lower wages or lock out striking workers – at a particular time and thus were short-lived. But the Holland woollen cloth manufacturers' synod, which had members in several cities (and for a while nurtured a separate national organization), lasted from the mid-seventeenth to the end of the eighteenth century, its directorate actively corresponding to warn of walkouts and circulating blacklists of alleged troublemakers.

What issues mobilized employers and employees? And how did they press their demands? Across Europe, no matter what the trade, pay was always a matter of great contention, but in the eighteenth century, when capitalist relations increasingly penetrated workplaces, wages became the single issue most likely to mobilize workers. As ever larger numbers of workers came to regard their labor as a commodity they sold in the market, they became determined to get the highest possible price for it. According to a study that examined 383 strikes in Britain between 1717 and 1800 (by no means all the strikes that occurred, nor were strikes the sole type of workers' collective action), requests for pay increases figured in half the disputes, attempts to block wage reductions in another 7 percent. Closely related matters such as payment in truck or below statutory or agreed-upon rates, unilateral changes in types of pay or in output per piece rate, withdrawal of customary entitlements, arrears, and unfair deductions were implicated in a further 11 percent of strikes. Disputes focused on other issues were likely to have a wage dimension as well, notably alterations in hours (listed in 4 percent) and the employment of apprentices, women, or other "unqualified" persons in place of journeymen (9 percent). The interlacing of such matters was evident around Manchester in 1758, when thousands of cotton weavers turned out for higher wages, precise description of the fabric size that determined piece rates, and the firing of "unfair" (that is, below-rate) workers.

Labor-displacing technological innovation had given rise to contestatory movements in earlier centuries. To take just one example, in the 1660s small producers in the southern Netherlands had successfully rebelled to thwart the use of looms that could make twelve to fourteen ribbons at once. But in the eighteenth century – especially during the second half – the introduction of new or improved machinery also became a more frequent bone of contention. Not mentioned in any of 137 British strikes tabulated for 1717–60, it was cited in 7 percent (8 of 113) between 1761 and 1780 and 10 percent (15 of 153) in 1781–1800. Hand sawyers might object to the opening of a wind-powered sawmill, but the great majority of protests arose in the textile trades as the innovations that would transform clothmaking began to make their appearance, threatening the livelihoods of thousands.

Despite the growing importance of these issues, even in the eighteenth century collective actions were typically multi-faceted, for workers remained concerned with their standing, prerogatives, and workplace environments as well as their pay packets. Along with an adequate income and a tolerable pace of work, workers demanded the maintenance of rights, privileges, and practices that defined their identity and status or, as they were likely to express it, their "honor." The 1731 strike in the

Newcastle (England) coalfields sought not only a living wage but more say in deciding the conditions of work and abatement of discipline that miners considered arbitrary. When Parisian journeymen locksmiths rebelled in 1746 against new registration and job-leaving rules, they wanted to defend not just their mobility but some degree of freedom to dispose of their own labor in ways to which they were accustomed. Shipyard workers of Guarnizo (Italy), on strike in 1766, insisted on better pay but also less expensive, better quality food, lower rents, on-site medical care and religious facilities.

Just as any single movement might voice multiple demands, so it was likely to include several types of collective action, although they frequently shaded into one another. Like individuals, whole groups repeatedly resorted to slowdowns of various kinds – quitting early, taking whole days off, working at a leisurely pace, ignoring or "misunderstanding" directives – especially, it seems, when employers tried to impose new work schedules or routines. Changes of this sort also frequently provoked litigation, most of all in the corporate trades, which after all were based substantially on statute and in which recourse to the courts was a time-honored way of dealing with matters of all kinds. Taking a page from their employers' book, journeymen argued that laws and regulations designed to limit both the number of masters and competition among them also authorized journeymen's own attempts to exclude "illegal" workers and sanction "dishonorable" masters.

Rarely, however, were court cases speedily adjudicated; many dragged on for years, even decades. Petitions brought quicker decisions and were cheap to mount; often they represented the initial step taken by a group that otherwise lacked organization. The earliest known collective action by Whickham coal miners was a 1662 petition, signed by 2,000 individuals, protesting unpaid wages and high food prices; even earlier, Holland wool workers had petitioned municipal governments for higher wages. Petitions were especially favored in England, where it was legal to combine to ask Parliament to relieve grievances or to regulate wages, whereas many other forms of collective action were outlawed and risked severe punishment.

Workers faced with reductions often petitioned the authorities to set wages at a level that would ensure subsistence or to enforce existing regulations. The assumptions informing these pleas may have been related to the "moral economy" ideas that historians have identified as permeating the consumer consciousness of the period. These notions grounded their legitimacy in paternalist laws enacted during especially bad bouts of inflation during the long sixteenth century. They held that minimum wages – like maximum grain prices – should be set by reference to basic needs and equity rather than by the competitive market alone, by non-economic as well as purely economic criteria. But whether or not such concepts of justice informed them, wage petitions were clearly motivated by an attempt to right an unfavorable balance of forces by calling for state intervention. Employers used them for the same purpose. When in 1720 London journeyman tailors, taking advantage of good times, struck to compel higher pay for an hour's less work, masters petitioned Parliament, which passed an Act fixing wages and hours – a resolution that only set the stage for decades of agitation to force its repeal.

Workers' petitions were often rewarded. When four prominent Bruges entrepreneurs unilaterally lowered combers' wages in August 1703, the city government responded to an appeal from the aggrieved workers and forbade the reduction. But success was far from assured. When the combers subsequently asked the magistrates to boost their wages by statute, on the grounds that they had traditionally been linked to the thread price, which had risen, the request was refused and employers were ordered not to grant any hike. Despite the authorities' intentions, such a decision was rarely the end of the matter: the Bruges combers, for instance, went on strike.

Whatever the specific trigger, strikes were not uncommon in early modern Europe; in fact, they continued a form of collective action used at least since the mid-thirteenth century. Just in sixteenth-century Antwerp, masons walked out (alone or with carpenters) in 1522, 1532, and 1552, dyeing workers in 1553, 1560, and 1563, finishing workers in 1565 and 1574. Workers did not like to strike, however. For one thing, they were likely to face employers with ample organizational, political, and economic resources with which to wait out workers or combat them more actively. In 1720, London master tailors not only invoked the Act of Parliament that they had secured but hired strikebreakers and set up new houses of call to engage journeymen who did not belong to the association on strike. In addition, governments tended to define strikes as "conspiracies," "mutinies," or "insurrections," and to prosecute real or ostensible leaders as political criminals. (This was not simply hysterical overreaction but was founded on historical and contemporary realities. Most medieval strikes had embodied political as well as economic aims – the famous Ciompi Revolt of Florentine wool workers in 1377–78 had overthrown the existing state – and due to the continuing economic involvements of governments, early modern collective action nearly always had political overtones.)

Still, workers struck and sometimes succeeded when they did, as a particularly well documented example from late eighteenth-century Basel illustrates. Upon learning, one October morning, that the owners of the city's six flourishing calico-printing manufactures had just agreed not to hire any printer or engraver without his previous employer's consent – thereby eliminating job mobility, one of workers' chief ways of bargaining for better wages and working conditions – the employees of one shop unanimously voted to lay down their tools at once. That afternoon, after delegations had visited the other manufactures and persuaded nearly all workers to cease work, several hundred strikers assembled in a hall, ate and drank, and discussed their bosses' act of (in their words) "tyranny" that threatened them with "slavery." Following considerable (and carefully recorded) deliberation, they elected a strike committee, voted to refuse to return to their jobs as long as the employers stuck to their compact, sent a deputation to the city fathers, and vowed solidarity.

The Basel magistrates promised to investigate on condition that the strike be abandoned, but the employers' front cracked first. The owner of the newest enterprise – where the strike had begun – repudiated the agreement. Once his workers returned – on their side pledging not to participate further in the strike movement – the rest quickly followed. Nevertheless, the city proceeded with its inquiry, finding in favor of the workers while also condemning their action. The magistrates then forbade the manufacturers to take any similar step without prior notification to both employees and city government; they also tried and fined three workers as instigators.

As this instance suggests, strikes could be resolved quickly and on terms favorable to workers – even if not planned ahead of time – so long as employers' orderbooks were full, the issues were clear, the action won and maintained wide support, and the authorities could be neutralized if not won over. Conversely, strikes that lacked such auspicious conditions were not likely to triumph. A walkout that Bruges woolcombers had called a century earlier is instructive. After a decade of repeated wage cuts during a period of both reduced output and high inflation, combers finally petitioned the drapers who employed them for a raise; the response was a further decrease, instituted in January 1674. At the news, four combers went around to fellow combers' houses (all lived on neighboring streets), urging them to refuse to work for the new low wage. At each stop, other combers joined them, and eventually the group numbered about forty men. At that point, they fell violently upon a comber who had not laid down his tools and forced him to stop, an act that provoked the magistrates to intervene. They ordered the militia to seize the original four and clapped them in jail, quickly bring the movement to a halt. Once the agitation calmed and the combers went back to work – for the new rate – the four were released with no further penalty.

A specific form of strike was the walkout, when workers laid down their tools and left not simply their shops but the city itself (because this was a breach of contract, and thus illegal, amnesty was always insisted upon, although rarely granted to all involved), to return only when their demands had been met by employers or town government. This was the preferred weapon of Holland fullers, who in the later Middle Ages and early sixteenth century repeatedly and ably exploited the weakness of the central government and rivalries among cities. But it was also resorted to by eighteenth-century French shearers, who thought nothing of quitting Sedan for the Verviers region of the southern Netherlands or even Brandenburg (in eastern Germany) to better their condition, although this now proved a two-edged sword, since employers started bringing in outside shearers as strikebreakers.

Against such tactics, however, strikers had several means of enforcing solidarity with their movement. One of the most powerful was declaring scabs or those who held out to be "dirty" or "foul" (that is, without honor). Anyone so labelled was shunned not only in the workplace but everywhere else; a shop that employed such a person would itself be designated dirty and would face a boycott. Shunning was a powerful disciplinary measure in close-knit industrial towns and villages – so persuasive that it was used to regulate daily social life (and, among sects, to enforce religious conduct) as well as during industrial actions. Becoming "clean" entailed a public "washing" or confession, normally capped by buying drinks for a large crowd of fellow workers and neighbors to reestablish the bonds of conviviality.

Intimidation was another way of encouraging participation in collective actions or frightening away the "dirty," strikebreakers, and workers who had agreed to work below the going rate. Humiliating rituals like charivari or "rough music" were favored stratagems, but informers could expect violent treatment, up to and including murder. Employers, too, were targeted: they received large deputations and threatening letters or faced machine breaking and arson. Well before the Luddites smashed looms in the early nineteenth century, machines were being attacked. Shearers in Warminster (England), for instance, destroyed a mechanical gig-mill in 1767, alleging that it allowed a man and a boy to teasle as much cloth in two hours as thirty trained men could in a day, threatening mass unemployment. Two decades later, eleven individuals pledged in writing to burn down calico-printing plants around Manchester on the grounds that cylinder printing machines had destroyed journeymen's livelihood.

These forms of industrial direct action may have gained sanction from contemporary types of pressure – from menacing demonstrations to seizures and forced sales of grain at "just prices" – by crowds convinced that they had the right, derived from law, decree, and custom, to assure their subsistence if the authorities failed to fulfill their duties. It was known, for example, that laws passed as early as 1551 had proscribed gig-mills. But even in the absence of such (implicit) warrant, direct action was generally an effective form of collective bargaining, since police forces were sufficiently weak that both perpetrators and potential victims knew that physical harm or destruction of capital equipment could easily be accomplished.

Although most evidence about industrial collective action refers to urban journeymen, rural workers were far from passive. Swedish peasants who also produced charcoal, for example, repeatedly boycotted the iron industry to raise the price they received; they also turned with success to the courts. Putting-out was singularly fertile soil for conflicts, most notably over the quality and quantity of both the raw materials that entrepreneurs distributed and the finished products they collected. To press their demands, village laborers on occasion resorted to measures favored by their urban counterparts. But because of their isolation and dependence on the Verleger, they often found face-to-face individual negotiation, embezzlement, or, at the extreme, sabotage, more effective. Strikes and similar mass actions were most likely in such centralized rural units of production as mines. In Germany and east central Europe, pitmen formed associations that used strikes, slowdowns, and unauthorized absences to regulate output and gain control over working conditions. Indeed, even enserfed Scottish miners organized and struck.

Sailors were probably the most turbulent of all laborers, for their protests against frequently atrocious working and living conditions commonly erupted in riot and mutiny. Seamen engaged in long-distance shipping, whether trans-Atlantic or to the East Indies, were the most notorious; sailors who plied intra-European routes were more peaceful. The latter were also much more organized than the former, participating in guilds, confraternities, and insurance boxes. These not only helped them secure the more desirable jobs that involved shorter journeys and paid better, but also fostered less disruptive means of collective action on their part.

The largest collective movements on the part of early modern Europe's working people (as among their medieval predecessors) involved peasants – the German Peasant War in the mid-1520s, regional risings in early seventeenth century England, revolts that repeatedly shook entire French provinces from the Religious Wars to the end of Louis XIV's reign – and beyond these major outbursts were countless others of more limited scope. Many were grounded in peasant resentment of excessive landlord exactions or innovations that threatened their very existence: steeply rising rents and obligations, enclosure and eviction, privatization of common resources. Thus in the 1620s, farmers in southwestern England tried to block the crown's sale of forests, where villagers had long grazed their livestock; a few years later, drainage of the fens, which would deprive peasants of valuable hunting, fishing, and pasture grounds, set off opposition movements in the eastern part of the country.

Radical voices occasionally called for the abolition of tithes or dues, and in the eighteenth century, when population growth made viable holdings scarcer, demands for land redistribution were sporadically raised. But peasants usually had defensive or restorative goals: the confirmation of traditional tenures, rents and fines set at reasonable levels, fair tithes, the reestablishment of legitimate rights. Peasants exhibited a strong sense of moral outrage, denouncing specific lords and particular actions as oppressive and wrong. They did not, however, attack either structures of property ownership or the seigniorial system. What they sought was not a new order but the reinstatement of one that they felt slipping away. Similarly, the grain riots that frequently broke out when cereals were shipped out of an area suffering a subsistence crisis wanted only to halt the exports so that local people could be supplied, not to abolish grain sales, much less abandon commercial farming.

Agrarian protests were often mixed with and heightened by other issues. In the sixteenth century, these were typically religious matters; the close implication of states with churches inevitably added a political dimension. The English Revolt of the West in 1549 both opposed changes in doctrine and liturgy that the government had recently imposed and demanded that the tithe be commuted to a fixed cash payment. Religious and secular concerns were much more thoroughly fused in the series of conflicts known as the German Peasants' War of 1524–25. Culminating decades of peasant resistance to a lordly feudal offensive, the rebels insisted not only that lords respect commons, lighten corvées, and cut rents and dues. Based on their reading of Scripture, they also refused to pay tithes on cattle, requested that the grain tithe be collected honestly and devoted only to supporting pastors and the poor, and refused to pay the heriot (lordly death duty) any longer. The Reformation did not cause the Peasants' War, and indeed Martin Luther furiously disowned it. But it focused and legitimated pre-existing discontents, furnishing both an idiom in which to express them and a powerful new justification for taking steps to remedy them. Thus the freedom of the Christian man promised in the Bible was taken to mandate the abolition of serfdom.

In later sixteenth- and seventeenth-century France, political aspects became much more pronounced, as escalating tax burdens introduced first during the Religious Wars and subsequently – and much more heavily – by the centralizing monarchy to pay for its absolutist and war-making policies set off numerous peasant revolts. Although seigniorial mistreatment was a prominent target in risings in the Vivarais in the 1570s and among the Breton *Bonnets rouges* or "Redcaps" a century later, explicit agrarian demands were usually a minor element in these movements. Nevertheless, peasants were keenly aware that taxes directly impinged upon their well-being. Thus peasant anger and action focused on tax farmers, fiscal officials, and other government agents; it was they who were reviled as cannibals; they who were roughed up or, at times, murdered; they whose offices were vandalized and put to the torch. And it was they who, it was believed, had duped and robbed the king, who would soon be undeceived by his faithful subjects' deeds. These peasant revolts hence took the form, in part, of rites of unmasking and purification. The golden age – increasingly identified with the reign of Henry IV (1589–1610), before Richelieu's tax hikes – was to be revived rather than a new society introduced.

Fiscal pressures, enclosure, baldío sales, and other agrarian change, together with the emergence of elites pursuing distinctive activities, disrupted village communities, as we have seen. But village institutions typically led protests because both the substantial peasants who controlled them and the mass of poorer inhabitants continued to find them useful instruments for defending their interests against state and landlord. Like industrial workers' associations, peasant communities often resorted to petitions, litigation, and similar kinds of formal and informal negotiation, not to mention demonstrations in which crowds marched, made humiliating rough music, and tried to overawe by sheer numbers. Nor were they averse to direct action, whether against fences and hedges that demarcated privatized land, grain convoys, tax-collectors' houses, or persons.

At times, entire rural districts went on war footing, mobilizing thousands of peasants: 12,000 *Tard-avisés* in Bas-Limousin in 1593, 8,000–10,000 *Croquants* ("clodhoppers") in Périgord in 1637, up to 15,000 *Tard-avisés* (the name was proudly resurrected) who attacked Cahors in Quercy in 1707. Numbers were no guarantee of success, however, and even the largest movement was likely to be drowned in blood. Yet although resistance did not derail agrarian transformation or reverse state development – the golden age was not reborn – it frequently did have immediate, positive effects for peasants. Court cases were often settled by arbitration resulting in favorable compromises; petitions were granted; torn-down fences stayed down; terrified excisemen fled. Grain riots not only blocked specific exports but discouraged further attempts by merchants of the affected region. Because governments did not always have sufficient military force to compel payment from refractory communities or might decide that the costs of collection would outweigh anticipated receipts, even districts that suffered defeat in insurrectionary battle might well find their taxes reduced or suspended, if not permanently then for a few years.

Most associations and conflicts in early modern Europe were limited to one craft, town, or district. It was exceptional when Protestant and Catholic peasants in the late sixteenth-century Vivarais (France) laid aside their religious differences to join in concerted attack on despotic seigniors, or when Dutch woollen-cloth shearers struck in Gouda, Haarlem, Hoorn, and Rotterdam in 1636–39. It would be a mistake, however, to dismiss either their organizations or their actions as ineffective. On the contrary, they were entirely appropriate to an era when predominantly small-scale production units, tenaciously held craft privileges and monopolies, and sturdy worker pride in skill and honor remained dominant but faced pressures that would ultimately undermine them. Superior resources and privileged access to political power gave landlords, entrepreneurs, masters, and officials considerable economic and non-economic leverage over tenants and laborers. For all that, brotherhoods, village communities, and other bodies proved able repeatedly to marshal people for collective action both to advance their material interests and to uphold what they regarded as correct economic and social arrangements.

Women and children last

Most women worked for remuneration in early modern Europe: three-quarters of London women in the 1695–1725 period, probably even higher proportions in commercial agricultural and proto-industrial areas. They were found in a remarkable variety of trades. Female drawers hauled tubs or sledges heavily laden with coal out of underground pits. Women nailers scandalized contemporaries by working at their forges stripped to the waist. Languedoc women monopolized the manufacture of verdigris used in green paint, dyes, and inks, and a few even became rich brokers. Nevertheless, the great majority of women were employed in a small number of occupations preponderantly in the tertiary sector (domestic service, laundering, nursing, retailing); in the textile and clothing trades; and in gardening, dairying, and unspecialized agricultural work.

These patterns were not unique to the early modern period: they had already existed in the later Middle Ages and persisted throughout the nineteenth century. Nor were gender divisions of labor that favored men with more skilled, higher status, more regular, and better paying jobs specific to this era. But between the sixteenth and eighteenth centuries women's work opportunities were further constricted, the lines of demarcation between male and female work were more sharply drawn, specific occupations and types of labor became more decidedly identified with each gender, and women's work was widely devalued. Children's work underwent a similar restructuring. These developments cheapened the cost of female and child labor, making it especially attractive to entrepreneurs, who responded by massively employing women and the young in many a Verlagssystem and manufactory. The feminization and "juvenilization" of proto-industries and proto-factories explain much of their dynamism.

In both agriculture and industry, women lost jobs they had once shared with men, leading to a greater degree of workplace segregation by gender. On farms, the growing division often resulted from increasing specialization in garden-grown fruits and vegetables, in permanently stabled livestock, and in industrial raw materials such as silk, dyestuffs, hemp, and flax – the raising of all of which was largely delegated to women. At times, technological change separated the genders at work. On some large English farms, for instance, the sickle, wielded by both men and women, began to give way to the scythe. Although it cut grain faster and thus raised labor productivity, the scythe was much heavier and more cumbersome than the sickle, so men came to monopolize harvest work, whereas women were hired for sowing and weeding. New technologies could also have similar effects in crafts. When the more productive Dutch engine looms were adopted by Coventry (England) ribbon weavers, they were assigned to men, whereas women were relegated to slower single hand looms. In mines, the labor-saving machines that eliminated many unskilled washing, sorting, and hauling jobs traditionally held by women were reserved exclusively for men; Genevan women who assisted in the watchmaking and jewelry trades were likewise displaced by new equipment. In none of these cases did innate physical or mental capacities disqualify women, yet only men got to operate the new machines.

Technology was not necessarily linked to either gender, however, and occasionally women monopolized it. The history of the water-powered lintmill shows, in fact, just how arbitrary the identification of technology with gender was. This eighteenth-century invention, which mechanized scutching (the arduous task of scraping pieces of woody stalk from flax fibers destined for weaving linen), became the basis of an exclusively women's trade in Sweden – and an entirely male one in Ireland. In both countries, mechanized scutching was regarded as highly skilled labor, and in both it was performed in the same way. Yet the lintmill also demonstrates how even in a situation where the genders could easily carry out each other's work, male workers kept the upper hand. For in Ireland scutching was the labor of male professionals employed full-time during the entire year, whereas in Sweden it was the seasonal employment of peasant women during periods when they were not occupied on their family farms. Their husbands, moreover, had more lucrative seasonal jobs as woodcutters and charcoal makers, and these remained wholly male.

The rise of centralized workplaces and labor gangs on commercial farms often provided new but sex-segregated jobs for women, especially those without significant burdens at home. Large groups of women sowed, weeded, and hoed in the fields, and others assembled in big sheds or "jenny factories" to operate spinning jennies under the watchful eyes of male supervisors. But these developments disadvantaged married women with young children – the condition of most European females during a significant part of their adult lives. Small family farms and household work units allowed such women more latitude for setting their own work rhythms and thus to combine domestic responsibilities – particularly the bearing and rearing of children – with production for the market. In many poor upland farming communities, indeed, wives and younger children stayed home to till smallholdings while husbands and older sons performed migrant agricultural labor, found seasonal urban jobs as masons, chimney sweeps, or carriers, or shipped out on fishing boats; older daughters often moved to town to seek employment as servants. But this linkage was disrupted when production moved away from the home and the workday became more continuous, for these changes made it difficult to accommodate the specific needs of women.

The movement of industry to towns could also lead to the displacement of women. Woolcombing had long been an unregulated female occupation practiced in rural areas of French Flanders, Artois, and Hainaut in the southern Netherlands. But as light drapery developed in towns during the first half of the sixteenth century, the associated urban trade of combing quickly became organized into corporations – and entirely male. For neither technological innovation nor more centralized workplaces impeded female labor as much as guilds did. Organizing trades within a corporate framework was, in fact, often tantamount to excluding women. As Geneva's taffeta-makers, ribbon-makers, pin-makers, and other crafts assumed guild structure after 1560, for example, they shut out the working women they had previously welcomed. By the end of the sixteenth century, guilds' gender exclusivity was virtually complete throughout Europe. Small groups of women did continue to participate in some mixed-gender corporate trades thereafter; there were even guild-based female building contractors in eighteenth-century Brittany. But increasingly women were confined to single-sex guilds in a narrow range of occupations that came to be defined as women's work. In Bristol, England, for example, some girls apprenticed in carpentry, bellfounding, and other predominantly male professions in the 1530s–40s. By the early seventeenth century, however, girls trained only for so-called "female" vocations, mainly textile and needle trades such as knitting, sewing, spinning, hosiery, lacemaking, and buttonmaking.

Some girls did pick up craft knowledge in their families' shops, and a few – usually masters' daughters – always managed to apprentice in male-dominated trades. Even after successfully completing their training, however, they rarely won admission to mastership and thus were effectively excluded from operating their own businesses. Probably the best that such women could hope for was employment at relatively high wages. During the 1770s, Josiah Wedgwood paid female flower painters 3 shillings 6 pence a day; although at the top of women's rates, this wage was just two-thirds of what men received. When women did persevere and become masters, they rarely had sufficient capital or contacts to thrive. Although 15 percent of master linen weavers in Augsburg about 1600 were women, they employed just 5 percent of the journeymen and apprentices and were among the poorest of the city's residents. Admittedly, a few female printer/publishers stood at the top of their profession, but all were widows of already successful printers. Moreover, their ranks rapidly thinned after 1550, as the industry became more organized and capital-intensive; thereafter, the rare women publishers, like their sisters in other crafts, clustered at the bottom of their trade.

Early modern guilds hindered women's work for a variety of reasons. In some cases, political factors played a role. Guilds in south German cities, for instance, agitated for the exclusion of women to assert corporate independence from municipal authorities, and, in Low Countries towns, guild entry into public life was taken to mandate the proscription of females from what was accepted to be a male preserve. Even guilds that allowed widows to continue practicing their late husbands' crafts wholly excluded them from all public activities as well as from corporate office. Guild attitudes to women's work were also affected by the state of the labor market. Where a chronic shortage of skilled workers obtained, as in booming sixteenth-century Gdansk, guilds put few roadblocks in the way of female artisans. Conversely, where job competition was more intense, or in times of crisis or decline, women were condemned for taking jobs more urgently needed by their male colleagues or – more frequently – were simply debarred without comment. Geneva's male carders tried to prevent merchants from employing women during periods of unemployment; as Saxon silver mines were exhausted in the 1570s and 1580s, newly formed miners' fraternities helped men frantic for any work to take even the most poorly paid jobs from women (so desperate were the men, in fact, that they even started making lace, braid, and trim, work stereotyped as female), and craft organizations agitated to ensure that male miners would monopolize labor-saving machines. But correlations between prosperity and welcoming women workers, and depression and hostility to them, were far from watertight. Lille's light woollens output swelled across the sixteenth century, yet female apprentices and mistresses progressively lost the rights and privileges initially guaranteed them by craft statutes. Conversely, declining trades – such as woollens in seventeenth-century Italy – accepted women as men abandoned them for better opportunities.

Such responses were not "natural," inevitable, or even economically rational – especially as artisans' own wives and daughters bore the brunt of the prohibitions. They stemmed from cultural, social, and ideological assumptions about appropriate gender roles and behavior which themselves were being redefined to women's detriment. The Renaissance and Reformation revivals of classical and early Christian learning, together with attempts by secular and religious officials to enhance social discipline by reconstructing morality, marriage, and family, reinforced patriarchal values that justified and perpetuated male dominance. Sharply delineating a female domestic sphere from the male public arena, these beliefs delegitimated women's authority in the workplace, now considered an inversion of proper order, and condemned mixed shops as occasions for lewdness. Such strictures, as we have noticed, made it difficult for masters' wives to wield effectively the power their husbands delegated to them, and they also made it much tougher for all females to acquire training and mastership. In many trades, a widow had long been permitted to take on apprentices and journeymen to keep her late husband's shop in operation until it could be transferred to her new mate or a male heir came of age. Even in these crafts, it was now assumed that she would wind the business up, an expectation underlined by the decreasing amount of time granted her to do so.

The increasingly numerous and assertive male journeymen's associations were often at the forefront of efforts to exclude women and for this purpose mounted singularly aggressive campaigns. Although fostered by economic circumstances, their position was expressed in terms of honor. At a time of declining opportunities for upward mobility into the ranks of masters, that is, journeymen argued that women should be shut out of shops not because they were rivals for jobs that were now journeymen's permanent lot but because they debased any shop harboring them. Success in these offensives tightened the labor supply to male workers' advantage, of course. It also provided them a new form of differentiation as journeyman rank lost its former prestige.

Precluded from positions that they or their mothers had once held, and attentive to changing standards that praised the leisured rather than the working wife, some women withdrew from market production altogether. By the later seventeenth century, wives of masters in London usually did not hold paying jobs. But most women could not afford this option, and many may not have wanted it. On the one hand, inflationary pressures during the long sixteenth century and again from the 1730s drove down real wages; on the other, a broadening array of new consumer goods was becoming available from the later seventeenth century. At the same time, entrepreneurs seeking to cut their labor costs feminized the labor force. In Bologna, women were just 7.5 percent of the weavers of silk *drappi* (fabrics such as brocades, damasks, and taffetas woven on commission for merchants) in 1610, but 62 percent in 1726 and 83 percent by 1796. Women were pulled into the workplace with particular urgency by consumer goods trades, since few required any sort of formal apprenticeship, many were based on work once performed by females at home but now transferred into market production, and all expanded sales by cutting prices, mainly by employing cheap labor. Commercial farmers, too, relied more and more on ill-paid women to perform labor-intensive specialized tasks such as dairying, caring for small animals and gardens, repeated hoeing of fodder crops, cultivating and replanting seedlings, soaking and breaking flax. On one large farm near Béziers on the Mediterranean coast of Languedoc, women worked for 2,969 days at 8 sous a day in 1773–74; men for 1,486 days at 25–30 sous.

On a few occasions, female artisans excluded from male-controlled trades managed to form separate, recognized guilds enjoying distinctive privileges and monopolies: Paris seamstresses were chartered in 1675 to make women's and children's garments, despite the strident opposition of the tailors' corporation. More often, however, women were limited to performing work similar to men but which corporate artisans deemed dishonorable or insufficiently remunerative. Thus whereas German guildsmen fabricated new hats, women workers repaired them; female seamstresses could mend used clothing, but tailoring new garments was reserved to men. Many women worked in proto-industrial household production units in which tasks were typically assigned by gender, although in the interests of maximizing income conventional patterns might be violated. In most Leicestershire hosiery families, for example, the husband operated the knitting frame while his wife seamed the finished stockings and the children wound bobbins, but some rented a second frame to be run by the wife or adolescent son while daughters seamed. Norwegian women were so central to textile production that during the long winters they wove or spun while men cared for children and cattle. Often servants – who formed the largest single female occupational group – also participated in household-based market production by spinning, doing needlework, knitting stockings, embroidering, or making lace.

The major female proto-industrial occupations were those that required little capital, were interruptible and thus easily integrated with

13 This view of a spinning and carding room at the Waldstein cloth works reveals the importance of female and child labor in proto-factories. Only the spinning master at the table to the right is male; his task was to check the thread, for the reason that spinners were put in large rooms was to cut down fraud and maintain quality. In 1728, the year when this plate was published, the Waldstein mill counted 164 spinners and 100 carders out of a total labor force of about 390. They supplied twenty-two looms, each operated by two weavers, who worked separately, mostly in sheds attached to their cottages.

family responsibilities, and were based on empirical knowledge transmitted informally within a domestic setting. Trades from stocking knitting to verdigris making had these characteristics. But the vast and continued strong demand for wool, silk, flax, and cotton thread made spinning women's preeminent craft throughout Europe. The big putting-out networks that supplied manufactories indicate the scope of the trade. Recall that 85 percent of the Osek woollen mill's 766 workers were females spinning at home; the far larger Linz woollen manufactory contracted with some 28,000 domestic spinners.

Across the early modern period, households and individuals of both genders became increasingly subject to capitalist employers who bought their labor rather than the products of their labor. Yet women also worked under unfavorable conditions specific to their sex that disadvantaged them as a group relative to men as a group. Job segregation created dual labor markets defined by gender. The asymmetrical nature of the discrimination allocated women to a restricted number of overcrowded trades characterized by low pay, skill levels, and status; by casual, irregular, or seasonal employment; by minimal formal or only informal training; by little supervisory responsibility; by weak or no regulations; and by the use of few and rudimentary tools. Women were frequently forced to work at the margins or in the interstices of the economy, accepting jobs that were undesirable, unhealthy, even illegal.

Unmarried women from "respectable" artisan or middling families faced the bleakest prospects, for only a few needle trades were considered proper. As a result, these crafts enjoyed exceptionally abundant labor supplies and paid the lowest wages; ironically – given the moral preoccupations that drove young women into them – such trades frequently became little more than breeding grounds for prostitution. Able to choose from a broader, although hardly optimal, range of options, other women pieced together their living from several sources, although they could usually earn just enough to support a single adult in minimal comfort. A widow with children thus urgently needed to remarry; failing that, she could abandon her children or enter the poorhouse (which often amounted to the same thing). Given their work experiences, women's professional identities were understandably thin, and lacking autonomous craft or worker organizations, they had no way to give voice to their occupational interests. Little wonder, then, that they rarely mounted collective labor movements but focused on family concerns: women led grain and bread riots rather than strikes.

Surviving family production units provided women with their best opportunities to work outside gender-separate situations. Family farms always remained the most common of these, but they were also numerous in all manner of crafts even in the late eighteenth century. One of the two or three looms in the average-sized family shop in the Lyon silk industry in 1788, for example, was occupied by the master's wife, who usually sent her youngest child to a wetnurse so that she could work without interruption, as was vital for the household's survival. At the same time, many women continued to be employed in mines as part of family groups that in time-honored fashion exploited small pits. Apart from these kinds of enterprises, women were most likely to find jobs that violated sex-linked stereotypes when men were scarce – most notably during wars – or in crafts that men were abandoning for superior prospects in other trades. Thus women in seventeenth-century Florence were able to enter both woollen weaving, a dwindling craft, and silk weaving, which although healthy provided work for only part of the year; men moved into crafts where they could find full-time jobs. Despite its necessity to the well-being of her and her family, however, a woman's productive employment was slighted – if not condemned – by many contemporary commentators, who instead emphasized her moral and religious roles, albeit ranking them subordinate to a husband's or father's.

Many attributes of women's work also marked the labor of the numerous children engaged in production during the age of manufacture. To be sure, not all children were equal: boys were generally privileged. For one thing, they tended to enter the labor force later and with better qualifications than girls. In Norwich, only a third of boys between six and twelve was working in 1570, while another third was in school, whereas four-fifths of girls in that age group were already employed. Once in the labor force, moreover, boys could anticipate some upward mobility, even if they were not fortunate enough to be apprenticed in a still-open corporate trade. In mines, for example, boys began as stampers but usually became pit-face hewers as adults, whereas girls started as washers or haulers and remained in those low-level jobs for the rest of their lives – if they were lucky enough not to lose even them. Before reaching their majority, however, children of both genders received equally low wages yet often contributed crucially to their own or their families' income. Leiden's woollen industry employed at least 9,000 boys and girls taken from orphanages and poor families throughout Holland, western Germany, and the prince-bishopric of Liège between 1608 and 1664. Although registered as apprentices, virtually none received any training; instead, they formed a kind of juvenile proletariat whose members could never hope to attain mastership. So little were they paid that they even undersold adult female labor.

Children could commence work at a very early age. Although most London girls started between the ages of fifteen and seventeen, some began at ten. Lille's light-woollens weavers averred that their nine- or ten-year-old sons could readily operate looms, and more than a few of the young people brought to Leiden were set to work when they were just six years of age. Rural children seem to have had the highest rates of participation in the labor force, for both proto-industries and farms employed them and few guilds existed to throw up obstacles to their work. Many towns tried to compensate for their relative lack of opportunities by establishing charity "schools" and workshops. But like those designed for adult paupers, institutions for unemployed children had trouble finding adequate supplies of raw materials and competent teachers, so the frequently flawed products usually proved unsaleable.

Children were employed along with women in trades from coal mining to turf digging to metallurgy: by the end of the eighteenth century, half the nailers in England were women, adolescent girls, and children of both sexes under fourteen. But children were concentrated in female-dominated branches of agriculture and in the textile industry, many branches of which could not have survived without female and child labor. Among the 115 people employed in the four Ghent say weaving enterprises operating in 1786, only eight were adult males. The large mills for winding, twisting, and doubling silk thread that spread through northern Italy in the seventeenth and eighteenth centuries were equally dependent on women and children. A typical mill, headed by five men (a manager, two winding masters, and two master carpenters to keep it in repair), employed a few men but mainly youths among the thirty-six workers who spun and threw the raw silk. Otherwise, it relied on ninety-eight boy and girl children to do the winding and ninety-six women who doubled silk at home. The children received 9 soldi a day, spinning workers 15, throwsters 24. The most extreme case of gender and age segregation was lacemaking, which produced vast quantities of luxury goods while paying its substantial workforce, with rare exceptions entirely composed of women and girls, some of the lowest wages of the time. The fabrication of lace was often urged as the ideal occupation for single women seeking to earn dowries or to support themselves. Yet for the vast majority, the reality was cruelly different, since the wages for fourteen, sixteen, or more hours of enervating, vision-destroying labor six days per week could barely buy a few scraps of bread.

Proletarianization and consciousness

Wage labor had existed far back into the Middle Ages, as we have seen. But for many centuries permanent wage-earners formed only a minority of the working population; when other workers labored for a wage they were supplementing their major source of income or were at a temporary stage before opening their own businesses or acquiring agricultural holdings. In the early modern period, however, the proportion of the population wholly dependent on wages for their livelihood increased substantially. In country and in city, in corporate as well as in free trades, on aristocratic estates and tenant farms, in large shops, in manufactories, and in proto-industries, more and more working people yielded control over both the means of production – land, livestock, tools, raw materials – and the production process. At the same time, they entered into new relations with the capitalist entrepreneurs who came to own the productive resources and employed wage labor to operate them. Much of the European population was proletarianized, in short, long before and in the absence of capital-intensive, power-driven factories.

Master light-woollens weavers in mid-sixteenth-century Lille who dreaded being turned into employees of would-be entrepreneurs decried the poverty – indeed, the "extreme want" – that, they predicted, would inevitably be their fate. But in fact to become a proletarian did not necessarily mean becoming impoverished, for a wage-paying job – or better, jobs for a previously underemployed household – might well provide a better living than a tiny holding or a marginal workshop could. But it did mean – as the Lillois also foresaw – a loss of autonomy, the replacement of a proud if often modest independence by dependence, most directly on capital, as embodied by the entrepreneur, and, more generally, on the labor market. In their words, proletarianization entailed exchanging their "honorable way of life," in which seven-eighths of all masters wove in their own petty shops, for "oppression" as "dependents and laborers" under a handful of "powerful" employers who would "set to work fifty, sixty, 80 or 100 looms" apiece.[4] Instead of selling commodities that they made, they would sell their commodified labor power.

Proletarianization was a protracted process. Although the number of wage-earners mounted during the long sixteenth century, the increase may have been outstripped by the creation of new peasant holdings and artisanal shops. But in the long eighteenth century, a time of revitalized agrarian change, spreading proto-industry and proto-factories, and renewed demographic growth, the pace of proletarianization quickened. Across these decades, workers entered into a bewildering variety of relations with capitalists, ensuring that proletarianization was as complex a process as it was lengthy. As a proletarian, you might receive a wage yet own your tools, as in most proto-industry, or the entrepreneur might

---

[4] Quoted in Robert DuPlessis, *Lille and the Dutch Revolt* (Cambridge, 1991), pp. 112–14.

supply both, as in many proto-factories. You might be paid a wage as a subcontractor, yet yourself employ wage-earners to perform the actual task. You might work for wages for several employers, thereby retaining a degree of bargaining power, or you might be in the sole employ of one capitalist. You or your household might retain some grazing rights, a garden, or some other additional source of income, or you might rely entirely on wage labor. You might retain a say in how you mined coal or wove cloth, or you might have to follow orders closely. You might labor for a wage your entire working life, or, like many villagers, eventually buy land and take up peasant farming – or even, like a decreasing number of journeymen, become an independent master.

Males were generally in the strongest position to influence the tempo and character of proletarianization, for they possessed most property and monopolized the resources afforded by collective organization. Fewer material reserves and exclusion from most institutions gave women and children less ability to determine the contours of their worklife. The loss of common grazing, forest, and gleaning rights hit females and the young hardest of all; because they had exploited these resources most intensively to help achieve household subsistence, they now had little choice but to take on wage labor. The initiative was in the hands of those with capital, for it allowed them to expropriate independent masters and peasants, create jobs in putting-out systems, centralized workplaces, and commercial farms, and discipline labor. When the Aachen (Germany) guilds kept urban wages too high and output too low, Bernard Scheibler founded a competing fine-cloth industry at guild-less, rural Montjoie (Monschau); by 1762, his enterprise employed 6,000 workers. At Igualada in Catalonia, clothiers deliberately shifted work from independent corporate masters to unprotected journeymen in order to gain dominion over production; the owners of the Montgolfier papermill at Vidalon-le-Haut (France) simply fired workers who refused to accept a strict new discipline that eliminated practices which had given them a large measure of autonomous control over their work.

Entrepreneurs did not act unassisted; state aid ranging from acquiescence to active support was critical to proletarianization. Governments consolidated property rights to the advantage of capitalist owners, abolishing customary rights to commons and to surplus raw materials that had allowed workers income not dependent on wage labor. In deference to entrepreneurial pressure, rules protecting artisan independence could be loosely enforced, modified, or repealed. Restrictions on vagrancy and begging, coupled with other policing methods, helped to discipline the laboring population; in extreme cases, the militia or regular troops might intervene against strikers or other disorderly workers.

Because proletarianization was a gradual, uneven, and varied process that occurred largely within existing structures, the laboring population – at least that male segment for whom we have most records – retained a primarily craft or trade consciousness. Particularism was a prominent feature of such an outlook. One was a "sayeteur" not a "bourgeteur," even if both wove many of the same types of light drapery and even if numerous people moved between the two crafts, or one was a shoemaker rather than a cobbler, even if each knew equally well how to fashion and to repair shoes. Maintaining such distinctions was economically vital, for they demarcated boundaries and thereby restricted competition. For that reason, Lille's sayeteurs and bourgeteurs – many of them related by blood as well as marriage – vied during more than two centuries for a monopoly of weaving changéants and related mixed-material cloth, while Bologna shoemakers fought for decades to reverse the city council's 1688 decision that cobblers could recondition used shoes.

Trade consciousness did not dictate absolute separatism among artisans in different trades. In his autobiographical chronicle, Pierre-Ignace Chavatte, a Lille sayeteur of the second half of the seventeenth century, repeatedly communicated his disdain for bourgeteurs. Nevertheless, he ardently participated in a religious confraternity whose leaders included bourgeteurs and members of other crafts. Craft-oriented sensibilities tended to dominate, however, since they were undergirded by the structures of work, embodied in an assortment of institutional forms (guild, confraternity, brotherhood, box), expressed in rituals, symbols, charity, shared conviviality, and other manifestations of solidarity, and honed by court cases, street brawls, and other types of contention with rival crafts.

Workers' language, like that of their employers, often postulated a perduring unity of common interests among all those engaged in a trade, concerns that allegedly transcended distinctions of rank, activity, and wealth and that should be recreated after any clash, whatever its particular content. But this conception of solidarity did not preclude a keen awareness of the distinctions and different interests that separated employers and workers. Printers' journeymen in Lyon may have called for "mutual and reciprocal love between" their masters and themselves, but they also knew that masters' wealth was the result of journeymen's "sweat and marvelous toil" which merited being rewarded with appropriate wages and grants of food.[5] Such compounds of attitudes were not confined to the sixteenth century but continued to inform even proletarianized workers two hundred years later. In the aftermath of a decade of

[5] The quoted passages come from Natalie Davis: "A Trade Union in Sixteenth-Century France," *Economic History Review*, 2nd ser., vol. 19 (1966), pp. 53–4.

violent protests that had wracked Spitalfields (London) before an Act of Parliament brought peace in 1773, an anonymous silk weaver denounced "treacherous, base, designing men" who had trampled on the "rights" of workers. He then went on to express his hope for the future: "May upright masters still augment their treasure, / And journeymen pursue their work with pleasure . . ."[6] In both cases, a hierarchic or "vertical" conception of community coexisted with a more class-based "horizontal" notion that emphasized the common interests unifying those located at the same level in the production structure.

Early modern European workers learned to criticize and resist the forces that were, if slowly and unevenly, reshaping their economic environment. Because many established structures long remained vital, workers' outlook – like their organizations and actions – was most firmly rooted in specific circumstances of craft and location. Hence their efforts to make sense of, operate within, and – if possible – affect the emergent capitalist order were cast only partly in the inclusive discourse of class, the idiom of the era of factory industrialization. More often, they used a particularistic trade-based language that emphasized privilege, custom, liberty, and independence. Their consciousness was not, however, simply atavistic traditionalism, a nostalgic throwback to an unrecoverable and undoubtedly idealized past. Rather, their understandings of their situation – in common with their collective associations and contestations designed to challenge it – were born of and appropriate to an age of transitions.

SUGGESTED READING

A good introduction to many of the issues discussed in this chapter is *The Workplace before the Factory. Artisans and Proletarians, 1500–1800*, ed. Thomas Safley and Laurence Rosenband (Ithaca, NY, 1993). For England, see John Rule, *The Experience of Labour in Eighteenth-Century Industry* (London, 1981), and R. W. Malcolmson, *Life and Labour in England 1700–1780* (New York, 1981). For France, see *Work in France: Representations, Meaning, Organization, and Practice*, ed. Steven Kaplan and Cynthia Koepp (Ithaca, NY, 1986); William Sewell, *Work and Revolution in France: The Language of Labor from the Old Regime to 1848* (Cambridge, 1980), chs. 1–3; Michael Sonenscher, *Work and Wages. Natural Law, Politics and the Eighteenth-Century French Trades* (Cambridge, 1989); Arlette Farge, *Fragile Lives* (Cambridge, Mass, 1994; orig. publ. Paris, 1986), part II; and William Reddy, *The Rise of Market Culture: The Textile Trade and French Society, 1750–1900* (Cambridge, 1984). More generally, see *The Historical Meanings of Work*, ed. P. Joyce (Cambridge, 1987).

Particular labor systems are discussed in R. Vergani, "Technology and the

---

[6] Quoted in John Rule, *The Experience of Labour in Eighteenth Century Industry* (London, 1981), p. 209.

Organization of Labour in the Venetian Copper Industry (Sixteenth–Eighteenth Centuries)," *Journal of European Economic History*, vol. 14 (1985); Robert Darnton, "Work and Culture in an Eighteenth-Century Printing Shop," *Quarterly Journal of the Library of Congress*, vol. 39 (1982); Milan Myska, "Pre-Industrial Iron-Making in the Czech Lands: The Labour Force and Production Relations *circa* 1350–*circa* 1840," *Past and Present*, no. 82 (1979); James Farr, *Hands of Honor: Artisans and their World in Dijon, 1550–1650* (Ithaca, NY, 1988). For discipline, see E. P. Thompson, "Time, Work Discipline and Industrial Capitalism," *Past and Present*, no. 38 (1967), the starting point of much recent thinking; Neil McKendrick, "Josiah Wedgwood and Factory Discipline," *Historical Journal*, vol. 4 (1961); the early chapters of Sidney Pollard, *The Genesis of Modern Management* (Cambridge, Mass., 1965); and Robert C. Davis, *Shipbuilders of the Venetian Arsenal* (Baltimore, 1991). Peter Mathias, "Leisure and Wages in Theory and Practice," ch. 8 of his *The Transformation of England* (London, 1979); and Kristine Bruland, "The Transformation of Work in European Industrialization," in *The First Industrial Revolutions*, ed. P. Mathias and J. Davis (Oxford, 1990), examine changes in notions and practices of work.

For incomes, see Giovanni Vigo, "Real Wages of the Working Class in Italy: Building Workers' Wages (14th to 18th Century)," *Journal of European Economic History*, vol. 3 (1974); Jan de Vries, "An Inquiry into the Behaviour of Wages in the Dutch Republic and Southern Netherlands, 1580–1800," *Acta Historiae Neerlandicae*, vol. 10 (1978); Wilhelm Abel, *Agricultural Fluctuations in Europe from the Thirteenth to the Twentieth Centuries* (London, 1980; orig. 3rd edn publ. 1978); H. Phelps-Brown and S. Hopkins, *A Perspective of Wages and Prices* (London, 1981); L. A. Clarkson, "Wage-Labour, 1500–1800," in *The English Labour Movement, 1700–1951*, ed. K. Brown (Dublin, 1982). The criminalization of entitlements is the subject of John Styles, "Embezzlement, Industry and the Law in England, 1500–1800," in *Manufacture in Town and Country before the Factory*, ed. Maxine Berg, Pat Hudson, and Michael Sonenscher (Cambridge, 1983); and Peter Linebaugh, *The London Hanged. Crime and Civil Society in the Eighteenth Century* (Cambridge, 1992).

Living standards are discussed from varying perspectives in Daniel Roche, *The People of Paris. An Essay in Popular Culture in the Eighteenth Century* (Berkeley, Calif., 1987; orig. publ. 1981); W. W. Hagen, "Working for the Junker. The Standard of Living of Manorial Laborers in Brandenburg 1584–1810," *Journal of Modern History*, vol. 58 (1986); Donald Woodward, *Men at Work. Labourers and Building Craftsmen in the Towns of Northern England, 1450–1750* (Cambridge, 1995); L. D. Schwarz, *London in the Age of Industrialisation. Entrepreneurs, Labour Force and Living Conditions, 1700–1850* (Cambridge, 1992); Margaret Spufford, *The Great Reclothing of Rural England. Petty Chapmen and their Wares in the Seventeenth Century* (London, 1984).

Associational life is treated in *Before the Unions. Wage Earners and Collective Action in Europe, 1300–1850*, ed. C. Lis, J. Lucassen, and H. Soly (Cambridge, 1994); Natalie Davis: "A Trade Union in Sixteenth-Century France," *Economic History Review*, 2nd ser., vol. 19 (1966), and "Strikes and Salvation at Lyon," ch. 1 of her *Society and Culture in Early Modern France* (Stanford, Calif., 1975); Cynthia Truant, *The Rites of Labor. Brotherhoods of Compagnonnage in Old and New*

Regime France (Ithaca, NY, 1994); David Garrioch and Michael Sonenscher, "*Compagnonnages,* Confraternities and Associations of Journeymen in Eighteenth-Century Paris," *European History Quarterly,* vol. 16 (1986).

On collective action, see C. R. Dobson, *Masters and Journeymen: A Pre-history of Industrial Conflict 1717–1800* (London, 1980); Rab Houston, "Coal, Class and Culture: Labour Relations in a Scottish Mining Community, 1650–1750," *Social History,* vol. 8 (1983); Rudolf Dekker, "Labour Conflicts and Working-class Culture in Early Modern Holland," *International Review of Social History,* vol. 35 (1990); Carlo Poni, "Norms and Disputes: the Shoemakers' Guild in Eighteenth-Century Bologna," *Past and Present,* no. 123 (1989); G. Benecke, "Labour Relations and Peasant Society in Northwest Germany, c. 1600," *History,* vol. 58 (1973); Marcus Rediker, *Between the Devil and the Deep Blue Sea: Merchant Seamen, Pirates, and the Anglo–American Maritime World 1700–1750* (Cambridge, 1987). The classic study of the moral economy is E. P. Thompson, "The Moral Economy of the English Crowd in the Eighteenth Century," *Past and Present,* no. 50 (1971). See also his later thoughts in "The Moral Economy Reviewed," ch. 5 of his *Customs in Common* (New York, 1991), the footnotes of which give guidance to other work on the issue, and John Stevenson, *Popular Disturbances in England 1700–1870* (London, 1979), ch. 6. Yves-Marie Bercé, *History of Peasant Revolts* (Ithaca, NY, 1990; orig. publ. 1986), and Peter Blickle, *The Revolution of 1525* (Baltimore, 1981; orig. publ. 1977) analyze peasant resistance.

Two earlier books on women's work, both focused on England, are still worth consulting: Alice Clark, *Working Life of Women in the Seventeenth Century* (London, 1919), and Ivy Pinchbeck, *Women Workers and the Industrial Revolution, 1750–1850* (London, 1930). Reviews of more recent scholarship can be found in Katrina Honeyman and Jordan Goodman, "Women's Work, Gender Conflict, and Labour Markets in Europe 1500–1900," *Economic History Review,* 2nd ser., vol. 44 (1991), and Janet Thomas, "Women and Capitalism: Oppression or Emancipation?" *Comparative Studies in Society and History,* vol. 30 (1988). More detailed studies are to be found in the essays in *European Women and Preindustrial Craft,* ed. Daryl Hafter (Bloomington, Ind., 1995). For England, see Bridget Hill, *Women, Work, and Sexual Politics in Eighteenth-Century England* (Oxford, 1989); Mary Prior, "Women and the Urban Economy: Oxford 1500–1800," in *Women in English Society 1500–1800,* ed. M. Prior (London, 1985); Peter Earle, "The Female Labour Market in London in the Late Seventeenth and Early Eighteenth Centuries," *Economic History Review,* 2nd ser., vol. 42 (1989); Michael Roberts, "Women and Work in Sixteenth-Century English Towns," in *Work in Towns 850–1850,* ed. Penelope Corfield and Derek Keene (London, 1990); Diane Willen, "Guildswomen in the City of York, 1560–1600," *The Historian,* vol. 46 (1984); Ilana Ben-Amos, "Women Apprentices in the Trades and Crafts of Early Modern Bristol," *Continuity and Change,* vol. 6 (1991); Carol Shammas, "Women Workers in the North of England during the Late Seventeenth Century," in *The World of William Penn,* ed. Richard and Mary Dunn (Philadelphia, 1986).

Women's work on the Continent can be studied thanks to Merry Wiesner, *Working Women in Renaissance Germany* (New Brunswick, NJ, 1986); Wiesner, "Spinsters and Seamstresses: Women in Cloth and Clothing Production" and

Judith Brown, "A Woman's Place Was in the Home: Women's Work in Renaissance Tuscany," both in *Rewriting the Renaissance: The Discourses of Sexual Difference in Early Modern Europe*, ed. Margaret W. Ferguson *et al.* (Chicago, 1986); Susan Karant-Nunn, "The Women of the Saxon Silver Mines," in *Women in Reformation and Counter-Reformation Europe*, ed. Sherrin Marshall (Bloomington, Ind., 1989); Natalie Davis, "Women in the Crafts in Sixteenth-Century Lyon," *Feminist Studies*, vol. 8 (1982); James Collins, "The Economic Role of Women in Seventeenth-Century France," *French Historical Studies*, vol. 16 (1989); Gay Gullickson, "The Sexual Division of Labor in Cottage Industry and Agriculture in the Pays de Caux: Auffay, 1750–1850," *French Historical Studies*, vol. 15 (1981); Elizabeth Musgrave, "Women in the Male World of Work: the Building Industries of Eighteenth-Century Brittany," *French History*, vol. 7 (1993); Judith Coffin, "Gender and the Guild Order. The Garment Trades in Eighteenth-Century France," *Journal of Economic History*, vol. 54 (1994); Judith Brown and Jordan Goodman, "Women and Industry in Florence," *Journal of Economic History*, vol. 40 (1980).

For women's agricultural work, see K. D. M. Snell, *Annals of the Labouring Poor. Social Change and Agrarian England, 1660–1900* (Cambridge, 1985); Michael Roberts, "Sickles and Scythes: Women's Work and Men's Work at Harvest Time," *History Workshop*, no. 7 (1979); Jane Humphries, "Enclosures, Common Rights, and Women: The Proletarianization of Families in the Late Eighteenth and Early Nineteenth Centuries," *Journal of Economic History*, vol. 50 (1990); Deborah Valenze, "The Art of Women and the Business of Men: Women's Work and the Dairy Industry c. 1740–1840," *Past and Present*, no. 130 (1991). Hugh Cunningham, "The Employment and Unemployment of Children in England c. 1680–1851," *Past and Present*, no. 126 (1990), provides a fine overview of the literature on children's work as well as a new interpretation.

Issues of consciousness are touched upon in many of the works already cited. But also see E. P. Thompson, "Eighteenth-Century English Society: Class Struggle without Class?" *Social History*, vol. 3 (1978), and Harold Perkin, *The Origins of Modern English Society 1780–1880* (London, 1969). Few artisan or worker autobiographies survive, even fewer talk much about work, and yet fewer are available in English. For one, see Jacques-Louis Ménétra, *Journal of My Life*, intro. by Daniel Roche (New York, 1986; orig. publ. 1984).

The best essays focused on proletarianization are in *Proletarianization and Family History*, ed. D. Levine (Orlando, Fla., 1984), but the topic is considered in many of the works listed above. Christopher Friedrichs, "Capitalism, Mobility and Class Formation in the Early Modern Germany City," in *Towns and Societies*, ed. P. Abrams and A. L. Wrigley (Cambridge, 1978) is an exemplary case study. For a brief introduction to the issue considered from the perspective of proto-industrialization, see Charles Tilly, "Flows of Capital and Forms of Industry in Europe, 1500–1900," *Theory and Society*, vol. 12 (1983).

Epilogue: Transitions and traditions

By the end of the early modern centuries, capitalist structures and relations of production had taken firm root in country and city across much of Europe. Landlords had dispossessed numerous peasants of land and claims to common resources; entrepreneurs had taken control of many workshops, tools, and raw materials formerly in the hands of artisans. On farms and in shops, Europeans concentrated on producing commodities for sale in competitive markets; land, labor, and capital markets increasingly allocated the factors of production; and cost-reducing organizational innovations based on new forms of tenancy and the employment of wage labor had been widely introduced.

Most of these changes had begun earlier, but during the long eighteenth century far-reaching developments abroad and at home accelerated and widely diffused them. More systematic exploitation of routes previously opened and territories previously claimed furnished raw materials for dynamic new industries, as well as expanding markets for Europe's trades old and new. Conditions within the Old World were also undergoing alterations with important ramifications for demand and supply. Novel crops and manufactures (including many of overseas origin) engendered new consumption patterns, and together with rising state and landlord levies, fresh government and particularly private entrepreneurial initiatives, and revived demographic expansion, both drew and pushed more – and more intensively working – Europeans into production of marketable goods.

The transitions to capitalism involved broad and disruptive innovations, and for that reason they evoked prolonged, creative, forceful, and frequently rancorous challenges that could delay and modify the new economic order. Changes that threatened long-established and morally condoned production structures, property relations, modes of surplus appropriation, economic and non-economic values, technologies, and work practices were opposed by entrenched groups and institutions with significant political and social leverage. Although guilds were turning ever more overtly into instruments of merchant, employer, and state domina-

303

tion of proletarianized workers, they clung to significant regulatory functions that curbed the free operation of labor and consumer markets. Village communities retained a good deal of authority over agricultural matters, frequently with the backing of powerful landlords and government officials. All of the protagonists had distinct – often conflicting – goals and priorities, of course, but both separately and together they could materially affect the pace and direction of structural change. And if all else failed, they had recourse to an array of time-tested legal and extra-legal judicial, associational, and confrontational forms of protest and resistance.

The interaction of these many forces ensured that the transitions were far from uniform over time and space. As a result, even while urban–rural dichotomies diminished, disparities appeared among regions and countries. Early pre-eminence was no guarantee of continued leadership, as witness the fates of Renaissance Italy and the Dutch Republic of the Golden Age; by the same token, England rose from the second rank to economic primacy. The new order was most completely realized in the northwestern core, which wielded a growing hegemony over the rest of Europe and substantial portions of the globe; yet this area, too, had its more and less dynamic countries, districts, and economic sectors. Conversely, even in East Elbia, where feudal structures in the guise of neoserfdom still substantially held sway, the commercial orientation of both landed estates and peasant producers, the rising employment of wage labor, and the appearance of large putting-out networks and manufactories betray the impact of expansive capitalism.

A variety of interpretive frameworks have been deployed in this book to help clarify these multiple and complex changes and continuities; at the same time, we have also found that these explanations are in need of some revision. The Smithian emphasis on market expansion that stimulated agricultural and industrial specialization and consequent productivity gains has found much justification in the historical record. Similarly, Smith's negative appraisal of corporate and state intervention in the economy has often been borne out: such policies could divert investment into unproductive if prestigious ventures or yield profits for the few at the expense of the many. Yet the expansive possibilities of early modern markets were not endless: the Dutch constructed an integrated and highly profitable commercial system that nevertheless did not induce ongoing industrial development, while in many places heavy state and landowner levies on the agrarian surplus constricted demand. Conversely, neither guilds nor governments turn out to have been so consistently harmful as Smith believed: the different types, goals, and scope of their endeavors, and the diverse contexts in which they occurred, made for beneficial as well as injurious outcomes.

Finally, the tenacious authority over economic behavior that non-economic values and purposes long retained suggests that Smith's account of human propensities needs emendation. "Economic man" was as much a historical creation as were the arrangements by which he (and, to a greater extent than is usually acknowledged, she) produced material wealth. That new economic beliefs spread and influenced behavior seems reasonably clear: in increasing numbers, landlords, big tenant farmers, yeomen, merchants, and artisans eschewed present consumption for investment in enclosures, drains, better seed and breeding stock, raw materials to be put out, equipment, and much else. What spurred them to take these steps remains obscure, however. The "Weber thesis" positing an unprecedented and uniquely galvanic capitalist spirit grown unexpectedly – almost perversely – out of religious imperatives has not won wide acceptance among economic historians. They prefer to attribute changed mentalities – or, more precisely, changed actions – to new opportunities and constraints caused by innovative production arrangements, falling transactions costs, novel consumer wants, urbanization. But this position often fails to acknowledge the power of moral, ideological, and spiritual commitments. Most likely the process was complexly interactive, even if the operative mechanisms have yet to be specified.

The processes that Marx fused into the concept of original accumulation were likewise visible across early modern Europe, and with increasing force during the long eighteenth century. Expropriation and proletarianization went on apace both on the land and in crafts; correlatively, a heterogeneous class that productively invested capital and employed wage labor came into existence. Colonial trade took on growing importance, most of all for those countries that were becoming the heartlands of capitalism. These developments had broader causes than Marx and his followers were often willing to recognize, however. Fragmented holdings and proletarianization resulted not only from the actions of rapacious landlords but also from demographic growth. The decline of artisanal crafts owed much to closing of the guilds, which relegated journeymen, artisans, and most women to permanent wage labor. As elucidated by scholars of proto-industrialization, moreover, rural putting-out (more accurately, given recent attention to the urban Verlagssystem, small production units and limited amounts of capital) had a more major part in the emergence of capitalism than Marx had thought, proto-factories a reduced one. Scale of the individual entities and degree of mechanization achieved through the concentration of capital turn out to have been less significant than organizational change and the linkage of agriculture and manufacturing. Correspondingly, capital in the form of New World treasure and booty mattered less for Old World development than did colonial raw materials for Europe's new industries. The world-system took longer to fashion and benefited Europe later and more narrowly than its theorists have often imagined. Most of all, it had the effects it did because of developments within Europe: the efforts of its modernizing landlords, merchants, and entrepreneurs, to be sure, but also peasant and artisanal initiatives and responses.

Significant economic growth and capitalist transformation occurred in early modern Europe, and frequently – though by no means always – they paved the way for the subsequent emergence of mechanized factory industrialization. First of all, they had given rise to sufficiently large markets at home and abroad to assure entrepreneurs a steady return on manufacturing establishments embodying substantial fixed capital investments. We have seen, moreover, that many innovations commonly associated with the factory system had already begun to develop in the prior period. Most obvious was the creation of a large proletarianized labor force. In addition, machines such as spinning jennies, water frames, and spinning mules originated within the domestic system and only later transferred into factories. At the same time, large centralized workshops that assembled several stages of manufacture had already made their appearance in numerous trades, and some contained machines powered by water, horses, or steam. Even those that relied on handicraft methods, moreover, separated the workplace from the household and helped impose new work rhythms and discipline. Putting-out systems and manufactories alike both employed throngs of women and children and segregated them into certain types of work, establishing patterns that persisted into early cotton mills, those paradigms of the initial phase of the Industrial Revolution.

That period of sustained change sped up and extended these earlier innovations, along with such critical trends as focused urbanization, the use of new raw materials to produce novel goods, growing interconnections among geographic areas and economic sectors, northwestern Europe's economic hegemony. The Industrial Revolution was momentous, and thus eventually thoroughly deserving of its traditional characterization. Yet outside a handful of industries – cotton, iron, and machine-making – it, like the previous economic transformation, was drawn out and uneven.

The mechanization of some procedures did not spell the quick demise of handicraft production, sometimes because technical problems proved hard to overcome or capital difficult to obtain, but especially because abundant, low-wage (and thus mainly female and youthful) labor remained available for that large share of productive activities that did not require close supervision to assure quality or rapid completion. Sometimes this condition resulted in the expansion of the home-based workforces associated with manufactories when other operations began to be performed on machines in factories. Thus was perpetuated a mixture of centralized and dispersed work, the former typically performed by a small nucleus of well-remunerated full-time male workers, the latter by a much larger penumbra of miserably paid seasonal, temporary, or part-time female workers. In the Nová Kdyne (Bohemia) woollens enterprise, for instance, the ratio of finishers, employed in a mill, to the domestic workers, who performed every other stage of production, fell from 1 : 5 in 1775 to 1 : 13 in 1838. At Barcelona, entrepreneurs actually moved cotton manufacturing out of big urban factories into smaller workplaces in towns and villages between the 1780s and the early 1830s in order to tap a supply of labor that was not only cheaper but preferred domestic work to the long unbroken shifts, constant supervision, and general environment of factories.

Not only was there no necessary, unidirectional progression from shop to factory, but, over the industrial sector as a whole, factories were long in a minority and those that existed were mostly small. Other forms of production remained viable in many trades. Small metalworking shops followed a long-established path of innovation and market enlargement by introducing cheap new products made from less costly raw materials. "Company mills," common in the English woollen industry from the 1780s to the later nineteenth century, likewise served to perpetuate small, labor-intensive domestic shops. Owned cooperatively by the artisans who used them, these concerns prepared raw wool (some also spun and dyed it), while weaving and most spinning continued to be performed in modest workshops.

Furthermore, the pace of factory industrialization varied greatly, even among the different branches of a single industry: spinning, for instance, was transformed decades before weaving and knitting. The mechanization of one stage typically spawned additional jobs in those that remained unmechanized. In England, 20,000 framework knitters were counted in 1782; nearly 30,000 in 1812; just under 50,000 in 1844. Similarly, there were 75,000 English handloom weavers in 1795; in 1811, 225,000; in 1833, 250,000. Exactly the same held true on the Continent. In the Haut-Rhin Department of France, for instance, 1,900 hand looms were in operation in 1786, but 18,000–20,000 in 1822 and 31,000 in 1834. In the Pays de Caux, domestic weaving – indeed, the classic proto-industrial combination of agriculture and rural industry – throve for half a century after factories took over spinning.

Even inside factories, work cultures showed many resemblances to earlier types. Skilled metal workers using a variety of highly specialized tools long continued to set their own pace, following procedures learned by practical apprenticeship. Weavers in mid-nineteenth-century British textile mills were employed on the same terms as their proto-industrial predecessors laboring at home. They purchased their raw materials from the entrepreneur, were charged deductions for loom rent, candles, and other operating expenses, and were liable to sudden variations in work availability and piece rates according to oscillations in demand. At the end of the nineteenth century, many French cloth factories still used the family to recruit and discipline their labor forces, and this structure continued to shape and focus worker agitation. Understandably, many of the forms, as well as much of the vocabulary, of nineteenth-century factory-workers' organizations and protest can be traced back to the skilled artisans of the age of manufacture.

Just as mechanized factory production relying on inanimate power developed unevenly within and between trades, so its advance was irregular among regions. In Britain, where change was most rapid, in 1841 the proportion of all male workers holding jobs in industries that had undergone significant change approached two-fifths in Lancashire and the West Riding of Yorkshire but was a tenth or less in twenty-three of the fifty-one counties or districts tabulated. Industrialization was correspondingly disparate among countries. By that same date, nearly half of all British males worked in some sort of industry, but just a quarter in Europe as a whole, and in Iberia, east central Europe, and Scandinavia the figure was closer to an eighth, if that.

The British Industrial Revolution was one path to factory industrialization; it was not, however, the sole model – nor even so rapid and thorough as is often imagined. In 1851, more than half of all British industrial enterprises had five or fewer employees, labor productivity had risen only modestly, and textiles continued to account for two-thirds in value of all British exports. Throughout Europe, capitalists sought to harness cheap, docile labor, but the means they chose to do so varied according to the different agrarian orders, market conditions, worker organizations and actions, government regulations, and property rights that they encountered. The complex histories that we have charted across more than three centuries from the Mediterranean to the Baltic, from east Elbia to the Atlantic coast, ensured that the transitions to factory industrialization would be as diverse as the transitions to capitalism.

SUGGESTED READING

The literature on factory industrialization is enormous. David Cannadine, "The Past and the Present in the English Industrial Revolution, 1880–1980," *Past and Present*, no. 103 (1984), provides a recent survey of the historiography regarding England. For classic interpretations emphasizing rapidity and thoroughness, see

W. W. Rostow, *The Stages of Economic Growth* (Cambridge, 1960); E. J. Hobsbawm, *Industry and Empire* (London, 1968); David Landes, *The Unbound Prometheus* (Cambridge, 1969). More recent statements include Joel Mokyr, "Has the Industrial Revolution been Crowded Out?" *Explorations in Economic History*, vol. 24 (1987), and Mokyr, "Was There a British Industrial Evolution?" *Research In Economic History, Supplement IV* (Greenwich, Conn., 1991).

More gradualist accounts can be found in J. G. Williamson, "Why was British Economic Growth so Slow during the Industrial Revolution?" *Journal of Economic History*, vol. 44 (1984); Williamson, "Debating the British Industrial Revolution," *Explorations in Economic History*, vol. 24 (1987); N. F. R. Crafts, *British Economic Growth during the Industrial Revolution* (Oxford, 1985); Rondo Cameron, "A New View of European Industrialization," *Economic History Review*, 2nd ser., vol. 38 (1985); Jordan Goodman and Katrina Honeyman, *Gainful Pursuits. The Making of Industrial Europe 1600–1914* (London, 1988), ch. 11.

The best recent overview of the controversy is Maxine Berg and Pat Hudson, "Rehabilitating the Industrial Revolution," *Economic History Review*, vol. 45 (1992), which while recognizing continuities emphasizes the radical departures involved. Pat Hudson, *The Industrial Revolution* (London, 1992), also reviews the current state of scholarship while emphasizing fundamental shifts. *The Industrial Revolution and British Society*, ed. P. O'Brien and R. Quinault (Cambridge, 1993) is a wide-ranging survey.

The continuing diversity of organizational forms within industry are detailed in Raphael Samuel, "The Workshop of the World," *History Workshop*, no. 3 (1977); *The Historical Meanings of Work*, ed. Patrick Joyce (Cambridge, 1987); Patrick Joyce, "Work," in *Cambridge Social History of Britain*, vol. II (Cambridge, 1990). For the persistence of work cultures and organization, see E. P. Thompson, *The Making of the English Working Class* (Harmondsworth, 1963); William Sewell, *Work and Revolution in France: The Language of Labour from the Old Regime to 1848* (Cambridge, 1980); William Reddy, *The Rise of Market Culture: the textile trade and French society 1750–1900* (Cambridge, 1984); L. D. Smith, "Industrial Organization in the Kidderminster Carpet Trade," *Textile History*, vol. 15 (1984).

Index

310